Public **8e**

Speaking

Concepts and Skills
for a Diverse Society

Public **8e**
Speaking
Concepts and Skills
for a Diverse Society

Clella Iles Jaffe
George Fox University

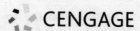

Andover • Melbourne • Mexico City • Stamford, CT • Toronto • Hong Kong • New Delhi • Seoul • Singapore • Tokyo

Public Speaking: Concepts and Skills fora Diverse Society, Eighth Edition
Clella Iles Jaffe

© 2016, 2013, 2007 Cengage Learning

This edition is reprinted with license from **Cengage Learning**, for sale in India, Pakistan, Bangladesh, Nepal and Sri Lanka.

ISBN-13: 978-93-86858-84-9
ISBN-10: 93-868-5884-3

Cengage Learning India Private Limited
418, F.I.E., Patparganj
Delhi 110092
India

Tel: 91-11-43641111
Fax: 91-11-43641100
Email: asia.infoindia@cengage.com

Cengage Learning is a leading provider of customized learning solutions with office locations around the globe, including Andover, Melbourne, Mexico City, Stamford (CT), Toronto, Hong Kong, New Delhi, Seoul, Singapore, and Tokyo. Locate your local office at: www.cengage.com/global

Cengage Learning Products are represented in Canada by Nelson Education, Ltd.

For product information, visit our website at **www.cengage.co.in**

Printed in India
Second Indian Reprint 2019

Disclaimer:
This book contains link to resources which are a part of the US edition. The same may not be available with the Indian edition. The buyer needs to purchase a copy of the US edition to have full access to those resources. In no event the publisher shall be liable for any limitation or performance due to unavailability of these resources.

BRIEF CONTENTS

CONTENTS

CHAPTER 15

Informative Speaking   198

CHAPTER   16

Foundations of Persuasion   214

PREFACE

Courage is what it takes to stand up and speak; courage is also what it takes to sit down and listen.

WINSTON CHURCHILL

THE EIGHTH EDITION of *Public Speaking: Concepts and Skills for a Diverse Society* continues to be a culturally informed text that maintains its fundamental purpose—to train students to be effective public speakers and listeners in an ever-changing world.

I originally wrote this text to emphasize the intertwined relationships between public speaking and culture because public speaking and listening combine to reinforce, transmit, change, and blend cultures. In fact, the very characteristics speakers aim to influence—beliefs, values, attitudes, and actions—are the basic elements of diversity. In addition, our cultural backgrounds influence our perceptions of our roles as public speakers and listeners. Culture also affects topic selection, research methods and resources, and reasoning styles. Consequently, this text combines 2,500-year-old principles from Western traditions with up-to-date research in a way that is sensitive to our pluralistic society.

The years between the first edition and this, the eighth edition, have seen monumental social, cultural, and technological changes, both in the United States and across the globe. Each new edition provides an opportunity to integrate developing trends into the text as well as to update research findings and pedagogical trends in the field of public speaking. I am grateful to all who have used the first seven editions and to the many professors and students who have given helpful suggestions to keep the text practical and current.

New to This Edition

I'm proud to say that this was the first public speaking textbook to focus on diversity, include an interpreted speech (given in Spanish and translated into English and now available in the online resources), describe invitational rhetoric, discuss receiver apprehension, and show alternative patterns of speech organization. Each edition has maintained several proven emphases:

- Cultural influences on public speaking and public speakers' influence on culture
- Gender, ethnic, and global diversity
- Civility and ethics in speaking and listening
- Emphasis on dialogical public speaking and listening
- Technological advances and public speaking
- Traditions dating back to classical rhetoric
- Nontraditional organizational patterns

This edition retains these features and includes a number of important changes in response to reviewer feedback. Here are some highlights of what's new or revised:

- **Information about online courses**. A Google search for "online public speaking course" resulted in thousands of links, indicating that nontraditional courses have an increasingly important presence nowadays. Consequently, this edition includes research about online courses (Chapter 1), some information about audiences in online courses (Chapter 6), and tips for videotaping speeches (Chapter 14).
- **New and updated information**. A new section on listening competencies incorporates up-to-date cognitive science research regarding basic skills (surface processing) versus advanced skills (deep processing) for listening. Chapter 7 includes new material about legacy journalism and native digital news outlets in the rapidly changing world of journalism; in the same chapter is a new strategy, (MAPit) for evaluating online materials. Chapter 12 includes a new section on powerful (versus powerless) language forms.
- **Revised chapters**. Many reviewers requested a shorter book, so I edited out some nonessential material to make a more concise text. Gone is the narrative chapter with its explanation of narrative theory, but the exemplum pattern for narratives is retained in a new Chapter 18 that now incorporates the guidelines for special occasion speeches that were in Appendix B in earlier editions.
- **Additional figures that summarize information**. Both student and faculty reviewers noted the helpfulness of visuals, such as Figure 2.1 that summarizes the five canons of rhetoric, so I added several such features throughout the text.
- **Updated references to social events**. Keeping a text current requires frequent updating to include accurate and relevant information. For example, between every edition, current issues—nationally and internationally—change. References in one edition become outdated in the next.
- **Enhanced online materials**. To meet reviewers' requests for a shorter book, sample speeches, the Stop and Check boxes, and the Build Your Speech features are now mostly in interactive online format. For more information about the speech videos for this book, see the Resources for Students section.

Proven Chapter-by-Chapter Features

In addition to chapter-opening lists of learning objectives, key term definitions in the margins of each chapter, and chapter-ending summaries, each chapter includes several acclaimed pedagogical features that improve student learning and performance.

- **Diversity in Practice boxes**. These boxes enhance the book's emphasis on diversity by presenting brief summaries of public speaking traditions from a range of perspectives. Examples include ancient cultures (Chapter 1), global groups (Chapters 7, 9, and 18), ethnic groups (Chapters 10 and 15), gender (Chapters 2 and 16), and co-cultures (Chapter 12).
- **Ethics in Practice boxes**. This text has always emphasized ethical speaking and listening. This edition includes an ethics box in most chapters. These boxes present short examples or cases that invite students to contemplate the ethical implications of chapter concepts, using probing questions that are appropriate for class discussions.
- **Critical Thinking Exercises and Application Exercises**. These end-of-chapter questions help students better understand and critically evaluate the chapter content and further apply the skills they've learned. Critical Thinking Exercises are designed for individual reflection on chapter concepts. Application Exercises are designed for group assignments and for in-class discussions.

- **Sample speeches**. Many chapters include excerpts from student outlines or speeches. Appendix B also includes speeches and outlines that provide models showing how other students fulfilled a typical assignment. Chapter 17 provides a cautionary, negative model. Appendix B also features speeches by professional speakers. Most of these speeches and many others are available in online supporting materials. For more information about this book's speech resources, see the Resources for Students section.

Resources for Instructors

Public Speaking: Concepts and Skills for a Diverse Society, Eighth Edition, also features a full suite of resources for instructors. The following class preparation, classroom presentation, assessment, and course management resources are available:

- **Instructor's Website**. This website is an all-in-one resource for class preparation, presentation, and testing for instructors. Accessible through Cengage.com/login with your faculty account, you will find an Instructor's Manual, Chapter-by-Chapter Powerpoint presentations.
  - **Instructor's Resource Manual**. The Instructor's Resource Manual (available for download at the Instructor Companion site) provides a comprehensive teaching guide. Written by the author and updated by Miri Pardo, St. John Fisher College, this manual features sample syllabi, as well as suggested speaking assignments and criteria for evaluation. Each text chapter has the following resources: chapter goals, a chapter outline, suggestions correlating supplements and online resources, supplementary research notes, and suggested discussion questions.
  - *The Teaching Assistant's Guide to the Basic Course*. Katherine G. Hendrix, who is on the faculty at the University of Memphis, prepared this resource specifically for new instructors. Based on leading communication teacher training programs, this guide discusses some of the general issues that accompany a teaching role and offers specific strategies for managing the first week of classes, leading productive discussions, managing sensitive topics in the classroom, and grading students' written and oral work.

These resources are available to qualified adopters, and ordering options for student supplements are flexible. Please consult your local Wadsworth Cengage Learning sales representative for more information, to evaluate examination copies of any of these instructor or student resources, or for product demonstrations. You may also contact the Cengage Learning Academic Resource Center at 800-423-0563 or visit us at **cengage brain.com**.

Acknowledgments

Every book is a co-created product in which an author relies on the encouragement of others. I owe a long-standing debt to former Oregon State University colleagues (Victoria O'Donnell, Sean Patrick O'Rourke, Anne Zach Ferguson, and dozens of graduate teaching instructors). My colleagues at George Fox University have consistently and patiently supported my writing, for which I am grateful. I also thank generations of students at Oregon State, St. John's (New York), and George Fox University who provided insights, examples, speeches, and support.

Likewise, I want to thank the many people at or working with Cengage Learning who helped bring this new edition and its many supplements to fruition: Nicole Morinon, Jessica Badiner, Kathy Sands-Boehmer, and Yashmita Hota. I would like to thank the reviewers who contributed valuable comments about this edition: Beverly Borawski, Pasco-Hernando Community College; Janet Colvin, Utah Valley University; Carla Harrell, Old Dominion University; Brian Heisterkamp, California State University, San Bernardino; Susan Kilgard, Anne Arundel Community College; Chris Lancaster, Southern Illinois University, Carbondale; Sherry Lewis University of Texas, El Paso; Nancy Tobler, Utah Valley University; and Stephanie Webster, University of Florida.

I would also like to thank the reviewers for previous editions of this book. Reviewers for the First Edition were Martha Ann Atkins, Iowa State University; Dennis Beaver, Bakersfield College; Carol Berteotti, University of Wisconsin–La Crosse; Carole Blair, University of California–Davis; Cynthia Brown-El, Macomb Community College; Ferald J. Bryan, Northern Illinois University; Bruce G. Bryski, Buffalo State College; Jacquelyn Buckrop, Ball State University; Michelle Burch, Clark State University; Kathleen Farrell, Saint Louis University; Norma Flores, Golden West College; Franklin L. Gray, Ball State University; Charles Griffin, Kansas State University; Susan Hellweg, San Diego State University; Mark Hickson, University of Alabama–Birmingham; Janet Hoffman, Southern Illinois University at Carbondale; Susan Huxman, Wichita State University; Karla Jensen, Texas Tech University; Tina Kistler, Santa Barbara City College; Shelley D. Lane, Collin County Community College; Jo Ann Lawlor, West Valley College; Steven March, Pima County Community College; Victoria O'Donnell, Montana State University; Sean Patrick O'Rourke, Vanderbilt University; Patricia Palm McGillen, Mankato State University; Mark Morman, Johnson County Community College; Teresa Nance, Villanova University; Patricia O'Keefe, College of Marin; Mary Pelias, Southern Illinois University; Mark Stoner, California State University–Sacramento; Patricia Sullivan, State University of New York at New Paltz; Marsha Vanderford, University of South Florida; Donald E. Williams, University of Florida; Lee Winet, State University of New York–Oswego; and Anne Zach Ferguson, University of California–Davis. Reviewers for the Second Edition were Thomas E. Diamond, Montana State University; Kevin E. McClearey, Southern Illinois University at Edwardsville; Susan Messman, Arizona State University; Karla D. Scott, Saint Louis University; Jessica Stowell, Tulsa Community College; and Lori Wisdom-Whitley, Western Washington University. Reviewers for the Third Edition were Clifton Adams, Central Missouri State University; Linda Anthon, Valencia Community College; Jay Baglia, University of South Florida; Carol Barnum, Southern Polytechnic State University; Lori Basden Arnold, Rowan University; Julie Benson-Rosston, University of Montana; John Bourhis, Missouri State University; Cheri Campbell, Keene State College; Faye Clark, Georgia Perimeter College; Risa Dickson, California State University at San Bernardino; Hal Fulmer, Georgia Southern University; Matthew Girton, Florida State University; Sherrie L. Guerrero, San Bernardino Valley College; Robert Gwynne, University of Tennessee–Knoxville; Fred Jandt, California State

University at San Bernardino; Laura Nelson, University of Wisconsin–La Crosse; Jean E. Perry, Glendale Community College; Susie Richardson, Prince George's Community College; Paula Rodriguez, Hinds Community College; Scott Rodriguez, California State University at San Bernardino; Cathy Sargent Mester, Pennsylvania State University; Kristi A. Schaller, University of Hawaii; Ann M. Scroggie, Santa Fe Community College; Karni Spain Tiernan, Bradley University; David Walker, Middle Tennessee State University; June D. Wells, Indian River Community College; Nancy J. Wendt, Oregon State University; L. Keith Williamson, Wichita State University; and Marianne Worthington, Cumberland College. Reviewers for the Fourth Edition were James E. Bruce, University of Tennessee at Martin; Ferald J. Bryan, Northern Illinois University; Nanci Burk, Glendale Community College; Helen Chester, Milwaukee Area Technical College; Omar Guevara, California State University at Bakersfield; Janice D. Hamlet, Northern Illinois University; Jeff Przybylo, William Rainey Harper Community College; Diana D. Roberts, Community College of Southern Nevada; Amy R. Slagell, Iowa State University; Lisa Waite, Kent State University; Diane E. Waryas, Community College of Southern Nevada; and Kathryn Wylie-Marques, John Jay College, City University of New York. Reviewers for the Fifth Edition were Christian Blum, Bryant & Stratton College; Bryan Crow, Southern Illinois University; Linda Czuba Brigance, SUNY Fredonia; Jonathan M. Gray, Southern Illinois University, Carbondale; Roxanne Tuscany, Grossmont College; Alex Wang, University of Connecticut, Stamford; and Melinda Williams. Reviewers for the Sixth Edition offered helpful suggestions for the Seventh: Kim Harris, William Jewell College; Terri Main, Reedley College; Anna Roseboro, Calvin College; Ken Sherwood, Los Angeles City College; Elizabeth Simas, Diablo Valley College; Cheryl Skiba-Jones, Ivy Tech Community College; Sheri Strothers, Grossmont College; Ed Sweda, Pasco Hernando Community College; Margaret Wick, The College of Wooster; and Tina Zagara, Georgia Perimeter College.

Writing takes a toll on an author's family. I am grateful for Jack, Sara, Josh, J. C., and all the little ones who make a difference in my life.

Clella Iles Jaffe, Ph.D.

Public 8e
Speaking
Concepts and Skills
for a Diverse Society

THIS CHAPTER WILL HELP YOU

- Define public speaking

- Define culture in the context of public speaking

- Give reasons for studying public speaking from a cultural perspective

- Identify ways that culture affects public speaking

- Explain how public speaking influences culture

- Explain the value of public speaking for individuals

- Identify elements of the transactional model of communication

Diana Ong/SuperStock

Introduction to Public Speaking and Culture

MindTap

view
e chapter
arning
bjectives
*d **Start***
th a quick
rm-up
tivity.

IN THE FINAL WEEK of his senior year, Josh presented the results of his honors thesis to professors and other physics majors. During her internship, Whitney helped organize a large fund-raising event, which required her to make regular reports to her supervisors. Mary worked with student volunteers, who spent their Friday nights interacting with homeless people in her city; she often gave public announcements about upcoming events. These students drew on concepts and skills they sharpened in their public speaking course.

In many languages and dialects and in formal and informal settings, speakers such as these inform, persuade, entertain, and reinforce community values. Public speaking is vital in a culture where each person has the constitutional

public speaking a person delivers a presentation to a group that listens, generally without interrupting the speaker's flow of ideas

right to express ideas freely. By definition, **public speaking** occurs when one person prepares and delivers a talk for a group that listens, generally without interrupting the speaker's flow of ideas. This very idea fills some people with dread, but over the coming weeks this course will help you assess your current abilities, identify areas for improvement, and work out ways to deal with the challenges of speaking and listening in a free society. As you create first one speech and then another, you will add competencies and refine those you already have.[1]

Although this text includes the word *speaking*, speech-*making* is only one element of the course. More often than not, you will be in the audience, listening to speeches in an increasingly diverse culture and world. Consequently, learning to better understand and evaluate the messages you hear daily is another major course goal. The competencies needed for these two roles—speaker and listener—are the focus of this text.

Diverse society is also part of the book's title because you will better understand our nation and our world if you understand how cultural diversity affects communication. To meet this goal, this text presents the most common public speaking norms in the United States, while introducing a variety of speaking traditions from other cultural groups.

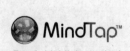

Read, highlight, and take notes online.

culture an integrated system of learned beliefs, values, behaviors, and norms that include visible (clothing, food) and underlying (core beliefs, worldview) characteristics of a society

Cultures are somewhat like onions because of their many integrated layers that surround an inner core of beliefs, values, and attitudes.

Culture and Public Speaking

A **culture** is an integrated system of learned beliefs, values, attitudes, and behaviors that a group accepts and passes along from older to newer members. Don Smith,[2] founder of Daystar University in Kenya, compares cultures to onions with outer layers (clothing, art, food, language, and so on) and embedded cores that filter how we view the world (ideologies, folk beliefs, attitudes, values, and the like).[3] In other words, cultures exist at both visible and conscious levels and at invisible and subconscious levels; they have relatively stable elements, but they can and do change.

© anyamuse/Shutterstock.com

Although members of a society share many commonalities, there is no single "U.S. culture"; instead, this nation consists of many **co-cultures**[4]–groups that share many aspects of the dominant culture, but diverge in some way. The TV show *Modern Family* illustrates co-cultural diversity. Phil and Jay are white heterosexual males; Mitch and Cam are gay; their daughter Lily is Asian American; Gloria is Colombian; and so on. The family members work together to create a humorously supportive family system.

co-cultures subgroups of culture, characterized by mild or profound cultural differences that coexist within the larger culture

Public speaking is essential within cultures. Professor Charles Conrad explains that

cultures are communicative creations. They emerge through communication, are maintained through communication, and change through the communicative acts of their members. Simultaneously communication is a cultural creation. Persons' perceptions of the cultures in which they live…form the situations that guide and constrain their communication.[5]

Public Speaking in Ancient Cultures

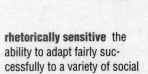

DIVERSITY IN PRACTICE

Public speaking has its place in every society. For example, fragments of an ancient manuscript, *The Precepts of Ke'gemni and Ptah-hotep* (ca. 2100 bce), provided young Egyptians with guidelines for speaking, including (1) do not pervert the truth and (2) avoid speech subjects about which you know nothing.[6]

The medieval Arab scholar Muhammad ibn 'Abd al-Rahman al-Qzawini (d. 1338) classified the science of eloquence into three parts: (1) *'ilm al-ma' ānī* (the science of meanings), (2) *'ilm al-bayān* (the science of clarity), and (3) *'ilm al-badī* (the science of ornamentation).[7]

The ancient Chinese scholar Lao-Tzu advised, "[a] virtuous person does not speak with high-sounding words; one who speaks with high-sounding words is not a virtuous person."[8]

You can see the practicality of the advice and analysis, both then and now.

A cultural perspective will enable you to communicate more competently. Identifying audience expectations regarding the specific setting and determining what is most appropriate in it will make you a more **rhetorically sensitive** person who "can adapt to diverse social situations and perform reasonably well in most of them."[9] In other words, each audience has expectations for a presentation regarding the length, appropriate delivery, and so on. You will be more effective if you understand and adapt to these cultural expectations.

rhetorically sensitive the ability to adapt fairly successfully to a variety of social situations

Culture Affects Public Speaking

Cultures influence speaking by providing core resources, communication technology, and cultural expectations for speakers and listeners.

Cultures Provide Core Resources

Each culture offers a pool of **core cultural resources**—systems of intertwined beliefs, attitudes, and values (BAV) that underlie our behaviors in every area of life, including public speaking.[10] (See Figure 1.1.)

core cultural resources beliefs, attitudes, and values (BAV) along with behaviors that provide a logical basis for a culture to define what is necessary, right, doubtful, or forbidden

Figure 1.1
Intertwined beliefs, values, attitudes, and actions comprise our core cultural resources.

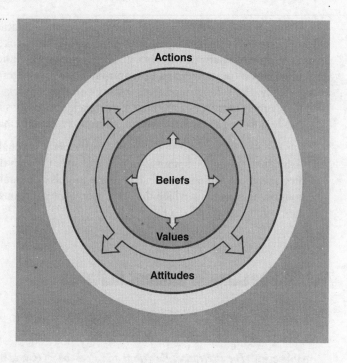

Beliefs are the ideas we mentally accept as true or reject as false. Attitudes are our predispositions to evaluate—either negatively or positively—persons, objects, symbols, and the like. Values are our underlying evaluations of what is important, significant, moral, or right. Finally, behaviors are the actions we consider appropriate or normal. (Chapters 6 and 17 provide more detail about this.) Some foundational cultural resources that affect public speaking in the United States include:

- A *belief* that we can change society by speaking out and creating public policies instead of giving in to fate.
- Positive *attitudes* toward open forums and negative *attitudes* about suppressing dissent.
- A *value* on individuality over conformity.
- Standards for predictable speaking and listening *behaviors* that vary according to context.

As you can see, these core resources underscore the importance of free public expression in the United States.

Cultures Provide Technological Aids

The technology available to a culture greatly affects how its members create and exchange messages. A strictly **oral culture** has no way to record, store, or transmit ideas, so speakers and audiences *must* meet face-to-face. Because everything they know must be memorized, oral groups rely on poems, chants, proverbs, and stories that help them learn and remember their values, beliefs, and traditions.[11]

oral culture culture with no writing and no technology for recording messages apart from face-to-face interactions

In contrast, most cultures today provide at least some access to literacy and to electronic devices that allow people to record their ideas and convey them to audiences separated by both distance and time. You can access an overwhelming amount of available resources for speech materials, including printed materials, digitally stored databases, the Internet, audiovisual resources, and so on. Additionally, microphones, cameras, sophisticated projectors, and resources such as YouTube enable you to record and present your ideas to a wide audience.

Alicia Nilo

Today's technology allows students to take speaking courses online where they create videos of their speeches and post them online for classmates to see and critique.

The amount and types of available electronic resources allow students to take public speaking courses in hybrid (partly online and partly face-to-face) or in entirely online formats. Students who choose these courses like the flexibility of learning on their own schedule. Of course, they need access to a computer, the Internet, and in entirely online courses, some form of recording equipment. Research shows the outcomes to be very similar between online and traditional courses, although the percentage of students who complete the face-to-face course is higher than those who take it online. Key factors for online success include the ability to work well independently and the match between the online mode and the student's learning style.[12]

Cultures Provide Expectations about Speaking and Listening

According to the Dutch theorist Geert Hofstede,[13] national cultures vary along an individualistic-collectivist dimension. People in **individualistic cultures** depend more on themselves and their immediate families. They're judged on the basis of individual achievement and merits, and they learn to speak up to solve problems. The United States, Australia, and Western European countries score highest on individualism. Members of **collectivist cultures**, in contrast, are born into strong, cohesive in-groups that protect them and to whom they are loyal. They may feel uncomfortable if they, and not the group, are singled out for an honor, and they try to avoid shaming others. Many Latin American and Asian countries score highest on collectivism.[14] Compare their pronouns: People from individualistic cultures use comparatively more "I" and "my" words than do people from collectivist cultures who prefer "we" and "our" pronouns. (Have you ever noticed that English is the only language that capitalizes the word for "I" and not the word for "you"?)[15]

individualistic cultures members of these cultures depend mainly on themselves and are judged on personal merits

collectivist cultures members of these cultures are integrated into an in-group that protects them throughout their lives

nonexpressive cultures
cultures that value privacy
and encourage members
to keep their emotions and
ideas to themselves rather
than to express them publicly

expressive cultures cultures
that encourage members to
give their opinions, speak
their minds, and let their feelings show

digital oratory an emerging form of public address
housed online in new media
platforms such as YouTube,
Vimeo, or iReport

communication style a
culture's preferred ways of
communicating, given its
core assumptions and norms

taboo topics a culture considers inappropriate

bicultural knowing and
applying different rules for
competent behaviors in two
cultures

Cultures range in the amount and kinds of information they encourage members to express. **Nonexpressive cultures** expect people to guard their emotions and ideas rather than express them indiscriminately. Japanese, Chinese,[16] Finnish,[17] and many Native American groups are comparatively nonexpressive. As you might guess, someone from these cultures could be overwhelmed at the thought of speaking in public.[18] In contrast, **expressive cultures** encourage people to give their opinions, speak their minds, and let their feelings show. Koreans, Puerto Ricans,[19] African Americans, and many African cultures[20] are more verbal and confident in speaking out. President Obama is just one example of the many African Americans considered to be a highly skilled speaker.

Cultures also influence "who" speaks—and "to whom." Some cultures allow only older adult men who are considered wisest or most knowledgeable to speak, leaving children, young people, nonexperts, and women without a voice in public arenas.[21] Sometimes ridicule, misunderstanding, or punishment await the poor, members of minority groups, or people with divergent political views who try to speak out.[22] In addition, access to specific venues is commonly limited. For example, could a minimum-wage worker at a local motel chain enter corporate headquarters and ask for a better retirement plan? Not likely. Can just anyone testify before Congress? No, only those who are invited.[23] On the other hand, sites such as Vimeo, CNN's iReport, and YouTube open up possibilities for young and old alike to participate in **digital oratory**—an emerging form of public address housed online in new media platforms.[24]

In addition, cultures develop a preferred **communication style**[25]—underlying ideas for how to speak most appropriately within the culture. The dominant style in the United States includes the following:

- *Problem orientation.* We assume that the world is rational and that we can create solutions to problems by acting on them.
- *Directness.* We expect ideas to be logically organized and go straight to the point.
- *Explicitness.* We prefer clear, concise, and precise language instead of indirect or vague statements.
- *Informality.* Cultural values of equality and individuality lead to conversational delivery.
- *Personal involvement.* Speakers commonly share personal experiences that establish common ground with their audiences.

Cultures also influence topics. The Polynesian word *tabu* or **taboo** (inappropriate topics) contrasts with *noa* (discussable topics). Each culture designates some topics as discussable and some as taboo. General topics such as current events are typical of *noa* topics, acceptable in many cultures.[26] However, issues related to human sexuality,[27] one's personal religion, death,[28] or criticism of the government—these topics can be taboo or confined to an "appropriate" time and place.

Cultural factors such as these can affect how comfortable you feel in a public speaking classroom that teaches Euro-American cultural norms. Appropriate speaking and listening in classrooms or workplace settings may be quite different from your cultural traditions. If so, you can become **bicultural**, knowing how to speak in the dominant culture while appreciating and participating in your own ethnic speech community. In the following example, a Nigerian woman living in the United States explains how she accomplishes this:

At work,…I raise my voice as loud as necessary to be heard in meetings. At conferences where I present papers on "Women from the Third World," I make serious arguments about the need for international intervention in countries where women are deprived of all rights.…Yet as easily as I switch from speaking English to Ibo (her Nigerian language),…I never confuse my two selves.

Hundreds of thousands of women from the Third World and other traditional societies share my experience. We straddle two cultures, cultures that are often in opposition. Mainstream America, the culture we embrace in our professional lives, dictates that we be assertive and independent—like men. Our traditional culture, dictated by religion and years of socialization, demands that we be docile and content in our roles as mothers and wives—careers or not.[29]

In summary, our cultures provide a range of appropriate communication behaviors. Consequently, students from many traditions bring contrasting expectations of "how to" speak into the college classroom. If you judge other traditions by your own culture's standards, misunderstandings and negative evaluations can result.

Public Speaking Affects Culture

New technology, new leaders, and new ideas can and do change cultures. Often changes come through skillful public speakers who transmit, reinforce, repair, or transform their cultures.[30]

- Speakers who *transmit* cultural resources teach cultural beliefs, values, and behaviors. For example, English-language professors teach foreign students how to navigate this culture. Religious leaders teach their beliefs to youth and to converts.
- Those who *reinforce* or support existing cultural elements encourage listeners to persist in positive behaviors or beliefs. Examples include politicians who urge people to keep on voting or inspirational speakers who stress the importance of teamwork.
- Speakers who *restore* matters to a healthy state step in when events threaten to tear apart a community. For instance after a community tragedy, officials provide information essential for reestablishing order and a sense of security.
- Those who *transform* societies become instruments for social change. Health insurance reform, gay rights legislation, environmental protection—skilled speakers argued for all these changes. Even relatively well-functioning societies can be improved, and people currently argue for hundreds of changes including reforms in sports and media.

Whether the goal is to transmit, reinforce, repair, or transform culture, we depend on communicators who are willing and competent enough to speak out and perpetuate positive cultural characteristics or, when necessary, who will resist and change cultural elements that need improvement.

David J. & Janice L. Frent Collection/Historical/CORBIS

GIVE MOTHER THE VOTE
WE NEED IT

VOTES FOR OUR MOTHERS

OUR FOOD　OUR HEALTH　OUR PLAY
OUR HOMES　OUR SCHOOLS　OUR WORK
ARE　RULED　BY　MEN'S　VOTES

Isn't it a funny thing
That Father cannot see
Why Mother ought to have a vote
On how these things should be?

THINK IT OVER

Many cultural transformations have come about because people willingly argued for change. Women's suffrage was a major theme one hundred years ago; today, the themes are different, but reformers still speak out to create a more just, equitable, and safe society.

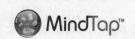

Public Speaking Affects Individuals

Most universities not only offer public speaking courses, they require them for at least two good reasons: they emphasize critical thinking, and they focus on skills that are important in professional, civic, and personal contexts.

ETHICS IN PRACTICE

Vir Bonum, Dicendi Peritus

Every culture has sayings that capture cultural ideals in short, pithy statements. The Latin phrase *Vir bonum, dicendi peritus*—"The good person, skilled in speaking"—is a slogan that Quintilian, a Roman speech teacher who lived during the chaotic rule of the notorious Emperor Nero, instilled into his students. He knew that persuasive words have power to move people; therefore, they have ethical implications. Put simply, speakers can urge others to act out horrors or to make the world better. Today, "good people, communicating skillfully" are more important than ever in a world where technology opens the possibilities for millions of people to get a wide hearing.

Questions

1. Make a list of individuals, skilled in speaking, but who were not "good" persons. (Hitler tops many people's list.)
2. Add to this list some Internet sites you think promote negative values or behaviors. (For example, you can find pro-anorexia websites or uploaded videos that demean a specific religion.)
3. How might the principles in the slogan mentioned above apply to the Internet and YouTube generation?
4. Identify situations, real or hypothetical, in which good people want to do something to better their world but lack the skills to present their ideas to those who could support their efforts.

Critical Thinking Skills

critical thinking the ability to think analytically about ideas

rhetoric the study of persuasion in its various forms; this helps develop critical thinking skills

The California State Senate defined **critical thinking** as "the ability to engage in reasoned discourse with intellectual standards such as clarity, accuracy, precision, and logic, and to use analytic skills with a fundamental value orientation that emphasizes intellectual humility, intellectual integrity, and fair-mindedness."[31] For centuries, critical thinking has been linked with the study of **rhetoric**, or "the strategic use of communication, oral or written, to achieve specifiable goals."[32] In fact, rhetoric is one of the original seven liberal arts, developed by the Greeks and Romans and continued into today's universities, where researchers study effective and ineffective communication.

However valuable rhetoric may be, people today often view the word negatively. For instance, you may hear someone say, "That's just rhetoric!" or "We want action, not rhetoric!" But is rhetoric just words? Or is it a way to sharpen critical thinking skills? Here are four additional definitions:[33]

- The faculty of discovering in any particular case all of the available means of persuasion (Aristotle)
- The study of misunderstandings and their remedies (I. A. Richards)
- The use of words by human agents to form attitudes or to induce actions in other human agents (Kenneth Burke)
- The use of reason and evidence by both sides, who express their opinions on matters and issues, expose their opponent's weak points, and finally achieve a correct viewpoint and mutual understanding (*Modern Chinese Dictionary* definition of the Chinese word *bian*)[34]

As you can see, most definitions associate rhetoric with some form of persuasion. Because persuasion surrounds you in speeches, ads, films—to name just a few—this text describes rhetorical principles that will help you develop competencies you can use every day to think critically about information, sort through persuasive appeals, discriminate faulty arguments from valid reasoning, and follow ideas to logical conclusions.[35]

Professional, Civic, and Personal Skills

Employers look for more than just "technical skills" or a particular major when they evaluate job candidates. In a recent national survey of business and nonprofit leaders, 93 percent marked critical thinking, clear communication, and the ability to solve complex problems as vitally important skills.[36] They want new hires who can listen effectively, think ethically, work in diverse situations, and understand global realities.[37] Public speaking competencies are used daily in occupations as diverse as law, medicine, engineering,[38] and accounting.[39]

Skills from this course also enable you to participate more effectively in society. Stop and think for a moment. What social issues concern you? Human trafficking? The environment? Something else? Instead of remaining silent about significant problems, you can take part in **civic engagement** by contributing your ideas and working with others to seek resolutions to issues of public concern.[40] On blogs, social network pages, news sites,[41] and other discussion forums, you can share your well-thought-out ideas about issues as varied as sport controversies to movies to politics. The most skillful communicators influence thinking and actions about local, national, and international issues.

civic engagement working with others to help solve issues of public concern

Finally, a course in public speaking can help you personally in two ways. This text gives guidelines on how to create speeches for a variety of social situations; for example, you may be asked to give a wedding toast or funeral eulogy, a tribute, or an inspirational talk. In addition, many—even most—students enter this course with some anxiety;[42] they dread even the thought of giving a speech. If you're one of them, there's good news. Most people feel both more competent and more confident after they complete the course.[43]

In short, studying public speaking adds to your communication abilities within a culture that values them. You can develop critical thinking skills and presentational skills that will serve you well in almost any profession, while you sharpen your ability to engage in the broader cultural conversation that makes a difference in the world. On top of these benefits, you can gain confidence as you face your fears and meet the challenge of preparing and giving speeches.

A Model of Communication

The word *communication* is so common that you may not think much about what actually happens when people communicate. However, scholars study the interrelationships among speakers, messages, listeners, and situations. The **transactional model**,[44] shown in Figure 1.2, is one of many ways to think about what happens during communication, and it is the most common. It includes the following components, described by showing how they interact when you give a speech.

transactional model of communication represents communication as a process in which speakers and listeners work together to create mutual meanings

- As a *sender-receiver* (or source), you originate or *encode* a message by selecting words (a verbal code) to represent your ideas. As you prepare, you consider your audience, reflecting on what you know about them and their knowledge of and interest in your topic.
- Your *message* has a purpose. For this course, your instructor might assign a speech to inform or persuade. In other settings, you might give a report, honor another

Figure 1.2
The transactional model depicts communication as a dialogical process in which communicators co-create messages in culturally appropriate situations.

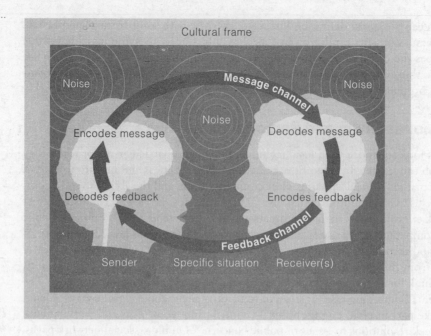

person's achievements, or make your audience laugh. You craft your message in language your audience will understand, using reasoning they accept and illustrations that relate to their lives.

- The face-to-face, voice-to-ear *channel*, along with nonverbal channels such as gestures or tone of voice, is the most common in classrooms. In other settings you might speak in a videoconference or record your message digitally and upload it to a file server or Internet site where your audience can listen at their leisure.

- *Receivers-senders* hear your words and *decode* or interpret them. They create meanings out of their personal backgrounds and heritages, plus their individual beliefs, values, worries, and judgments.

- Your audience sends *feedback*. Face-to-face audience members can ask questions, nod, frown, smile, or clap. Some may even heckle you. You decode their feedback and adapt to it. For example, if you see confused faces, you might add details to clarify your point. Were you to use another channel, such as YouTube, feedback would come in the form of written remarks below your video. In this transactional process of mutual sending-receiving-responding, you and your listeners cooperate in creating meaning.

- *Noise*, or static, can interfere with both the message and its reception. A mild case of laryngitis might make your words difficult to hear. A lawnmower outside the window (*external noise*) might overwhelm your words. *Internal noise*, such as listeners' worries about being overdrawn at the bank or their hunger pangs, can also disrupt the process. Finally, *cultural noise* occurs when cultural differences make the message irrelevant or offensive, as when the topic or the manner of the presentation runs counter to a listener's cultural norms.[45]

- Each speech takes place in a specific situation. During the term, you'll speak in a classroom or perhaps an online setting. But in the workplace or community, the situations will be more varied. Regardless of the context, room temperature, lighting, room decor, available technology, and seating arrangements all can affect your presentation.

- Finally, as this chapter explained, each speech takes place within a larger cultural framework. Class speeches come with expectations about grades and higher education. Other organizations have their ideas about public speaking, and these affect what is considered appropriate and inappropriate in the context.

Although imperfect, the transactional model effectively depicts communication as a complex, dynamic process. It further identifies and clarifies some of the many variables that affect the way we cooperate with one another to co-create meanings.

Summary

This chapter introduced some benefits you can gain by studying public speaking from a perspective of cultural diversity. By definition, cultures emerge, maintain themselves, and change through communication. Cultures include both the visible and the underlying (embedded) aspects of a society; they are complex and contain many co-cultural groups, which often have different norms for speaking and listening. Culture affects public speaking, and public speaking affects culture.

Our cultures provide us with core beliefs, values, attitudes, and behaviors that shape our own speeches and our responses to others' messages. In addition, our technology provides a variety of resources we can use to research topics and present our speeches, face-to-face as well as online. Finally, our cultural heritages provide expectations regarding the *how*, the *who*, and the *what* of public speaking. Of course, within each culture individual personalities and preferences also shape the ways we communicate.

Public speaking allows us to transmit core cultural beliefs, values, and attitudes to newcomers. Speaking reinforces or supports culture as it is, and through speaking we repair or restore community when it is threatened. We also change or transform cultural elements that are outmoded or dysfunctional.

The study of rhetoric, a cornerstone of a liberal arts education, can equip you personally with critical thinking skills that are useful in everyday and workplace interactions. Throughout this course, you will learn skills that are personally and professionally valuable in a culture that relies on skilled speakers and listeners.

The chapter closed with the transactional model of communication that depicts in visual form the transactional nature of communication. It emphasizes that both the originator of the message and the receiver must cooperate if they are to *transact* or negotiate meaning. Although public speakers originate messages, they should remember to adapt to feedback both as they prepare and as they speak. Listeners participate by actively decoding information and encoding feedback. All this communication, which can be negatively affected by both internal and external noise, takes place within a specific situation and cultural frame.

STUDY AND REVIEW

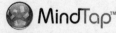

Reflect on what you've learned.

Public Speaking: Concepts and Skills for a Diverse Society offers a broad range of resources that will help you better understand the material in this chapter, complete assignments, and succeed on tests. Your MindTap resources feature the following:

- Speech videos with viewing questions, speech outlines, and transcripts
- Activities to help you check your understanding and to apply what you've learned to your own life
- Stop and Check and Critical Thinking exercises
- Outline Builder
- Web Links related to chapter content
- Study and review tools such as self-quizzes and an interactive glossary

You can access your online resources for *Public Speaking: Concepts and Skills for a Diverse Society* at cengagebrain.com using the access code that came with your book or that you purchased online.

Review *your Flashcards.*

KEY TERMS

The terms below are defined in the margins throughout this chapter.

bicultural 6

civic engagement 9

co-cultures 3

collectivist cultures 5

communication style 6

core cultural resources 3

critical thinking 8

culture 2

digital oratory 6

expressive cultures 6

individualistic cultures 5

nonexpressive cultures 6

oral culture 4

public speaking 2

rhetoric 8

rhetorical sensitivity 3

taboo 6

transactional model of communication 9

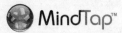

CRITICAL THINKING EXERCISES

1. If people define the word *public* too narrowly, they may think of public speakers as politicians speaking at conventions but not as teachers making an announcement at a PTA meeting. Write your definition of "public." Then, make a list of specific publics you have already addressed and those you may address someday.

2. Many online speeches can help you see the relationship between public speaking and culture. One such example is Barack Obama's speech on race, "A More Perfect Union," given in response to widely disseminated video clips of controversial statements by his pastor. It's available online. Watch it outside of class and then come to class prepared to discuss how it might function to transmit, reinforce, restore, and/or transform culture.

3. The Internet has many sources of information on the topic of rhetoric. Visit the American Rhetoric website and do some of the "Cool Exercises." Then watch at least two speeches you find there. Identify whether each speech functions to transmit, reinforce, repair, or transform culture.

4. Elaborate on the transactional model of communication by selecting a communication event from your own life and analyze it by identifying and explaining each element of the model.

APPLICATION EXERCISES

1. To gain experience in speaking publicly, look for upcoming campus or community events that would interest your audience. Then prepare an announcement using the guidelines in Chapter 18, and deliver it to your classmates.

2. Work with a group to evaluate the role of public speaking in creating and maintaining your college or university.
   - What role did public speaking play during the founding years?
   - How does your school currently use public speaking to recruit new students and donors?
   - What role does ceremonial speaking, such as a convocation or commencement speech, have in maintaining the vision and the values of your institution?
   - When issues threaten to divide your campus, how do groups and individuals use public speaking to negotiate differences?

3. To understand the importance of critical thinking skills, work with a group to select a short video on YouTube, a news report, or an ad to analyze. Begin by giving your first

impressions. What does your piece say or suggest? Then probe deeper and identify the assumptions on which it relies. Next, ask question about those assumptions. Finally, compare your first impressions with your impressions about the selection after you've examined it more carefully. Discuss with your classmates the value of critical analysis.

4. Interview a person working in the career you hope to enter after you graduate. Ask what opportunities exist for public speaking within that occupation. Ask if and how public speaking is related to the higher-paying, more prestigious jobs within that career.

CHAPTER 2

THIS CHAPTER WILL HELP YOU

- Acquire skills to overcome process anxiety

- Explain the five canons of rhetoric: invention, disposition, style, memory, and delivery

- Develop strategies to deal with performance anxiety

- Develop strategies to deal with physiological anxiety

- Develop strategies to deal with psychological anxiety

- Learn skills for effective rehearsal

Diana Ong/SuperStock

Giving Your First Speech: Developing Confidence

WHEN ASKED "What's the worst part about giving a speech?," these students responded:

Knowing what to speak about.

JONATHAN

I turn red and I think that's embarrassing.

MALIA

English is not my first language.

DMITRY

I'm very shy and I don't like to talk much to a single person, let alone a group.

REESE

MindTo

Review the chapter Learning **Objective** *and* **Start** *with a quic warm-up activity.*

These students all identified elements of **communication apprehension (CA)**,[1] which is commonly defined as "the fear or anxiety associated with either real or anticipated communication."[2] It is the dread of possible negative reactions you might experience when you communicate.[3] Although CA is linked to inborn temperament traits such as shyness,[4] even self-confident people can and do experience it.

Public speaking strikes fear into many, even most hearts. Whether you call it stage fright or **public speaking anxiety (PSA)**, it is a form of CA that refers to the common feelings of dread people experience at the thought of performing a speech in front of an audience.[5] There are two types of PSA: **process anxiety** (not knowing how to create a speech) and **performance anxiety** (worries about actually giving the speech). The goal of this chapter is to demystify the speech-making process and give you strategies for dealing with your performance anxiety. Putting this information into practice will increase your overall speaking competence.

Causes of Stress

Athletes commonly experience stress when they must perform under pressure. Consequently, sports psychologists have developed strategies to help athletes manage their anxiety. Rainer Martens,[6] a psychologist from Michigan State University, came up with a useful model that includes both process and performance anxiety. It's applicable not only to athletes, but to beginning speakers as well. Martens says, stress comes from your uncertainty about an outcome and the importance of that outcome. Consequently, stress results from three perceptions: your perceived imbalance between an *objective demand* and your perceived *response capability*, where you perceive failure to have *serious consequences*. Martens's model gives three areas to manage, change, or improve:

1. Sometimes you can change the *objective demand*; sometimes you can't. In this course, you don't create the speech assignment, so you can't really change it. But you can start your preparation long before the speech is due, leaving you enough time to meet the objective demands of the assignment.
2. You can increase your *response capability* for the required task. Think of an old-fashioned scale where you pile the demands on one side and your response capability on the

communication apprehension (CA) the fear or dread of negative responses you might experience because you speak out

public speaking anxiety (PSA) fear or dread specifically related to speaking in public

process anxiety fear due to lack of confidence in knowing how to prepare a speech

performance anxiety fear of forgetting or of poorly presenting a speech

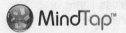 MindTap™

Read, highlight, and take notes online.

Stress results from a perceived imbalance between your capabilities and the requirements and importance of the task. To relieve stress, increase your abilities to create and perform speeches.

© iStockphoto.com/zothen

other. One way to balance the scale is to increase your response capability by studying harder, preparing better, and practicing in ways that improve your speaking abilities.

3. Changing *perceptions* is the third strategy. You might exaggerate the objective demands, or you may not give yourself enough credit for your response capability. In contrast, you might *reevaluate the consequences* and see if they really are that serious. There's a difference between not succeeding and not succeeding completely, and in the big scheme of things, doing poorly on a speech won't destroy your life.

The remainder of this chapter gives you ideas for implementing these strategies.

Develop Skills to Overcome Process Anxiety

anticipatory speech anxiety tension experienced at the mere thought of giving a speech

"Next week, your speech is due"—Martens would call this the "objective demand." When you first receive the assignment you may begin to experience **anticipatory speech anxiety**,[7] which is typically high just after the speech is announced.[8] Why? Perhaps you fear the unknown—it's like finding yourself in a dark, unfamiliar place without a flashlight.[9] Or, as Martens would say, you doubt your ability to respond. Fortunately, understanding the objective demand by studying speech principles and observing others speak, plus gaining response capability by actually giving speeches removes some of the mystery from the process. As speech-making becomes more familiar, most people experience less process anxiety and the panicky feelings that accompany it.[10]

canon a set of principles, standards, norms, or guidelines

canons of rhetoric principles, standards, norms, or guidelines for creating and delivering a speech

To teach the principles of speech-making, Roman educators identified five major categories of good speech-making—each one containing a set or **canon** of principles, standards, or guidelines that students should master to become effective speakers. The **canons of rhetoric**[11] are (1) *invention*—creating speech content; (2) *disposition* or arrangement—organizing speech materials; (3) *style*—choosing effective language; (4) *memory*—learning the major ideas; and (5) *delivery*—actually performing the speech. Learning the principles in the canons will give you the how-to skills you need to relieve some of your process anxiety.

Create Your Speech: The Canon of Invention

canon of invention principles for designing a speech that meets a need of a specific audience

The **canon of invention** provides guidelines for creating your speech content. Just as an inventor designs a product to meet a particular need, you design your presentations to meet a need for a specific audience in a specific situation. With any speech assignment, be sure you understand the expectations regarding general requirements and time limits. This text devotes nine chapters to this vital canon, but as a general introduction and to help you prepare your first speech, several principles are briefly summarized here.

Choose a Topic

Finding a classroom topic that will interest your listeners is challenging. (In some contexts, such as in an organization or workplace, your topic will be obvious.) The first class assignment is often either a self-introduction or the introduction of a classmate. If so, topic choice is partly chosen for you, but you must also find an interesting focus. Avoid boring your audience with well-known material presented in a predictable way. (Chapter 5 covers topic selection, and Appendix B plus the text's online resources show how other students successfully chose topics.)

Consider the Audience and the Setting

Another major task is to think from the diverse perspectives of your audience. What interests them? What is relevant to their lives? Analyze your listeners for *demographic information*, such as gender and age. Features such as religious jewelry or clothing also suggest interests, affiliations, and perspectives. Analyze *psychological factors* including what they already believe about your topic and their attitudes toward it. Finally, *the situation* in which you will speak—the lighting, ventilation, acoustics, and room layout—can make a difference in their attention and comfort. Other factors, such as time of day, matter as well. (Chapter 6 describes audience analysis in detail.)

Identify Your Purpose

What response do you want from your audience? Your answer determines your general purpose. If you want listeners to learn something, your general purpose is *to inform*. Do you want them to respond by believing or doing something? Or are you trying to reinforce their beliefs or behaviors? If so, your general purpose is *to persuade*. If you want them simply to laugh and enjoy themselves, your major purpose is *to entertain*. Finally, if you want to highlight and reinforce a particular cultural ideal, your general purpose is *to commemorate*. (Chapter 5 describes these purposes in greater detail.)

Gather Speech Materials

Even if you know your topic fairly well, you generally need to fill some gaps or update your knowledge by doing research. Search in library holdings or find materials in interviews, videos, radio or television programs, and the Internet. Of course, you should think critically about what you find in each source. (Chapters 7 and 8 describe research and supporting materials.)

If you are assigned to introduce a classmate, schedule an interview for an uninterrupted time in a quiet place—and then be on time. Bring a list of questions and record your conversation (with permission only) or take notes as you talk. Be sure you understand what you are told by asking questions such as, "Could you explain that in more detail?" To avoid any misunderstandings, read back your notes as you conclude.

Organize Your Ideas: The Canon of Disposition or Arrangement

Once you have your information in hand, your next step is to arrange your ideas so that they make sense. The principles of speech organization make up the **canon of disposition or arrangement**.

canon of disposition or arrangement guidelines for organizing a speech

If your first speech is a self-introduction, consider telling a story about a significant experience. For example, Heidi created a speech around the theme "wounded warrior." She narrated an intense experience she had as an Army translator in Afghanistan. The exemplum pattern in Chapter 18 is a good way to organize a story.

Most speeches in the Western speaking tradition have three major parts: the introduction, the body, and the conclusion. Taken as a whole, the outline looks like this:

I. **INTRODUCTION** This section orients your audience toward the subject. In general, introductions have four major functions that the first-century Roman Quintilian taught his students:[12]
   A. Draw audience attention to the topic.
   B. Relate the topic to their concerns.
   C. Link yourself to the subject.
   D. Preview the major points.
II. **SPEECH BODY** Here, you present your major ideas, using enough evidence to clarify and support each point; this part of the speech takes up most of your speaking time.

(continued)

There are many ways to organize speeches, and Chapters 9 and 17 describe common patterns in more detail. A speech outline typically looks like this:

    A. First main point
      1. Support
      2. Support
    B. Second main point
      1. Support
      2. Support

III. **CONCLUSION** Instead of ending abruptly, provide a sense of closure that ties your ideas together and leaves the audience with a takeaway thought. Conclusions typically have these elements:

    A. A transition to the conclusion
    B. A summary of the major ideas
    C. A reference to the introduction
    D. A final memorable statement

connectives words, phrases, and sentences used to lead from idea to idea and tie the parts of the speech together smoothly

Link your ideas to one another so that your speech flows smoothly from point to point, using **connectives** such as *first*, *next*, and *finally*. More complex transition statements, such as "After I left my job as a barista, I had more time to devote to my acting," summarize where your speech has been and where it is going. Connectives help your listeners keep their place in the speech.

After you have gathered materials and selected an organizational pattern, you can then choose precise wording and learn your speech well enough to present it. The skills for these tasks are found in the final three canons of rhetoric: style, memory, and delivery. (See Figure 2.1.)

Choose Suitable Language: The Canon of Style

style in rhetoric, style refers to language

canon of style principles for choosing effective language

Style can mean your individuality as expressed in your actions and tastes, your personality, and the way you dress and present yourself.[13] However, in rhetoric, **style** refers to language; consequently, the **canon of style** contains principles for using language effectively in both speaking and writing. (You probably consult a style manual for your writing classes.)

Finish your speech by polishing your wording, always with an ear tuned to your listeners. Here are a few general guidelines for effective use of language in public speaking:

Figure 2.1
The Romans identified the canons of rhetoric. Each canon contains principles, standards, norms, or guidelines for one aspect of speech-making.

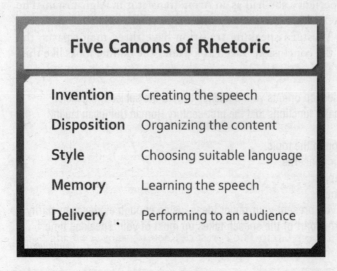

Five Canons of Rhetoric

Invention	Creating the speech
Disposition	Organizing the content
Style	Choosing suitable language
Memory	Learning the speech
Delivery	Performing to an audience

- Choose vocabulary and grammar that fit both the occasion and the audience.
- Omit offensive language such as swear words or demeaning language.
- Choose understandable words. Either define technical jargon or replace it with more familiar terminology.
- Instead of writing your speech like an essay, use an oral style that reflects the way people actually speak. However, use fewer slang expressions.

More detailed information on the canon of style is provided in Chapter 12.

Learn and Present Your Speech: The Canons of Memory and Delivery

Previous generations lacked index cards, teleprompters, and other memory aids, so speakers often memorized their speeches. However, the **canon of memory** is often called *the lost canon* because so few people in this culture rely on memory alone and because **memorized delivery** can be risky. Forgetting even a few words can lead to embarrassment—something you definitely want to avoid. **Manuscript delivery**, in which you write out your entire speech and then read it to your audience, helps you remember your ideas, but it is generally more useful for formal talks than for classroom or workplace speeches. Also, spur-of-the-moment **impromptu delivery**, where you stand up and speak with little advanced preparation, is not recommended for most classroom assignments, although it is common in workplace settings or social events for someone to be asked to "say a few words" on a familiar topic.

Instead, most classroom and workplace settings prefer **extemporaneous delivery**. Here, you gather your materials, organize them carefully, and then jot down key ideas on note cards that you later use to jog your memory during your talk. Chapter 14 elaborates on these four delivery methods, and Chapter 11 further explains content outlines and speaking outlines.

Rehearsal is a vital part of the preparation process, but the amount of time needed for rehearsal depends on several factors including your level of experience, your familiarity with the topic, the speech length, and your anxiety level. Interestingly, in a recent study researchers asked students to log the amount of time they spent in each of the canons. Rehearsal was the area that made a difference in grades.[14]

Here are a few rehearsal tips: Practice your speech orally and silently, using your note cards. Recruit friends or family—basically anyone who can act as an audience, provide feedback, troubleshoot problems, and let you deliver your speech to actual listeners. Or make a video of your speech and watch it to identify areas to improve. Go through the speech several times, each time selecting slightly different words. Focus on looking away from your notes and communicating conversationally. Although practice may not make perfect, you can at least have the confidence that comes from careful preparation.

Principles found in the **canon of delivery** provide guidelines for the four delivery methods described earlier and for nonverbal behaviors, such as gestures and eye contact. Good delivery includes pleasant facial expressions, smiling at appropriate times, and a posture of confidence. Good speakers speak conversationally, not in a monotone. Focus throughout on creating something *with* your listeners instead of giving something *to* them.

In summary, the guidelines found in the five canons of rhetoric build process competence and increase your response capability. You learn the skills of audience analysis, topic and purpose selection, and research (invention). Then you develop skills in organizing or arranging your ideas into meaningful patterns (disposition), choosing appropriate language (style), and learning your major points (memory), so that you can present them effectively (delivery). Go to The Forest of Rhetoric website for additional information about the canons of rhetoric.

canon of memory guidelines to help you remember your ideas

memorized delivery learning the speech by heart, then reciting it

manuscript delivery reading a speech

impromptu delivery speaking with little advanced preparation

extemporaneous delivery preparing a speech carefully in advance but choosing the exact wording during the speech itself

canon of delivery rules or standards for presenting a speech

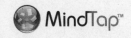

Outline Builder

 **Your First Speech**

Using the five canons of rhetoric, prepare a self-introduction or the introduction of a classmate. Throughout your preparation, consider the following questions:

1. Do I understand the assignment?
2. Is my topic somewhat unusual? If not, do I have a unique or novel approach?
3. What is my purpose in speaking?
4. How will I adapt this speech to this audience?
5. Is my speech clearly organized?
6. Are my language choices appropriate to the audience and the situation?
7. Which friends can I ask to listen to me rehearse?

Develop Strategies to Overcome Performance Anxiety

Physiological anxiety bodily responses to a perceived threat (increased heart rate, adrenaline rush)

Psychological anxiety mental stress about a perceived threat

Performance anxiety comes in two forms: physiological and psychological. **Physiological anxiety** is how your body responds to the feared event. **Psychological anxiety** is your mental worry, dread, and feelings of inadequacy about the performance itself. In Rainer Martens's model, this is your perceived response capability in light of the real or perceived seriousness of the consequences. In the following pages, you'll find a number of specific ideas you can use in combination to overcome both kinds of nervousness.

Strategies to Deal with Physiological Responses

fight-or-flight mechanism physiological mechanism your body automatically activates when threatened; helps you fight or flee

You know from experience how your body responds to danger. You might freeze. Or you might experience the **fight-or-flight mechanism**—a rush of adrenalin that prepares you to run or stay to fight the threat. Unfortunately, bodies don't distinguish between physically threatening situations (where you need extra physical energy to escape) and psychologically threatening experiences (where your rapid heart rate, butterflies, and adrenaline rush only add to your stress). Chris Sawyer and Ralph Behnke[15] identify four milestones of anxiety-producing events: (1) *anticipation*, the prespeaking period; (2) *confrontation*, beginning the speech; (3) *adaptation*, completing the speech; and (4) *release*, the period lasting one minute after the speech. Anxiety peaks in the anticipation period and steadily decreases, virtually disappearing in the release milestone, although some symptoms may linger.[16] (See Figure 2.2.)

Here's how Hattie described the process:

On speech day, I try to eliminate unnecessary stress. I sleep well the night prior, eat well, and especially make sure I exercise, as this has the biggest calming effect aside from good preparation. I feel well up until I step into the classroom when my heart begins to race. I start to question if I used deodorant and if my outfit is appropriate. When my name is called I feel a surge of anxiety similar to what I imagine a heart attack feels like, but I also feel relief, as all the anxiety will soon be over. During the speech I try to be mindful to purposefully breathe and pause. If I don't, I tend to race to the end. Once I have finished, I think of ways to improve next time but mostly I relish the fact that it is over!

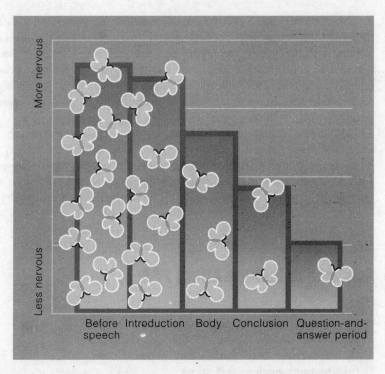

Figure 2.2
Performance Anxiety
Knowing that anxiety is greater at certain periods can help you control your nervousness by planning strategies that enable you to get through these periods.

To counteract nervous tension, get a good night's sleep the night before and then on speech day, work off your excess energy by doing some form of physical exercise such as weight lifting, brisk walking, or running. Try to relax by listening to soothing music. Eat breakfast and lunch, but limit your sugar and caffeine intake if these substances make you feel wired. Just before you speak, focus on relaxing your major muscle groups and breathe slowly and deeply.

Systematic Desensitization

If you are extremely nervous, you can try **systematic desensitization**,[17] a technique designed to minimize the physical effects of PSA. Theoretically, you can't be relaxed and tense at the same time, so this process teaches you how to relax physically as you think your way through increasingly intense scenarios. Although psychologists developed it to deal with irrational fears of snakes, researchers have found the techniques useful in alleviating public speaking anxiety.

systematic desensitization process designed to lessen physical reactions to stress; teaches how to relax while thinking about frightening speech events

This method involves three basic activities: (1) construct a list of frightening activities and put them in order, from least to most frightening; (2) learn some principles of relaxation; and (3) learn to relax as you think your way through progressively threatening situations.

To apply the techniques, first, list about fifteen public speaking activities and order your list, from the least to the most frightening. Your list might range from reading about a speech (not threatening) to giving a live speech on national television (terrifying). Receiving a speech assignment and giving a classroom speech will lie somewhere in between. Include things you can imagine happening but that you've never seen, such as fainting during your speech. Make each incident detailed and vivid. Interestingly, researchers have found that humor is helpful, so something as crazy as "during my speech a bird flies into the room and lands on my head" can go on your list. Sort your list into five piles: low, medium low, medium, medium high, and high, then order items from lowest to highest within the pile. Set this aside for a day.

Next, practice some progressive relaxation techniques. First, breathe deeply . . . hold the breath . . . release it . . . repeat several times. Next, tense and relax muscle groups, starting with the legs. Tighten your muscles . . . hold . . . hold . . . relax. Breathe, hold, and release your breath again. Continue the tighten-hold-relax process as you move up your body, from foot to head. Breathe-hold-release between each group of muscles. After you have tensed and relaxed all your muscle groups, completely relax, breathing deeply.

While you're still relaxed, pull out an anxiety pile; start with the lowest item, and imagine yourself doing it for a tolerable time. Stop. Assess your anxiety level (1–10 scale). Relax again. Return to the item and repeat the process, assessing your anxiety level each time you end. When you no longer feel anxious about one item, move to the next. Do just a few per day. The next day, begin with the last item from the previous session.[18]

DIVERSITY IN PRACTICE

Gender and Culture Affect PSA

Do women experience more PSA than men? In a variety of stressful situations, such as test taking, numerous studies indicate that females in general have stronger physical and psychological reactions than males. Consequently, communication researchers wanted to know if this trend carried over into public speaking contexts. They found that females do, in fact, report more communication anxiety than males. In the public speaking classroom, both males and females went through all four milestones of speech anxiety, but females were likely to react more strongly than males, possibly because they tend to be more cautious about communicating when they know they will be judged on their performance.[19] One of the best ways for both males and females to lessen high levels of anxiety is to reduce uncertainty about the assignment—in other words, to develop process competence.

As you might expect, speakers whose first language is not English often have strong PSA. They especially fear that listeners will evaluate them negatively because of their English-speaking skills.[20] Individuals in other-directed societies, such as Japanese, Chinese, or Thai cultures, have a great deal of concern about how others perceive them, and they may experience more speaking anxiety. Being in an accepting classroom, where the other students react positively to their speeches, is most helpful.[21]

© iStockphoto.com/sjenner13

Strategies to Deal with Psychological Anxiety

Rainer Martens pointed out two areas of psychological vulnerability: your perceived response capability (I can't do this; I don't have good delivery skills; I won't be able to hold their interest) and your perception of the consequences (they'll make fun of me; they won't pay attention; I'll flunk). Self-talk is called **internal monologue (I-M)**.[22] Negative I-M contributes to negative stress, which adds to your discomfort, but it's not fatal.

internal monologue (I-M) self-talk

Cognitive Modification

Mount Sinai Medical Center[23] experts suggest **cognitive modification** as a method to change your perceptions. Identify negative thoughts and replace them with positive ones[24] in four areas: the message, the audience, yourself, and the assignment:

cognitive modification identifying negative thoughts and replacing them with positive ones

- To think positively about the message, select an interesting topic that your audience will find relevant. Increase your response capabilities by giving yourself enough time for research and organization, and check the dictionary for pronunciation of unfamiliar words. Keep in mind your speech goal. Do everything you can to feel confident about the speech content.
- To promote positive thoughts about the audience, think of each listener as an individual with personal quirks. Specific individuals are not threatening, so why should the group be intimidating?[25] Remember that audience members are probably just as nervous when they speak and that they are not experts in your subject. Assume that they want you to succeed. (If your first language is not English, think of how your audience would feel if they had to give a speech in *your* native language.)[26]
- Maintain a positive self-image by concentrating on things you do well. Remind yourself that your worth as a person is unrelated to your skill as a novice public speaker and that competence develops with experience.
- Finally, change your perception of the consequences by thinking realistically about the assignment. No one expects perfection for beginning speakers. Watch some examples of public speaking students, and use examples in this text and its accompanying materials to understand reasonable expectations for student speeches.
- Remember, too, that being nervous does not mean you're doing a bad job. Most students who watch videos of their speeches are surprised at how calm they appear, knowing how nervous they felt. The fact is that some nervousness can energize you and make you appear more vital and enthusiastic.[27]

Visualization

Athletes and musicians regularly use a form of mental strategizing called **visualization**. Here, you imagine yourself successfully performing a complex task. Many speech instructors have taught thousands of students how to ease their anxiety through visualization techniques, and these students commonly report being less apprehensive and having fewer negative thoughts as they spoke.[28] This is true even for speakers who tend to freeze under stress.[29] The suggested process goes like this:

visualization rehearsing by using your imagination to envision your speech from start to finish

1. Find a quiet place and picture every detail from the beginning to the end of your speech.
2. Mentally place yourself in the audience and pretend you are watching yourself give your speech.
3. Imagine yourself as a competent, well-prepared performer who stands confidently, stresses important words, pauses effectively, and makes appropriate gestures.
4. Think about the audience responding positively with nods, smiles, and interest.

5. Continue to visualize yourself completing your speech, gathering your notes, making final eye contact with the audience, and returning to your seat.

6. Finally, imagine yourself back in the audience, delighted to be through![30]

Two key elements accompany successful visualization: You must create vivid images, and you must control the images you generate.[31]

Power Posing

power poseing assuming the open and expansive postures associated with powerful people

Researchers from Harvard and Columbia University are exploring a new line of research that links power posing to physical changes that can actually affect our levels of self-confidence and control over our bodies, minds, and emotions. They studied whether or not assuming a **power pose** (open and expansive posture) for two minutes could actually cause power. They discovered that high-power posers showed increased dominance hormones, reduced stress hormones, more willingness to take risks and more feelings of power.[32] In a related study, researchers in the Netherlands[33] found that using a lowered voice pitch, which is also associated with power, influences a speaker's feelings of power as well as the ability to reason abstractly.

If you want to experiment with these techniques, copy some of the poses used by powerful people. Stand with open (unfolded arms and uncrossed legs) and expansive postures (taking up more space) for two minutes before you rehearse and again before you present your speech. Lower your vocal pitch during your rehearsals, and maintain lower tones when you speak.

To find out more about this research, do an Internet search for "TED Talks" and link to Amy Cuddy's speech, "Your Body Language Shapes Who You Are."

habituation lessening anxiety by successfully repeating an experience over time

Fortunately, research shows that most highly anxious students finish their speech class feeling less anxious[34] because of **habituation**, which means that anxiety lessens

© rudall30/Shutterstock.com

© wavebreakmedia/Shutterstock.com

Researchers are exploring the relationship between power poses, more confidence, and less stress.

when an experience is repeated over time and the anticipated negative outcomes are not as bad as expected.[35] Jennifer's comments support this idea:

> I think it was really good that we did so many speeches because when we did it so many times, I was less nervous each time.

Online courses and traditional courses had similar results. In both formats, students learned the processes of speech-making and developed strategies for ridding themselves of some of their performance anxiety.[36]

Summary

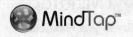

Many people experience public speaking anxiety (PSA) that results from the relationship between their uncertainty about the outcome and the importance of that outcome. Stress results from three perceptions: your perception of an imbalance between an objective demand and your perceived response capability, where you perceive failure to have serious consequences. To overcome stress, work on increasing your process and your performance capabilities.

To increase your process competencies, develop skills in five areas of speech-making (what Greeks and Romans identified as the five canons of rhetoric): invention, disposition, style, memory, and delivery. Use guidelines from the canon of invention to consider your audience's characteristics and interests, and take into account their responses to the specific situation. After that, select a unique, significant, and appropriate topic and focus. Decide whether your major purpose is to inform, persuade, entertain, or commemorate; then gather information from oral, print, or electronic sources that will support your topic adequately.

Organize your ideas to create an introduction, body, and conclusion using norms from the canon of disposition. Choose appropriate wording (canon of style), and learn your major ideas (canon of memory) so that you can extemporaneously deliver your speech (canon of delivery).

To increase your performance competencies, plan strategies for dealing with your nerves. Know when to expect the highest levels of physical symptoms, and prepare accordingly. Plan specific activities to counteract the physical tension brought on by the fight-or-flight mechanism. Systematic desensitization works for some people with extreme physical reactions. Then work on your psychological stress. Control your internal monologue by cognitive modification, substituting positive thoughts for negative ones. Or visualize yourself performing your speech successfully from beginning to end. Use vivid images and control your imaginary scenario. A third strategy is to experiment with power posing and lowering your voice as a way to increase your feelings of competency.

Doing these steps thoughtfully and thoroughly can give you confidence on speech day, and they equip you with the necessary knowledge and skills to be a more competent public speaker.

STUDY AND REVIEW

Reflect on what you've learned.

Public Speaking: Concepts and Skills for a Diverse Society offers a broad range of resources that will help you better understand the material in this chapter, complete assignments, and succeed on tests. Your MindTap resources feature the following:

- Speech videos with viewing questions, speech outlines, and transcripts
- Activities to help you check your understanding and to apply what you've learned to your own life

- Stop and Check and Critical Thinking exercises
- Outline Builder
- Web Links related to chapter content
- Study and review tools such as self-quizzes and an interactive glossary

You can access your online resources for *Public Speaking: Concepts and Skills for a Diverse Society* at cengagebrain.com using the access code that came with your book or that you purchased online.

Review your **Flashcards**.

KEY TERMS

The terms below are defined in the margins throughout this chapter.

anticipatory speech anxiety 16
canon 16
canon of delivery 19
canon of disposition or
    arrangement 17
canon of invention 16
canon of memory 19
canon of style 18
canons of rhetoric 16
cognitive modification 23
communication apprehension
    (CA) 15
connectives 18
extemporaneous delivery 19
fight-or-flight mechanism 20

habituation 25
impromptu delivery 19
internal monologue (I-M) 23
manuscript delivery 19
memorized delivery 19
performance anxiety 15
power pose 24
process anxiety 15
physiological anxiety 20
psychological anxiety 20
public speaking anxiety
    (PSA) 15
style 18
systematic desensitization 21
visualization 23

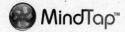

CRITICAL THINKING EXERCISES

1. Many factors affect communication apprehension (CA). An interesting study found that athletes have less CA than nonathletes, and those who play team sports have less CA than individual athletes.[37] From your own experiences, does this seem true? What factors might contribute to these differences?
2. Rank from 1 to 5 (easiest to hardest) the five canons of rhetoric in order of difficulty for you.

   ___ Invention: audience analysis, topic selection, purpose, research
   ___ Disposition: organization or arrangement and connection of ideas
   ___ Style: choice of appropriate language
   ___ Memory: remembering what you want to say
   ___ Delivery: actually presenting your speech

   Why did you rank them in this order? Identify some strategies you can use to work on the areas that challenge you most.
3. Write down an occupation that interests you. Then list the five canons of rhetoric. Beside each canon, identify ways that the skills developed within that canon will be useful in the job you named. For example, how will identifying a purpose or doing research help in a career such as nursing or engineering? How might organizing ideas help in teaching or computer programming?
4. Consider the ways that careful preparation and adequate rehearsal might contribute to your speaking competence. What effect does last-minute preparation have on competence? What effect does it have on anxiety? Knowing this, how do you plan to prepare for your next speech?

5. Make a list of your top ten suggestions for overcoming public speaking anxiety. For instance, your list might start with knowing how to create a speech, because you're always less comfortable when you don't know what to do. Develop a personal strategy for dealing with your anxiety.

APPLICATION EXERCISES

1. Work with a group to analyze your classroom audience, using the suggestions on pages 16 and 17. Then discuss some adaptations you might make to speak successfully to your class. For instance, how might your classmates influence your choice of topics? How might you adapt to diversity? How might the classroom itself, the time of day of the class, and other outside factors affect your speaking?

2. Often persuasive speeches require informing, and informational speeches have persuasive effects. Take, for example, the same general topic of study abroad programs. An informative speech could describe the various study abroad opportunities on campus; a persuasive speech could urge audience members to study abroad. With a small group of your classmates, identify at least three other topics and write down an informative goal and a persuasive goal for each.

3. Classroom speakers generally use extemporaneous delivery; however, the other modes of delivery are sometimes more appropriate. With a group of classmates, write down the four modes: memorized, manuscript, impromptu, and extemporaneous. Beside each, identify specific instances in which that mode would probably be the most effective. For instance, impromptu delivery goes with many wedding toasts; manuscript delivery works with commencement addresses. After you have identified several examples, discuss with your group some guidelines that you think speakers should follow for each type of delivery.

4. Memory is often considered the "lost" rhetorical canon because so little emphasis is placed on memorization in our digital age. Discuss these questions in your class: Is there any value in learning how to memorize speech information? If so, when and where might memorization be useful?

CHAPTER 3

THIS CHAPTER WILL HELP YOU

- Define ethical communication

- Describe three responses to diversity

- Explain three democratic principles for public speaking

- Identify characteristics of dialogical speaking and listening

- Discuss ethical responsibilities of listeners

- Define two kinds of academic dishonesty: plagiarism and fabrication

- Explain three types of plagiarism

- Paraphrase and cite sources correctly

Diana Ong/SuperStock

Ethics in a Diverse Society

FREE SPEECH. It's the cornerstone of US society. The nation's founders knew that limiting our right to express ourselves freely would limit our ability to engage fully in a representative form of government. So they crafted the First Amendment to the Constitution to read:

> Congress shall make no law … abridging the freedom of speech, or of the press; or the right of the people peaceably to assemble, and to petition the Government for a redressing of grievances.[1]

This does not mean freedom of speech is total. We can't legally joke about hijacking in an airplane,[2] and courts are increasingly ruling against hate

MindT

Review the chapter Learning ***Objectives*** *and* ***Start*** *with a quic warm-up activity.*

speech, discriminatory language, or language "intended to intimidate" a person or group.[3] Instead, we must balance our rights with our responsibilities into what Professor Vernon Jensen calls our "**rightsabilities**."[4] Jensen further defines **ethical communication** as the conscious decision to speak and listen in ways that you, in light of your cultural ideals, consider right, fair, honest, and helpful to others as well as yourself.[5]

Focusing on both rights and responsibilities brings up a number of ethical questions. On what basis should we determine right and wrong in public speaking and listening? Should some things be left unsaid? When? Who decides? What responsibilities do you have as a listener or as a researcher? This chapter presents some principles that have emerged from discussing these ethically challenging questions. We first examine common responses to diversity and then discuss guidelines for ethical speaking, listening, and researching in a complex culture.

Responses to Diversity

Diversity includes obvious differences such as language, ethnicity, religious beliefs and practices, as well as conflicting opinions about political and social issues that can seem irreconcilable, leading to tensions that can overshadow the many things that might otherwise bind people together.[6] However, diverse people and groups can and do come together in productive, civil, and ethical ways. Common responses to diversity include resistance, assimilation, and accommodation.[7]

Individuals and groups enact **resistance** in many forms. Some bolster and defend their beliefs and traditions. Others withdraw from challenging situations. Still others attack their opponents with mild challenges that ignore, discount, or ridicule divergent ideas or escalate to physical assaults, death threats, terrorism, or armed conflict.[8] Resisters often attack with words, so much so that Deborah Tannen, a professor of linguistics, says we live in an "argument culture."[9] Tannen is especially sensitive to the war metaphors we use. For example, think about all the battle terms you hear: culture *wars*, *fighting* for your ideas, *battleground* states. We *arm* ourselves for arguments; we *shoot down* ideas; we *target* our political enemies. You'll find dozens of additional examples.

Resistance is not inherently bad. In many cases, both in the United States and around the world, conscientious resistance leads to positive outcomes. Protest movements and activists often confront social, environmental, and global injustices and bring about necessary reforms. However, activism that justifies using questionable means for a good cause has ethical implications.

In **assimilation**, groups or individuals embrace new perspectives and lifestyles and reject or surrender some or most of their previous beliefs and actions. For example, a person might encounter religious diversity and convert to a different belief system, adopting a new religious vocabulary, new rituals, and changed concepts. Assimilation takes place over time and is rarely total.[10] Because choice is a dominant US value, people are free to change their ideas and lifestyles, but ethical implications arise when individuals feel coerced or manipulated into changing without critically examining good reasons for the change.

Another approach, **accommodation**, involves adjustment or adaptation.[11] Accommodating groups or individuals show a willingness to hear and evaluate diverse ideas

rightsabilities phrase coined by Professor Vernon Jensen to highlight the tension between our right to free speech and our responsibility for our speech

ethical communication the conscious decision to speak and listen in ways that you, in light of your cultural ideals, consider right, fair, honest, and helpful to all parties involved

 MindTap™

Read, highlight, and take notes online.

resistance response to diversity in which you refuse to change, and you defend your own positions or attack others

assimilation response to diversity in which you embrace new perspectives and lifestyles and reject or surrender some or most of your previous beliefs and actions

accommodation response to diversity in which you listen and evaluate the views of others; both sides adapt, modify, and bargain to reach mutual agreements

In an "argument culture," a war of words is a common form of resistance by those who are unwilling to accommodate diverse ideas.

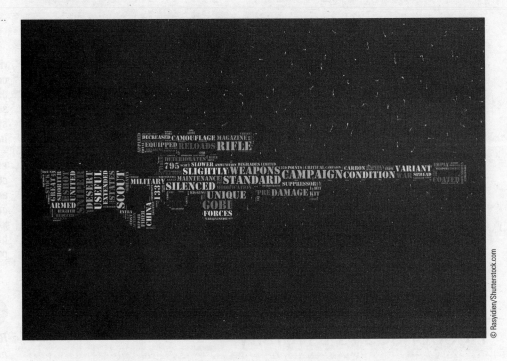

© Rasyidien/Shutterstock.com

multivocal society society that actively seeks expression of a variety of voices or viewpoints

with an open mind. They allow themselves to rethink their ideas and surrender some, modify others, and hold some relatively intact. Accommodation leads to a **multivocal society** that seeks out a variety of ideas, opinions, and visions and gives them an open, recognized voice. Here, co-cultural groups recognize their diversity yet work together to forge a civic culture that accommodates both differences and commonalities.[12] However, accommodation has its challenges:

> Participating in this form of communication requires a set of abilities, the most important of which is remaining in the tension between holding your own perspective, being profoundly open to others who are unlike you, and enabling others to act similarly.[13]

Study Rodney Smolla's inaugural speech in Appendix B and notice the ways he calls for accommodation on the college campus where he is assuming the presidency.

Resistance and accommodation have ethical implications. It's easy to label extreme forms of resistance (terrorist attacks, for example) or even taunting as unethical, but what about simply ignoring people who differ from you? What about cruel remarks in anonymous posts on Internet sites? Your decision to resist new ideas or to embrace them with relatively few questions, to block voices from being heard or to invite dialogue—all of these have ethical implications for both speaking and listening in a diverse society.

Let's now turn to specific cultural resources that can help you be a more ethical speaker.

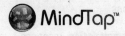 MindTap™

Speaking Ethically

Your concern with ethics should begin as soon as you receive your speech assignment because you have responsibilities to your audience, your topic, and yourself. Ethical principles fall into two major categories: democratic and dialogical. (The Credo for Ethical Communication, created by the National Communication Association and reprinted in the Ethics in Practice box, includes both perspectives.)

ETHICS IN PRACTICE

NCA Credo for Ethical Communication

Questions of right and wrong arise whenever people communicate. Ethical communication is fundamental to responsible thinking, decision making, and the development of relationships and communities within and across contexts, cultures, channels, and media. Moreover, ethical communication enhances human worth and dignity by fostering truthfulness, fairness, responsibility, personal integrity, and respect for self and others. We believe that unethical communication threatens the quality of all communication and consequently the well-being of individuals and the society in which we live. Therefore we, the members of the National Communication Association, endorse and are committed to practicing the following principles of ethical communication:

- We advocate truthfulness, accuracy, honesty, and reason as essential to the integrity of communication.
- We endorse freedom of expression, diversity of perspective, and tolerance of dissent to achieve the informed and responsible decision making fundamental to a civil society.
- We strive to understand and respect other communicators before evaluating and responding to their messages.
- We promote access to communication resources and opportunities as necessary to fulfill human potential and contribute to the well-being of families, communities, and society.
- We promote communication climates of caring and mutual understanding that respect the unique needs and characteristics of individual communicators.
- We condemn communication that degrades individuals and humanity through distortion, intimidation, coercion, and violence, and through the expression of intolerance and hatred.
- We are committed to the courageous expression of personal convictions in pursuit of fairness and justice.
- We advocate sharing information, opinions, and feelings when facing significant choices while also respecting privacy and confidentiality.
- We accept responsibility for the short- and long-term consequences for our own communication and expect the same of others.

Source: Endorsed by the National Communication Association, November 1999. Reprinted by permission of the National Communication Association.

Practice Democratic Principles

In society, we discuss issues of concern to individuals, the nation, and the world in face-to-face meetings, through the media, and on the Internet. The variety and amount of available opinions call for citizens who can think carefully about matters that affect our nation and world.

Develop a Habit of Research

Because you are your audience's primary source of information during your speech, you owe it to your listeners to know what you're talking about, so it's important to do your homework beforehand. Don't just settle for a surface understanding of your topic; instead, examine a variety of credible sources and search for diverse viewpoints from supporters as well as critics. Make sure your position is well reasoned. Present a variety of perspectives to give your listeners the breadth of information they need to form their own conclusions. This approach contrasts with the "argumentative mentality" that Deborah Tannen says "obscures the complexity of research"[14] and creates oversimplification, disinformation, and distortion of issues.

Be Honest and Fair

Present your information truthfully. Don't exaggerate a problem to make it seem greater than it actually is. Don't distort or twist evidence. Statistics can be particularly misleading, so find out as much as you can about the numbers you present. Strive for fairness, balance, and evenhandedness rather than simply giving the side that favors your position.

Practice Civility

Civility a social virtue grounded in courtesy that chooses to understand and work with others

Civility is a social virtue grounded in courtesy.[15] Civil speakers and listeners are more than simply polite; they *choose* to persuade, consult, advise, bargain, compromise, and build coalitions. Civility accommodates diverse opinions by striving for understanding, appreciating opposing perspectives, and accepting the possibility of losing the argument. Cultures from the ancient Greeks to modern Asian societies have promoted civility as an ethical principle.[16]

President Obama called for civility in a speech after yet another deadly shooting:

> [A]t a time when our discourse has become so sharply polarized . . . it's important for us to pause for a moment and make sure that we're talking with each other in a way that heals, not in a way that wounds. . . . As we discuss these issues, let each of us do so with a good dose of humility. Rather than pointing fingers or assigning blame, let's use this occasion to expand our moral imaginations, to listen to each other more carefully, to sharpen our instincts for empathy and remind ourselves of all the ways that our hopes and dreams are bound together.[17]

These concerned citizens are taking advantage of a town hall forum where they can discuss public concerns with the city's mayor. All speakers should enact dialogical and democratic principles and be mindful of their ethical responsibilities to other speakers, to audience members, and to themselves.

AP Images/Gerry Broome

Habits of research, honesty, fairness, and civility—these are by no means all of the democratic principles related to public speaking. However, this list gives you some specific ways to think about ethical speaking. Since diversity is pervasive in our society, you must create your own way to best respect (and live comfortably with) cultural differences.[18]

Does Facebook Encourage Civility?[19]

DIVERSITY IN PRACTICE

Communication researchers are currently exploring ways that digital media help or hinder high school and college students' civic engagement and involvement in issues of public concern. Early studies are finding that online groups based on common interests are not just "echo chambers" that only reinforce the participants' views. Instead, the more time students spend in online groups, the more exposure they have to diverse perspectives. Compared with youth who don't participate in online groups, these students are more likely to volunteer, give to charitable causes, and express their opinions about community issues.

Researchers next plan to explore questions related to civility. How do young people respond online to diverse viewpoints? When, how, and why do they attack the opposition? Do they present reasoned support for their own views? Rethink their perspectives? The answers, when they come, may be surprising.

Questions

1. Are you a member of online groups? If so, what are they? Do any of them deal with controversial social or political topics?
2. Do you find diversity of participants and of opinions in the groups? Read through some recent messages. How do the participants, in general, interact?
3. Go to an online news or opinion site and find an article about a controversial topic. Read the comments below the article. How do they support or contrast with the NCA's Credo for Ethical Communication?

Use Dialogical Principles

A dialogical perspective is not a set of "rules"; instead, it is a mind-set linked to cultural values of honesty, openness, and freedom of choice.[20] Taking a dialogical perspective can help you be more ethical as a speaker and listener. In *The Magic of Dialogue: Transforming Conflict into Cooperation*, Daniel Yankelovich[21] identifies three essential components of dialogue: equality, empathy, and examination. (See Figure 3.1.)

- *Equality* means you and your listeners respect each other and regard each other's opinions as important enough to consider.
- *Empathy* means you show compassion and a willingness to identify emotionally with others in an attempt to understand other perspectives.
- *Examination* means you put aside a know-it-all attitude and willingly scrutinize both your assumptions and those of others with an open mind. You may *never* agree with some people or you might eventually persuade them to adopt your views.

Figure 3.1
These are the three essential
components of dialogue.

A Dialogical Attitude

Equality: respect others; consider their opinions

Empathy: show compassion and identify emotionally with others

Examination: consider your assumptions and theirs with an open mind

Figure 3.1
These are the three essential
components of dialogue.

This perspective also helps create a multivocal society. What does it look like in practice? Amitai Etzioni,[22] who experienced Nazi persecution during his childhood, emphasizes both rights and responsibilities in the principles he proposes for discussions involving major differences:

1. Don't demonize the other side or only show it negatively.
2. Don't insult or offend the deep moral commitments of others; don't bring up dark moments from a group's history.
3. Talk less about nonnegotiable "rights" and more about negotiable needs, wants, and interests.
4. Don't feel you must deal with every issue; you can let some things drop.
5. Don't abandon your convictions, but balance your beliefs and passions against those strongly held by others.

Dialogue can help resolve international, national, and campus problems. For example, groups such as the Difficult Dialogues initiative provide space for people from various perspectives to come together in reasoned dialogue about controversial issues. On campuses, The Democracy Project develops "intentionally designed, permanent spaces on campuses for identifying, studying, deliberating, and planning action regarding pressing issues with ethical or social implications."[23]

Listening Ethically

You don't have time to listen to every person or every idea. But polite listening affirms another person's right to speak, and your respectful attention is one way to empower others. Think about how positive you feel when someone who disagrees with you still takes time to ask how you came to your conclusions. Sincere questions that are not meant as personal attacks show that the listener is really trying to understand your viewpoint.

Some situations pose ethical dilemmas for listeners. For example, when you hear someone saying something you know to be false or arguing for a viewpoint that does not seem well reasoned, what should you do? Should you respectfully confront the speaker in front of others? Should you prepare another speech to present more accurate information or provide a different perspective? Should you ask questions that help other listeners detect the misinformation or bias? Should you disrupt the speech by **heckling**— by interrupting or shouting down the speaker? These are all possible responses.

heckling disrupting a
speech by interrupting or
shouting down a speaker

Classroom listening also has ethical implications. Have you been in a class situation where disruptive or impolite students caused you stress and, as a result, you got less out of the session? For example, students who challenge the instructor or other students with whom they disagree can make a learning situation stressful and difficult. Nowadays, many universities are addressing classroom incivility—defined as actions that interfere with students' overall learning.[24] In addition to disruptive challenges, annoying behaviors such as arriving late and leaving early, noisily packing up before class ends,

Fotosports International/Photoshot

Incivility among audience
members can make it difficult
for others to hear and
understand the speaker.

texting, reading other materials, surfing the Internet, or having side conversations may
seem relatively minor, but they can add up to create a climate that interferes with both
your and other students' ability to listen and learn.[25]

Interestingly, one professor who taught in both face-to-face and online formats
reported that student feedback on controversial topics differed in these two formats.
In classroom discussions, students were often sarcastic, disrespectful, and dismissive of
opposite opinions; however, in online forums (where comments were graded on how
well ideas were developed, organized, and supported by evidence) students typically
gave professional and mature feedback, perhaps because they took time to evaluate
their reasoning before they submitted a post. You can follow the principles for ethical
feedback by holding yourself accountable for thoughtful but civil responses to ideas that
conflict with yours.[26]

To evaluate your ethical responsibilities as a listener, ask yourself these questions:

- Do I keep myself informed about significant issues by exposing myself to a number
of arguments, or do I listen only to the side with which I already agree? In short, do
I listen with an open mind?
- Do I fulfill my ethical responsibilities to other listeners by not distracting them?
- Do I fulfill my responsibilities to speakers by letting them know they are being heard?
- Do I encourage speakers to meet ethical standards? This may mean that I ask for
further information about their sources or that I point out relevant information they
omit.
- Do I evaluate my feedback to make sure my responses are civil and well reasoned?

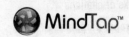

Academic Honesty

Kari's introduction was fine until she got to her thesis statement:

The National Collegiate Athletic Association (NCAA) is the main governing body of
collegiate sports, where students look to further their athletic careers....

Today, I will share with you the rule I would like to see changed—and that is athletic scholarships for Division III schools.

The professor thought, "Wait a minute! I don't assign a change-a-rule speech, but my colleague down the hall does." A quick check with him turned up an identical opening submitted by a student in another class. Kari's speech was plagiarized. She admitted that she had changed a couple of lines, but basically she'd given her friend's speech. Taylor failed to cite sources in her speech and on her PowerPoint slides. In a speech about drug cartels, Aaron made up a statistic—an act of fabrication, a second type of ethical breach. Plagiarism and fabrication are specific ethical violations, punishable by a failing grade, being fired from a job, and sometimes public humiliation. (Not every culture shares these concepts. See Diversity in Practice: Plagiarism and Culture for other cultural notions about intellectual property.) To avoid ethical problems with plagiarism or fabrication, it is important to understand what they are.

Avoid Plagiarism

plagiarism presenting the words, images, or ideas of others as if they were your own

Your degree is your college or university's official recognition and certification that you have personally learned the concepts and practical skills associated with your degree.[27] Because student learning is their purpose for existing, colleges and universities crack down on **plagiarism**. They reason that when you plagiarize, you don't personally do the work; instead, you present other people's ideas, words, or works as your own, without giving credit to the source. It would be somewhat like sending your roommate to the weight room to do your weight training; you don't benefit from the exercise.[28] Furthermore, it's not fair to your classmates who *are* doing the work.[29]

The Internet makes plagiarism easier than ever because it is so simple to access and download other people's material.[30] Consequently, someone who would never consider ripping a paragraph out of a *New York Times* column or cutting a sentence out of *Sports Illustrated* and gluing it onto an outline finds it easy to cut and paste the same material from those sources online into a computer document. To many people, electronically stored material is easier to conceptualize as somehow different in kind from hard copies of the same content.[31]

To avoid plagiarism, you should understand its various forms:[32]

Deliberate fraud knowing, intentional plagiarism

- **Deliberate fraud** happens when students knowingly and intentionally borrow, buy, or steal someone else's speech or outline and present it as their own work. Because Kari's speech on changing a rule, mentioned earlier, was deliberately borrowed, she was subject to her university's harsh penalties for plagiarism, which included an F on the assignment and a letter placed in her file in the dean's office.

Cut-and-paste plagiarism copying material word for word and then patching it together without quotation marks or citations

- **Cut-and-paste plagiarism** is when plagiarists copy entire sentences or paragraphs, word for word from an article or articles and piece them together into an outline or speech. They omit quotation marks around the copied words and fail to cite the sources in the speech or next to the material on the outline, even though they may supply a list of resources at the end of the outline.

Improper paraphrase changing some words of a source but keeping the basic structure and ideas intact without citing the source

- **Improper paraphrase** means changing words or moving phrases around but keeping the basic organizational structure and ideas of the original intact. Although these plagiarizers might list all sources in a reference list, they fail to credit the source *next to the paraphrased material itself*.

Accidental plagiarists plagiarists who lack knowledge about the rules

Plagiarism can be intentional or accidental. **Accidental plagiarists** don't intend to cheat, but they fail to properly paraphrase or give credit to their sources. Intentional or not, the consequences can be serious. For example, Allison created a series of PowerPoint slides with pictures she'd downloaded from the Internet without crediting the websites where she found the pictures. However, it never occurred to her that she should cite the

Plagiarism and Culture

Individualistic cultures like the United States consider plagiarism to be a serious intellectual breach.[39] First, writing something down is thought to be a concrete way to demonstrate your knowledge and skills. Turning in someone else's work does not show what *you* know.

Second, because individuality is emphasized, you should develop yourself to your highest potential and do creative, original thinking. Turning in someone else's work does not demonstrate your originality.

Finally, the cultural notion of personal property includes ownership of intellectual property. You can patent, copyright, or sell your ideas, creations, musical works, unique words, and writings because they are legally yours. Thus, if someone else uses all or part of your original work without giving you credit, you can charge that person with "stealing" your intellectual property.

In contrast, collectivist cultures view intellectual property differently. In a society that values the group over the individual, words and ideas can belong to the culture as a whole, not to a single person. Would stealing or pirating works be viewed with the same perspective? What might happen if a business headquartered in the United States moved into such a culture?

Also, consider the impact of the Internet on notions of "ownership" of words and ideas. For example, through hypertext, people can "write collaboratively and use nonlinear connections to create products that show few indications of who said what."[40] Wikipedia is just one example of a jointly created resource. Who really "owns" a Wikipedia entry? If you find two or more websites with identical information, who originated the material?

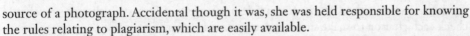

source of a photograph. Accidental though it was, she was held responsible for knowing the rules relating to plagiarism, which are easily available.

Where are these rules? Your university library or campus writing center provides guidelines for source citations. Here's an example from Purdue University's Online Writing Lab:[33]

- Give credit whenever you use somebody else's words, ideas, or creative works directly—whether you take them from library resources, the Internet, films or television shows, audio recordings, advertisements, letters from friends, or elsewhere.
- Provide sources for information learned in interviews, conversations, or email.
- Tell your audience the source of unique words and phrases that are not your own.
- Identify the sources of diagrams, illustrations, charts, photographs, and figures.

You do not need to document:

- Personal experiences, observations, conclusions, or insights.
- Results of experiments you personally conduct.
- Common knowledge, including folklore or traditions within your cultural group such as Cinderella or Robin Hood.
- Generally accepted facts—the kind of information every source provides or information your audience already knows or easily finds in reference material. For example, numerous sources say Presidents John Adams and Thomas Jefferson both died on the fourth of July in 1826, so citing a source may be unnecessary. To be

on the safe side, however, the Writing Center at the University of North Carolina counsels you to cite information that is new to you.[34] Maybe "everyone" knows the death date of Adams and Jefferson, but if *you* first learn it in a specific history book, cite that source.

Sources can be either published or unpublished. Of course, books and magazines are considered publications, but so are paintings, websites, and movies or audio recordings. Unpublished sources include letters and email, speeches, personal interviews, personal photographs, class lecture notes and handouts—even papers you've submitted for another class.[35]

To avoid plagiarism, name each source as you deliver your speech. For example, when you use a direct quotation, introduce it as such. When you paraphrase someone else's ideas, cite the originator. When you present a diagram or chart on a visual, write the source somewhere on the visual or on a reference list at the end of the presentation. Here are some specific examples of how speakers cited sources:

- *Published source, journal.* Products can be added to shows even after they've initially aired. In a February 1, 2008, article in *Teacher Librarian*, Keith McPherson reported that a scene from the *Friends* sitcom originally showed Ross sitting at a bare table; now a rerun shows a package of Oreo cookies in front of him.[36]
- *Published source, Internet.* To cite the source of a visual, Zitong provided information in a very small font beside the image. Alternatively, she could have created a reference list at the end of a series of visuals citing the source for each image used.
- *Unpublished source, personal conversation* [by a filmmaker]. The other day my friend Glen Basner told me that everything we've learned about financing films over the last 15 years we have to forget.[37]

Chapter 11 describes ways to document sources on your outline. Be sure to list your references at the end using a standard format such as MLA (Modern Language Association) style or APA (American Psychological Association) style. Look for the latest version of these style manuals and others that are available on the Internet or in the reference section of your library. They show you how to cite just about any source, from a book to a personal letter, from a DVD to a website. Many articles in your library's databases also show how to cite the article in a variety of formats, although you should check each citation to make sure it meets your instructor's criteria.[38]

Traditional Chinese Wedding

Source: iStockPhoto File #32257176

© iStockphoto.com/windcatcher

References

- The traditional Chinese wedding photograph was downloaded from iStock Photo (n.d.) Newlyweds – stock image.
  www.istockphoto.com/stock-photo-32257176-newlyweds.php?st=99778a3

To provide the source for a visual aid, either (1) give credit beside the image or (2) create a final reference list that tells the source for each image you use.

Avoid Fabrication

Plagiarism is only one form of academic dishonesty. Another is **fabrication**, which happens if you make up information or guess at numbers but present them as factual. Fabrication has serious consequences. For instance, a well-known researcher faked scientific data linking autism to vaccines. He was eventually disgraced, but not until the information was widely disseminated, frightening many parents away from vaccinating their children.[41] Until he was exposed, students had no way of knowing that his data were falsified, and many used them in their speeches on childhood vaccinations. After the news broke, however, the truth became widely available to everyone who double checks the facts, and speakers who continue to pass on the faked data as true can be held liable.

Citing a reference you did not actually read or passing along rumors or other unsubstantiated information are types of fabrication common in public speeches. Rumors—especially about politicians or celebrities or sports figures—sweep across Internet blogs, emails, talk radio, and whispered conversations. However, accurate information should be available to those willing to search for it. (Hypothetical examples, described in Chapter 8, are in a different category because the audience understands that these examples are not real.)

The best ways to avoid fabrication are to use a number of sources and to be alert for conflicting data. Thoroughly check out your information before you present it as factual. If something seems suspicious, don't use it. Many Internet sites exist to uncover hoaxes and false claims and to expose urban legends of all kinds.[42]

fabrication making up information or repeating information without sufficiently checking its accuracy

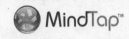

Summary

People in pluralistic cultures differ in beliefs, values, attitudes, and behaviors to degrees that range from superficial to fundamental, and responses to diversity vary. If you choose to defy or resist, you defend or bolster your position and (perhaps) attack or ignore diverse perspectives. If you choose accommodation, you accept differences and work with others to create a society in which all can live together.

Our culture provides both democratic and dialogical resources that you can combine to speak and listen ethically. Democratic principles remind you to develop a habit of research, to present your materials honestly and fairly, and to respond to diversity with civility. When you choose a dialogical relationship with your listeners, you respect them as equals, have empathy with their perspectives, and examine both your own and your listeners' assumptions in an honest, open manner.

Listening also calls for ethically responsible actions, which many people violate. Allowing people to speak empowers them, giving them a voice and enabling others to hear their ideas. However, when speakers present incorrect or misleading information, you face an ethical decision in which you must balance your rights and responsibilities against the rights and responsibilities of the speaker and other listeners. The term *rightsabilities* highlights this tension. Public speaking courses provide good opportunities to practice civility and behave in ways that help others listen and learn without the stress of disruptions.

As you present your materials, be sure to cite your references and check a variety of sources to avoid the ethical problems of plagiarism or fabrication. Plagiarism occurs when you present the ideas, words, organizational pattern, or images created by another person as your own without giving credit to the original source. Fabrication occurs when you make up material or present something as factual when it is not.

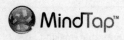

Reflect on what you've learned.

STUDY AND REVIEW

Public Speaking: Concepts and Skills for a Diverse Society offers a broad range of resources that will help you better understand the material in this chapter, complete assignments, and succeed on tests. Your MindTap resources feature the following:

- Speech videos with viewing questions, speech outlines, and transcripts
- Activities to help you check your understanding and to apply what you've learned to your own life
- Stop and Check and Critical Thinking exercises
- Outline Builder
- Web Links related to chapter content
- Study and review tools such as self-quizzes and an interactive glossary

You can access your online resources for *Public Speaking: Concepts and Skills for a Diverse Society* at cengagebrain.com using the access code that came with your book or that you purchased online.

Review your Flashcards.

KEY TERMS

The terms below are defined in the margins throughout this chapter.

accidental plagiarists 36	fabrication 39
accommodation 29	heckling 34
assimilation 29	improper paraphrase 36
civility 32	multivocal society 30
cut-and-paste plagiarism 36	plagiarism 36
deliberate fraud 36	resistance 29
ethical communication 29	"rightsabilities" 29

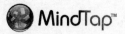

CRITICAL THINKING EXERCISES

1. Conduct an Internet search for the phrase "hate speech," and come to class prepared to share an example you found. With your classmates, discuss the importance of First Amendment rights to free speech, balanced against the ethical responsibilities described in this chapter.
2. Use your own values and beliefs as well as the guidelines described in this chapter to write an ethical code that states your personal principles for speaking and listening.
3. For an example of a famous speech that addresses religious diversity, read or listen to streaming video of John F. Kennedy's Address to the Greater Houston Ministerial Association in June 1960, which is available on the JFK Presidential Library and Museum site. Kennedy became the first Catholic president in 1960, but five months before the election, some voters worried that his allegiance might be to the pope, not to the American people. Notice how JFK lays out his views on religious diversity and how he affirms core American values.

APPLICATION EXERCISES

1. Using the NCA credo as a guide, work with a small group of your classmates to create a class code of conduct. Visit the National Communication Association site for additional information.
2. With a small group of your classmates, choose a specific international, national, or local situation in which conflicting beliefs, attitudes, values, or behaviors caused a conflict. Identify which of the ways of dealing with differences—resistance or accommodation— the various participants used to respond. Assess the ethicality of their responses.

3. With a small group in your classroom, discuss ways that people who hold diverse perspectives on a controversial topic might engage in dialogue (for example, pro-choice advocates meeting with pro-life activists; born-again Christians talking with committed Muslims; animal rights activists meeting with research scientists; leaders of NATO meeting with leaders of the African Union). How can each group listen to the other and explore its perspectives with an open mind?

4. Form small groups and choose a controversial issue about which you have moderate to strong disagreement. Discuss the topic within the group, and put into practice the principles for speaking and listening in this chapter.

5. Look up your campus's guidelines regarding academic honesty. What information do they provide to help students learn and practice ethical research procedures? What are the penalties for plagiarism?

6. Look up your campus library's information on source citation. What resources are available to help you format your reference list in the style your instructor prefers?

Diana Ong/SuperStock

Effective Listening

AN ANCIENT PROVERB emphasizes the comparative importance of listening: "We have been given two ears and but a single mouth in order that we may hear more and talk less."[1] Unfortunately, we often focus less on developing our listening competencies than on improving our reading, writing, and speaking skills.

Listening is more than simply **hearing**. I can **hear** traffic outside, a door slamming down the hall, rain against the window—that is, my ears pick up those sounds, but I'm not listening to them. Listening is an active mental process in which you interpret messages to understand and respond to them.[2] It takes motivation, effort, and concentration. Listening has at least five elements: (1) receiving sounds, (2) discriminating or distinguishing among them, (3) focusing attention, (4) assigning meaning to the sounds, and then (5) remembering the information. In contrast, something that goes in one ear and out the other is hearing.

MindT◉

Review the chapter Learning **Objectives** and **Start** with a quic◖ warm-up activity.

Because listening is so vital in many areas of life, this chapter first illustrates its importance and then looks at some factors that typically hinder effective listening. Finally, it presents strategies you can use to become a more effective listener.

listening active process that receives, distinguishes, attends to, assigns meaning, and remembers what you hear

hearing physical process involving sound waves, eardrums, and brain receptors

Listening Skills Are Valuable

A recent Internet search for "listening skills" linked to almost half a billion sites offering workshops, quizzes, advice, and activities that can improve listening in workplaces, in classrooms, and in relationships. Obviously, people definitely see room for improvement, and they value good listening for many reasons:

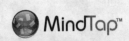

Read, highlight, and take notes online.

- *Listening takes up much of our time.* Listening is the most commonly used skill in the workplace; understanding and following instructions (skills linked to listening) come in second.[3] Furthermore, the average student spends fourteen hours each week listening in class; this is over and above the hours spent listening to friends and to media.[4]
- *Good listening skills are good job skills.* In one study, 80 percent of executives ranked listening as the most important work skill.[5] Other researchers found that physicians with good listening skills had fewer malpractice claims.[6] And Madelyn Burley-Allen, author of *Listening: The Forgotten Skill*, says the most common comment about well-liked bosses is "he or she really listens to me."[7] In occupations as diverse as dental hygienist,[8] interior designer,[9] roofing contractor,[10] tax preparer,[11] journalist, and politician, good listening makes a difference. President Calvin Coolidge once said, "No one ever listened himself out of a job."[12] In short, the most successful people are generally effective listeners.
- *Good listening skills are good academic skills.* Researchers administered a listening test to all incoming students at one university. At the end of the first year, 49 percent of low-scoring listeners were on academic probation, compared to less than 5 percent of high scorers. In contrast, 68.5 percent of high-scoring listeners were earning honors, compared to just over 4 percent of low scorers.[13]
- *You have an investment in the listening situation.* One university's counseling service advises students to develop a positive, consumer-wise attitude toward listening. The fact that you are in a particular listening situation means you have something at stake. Choosing to listen carefully and benefit from what you hear will help you gain the most from your time.[14]

These are only a few reasons that listening is important; you can probably think of many other ways that good listening makes life easier. Pause now, and ask yourself how your listening habits help or hinder your comprehension of course work. How are listening skills used in a job you currently hold or plan to hold someday? Keep these questions in mind as you study the remainder of the chapter.

Barriers to Listening

The Chinese character for listening (Figure 4.1) combines the symbols for ears, eyes, and heart; it reinforces the idea that good listeners are wholly involved in listening. Most likely, you intend to listen well, but linguistic, cultural, and personal barriers can hinder your effectiveness. Understanding these barriers and planning strategies to deal with them will build your listening skills.

Linguistic Barriers

Sometimes a speaker's language creates a barrier because diverse cultures include many language variations. Linguistic barriers show up in both language and vocabulary differences.

Figure 4.1
The Chinese character that translates as "listening" emphasizes its holistic nature by combining the symbols for ears, eyes, and heart.

- *Language differences.* Obviously, when you don't share a speaker's language, you won't understand without an interpreter. Even then, you'll probably miss some concepts or nuances of meaning because languages and the ideas they embody are so different. In addition, you may find it hard to figure out words when a person speaks with a heavy accent, whether the accent is regional, ethnic, or influenced by a first language.
- *Vocabulary differences.* Speakers with a more extensive vocabulary than yours may talk over your head. In addition, speakers who use technical jargon associated with a specific topic such as medicine or engineering will lose lay audiences unless they translate the terminology. And speakers who use slang or other specialized linguistic codes will reach some people but talk past others. Finally, a speaker can say a word, even one as simple as *taxes*, that listeners understand differently because each person has different ideas about and experiences with "taxes." The axiom "Meanings are in people" illustrates this.[15]

To overcome linguistic barriers, pay careful attention and try to figure out specific words from the general context of the speech. Listen for the main points. Take notes and jot down words to look up later. Speakers can help by translating jargon or slang, explaining confusing words, and displaying words visually (such as on a PowerPoint slide) so that listeners can see as well as hear what they're saying.[16] (Chapter 12 provides more information on language differences and comprehension.)

Cultural Barriers

cultural allusions reference to historical, literary, and religious sources that are culturally specific

Your ability to understand **cultural allusions**—references to culturally specific historical, literary, and religious sources—also affects your comprehension. You can probably think of many familiar things in your culture or co-cultures that would confuse someone from a different group. Here are a few examples:

- A Protestant or nonreligious person might be clueless about the Catholic Eucharist.
- Most people in the United States would not recognize allusions to the classic Japanese novel *The Tale of Genji*.
- Although he is one of the most famous African writers, many U.S. audiences would need an introduction to Ngũgĩ wa Thiong'o.

In our pluralistic society and multicultural world, each group draws from different cultural resources. Audiences may be unfamiliar with these culture-specific references, so each speaker should be sensitive to potential differences and explain allusions or choose areas of common knowledge. Listeners can also play their part by jotting down unfamiliar allusions and looking them up later.

Personal Barriers

physical factors bodily conditions that can limit your desire or ability to listen

Personal issues can also obstruct your listening. **Physical factors** such as hearing loss, sleep deprivation, hunger pangs, or illness can affect your ability or your desire to pay attention. **Psychological factors** such as an argument with a friend or a huge test coming up in your next class can lessen your motivation to listen. You may also experience **receiver apprehension (RA)** if you fear you'll misinterpret, inadequately process, or fail to adjust psychologically to a message that threatens or negatively challenges you.[17] And you may struggle to stay focused if you lack interest in the topic or find it difficult to understand.

Stereotypes and prejudices can also hinder listening. **Stereotyping** puts people into a category and then assumes they fit the characteristics of the category. Showing **prejudice** or bias means listening to topics or speakers with preformed judgments, whether negative or positive. To illustrate, supporters of gay marriage listened enthusiastically to a marriage equality advocate, but they approached a defense of marriage speaker with suspicion, and vice versa.

Because listening requires attention, maintaining focus is a major component. However, attention constantly fluctuates, as this student explains:

> I'm easily distracted.... It's easy for me to either focus on one particular thing that has been said, and then sort of drift off, exploring it further in my own mind, or—and this applies more specifically to someone whose speaking style or subject does not impress me—float off on unrelated topics ("I wonder where she gets her hair cut"). Also, depending on the subject, I can get easily bored.

Paying attention can be hard partly because you can think far more rapidly (about 500 words per minute) than the fastest speaker can talk (about 300 words per minute). Most people average about 150 words per minute, leaving you with 350 words per minute of a **speech–thought differential**.[18] The following four thought patterns, illustrated in Figure 4.2, are common during listening.[19]

- *Taking small departures from the communication line*. Small departures can distract and hinder your comprehension, but they can also help you follow a message if you use them to produce your own examples, relate the material to your personal experiences, answer the speaker's rhetorical questions, and otherwise interact with the ideas during the departure.
- *Going off on a tangent*. When you leave the speaker's line of thinking and seize on one idea, taking it in your own direction, your attention is deflected, and you stop listening. One distracting thought leads to another, and before you know it, you're several subjects removed from the topic at hand.
- *Engaging in a private argument*. If you carry on a running debate or mental argument that parallels the speech, you close your mind and stop trying to understand the speaker's reasoning. To counter this, identify arguments that don't make sense, but withhold your final judgment until you have heard the entire speech.
- *Taking large departures from the communication line*. Here, your attention wanders off into unrelated areas; you bring it back and focus on the speech for a while; then, off it goes again, and you find yourself thinking about a totally unrelated topic. This cycle repeats indefinitely.

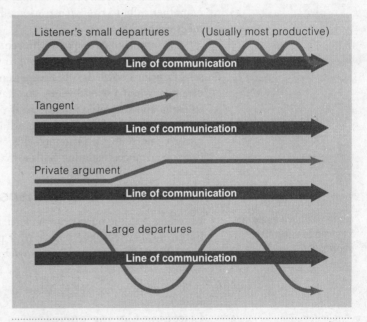

Figure 4.2
Listening Thought Patterns These four thought patterns are typical during listening. The first can be productive, but the rest characterize poor listening.

psychological factors mental stressors or distractions that take away from your desire or ability to focus

receiver apprehension (RA) anxiety that people experience while listening to messages that make them uncomfortable

stereotyping place someone in a category and then assume the person fits the characteristics of that category

prejudice preformed biases or judgments, whether negative or positive

speech–thought differential the difference between the rate you think (about 500 words per minute) and the average speaking rate (about 150 words per minute)

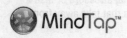

In summary, linguistic, cultural, and personal factors can challenge your listening competencies. To assess your skills, complete the Listening Skills Self-Assessment in your online resources. To improve your skills, use some of the tips described throughout the remainder of this chapter.

Strategies to Improve Listening

Margarete Imhof, past president of the International Listening Association, says that students do not usually think of listening as an active process they can control. Instead, they find it easier to criticize the speaker's mannerisms and characteristics rather than critically analyze the message. This section presents some of her suggestions for improving listening skills.[20]

Develop Advanced Skills

Throughout each day, you have listening goals, whether or not you think about them. You watch TV for entertainment, but when a commercial comes on, you might tune out or you might evaluate the claims, deciding whether or not the product is worth buying. You listen to a lecture for information and then you eat lunch with friends and listen empathetically to their frustrations. For each type of listening, you shift strategies to meet your goals.

Different goals require different competencies, ranging from basic to advanced levels. On the basic level, we listen to the message rather mindlessly, relying on cultural scripts, prior knowledge, past experiences, and the like to guide our understanding. For example, when a friend vents, you have in mind a "script" for venting that allows you to listen and respond empathetically. But more complex messages, such as lectures or political speeches, need more mindful attention and require more cognitive effort to analyze and reflect on the message.[21] (See Table 4.1.) This section focuses on ways to develop advanced listening skills for comprehending and evaluating messages.

Improve Your Comprehension

comprehensive listening
listening to understand information

Listening with the purpose of understanding information, also known as **comprehensive listening**, is useful every day: Your professor clarifies a complex process; your boss gives directions for your next project; your physician explains your medical condition;

TABLE 4.1
Listening Competencies

Basic Skills	Advanced Skills
Uses previous knowledge, experiences, scripts, and so on to process the message	Systematically examines messages and beliefs before coming to decisions
Takes less cognitive effort	Is mindful; requires more cognitive effort
Is comparatively rapid	Takes time and energy to control attention and focus
Gets the "gist" of the message	Elaborates, analyzes, and evaluates for broader and deeper understandings

Source: Burleson (2011).

a radio reporter tells where an accident blocks traffic. Several strategies can help you learn more competently.[22]

Prepare in Advance

Before the session, ask some pre-questions such as "What do I already know about this topic? What do I *want* to know? What do I *need* to know?" Your answers to these questions can help you set learning goals.

- Before a classroom session, review notes from previous sessions and then study the text, noting highlighted concepts, key terms, and headings; read the chapter summary. Look at the pictures and diagrams, or search the Internet for supplementary or background information.
- In the workplace, do your homework beforehand by brushing up on background information. This will help you ask more thoughtful questions.

Use Attention-Directing Strategies

Taking notes is a common attention-directing strategy. Focus on particular areas of the message; for example, listen for and write down the main ideas, list practical "things I must remember," or note examples that will help you recall concepts. Jot down unfamiliar words to look up later. Use what you know about speech organization to help you remember material. For instance, signals such as *first*, *next*, or *finally* can help you identify a series of steps. Be alert for words that connect ideas such as *therefore* or *in contrast*.[23]

Remember Your Goals

It's easier to pay attention when you consider your investment in the topic. For instance, a lecture on anatomy may seem boring, but the information is essential in many careers. So try to reframe your attitude about uninteresting material. Think of positive things about the topic and how the information can be of use. In the classroom, try to anticipate what might be on a test; in the workplace, look for the main things your boss wants you to remember.[24]

Taking notes and relating the material to your life are two helpful strategies to develop advanced listening skills.

© Michaeljung/Shutterstock.com

Use Elaboration Strategies

Link the material to yourself in ways that enhance the meaning. Create mental images or refer to what you already know or have experienced. For example, you might ask questions like: "Who do I know who is like that?" "What comes next?" "Does this match what I learned in another context?" "How does this relate to things I'm doing now?"

Use Strategies That Complement Your Learning Style

lecture capture use of technology to upload class materials in digital formats

If you are an auditory learner and your instructor uses **lecture capture** technology to upload class materials into digital formats, you can review them on demand. Or you might ask permission to tape the lectures and discussions. Replaying complex subjects can be especially helpful. You can skim over parts you understand easily and then replay the parts that are more difficult.[25] If you are a linear learner, outline the main points and the important supporting information. If you are more graphically oriented, make a mind map and draw connections between ideas, or sketch useful illustrations in the margins of your notes. I like to include the speaker's examples in my notes because I learn and remember abstract ideas better when I can tie them to real-life situations.

Don't Get Hung Up on Delivery

Some speakers with important things to say have annoying delivery habits that can take your focus off the main idea.

In summary, comprehensive listening corresponds with the general speech purpose of informing. Listening to learn requires advanced skills of understanding words and ideas, identifying major ideas and supporting materials, connecting new material with old, and recalling information. We now turn to critical listening skills that you should put into practice when you hear a persuasive speaker.

DIVERSITY IN PRACTICE

Cultural Listening Styles

schemas mental model that guides your perception, interpretation, storage, and recollection of a speech

Listeners from various cultural groups approach public speeches in ways that reflect their groups' different worldviews and listening behaviors. Knowing some cultural variations will make you more mindful of listening diversity. Here are a few examples:

- *Cultural schemas:* These are culturally developed mental plans, blueprints, or models that help the group's members perceive information and then interpret, store, and recall it.[26] For example, Native Americans from the Tlingit tribe have different schemas for *tlagu* stories (stories of long ago) and *ch'kalnik* tales (stories that really happened).[27]
- *African American schemas:* The entire audience participates in a "call and response" pattern that reflects African traditions. The speaker's statements (calls) are punctuated by the listeners' reactions to them (response), and in a real sense, the audience talks back to the speaker. No sharp line distinguishes speakers and listeners, and everyone cooperates to create the message.[28]
- *Asian cultural listening traditions:* Cultures that emphasize unity often expect speakers to develop oneness with listeners rather than present divisive ideas.

Both speakers and listeners share responsibility for making the speech successful. Some audiences remain silent, thinking that noise breaks their concentration and diverts their attention. Applause signals suspicion, similar to booing by US audiences; some cultures do not even applaud at the end of the speech, which allows the speaker to remain modest.[29]

- *Various student preferences:* A cross-cultural study of student listening preferences[30] showed that American students tend to like short, to-the-point messages given by speakers with whom they can identify. Disorganized presentations frustrate and annoy German students who are much less concerned about identifying personally with the speaker.

Think about your personal listening preferences. How are they shaped by your cultural background?

Improve Your Critical Listening Skills

Persuasive messages surround you, urging you to buy, sign up, donate, vote, change your beliefs, and so on. Consequently, **critical listening** skills help you sort through competing claims for your allegiance, your beliefs, your money, and your time. A critical approach means that you use advanced listening skills to analyze evidence, ponder implications, and evaluate merits of various appeals rather than accept them unreflectively. Critical listening skills build on comprehensive listening skills but add questions such as these:[31]

critical listening listening that requires you to reflect and weigh the merits of messages before you accept them

- What is this speaker's goal?
- Is this speaker trustworthy?
- Is he or she knowledgeable about *this* topic?
- Does this message make sense?
- Where does the supporting information come from? Are those sources reliable?
- What will I gain or lose if I adopt these ideas?
- What problems, if any, go along with this position?
- Am I being unduly swayed by my emotions?

Critical listening is your response to the speaker's general purpose to persuade. These skills help you live out the cultural saying "Don't believe everything you hear," and the principles guide you as you sift through all the persuasive appeals each day brings. Chapters 8 and 16 provide specific tests you can use to evaluate evidence and reasoning.

In a diverse culture, it's psychologically rewarding to seek out speakers who bolster and affirm your ideas, especially if the dominant society challenges them. The following examples may clarify this concept:

- Religious adherents gather regularly in churches, synagogues, mosques, and temples to reaffirm their beliefs.
- People who have strong political leanings assemble to hear passionate speeches that reinforce their ideologies.
- Every January 22, the anniversary of *Roe v. Wade*, supporters on both sides of the abortion issue attend rallies to hear speakers reaffirm their respective positions.

In similar contexts, you might find yourself clapping, nodding, or verbally encouraging speakers who affirm your biases. In fact, you might not notice questionable arguments or emotional appeals. However, you should submit all persuasive messages to critical evaluation, even those that reinforce positions you support.[32]

ETHICS IN PRACTICE   **Hecklers**

Hecklers are common at political speeches, and different speakers handle interruptions in different ways. During President Obama's speech at the National Defense University in 2013, the cofounder of Code Pink, an antiwar group, interrupted him frequently. At first, the president was restrained and tried to reason with her; he even paused for a while and let her rant, but eventually, because she was preventing others from hearing his message, security services escorted her out. As she was leaving, he commented that her voice was worth paying attention to.[33] In contrast, Michelle Obama was interrupted by a gay rights advocate. She stopped her speech and said, "One of the things I don't do well is this." She then left the podium and walked toward the heckler, saying, "Listen to me or you can take the mic but I'm leaving." The audience begged her to continue her speech, and the protestor was escorted out.[34]

- What do you think about President Obama's response to his heckler? About the First Lady's response to hers?
- To control meetings, many politicians today speak before carefully selected audiences, comprised of people chosen to prevent unwanted interruptions. How would you evaluate this practice?
- Have you ever been in a situation where a speaker was heckled? If so, discuss the situation and your responses to it.
- List your five top principles for ethical listening.

Practice Dialogical Listening

Remember the communication model introduced in Chapter 1? Because communication involves active participation from listeners and speakers alike, your feedback helps co-create the meanings that ultimately come out of the communication event. Feedback can come in nonverbal, verbal, or written messages. As you read the suggestions that follow, remember that cultural expectations affect what are considered appropriate feedback behaviors.

Give Appropriate Nonverbal Feedback

Your posture, movements, and eye contact, even the distance you sit from the speaker are all ways to provide meaningful feedback.

- *Posture.* Posture communicates involvement. Being "on the edge of your seat" means you are thoroughly engrossed, and a posture that faces the speaker squarely and leans slightly forward can help focus your attention. Even if you sit in a corner or off to the side, you can still turn in the direction of the speaker and let your body assume an open position.
- *Eye contact.* Watch the speaker instead of looking at another distraction. This not only helps maintain attention, it also establishes rapport and lets the speaker gauge your interest and comprehension.
- *Distance.* Think about the difference in your attentiveness when you sit far away from the speaker versus when you sit closer to the presenter where you have fewer distractions. Which seat contributes more to good listening? Choosing to sit where

the speaker can readily make eye contact with you puts more pressure on you to pay attention and give nonverbal feedback.[35]

- *Movements.* Avoid distracting behaviors such as fidgeting, shuffling papers, or playing with your pen. Instead, give nonverbal feedback in the form of smiles at amusing anecdotes or nods in support of a major point to further increase your involvement and provide additional interactions with the presenter.

Attentive listeners may actually help the speaker become more interesting. An old campus legend tells of a boring professor who always stood at the lectern and read his notes. His students decided to act *as if* he were fascinating whenever he moved away from the lectern. If he moved, ever so slightly, they all leaned forward a bit, made eye contact, and gave supportive feedback. According to the legend, the professor eventually was walking back and forth across the front of the room, speaking animatedly.

Give Verbal Feedback

"Where can I get more information?" "One article I read presented very different information." "How is he defining that word?" Questions and comments such as these arise as you listen. Question-and-answer periods provide opportunities to co-create meanings. Here are a few of the most common types of feedback:[36]

- If you are confused, ask **clarification questions** to gain more information. Examples: "Could you go over that third step again?" "What's your threshold level for 'poverty' "?
- **Closed questions** ask for brief, specific answers. Use them to gain precise information or to verify your understanding. Here are some examples: "Did you watch the documentary about dolphins?" (answer yes or no); "When was that law passed?" (answer a specific date).
- **Open questions** invite longer answers that could be developed in a variety of ways, as these examples show: "What do you think is the best new source of energy?"

clarification questions requests to clear up confusing ideas

closed question request for a brief, specific answer

open question giving opportunity for a range of answers or a more lengthy response

Asking questions or making comments are good ways to create a dialogue with a speaker.

"What suggestions do you have for recycling old cell phones?" "What is your personal plan for paying off your student loans?"

loaded questions questions containing implications intended to put the speaker on the defensive

- **Loaded questions** put a speaker on the defensive because of what they imply. Try to avoid them. For example, "When will you begin to look at both sides of the issue?" implies that the speaker was one-sided, and *when* is not really asking for a time. In other words, you wouldn't expect to hear, "I am going to research the other side tomorrow afternoon at 3:00."

request for elaboration question asking for more information

- To get a speaker to expand on an idea, make a **request for elaboration**: "You said the Electoral College was modeled on the system used in the Roman Republic; could you elaborate?" "Can you provide more details about the university's plan to expand its online offerings?"

comments information from personal experience or research

- Instead of questions, you can add **comments** or information from your own experience and research. For instance, after a speech on bullying, Tiffany shared statistics she had heard on a television show, and Jon told a story about a coach who bullied his team. If you know that data in the speech are incorrect (for example, the statistics are outdated), you could provide supplementary information.

Although question-and-answer periods are common in the United States, not all cultures participate equally in a co-creation of meaning process, as Diversity in Practice: Saving Face explains.

DIVERSITY IN PRACTICE

Saving Face

Question-and-answer periods are rare in some cultures. For instance, in traditional Chinese or Japanese public speaking contexts, listeners are supposed to understand the speaker. Asking a question is an admission that they lack the intelligence to unravel the speaker's shades of meaning. Furthermore, a question reflects on the speaker's communication abilities; in other words, if listeners are confused, the speaker has failed to communicate. Finally, to preserve the speaker's "face," it's considered inappropriate to publicly question a speaker's information and, thus, his or her character.[37]

Give Written Feedback

You may be asked to write a response to a classmate's speech. Just writing "I liked your speech" is too vague to be helpful. More effective comments focus on specific elements, using the **D-R-E method**: Describe-Respond-Evaluate.[38] *Describe* what you heard; *respond* with your personal interpretations and reactions; and *evaluate* by critiquing what you found effective and what could be improved. Phrase your comments objectively and positively. Here are some examples:

D-R-E method Describe-Respond-Evaluate; a feedback method that describes content, shares personal responses, and gives evaluation

- *Description*: "You used quotations from experts on both sides of this controversial issue" (content); "Your signposts and transition statements clarified your main points" (organization); "You touched your hair several times as you spoke" (delivery).
- *Response*: "I really connected emotionally with the story about the grandfather and the little boy" (content); "Because you alliterated your main points, I will be able to remember your ideas better" (style).

- *Evaluation*: "Using a variety of sources was good, because it showed you sought out opinions from many perspectives. Your use of examples balanced the statistics well. I think your speech would be stronger if you added a map to your visuals" (content); "Your ability to remember your ideas was impressive, but try to eliminate the phrase 'you know.' I found it distracting" (delivery).

Specific comments such as these are beneficial because they give the speaker an idea of the overall impression the speech made on you and why. In general, write out as many positive things as you can and then evaluate the performance by identifying a few things to improve.

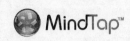

Summary

Listening is the communication activity that we do most and study least. Listening is more than just hearing sounds; it involves active processing and retention of what you hear. Listening is important in your personal and work life. However, different languages, vocabularies, and cultural allusions can hinder comprehension. In addition, personal and psychological factors—such as fatigue, stresses and worries, stereotypes and prejudices, and wandering attention—can be listening barriers.

Fortunately, you can devise strategies to improve your listening. Know your listening purpose, and plan ways to develop advanced listening skills that increase your ability to comprehend information or critically evaluate persuasive messages.

In addition, practice dialogical listening by contributing appropriate nonverbal, verbal, and written feedback. Nonverbal actions communicate that you are interested in the speech; they also help you pay attention. Useful nonverbal elements include a posture that communicates involvement, a distance that helps focus your attention, and movements that support rather than disrupt the speech. When you have an opportunity to interact verbally with a speaker, ask questions or provide comments that elaborate on the topic. However, be aware that after-speech questions and comments are inappropriate in some cultures. Finally, write out comments using the D-R-E method to describe what you heard, respond personally, and evaluate the overall presentation.

STUDY AND REVIEW

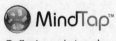

Reflect on what you've learned.

Public Speaking: Concepts and Skills for a Diverse Society offers a broad range of resources that will help you better understand the material in this chapter, complete assignments, and succeed on tests. Your MindTap resources feature the following:

- Speech videos with viewing questions, speech outlines, and transcripts
- Activities to help you check your understanding and to apply what you've learned to your own life
- Stop and Check and Critical Thinking exercises
- Outline Builder
- Web Links related to chapter content
- Study and review tools such as self-quizzes and an interactive glossary

You can access your online resources for *Public Speaking: Concepts and Skills for a Diverse Society* at cengagebrain.com using the access code that came with your book or that you purchased online.

KEY TERMS

The terms below are defined in the margins throughout this chapter.

clarification questions 51

closed question 51

comments 52

comprehensive listening 46

critical listening 49

cultural allusion 44

D-R-E method 52

hearing 43

lecture capture 48

listening 43

loaded questions 52

open question 51

physical factors 44

prejudice 45

psychological factors 45

receiver apprehension (RA) 45

request for elaboration 52

schema 48

speech–thought differential 45

stereotyping 45

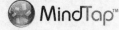

CRITICAL THINKING EXERCISES

1. Listening skills are important in thousands of jobs, ranging from academic advisers or financial aid officers on campus to hairstylists and real estate agents. Tell of a time when someone really listened to you while performing his or her job, and then tell of a time when someone failed to listen well. What was the outcome in each case?

2. Copy the Chinese symbol that stands for listening (see Figure 4.1), looking closely at each element. In what way do you use your ears, eyes, and heart when you listen to your classmates? Your professors? People at work? A speaker whose ideas support your own opinions? A speaker with whom you fundamentally disagree?

3. To face receiver apprehension head on, listen to a speaker who makes you anxious because he or she takes a position that differs dramatically from your views. You may find the person on radio, television, or the Internet (for example, a person whose lifestyle differs from yours, one whose views on a social issue, such as capital punishment, diverge from yours, or a person with different religious beliefs). Describe, respond to, and evaluate the content and delivery, and then assess how your apprehension affected your listening.

4. Watch a video of your choice from the Ted Talk site. As you listen, take notes on the speech content and jot down some personal responses and observations on the effectiveness of the speech. Then write a critique that (1) describes, (2) responds to, and (3) evaluates the speech. Discuss this critique with a group of classmates.

APPLICATION EXERCISES

1. Be quiet for thirty seconds and listen to what's going on around you. What sounds can you hear (such as traffic in the background) that you're not really listening to? Choose one of the sounds and really listen to it, keeping in mind the five elements of listening.

2. Using the diagrams in Figure 4.2 as models, draw a diagram that depicts your listening pattern during the most recent lecture you heard. Next, draw a diagram that depicts your listening pattern during the last conversation you had with your best friend. Draw a third diagram that shows your listening pattern during your last major conversation with a family member. Compare the three. What conclusions can you draw about your listening in various contexts?

3. The Utah State University Academic Resource Center provides many student aids. Under "Idea Sheets" link to "Note Taking and Listening." There you'll find three especially helpful worksheets: (1) "Note taking: Cornell method," (2) "Listening skills for lectures," and (3) "Effective note taking strategies." Use the suggestions in these handouts to create your Listening Skills Development Plan under your online resources for Chapter 4.

4. Practice the nonverbal skills of active listening in one of your courses. That is, use posture, space, eye contact, and movement to help focus your attention on the lecture. Afterward, evaluate how much your nonverbal behaviors helped you pay attention and recall the class material.

5. Verbally interact with one of the speakers in the next round of classroom speeches. During the speech, jot down several comments or questions to ask during the question-and-answer period. Use the D-R-E (Describe-Respond-Evaluate) method to give written feedback after a classmate's speech.

CHAPTER 5

THIS CHAPTER WILL
HELP YOU

- Choose your speech
  topic

- Narrow your topic to
  fit the situation

- Identify a general
  purpose and a specific
  purpose for your
  speech

- Write a thesis state-
  ment that states your
  subject and its impor-
  tance to the audience

- Write a preview that
  summarizes your main
  points

Diana Ong/SuperStock

Selecting Your Topic
and Purpose

WHAT SHALL I talk about? Many students find that choosing appropriate
topics for classroom speeches is challenging because the assignment is
so open-ended compared to other settings such as weddings or workplace
meetings where a topic is more obvious. For example, if you're scheduled to
present a report at work, the subject will be your most recent project. However,
in speech classrooms you're generally not assigned a specific topic so you
must choose from thousands of potential subjects. It can't be too broad or too
complex (after all, most classroom assignments are limited by time); it should
interest your audience, as well as you; it should be relevant; it should be novel—
you must consider many factors. Topic selection falls into the canon of invention,

Mind
Review t
chapter
Learning
Objectiv
and **Star**
with a qu
warm-up
activity.

and this chapter will give you guidelines for choosing your topic, narrowing it to a manageable size, and then selecting your purpose and focus.

Choose Your Topic

MindTap™

Read, highlight, and take notes online.

Is there a surefire method for selecting a topic that suits you, your audience, and the occasion? No. However, several guidelines can make the task easier. As you consider a specific topic, first think of your audience. Then look for things to talk about in four additional places: your personal interests and experiences, other courses you're taking, current events, and international and cultural subjects.

Assess Your Audience's Need to Know

Before you settle on a topic, keep two fundamental things in mind: significance and novelty. Everyday topics can result in interesting speeches.[1] However, the key is to find a significant subject—one that *needs* to be discussed in order to increase your audience's knowledge, bring about a desirable change, or highlight important cultural values and beliefs.[2] Try to think from your audience's perspective by asking questions such as these. Are they familiar with the subject? What more do they need to know? Do they care about it? Does it affect their finances? Their future? Their health? Will it appeal to their curiosity? Chapter 6 provides additional information on audience analysis.

Novelty is another fundamental principle for maintaining interest and speaking to a need. That is, either present something relatively unfamiliar or take a creative look at a familiar topic.[3] Going over well-known procedures such as how to make chocolate-chip cookies can waste your listener's time. But can these topics be appropriate? Yes, if you take a novel approach. For example, you might talk about the history of the famous Toll House recipe, explain why it is associated with the Nestlé company, or describe how the cookie became so popular.[4] Many of these facts would be novel and potentially valuable, even to a gluten-intolerant listener.

In summary, these two principles—choosing a topic that meets some audience need and presenting your subject in a novel way—are foundational. If your listeners already know a lot about your subject, dig for supplementary information, or select another topic.

ETHICS IN PRACTICE   **Are Any Topics Taboo?**

In a *BusinessWeek* article, "The Ethics of Talking Politics at Work,"[5] Bruce Weinstein argues that people should, for ethical reasons, avoid four topics at work: politics, religion, sex, and money. These topics cause disagreement and raise strong passions, which impair workplace productivity. Weinstein cites five ethical principles: do no harm, make things better, respect others, be fair, and be loving. While this advice may be reasonable for the workplace, should we in some contexts address topics that cause disagreement, raise strong passions, or make people uncomfortable? For example, some audiences might feel anxious about racial or religious topics, but *should* we publicly address race or religion, with their potential for creating discomfort? Arguably, directly tackling these topics can increase understanding of diverse perspectives, invite respect for a variety of viewpoints, and make American society better overall.

(continued)

Questions

1. Should students avoid topics such as abortion or sexual issues, which often have political and religious underpinnings and which arouse emotional responses? If so, what topics should be avoided and why?
2. How should your class balance First Amendment rights to speak freely—even about culturally taboo topics—against your responsibilities as outlined in Weinstein's five principles or the dialogical and democratic principles described in Chapter 3?
3. Identify a political, religious, sex-related, or money-related topic of your choice that *needs* to be discussed because honest discussion could actually *enhance* Weinstein's five ethical principles.

Consider Your Personal Interests

A basic principle of topic selection is to choose subjects you know and care about or those you wish to investigate further. Brainstorm your personal interests and experiences to generate a number of possible topics.[6] What is your major? Your occupational goals? Your hobbies? What music do you like? What irritates you? How should society change? Unique life experiences also make good topics. You are who you are because of what you know and what you've experienced. What topics in your family background, jobs, travel, or recreational interests might interest others?[7] Here are some ways students created speeches around their interests and experiences:

- Leif, an engineering major, actually built a hovercraft. He chose to explain the technology of that type of vehicle. (Read his outline in Chapter 11.)
- David, a nursing major, explored the topic of male nurses.
- Lishan, a student from China, compared and contrasted the Western celebration of St. Valentine's Day with the Chinese Double-Seventh Festival, sometimes called the Chinese Valentine's Day. (Read his speech in Appendix B.)
- Emily chose the topic of introversion to explain her personality.

Most people have never built a hovercraft like Leif, but they can still find topics among their interests and experiences.

Selecting a personal topic has obvious advantages. When you are interested in your subject, you can speak more passionately and focus more on your message than on yourself or your insecurities. Your enthusiasm can also energize your audience—after all, what is more boring than a bored speaker?

Look for Topics from Other Courses

Look for speech topics in your academic major or in other courses you are taking. Here are just a few examples:

- Music—dissonance, composer Hector Berlioz, music frisson
- Cognitive science—neuroimaging, brain anatomy, cognitive dissonance
- Health—prescription drug addiction, sleep deprivation, meningitis

Preparing a speech on an interesting topic from another class has the added advantage of helping you learn that subject better; however, some topics are obviously so complex that even an expert could not explain them in a short speech.[8]

Don't hesitate to use topics you have researched for a project in another course, if appropriate. For example, Bralee wrote a paper on product placement in the media for one course. She also used material from that research in her classroom speech. Although her speech included information that the paper did not, and vice versa, she adapted her purpose, her organizational pattern, and her language to meet two very different assignments.

Consider International and Cultural Topics

DIVERSITY IN PRACTICE

Explore your cultural heritage and experiences or consider global aspects of your major to find subjects. For instance, Ryan, who has Basque ancestors, chose to speak about the Basque artist, Jorge Oteiza. (His tribute is in Appendix B.) Bailey, who went on a service trip to Africa, chose the topic of AIDS in Swaziland. She helped students understand how US agencies and US tax dollars are involved in fighting AIDS in African countries. A film studies major might investigate a director or film genre from another country or a different cultural group. International trade, global investments, and international crime—all are topics of increasing importance in the twenty-first century. Contemporary cultural topics are easily found on the Internet.

As with all topics, it's essential to connect with your listeners' here-and-now concerns. For example, a subject such as drones in a war zone a continent away might seem far removed from your campus world. But there are ways to link your classmates with the topic. Would they empathize with people who lose family members to drone strikes? What about tax dollars that pay for military drones? What do they know about surveillance drones in the United States? Could you link the topic to fundamental values, such as the desire for a world at peace or for freedom and justice for all? Your challenge is to help your audience understand the significance and relevance of your subject.

Investigate Current Events

News sources and television shows are other good topic sources. Skim newspaper or magazine headlines or surf Internet news sites, jotting down current issues that interest

Figure 5.1
You can find novel topics that are significant or meet an audience need in personal and academic areas, in current events, and in your cultural background or interests.

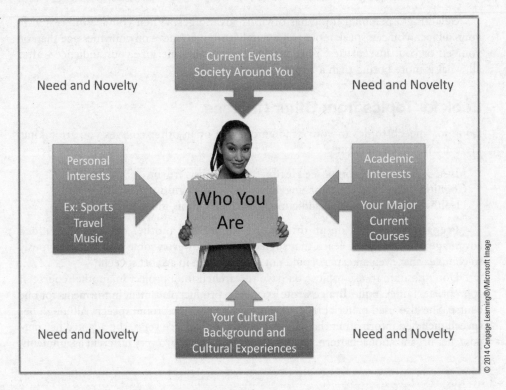

you. Major newspapers and news magazines, as well as trade and other specialized periodicals, can be accessed online. Here are some topics from a single day's news:

violent video games and youth	children whose parents overdose
airport control tower safety	immigration reform
professional athletes and marijuana	Stradivarius violins
drought in the West	low-fat yogurt and type 2 diabetes

Current event topics usually address a societal need. The fact that they show up in the news means that many people find them significant. Furthermore, you should be able to locate information easily. For example, a topic such as immigration reform will have thousands of related articles in your library's databases and on the Internet; even a topic such as Stradivarius violins can yield hundreds of credible sources. (See Figure 5.1.)

For additional ideas on how to find topics, check out Professor Ron St. John's website available in your *Public Speaking* Chapter 5 resources.

Narrow Your Topic

Once you have a topic in mind, your next step is to narrow your focus enough to discuss it within a designated time frame. This principle applies across all speaking contexts, from workplace project reports, sales presentations, and announcements to civic and ceremonial contexts. One professional speaker narrowed his topic like this:

I'm going to talk about technology and an introduction of technology into developing markets. I'm going to focus on agriculture . . . particularly in Africa and particularly in Sub-Saharan Africa . . . in Malawi . . . with a woman named Sabina Xhosa.[9]

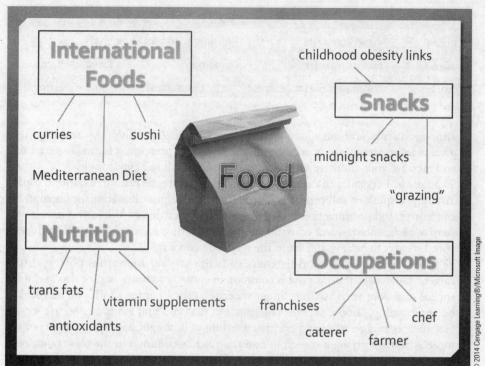

Figure 5.2
This mind map shows several food-related topics. You could find dozens more.

A mind map is a good way to let your ideas flow. Figure 5.2 illustrates how to create a mind map by starting with a broad subject such as food and narrowing it to a series of more realistic classroom topics, including personal, national, or international aspects of the topic. If you select and narrow your topic early, you will have plenty of time to gather and organize your materials and rehearse well enough to feel the confidence that a last-minute scramble won't produce.

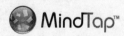

Choose Your Purpose and Focus

Public speeches aren't "accidental"; instead, you speak to accomplish specific goals or purposes,[10] so carefully clarify what you want to achieve by identifying your general purpose and tentatively formulating a specific purpose for your talk. Continue to refine your specific purpose as you go along. A thesis statement helps both you and your listeners understand your central idea, and a preview lays out your major points.

Identify Your General Purpose

Past teachers of rhetoric have consistently pointed out a few general goals for public speaking. In the fourth century, St. Augustine, who was originally a rhetoric professor, identified three **general purposes**: to teach, to please, and to move.[11] In the eighteenth century, George Campbell[12] identified four purposes: to enlighten the understanding, to please the imagination, to move the passions, and to influence the will. In the last century, Alan Monroe[13] said we attempt to inform, to entertain, to stimulate through emotion, or to convince through reasoning. Today's speech instructors commonly describe the following four general purposes (Table 5.1):

general purposes four general purposes are to inform, to persuade, to entertain, or to commemorate

- *To inform.* The goal here is to increase your audience's understanding by explaining, describing, or teaching about your subject. Lectures, how-to speeches, reports,

Table 5.1
General Purposes

To inform	To persuade	To entertain	To commemorate
curries	avoid trans fats	midnight snacks	a chef
sushi	take antioxidants	grazing	a franchise's values
franchises	childhood obesity causes	caterer moments	tribute to farmers

announcements, and introductions fall into this category. When you're assigned to give an informative speech, focus on discovering and presenting factual material that will increase your audience's knowledge or understanding of your topic.

- *To persuade.* Persuaders attempt to convince, motivate, or reinforce cultural ideals. You might speak to sell products, argue for ideas, request donations, campaign for candidates, and promote policy changes, among other things. When you have a persuasive assignment, select convincing and motivating materials that will influence your listeners to believe and act in the ways you advocate.

- *To entertain.* Here you want listeners to laugh at your humorous portrayal of a subject. Obviously, this purpose is common in comedy routines but it's also useful for special occasions such as after-dinner speeches. (See Chapter 18.) If you're asked to be entertaining, choose an event or situation that you find amusing and use strategies such as exaggeration and creative wording to highlight humorous aspects of the topic. Although giving a speech to entertain is less common in the classroom, each speech should always be interesting, regardless of its purpose.

- *To commemorate.* Special occasion speeches highlight and reinforce cultural ideals. Tributes, toasts, awards, eulogies, and other types of speeches described in Chapter 18 fall into this category. For a commemorative speech assignment, choose a worthy subject and develop it around cultural values.

Speech purposes often overlap because audiences are comprised of listeners with various levels of information and motivation. Take the example of Microsoft's Bill Gates, who recently vowed to work for the eradication of polio worldwide. In a single speech, he must tell uninformed listeners about polio's extent and effects globally; he must motivate informed listeners to get involved by donating money to worthy organizations. Throughout, he must hold their interest. Although his talk might not be specifically commemorative, he is reinforcing cultural beliefs about science and health and upholding cultural values on helping others.

Build Your Outline

Identify Your Specific Purpose*

Linnea became convinced that workers in a coffee-producing company were being exploited by her morning cup of coffee, so she chose to speak about "Fair Trade certified coffee." Her next step was to decide what she wanted her listeners to know or do about Fair Trade products. She needed a tool[14] to guide her research and organization— a **specific purpose** statement in the form of a phrase or sentence stating the cognitive, affective, or behavioral responses she desired from the audience.[15]

- **Cognitive effects** relate to the audience's beliefs, thoughts, or understandings. To achieve cognitive effects, Linnea should focus on providing information or on changing her listeners' beliefs about some aspect of coffee production.

- **Affective effects** are the feelings or emotions aroused in the listeners. Fair trade is a potentially emotional topic, and Linnea might hope to instill anger and perhaps guilt feelings over the treatment of workers in the coffee industry.

specific purpose the cognitive, affective, or behavioral response a speaker desires

cognitive effects influences on beliefs, understandings, and other mental processes

affective effects influences on listeners' feelings

*Excerpts from Linnea's sample student speech: Used by permission of Linnea Strandy.

- **Behavioral effects** relate to audience actions. She might ask them to change their purchasing habits and buy only Fair Trade-certified products.

behavioral effects influences on audience actions

In short, Linnea had to clarify what she wanted her audience to know, feel, or do and then create a specific purpose statement. One way to keep her desired response in mind is to write an infinitive phrase that includes the words "my audience." Here are some specific purpose statements that illustrate various general purposes.

- To inform my audience about the meaning of Fair Trade by decoding the meanings in five Fair Trade certification labels. (*Cognitive effect:* The audience will understand how to interpret Fair Trade labels.)
- To convince my audience that agricultural workers in the coffee industry often labor in unfair working conditions. (*Cognitive effect:* The audience will be persuaded that there is a labor problem at the production level of the coffee industry.)
- To persuade my audience to become angry about the abuse of agricultural workers in the coffee industry. (*Affective effect:* The audience will have an emotional response and thus develop a negative attitude toward coffee that is not fairly traded.)
- To persuade my audience to purchase only products with a Fair Trade certification label. (*Behavioral effect:* The audience will be motivated to do something specific as a result of this speech.)

Although many instructors want the specific purpose to include the phrase "to inform my audience," others ask students to write a statement that identifies the desired audience response:

- As a result of my speech, my audience will *understand* the principles of fair trade after learning the meanings of five Fair Trade labels.
- As a result of my speech, my audience will *believe* that agricultural workers in the coffee industry and others like it are not treated fairly.
- As a result of my speech, my audience will *feel anger* about unjust treatment of agricultural workers in the coffee industry.
- As a result of my speech, my audience will *purchase* only products that come with a Fair Trade certification label.

At this stage of preparation, Linnea had this much of her speech formulated:

Topic: Fair Trade-certified coffee

General purpose: To persuade

Specific purpose: To persuade my audience to purchase only products that come with a Fair Trade-certification label.

By formulating her general and specific purpose early on, she can focus her research more effectively. Facts, descriptions, and explanations are especially important in informative speeches. To prove links between coffee consumption and mistreatment of laborers on coffee plantations, she should look for opinions from experts in global economics. To motivate listeners to care or to act, she needs emotionally compelling examples of exploited workers. To urge listeners to purchase only Fair Trade-certified products in general, she needs specific information that will help listeners see this as a realistic goal.

After creating a specific purpose statement centered on your goals for your listeners, your next step is to formulate a *central idea* or *thesis statement* that captures the major idea of your speech.

central idea a synonym for thesis statement

Write Your Central Idea

Your **central idea** or **thesis statement** functions to communicate clearly your topic and purpose to the audience.[16] Consequently, write it out in the form of a single, declarative

thesis statement a single sentence that names the subject and establishes its significance

A speaker could develop a topic such as Fair Trade by focusing on the audience's knowledge or beliefs, attitudes, or behaviors related to Fair Trade-certified products.

© PhotoSGH/Shutterstock.com

sentence that names your subject and establishes your goal.[17] It's somewhat like a road map that summarizes your main idea and the direction you'll take. Here are some correctly and incorrectly written thesis statements:

Correct:	Workers in many countries are exploited by unfair labor conditions, but we can help improve their lives by buying only Fair Trade-certified products.
Correct:	My goal is to convince my audience that workers in many countries are exploited by unfair labor conditions, but we can help them by buying only Fair Trade-certified products.
Incorrect:	Why should we buy Fair Trade-certified products? (This is a question, not a declarative sentence.)
Incorrect:	Workers are exploited in many countries. This is unfair, but we can help by insisting on Fair Trade-certified products. (Use one sentence, not two.)
Incorrect:	Why care about Fair Trade products? (This is a fragment, not a complete sentence.)

Begin formulating your thesis statement when you select your topic and decide on your general and specific purposes. Then allow yourself plenty of time to explore and develop your ideas, narrow your approach, consider the point of view you'll develop, and choose your general direction.[18] The process of invention takes time and energy. New ideas will emerge and others will seem less important, so don't be afraid to revise repeatedly as you do additional research, preparation, and organization. As one student explained:

I tend to have running dialogues in my head, sometimes even out loud. While I talk to myself, I work out particulars. I answer questions I've posed to myself ("Well, really, Gail, if you argue that, where will you go? It's too huge!" or "Now does that really make sense?"). My answers often lead me to modify my central idea as I continue my preparation.

GAIL

When you actually give your speech, incorporate your thesis statement into your introduction, and follow it with a **preview**, or short summary of the major points you'll use to develop your thesis. Linnea previewed her speech like this:

> I will explain some problems associated with coffee production, show how Fair Trade certified products provide a solution, and challenge you to take action to promote and consume only fairly traded products.

The text of Linnea's speech appears on the book's online resources where you can watch it on video.

In summary, topic and purpose selection are important aspects of speech-making. Select and narrow an interesting subject, formulate general and specific speech purposes, and then write a thesis statement or central idea that summarizes your major ideas. During your speech, state your thesis in the introduction, and add a preview of the main points you will use to develop your central idea.

preview short summary of the major points you'll develop in the speech

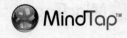

Summary

When you choose a speech topic, look for something that interests you, a subject that meets your audience's need to know and that you can treat in a novel manner. Then, examine your personal experiences, other courses, current events, and international or cultural possibilities for significant subjects. If you do careful work early in the term, you can produce a list or develop a series of files on topics that will interest both you and your listeners.

After selecting your topic, decide on your general intention or purpose for speaking. Will you inform, persuade, entertain, or commemorate? Follow that decision by writing your specific purpose statement that names the cognitive, affective, or behavioral response you want from your listeners. Focus on the speech's content by writing out the thesis statement or central idea, a single sentence that names the subject, alerts the audience to its significance, and establishes your goal. Begin to formulate this statement early in the speech, but revise it if necessary as you proceed in your research and preparation. Finally, write a preview of the major ideas you will develop in the speech.

STUDY AND REVIEW

Public Speaking: Concepts and Skills for a Diverse Society offers a broad range of resources that will help you better understand the material in this chapter, complete assignments, and succeed on tests. Your MindTap resources feature the following:

- Speech videos with viewing questions, speech outlines, and transcripts
- Activities to help you check your understanding and to apply what you've learned to your own life
- Stop and Check and Critical Thinking exercises
- Outline Builder
- Web Links related to chapter content
- Study and review tools such as self-quizzes and an interactive glossary

You can access your online resources for *Public Speaking: Concepts and Skills for a Diverse Society* at cengagebrain.com using the access code that came with your book or that you purchased online.

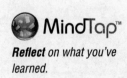

Reflect on what you've learned.

*Review your **Flashcards**.*

KEY TERMS

The terms below are defined in the margins throughout this chapter.

affective effects 62
behavioral effects 63
central idea 63
cognitive effects 62

general purposes 61
preview 65
specific purpose 62
thesis statement 63

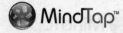

CRITICAL THINKING EXERCISES

1. Use a piece of blank paper to brainstorm ideas for speeches. Fold it into eight sections and label each, using a different category such as people, places, controversies, education, media, concepts from other courses, or historical events. Jot down possible topics in each category. After you've brainstormed in this way, select one or two of the most promising topic areas and make a mind map that further narrows the subject. File this paper for use during the term.
2. Obtain additional information on a site devoted to St. Augustine, one of the great figures of rhetoric, and read Chapters 12 and 13 of his treatise on rhetoric. He gave this advice seventeen centuries ago. Which principles still apply?
3. Some professors refer to the central idea or thesis statement by other names, including the core idea, the subject sentence, or the residual message. Which of these terms best clarify the concept for you? Why?

APPLICATION EXERCISES

1. Discuss in a small group some ways you could add the element of novelty to the following common topics: using seat belts, making a sandwich, watching television violence, writing a résumé.
2. For each of the following topics, tell how you could create one speech to inform, one to persuade, and one to entertain: negotiating a raise at work, attending an opera, evaluating cable news programs, planning spring break, taking a recreational hike.
3. Choose one of the topics above and write a general purpose, specific purpose statement, central idea or thesis statement, and preview that match the ideas you had for informative, persuasive, and entertaining speeches.
4. Work with a small group of your classmates to create a mind map based on a very general international topic such as China, global diseases, ethnic conflicts, or natural disasters. Record your mind map in such a way that you can show and explain it to the entire class.

Diana Ong/SuperStock

Audience Analysis

"AS A RESULT of my speech, my audience will understand how a hovercraft works, tell some advantages and drawbacks, and explain why these vehicles are not street legal." Leif's specific purpose statement lays out what he wants his talk to accomplish. However, to meet his goals, he must use **audience analysis** skills to think carefully about his listeners so that he can find the best way to communicate with that group. In doing so, he becomes a **listening speaker**[1] who considers his audience before, during, and after his presentation.

Like Leif, your relationships with your audience consist of complex connections among audience members, your topic, your situation, and yourself. Figure 6.1 depicts these relationships as a rhetorical triangle with three sides—audience, speaker, and situation—that converge around a message's topic,

The Rhetorical Triangle

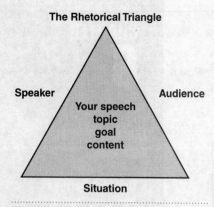

Figure 6.1
The Rhetorical Triangle The audience, the speaking situation, and the speaker come together around the message.

audience analysis
identifying audience characteristics to communicate more effectively

listening speaker dialogical speaker who hears audience interests and concerns before, during, and after a speech

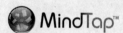

Read, highlight, and take notes online.

unmotivated audiences
listeners who lack a listening purpose or goal

random audiences listeners who are initially doing something else but are attracted by a message that catches their attention

content, and goals.[2] The previous chapter discussed the center of the triangle, the topic; however, a great topic, a specific goal, and significant content alone won't make a speech successful. Consequently, this chapter focuses on the three sides of the triangle—the audience, the situation, and the audience's perception of you.[3]

Analyze Your Audience

Good speakers prepare their speeches for a particular group at a particular time. Even politicians, sales reps, or university recruiters, who present similar material repeatedly, adapt the material to specific audiences in specific settings. This section explores ways to think about your audience's motivations and demographic characteristics.

Consider Audience Motivations

Think about why you listen to a speech. What attracts you? What holds your attention? What goals do you have for being there? Answering similar questions about your audience provides clues about their motivations and helps you tailor each message more effectively.[4] At one time or another, you've probably found yourself in each of these audiences:

1. **Unmotivated audiences** lack a purposeful listening goal. Listeners in **random audiences** are initially involved in another activity, but something attracts their attention, and they pause and listen for a while. A salesperson's demonstration at a street fair, the impassioned voice of an activist on a street corner, or the humorous stories of a sidewalk entertainer draw random audiences. Listeners may be browsing the radio dial or surfing YouTube when a speaker or topic temporarily captures

© iStockphoto.com/Izabela Habur

Classroom audiences are often passive audiences who listen to a speech, not because of their interest in the topic or the speaker but because they need course credit. Select a topic that is relevant and interesting.

their interest. A random audience requires you to attract and maintain attention long enough to present your message. If you communicate through a form of media, remember that your audience can easily change channels or tune you out, so focus on being interesting and relevant, and use conversational delivery as if you were addressing one listener at a time.

2. Members of **passive audiences** are present for a variety of reasons but *not* because they are motivated to hear a particular speaker or a particular topic. Some show up at a speech because a friend asked them to go, or they go as part of a job requirement. Most speech classes contain many passive listeners whose goal is to earn academic credit, not to hear you or to learn about your topic. Your challenge here is to do three things: (1) select a relevant, interesting topic; (2) gain and maintain interest; and (3) help them understand how the topic relates to their lives.

> **passive audiences** unmotivated listeners who listen to accomplish other goals

3. In contrast, **motivated audiences** want to hear a particular speaker or to know more about a topic. Consequently, they are **self-selected** by voluntarily and intentionally choosing to be at that speech. Here are some examples:

> **motivated audiences** listeners who listen for a reason

> **self-selected audiences** listeners who choose to listen to a selected subject or speaker

   - Students attend an evening lecture to hear best-selling author Susan Cain talk about the power of introverts.
   - Citizens across the country watch the president's televised State of the Union speech live.

4. **Homogeneous audiences** can be unmotivated, passive, or motivated. A shared attitude—whether positive or negative—toward the speaker, the topic, or both is their defining feature. Speaking when the audience likes you and is interested in your topic can be rewarding, but you must still develop your ideas clearly so that listeners can understand and accept them. **Hostile audiences**, in contrast, share a negative attitude toward the speaker or the topic. Chances are, your audiences won't be hostile toward you as a person—that sort of hostility is generally directed toward controversial public figures. Instead, listeners are more likely to be hostile toward your opinions on controversial ideas, especially if your conclusions conflict with theirs. Hostile audiences present unique challenges. Your best strategy is to emphasize common ground before you address areas of divergence. Chapter 17 discusses additional ways to design speeches for hostile audiences.

> **homogeneous audiences** listeners who are similar in attitude

> **hostile audiences** listeners who are negative toward the topic or the speaker

5. Technology as close as your handheld devices provide opportunities to speak to **absent audiences**. In this format, you are separate from your listeners, who watch or listen through some form of media, generally not in "real time." They can stop the speech or replay sections as they desire. Absent audiences don't give the instantaneous feedback of a face-to-face audience, but listeners can often contribute comments electronically. If you are taking this course online, you may be asked to upload your speeches to classmates who form an absent audience.

> **absent audiences** listeners who are separated from the speaker and receive the message through some form of media

As you might imagine, listeners in a single audience can have various motivations. A mostly self-selected audience may also include passive listeners who are just tagging along with friends, or a mostly passive audience can have some self-selected members. All things considered, try to discover the fundamental motivation of most people in the audience and design speeches that take their motivations into account.

Analyze Audience Demographics

One way to consider your audience is to do a **demographic analysis** and note some basic categories such as age, religious affiliation, ethnicity, and sex that are used in analysis of target groups. Demographic information can help you plan your remarks as long as you remember that, although we sometimes generalize about the experiences of different groups,[11] no one has a single fixed cultural or social identity.[12] Each audience

> **demographic analysis** identifying audiences by populations they represent, such as age or ethnicity

Spinning and Pandering

"So the peasants are unhappy.
Well do something about it.
You're my spin doctor."

Joseph Farris/ jfa1454/CartoonStock.com

Although spinning and pandering are common among politicians, journalists, universities, charities, and so on, these approaches have ethical implications. **Spinning** involves selecting materials that favor the *speaker's* interests and point of view; consequently, spin doctors may leave out inconvenient facts or carefully choose wording that nudges or bends the listener toward the speaker's position. For example, if crime were lower overall but burglary was up in an area, a speaker advocating for civilians carrying guns might present the "skyrocketing" increase in break-ins but omit the overall crime rates. [5] In contrast, **pandering** means providing a message the audience *wants* to hear, not necessarily what they *need* to hear. A politician, for example, might sidestep the truth about serious matters and play to potential voters' unrealistic hopes or fears.[6] Spin and pandering are not illegal, but they are arguably immoral if they keep audiences from hearing the information they need to make realistic and responsible choices.[7] Consequently, many spinners and panderers have a negative image.

In contrast, Dr. Martin Luther King Jr. was willing to speak unpopular sentiments.[8] His decision to speak out against the Vietnam War shocked and upset many civil rights leaders who believed that King's stance could undermine President Johnson, "the president who's done more for Black rights, how can you take him on?"[9] Even the National Association for the Advancement of Colored People (NAACP) came out in opposition to his position. However, Dr. King's core values, "the power of his faith, his love of humanity, and an irrepressible resolve to free black people, and other people too,"[10] led him to tell the truth as he saw it. As a result, Martin Luther King Jr. won the Nobel Peace Prize.

Questions

1. When, if ever, have you been aware that a journalist, politician, or other message provider was spinning a topic?
2. Is spinning immoral? Explain your answer.
3. In what instances, if any, have you heard a speaker pander to an audience? How did you respond?
4. Do you agree that pandering is immoral? Explain your answer.
5. Give an example of a historical or a current public figure who spoke unpopular truths that upset his or her audiences. What was the result?

spinning selecting material that favors the speaker's interests and point of view

pandering providing messages audiences want to hear, not necessarily what they need to hear

member's demographic characteristics become more **salient** (significant or relevant) in some situations than in others.[13]

For instance, no one is simply a "twenty something" or a "Cuban American" or "gay," but these characteristics are all elements of the person's identity. A young Cuban American may find that his identity as a gay man takes prominence in some contexts, whereas being twenty something or ethnically Cuban is more salient in others. The best advice is to consider your listeners' demographic characteristics *in light of the topic and your specific speaking situation*. How might membership in various categories influence their responses to your topic and your goal, given the speech situation? Let's briefly look at some common categories.

Ethnicity

Ethnicity refers to a group's common heritage and cultural traditions, usually national or religious in origin; it's often linked to language and dialects.[14] Ethnicity differs from **race**, which is a culturally constructed **social category** that categorizes people by such physical traits as skin color or facial features. These concepts are complex, however, because the criteria for grouping people into ethnic or racial categories is neither well defined nor universally accepted.[15] In addition, millions of people have mixed backgrounds.[16] President Obama's father was African, his mother was an American with Irish ancestors. Faulty as social categories are, being classified as Latino or Asian or African American can have real consequences on the life experiences and opportunities available to an individual.[17]

Religion

A single audience can represent a range of religious commitment from nonbelief to spiritual but not "religious"—from faith that's peripheral to one's identity to believers whose religion is a central factor in daily decision making. Because religion often evokes deep emotions, negative comments about a particular group's sacred texts, heroes, or rituals can create intense reactions—even among people who hold their affiliation loosely. Be sensitive to ways that religious commitment (or lack thereof) can affect a listener's response to you and your topic.

Sex, Gender, Sexual Orientation, Relationship Status, and Sexual Expression

These categories are not simply the "M for male" and "F for female" or the "single, married, divorced, partnered, or widowed" boxes that show up in demographic surveys. The biological category of **sex** is not the same as **gender**, which refers to culturally constructed concepts about what is feminine, masculine, or androgynous (not specifically masculine or feminine). Audience members also vary in their sexual orientation and their sexual expression. They may be in a relationship or not. Some are sexually active; others are not. Some are heterosexual; others are lesbian, gay, bisexual, transgendered, or questioning their orientation. For some topics and in some contexts, categories relating to sexuality become highly salient.

Age

Not surprisingly, age affects listeners' motivations and concerns. Demographers identify several general groups: mature Americans, baby boomers, Generation Xers, Generation Yers or millennials, and the newest "iGeneration" (Internet or individualized generation) sometimes called the Digital Generation, who use technology in ways previous generations never dreamed possible.[18] An era's history, culture, and technology offers each cohort different perspectives and goals.[19] Most traditional college students are millennials or iGeneration members; most professors are baby boomers or Gen Xers.[20] Although generational gaps can obviously be large, even minor age differences can play

---

salient relevant or significant

ethnicity heritage and cultural traditions, usually stemming from national and religious backgrounds

race category, often associated with stereotypes, based on physical characteristics

social category culturally constructed category such as race or gender

sex biological categories of male and female

gender clusters of traits culturally labeled as masculine, feminine, or androgynous

A single audience member is influenced by demographic factors that are interwoven with the individual's characteristics. In one situation, age is significant; in another, religion, gender, or other factors may be more salient.

© iStockphoto.com/Alina555

out differently. For example, college seniors and first-year students may have varying interest in a topic as seemingly simple as résumé writing.

Other Considerations

A variety of experiences and interests can also characterize audience members, and considering these can guide you in selecting topics and supporting materials.

- *Socioeconomic Status*. Socioeconomic status is related to *education* and *occupation*. Comfortably middle-class individuals and those who struggle in minimum wage jobs differ in many important ways, including the options available to them. Members of professions such as medicine or education share interests, backgrounds, and jargon.[21] Even in the classroom, engineering majors may be more interested in some topics than social work majors.

- *Group Affiliation*. Keep in mind that some political junkies nowadays are so committed to parties or policies that certain topics trigger passionate responses. In addition, members of groups as varied as Wheelchair Athletes, Alcoholics Anonymous, fraternities or sororities, and professional business organizations coalesce around shared interests that you should consider before you speak.

- *Region*. You'd expect to use different strategies for audiences in different countries, but factors such as climate, history, and the economic base create diversity between states or regions or from area to area within a single state. Such differences can even shape the types of cars people prefer; for example, hybrids are top choices in the West and full-sized pickup trucks in the South.[22] In the state of Oregon, for example, residents along the Pacific Ocean, those who live in the middle "wine country," and inhabitants of the eastern semiarid ranch lands all have different interests and concerns.

In summary, demographic audience analysis provides insights into your listeners' ethnicity, race, religion, gender concerns, and age as well as socioeconomic status, group affiliation, and regional identity. However, instead of stereotyping your listeners, try to use a more inclusive model that recognizes which demographic characteristics are most significant to your topic and the situation.

The Audience and the Topic

Just knowing demographic characteristics does not tell you how listeners will react to your topic. By taking their **psychological profile** through direct or indirect methods, you can discern some of their beliefs, attitudes, values, and behaviors related to your subject.

Direct Methods

Use **direct methods** by asking the audience members what they think and do, whether by an interview, a focus group, or a questionnaire. For instance, a commencement speaker interviewed several students about their campus experiences and their expectations for the future and then wove this information into his speech. Focus group consultants, especially in politics or organizations, invite a small group of representative respondents to answer a few questions about a policy or a product.

For classroom speeches, questionnaires are common. Create a paper-and-pencil test, or use Internet resources such as SurveyMonkey, Zoomerang, or Fluidsurveys that make it easy to distribute, collect, and analyze data, often free of charge. Although Leif was personally excited about hovercrafts, he wanted to know how to make his information understandable and interesting to first-year college classmates. So early in his preparation, he created an online questionnaire to assess his classmates' knowledge and beliefs about hovercraft technology as well as their attitudes, values, and behaviors regarding alternative vehicles.

As Chapter 1 briefly pointed out, a **belief** is a mental acceptance of something as true or false, correct or incorrect, valid or invalid.[23] Because beliefs are based on study and investigation, as well as on convictions developed without much factual information or knowledge, misconceptions are common. Leif used a **closed question** (one answer) such as this to gauge his listeners' knowledge of the topic:

Do you know what a hovercraft is?

_____ Yes

_____ No

_____ I'm not sure

He followed this with an **open question** that allowed listeners to explain what they knew about the physics behind these all-terrain vehicles:

In the box below, tell what you know about the "Summation of Force" or "Net Force" principle.

[ ]

Attitudes are our tendencies to like or dislike something or to have positive or negative feelings about it. **Scaled questions** typically measure attitudes along a range or continuum, from highly positive to neutral to highly negative. This scaled question relates to Leif's topic:

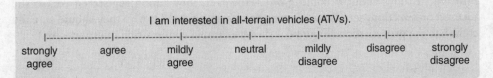

I am interested in all-terrain vehicles (ATVs).

|----------------|----------------|----------------|----------------|----------------|----------------|
strongly agree   agree   mildly agree   neutral   mildly disagree   disagree   strongly disagree

psychological profile assessment of an audience's beliefs, values, and attitudes regarding a topic

direct methods asking audience members directly for their opinion by questionnaires, interviews, and so on

belief mental acceptance of something as true or false, correct or incorrect, valid or invalid

closed question request for a brief, specific answer

open question giving opportunity for a range of answers or a more lengthy response

attitudes our tendency to like or dislike something or to have positive or negative feelings about it

scaled questions asking for responses along a continuum, used to assess attitudes

When listeners share your attitude toward your topic, whether it's negative or positive, your speaking task is usually easier than when audience attitudes are diverse. Listeners with neutral attitudes probably have not thought enough about the subject to form an opinion.

values standards used to make evaluative judgments such as good or bad

Values are standards for making evaluative judgments such as good or bad, beautiful or ugly, appropriate or inappropriate. Almost all your topics touch on your values in some way because you at least consider the subject significant enough to discuss. However, when you use words such as *right* or *wrong, moral* or *immoral, important* or *insignificant,* you are directly addressing value questions. **Ranked questions** such as this work well for value questions:

ranked questions asking for responses to be placed in an order

In vehicles, I care most about (rank these in order from most to least):

_____ Safety

_____ Fuel efficiency

_____ Versatility

_____ Noise pollution

Finally, this scaled question is a way to assess behaviors—what audience members do—or would do—given the chance.

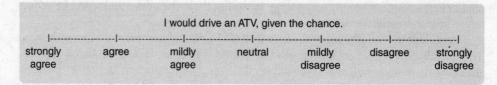

Leif found that only about one in four knew what a hovercraft was, so he organized his remarks around the vehicle itself and the principles that made it work. Respondents cared about fuel efficiency and safety but were less concerned about versatility and noise pollution, and he could use those values to explain that hovercraft, although noisy and hard to maneuver, were fuel efficient and safe. (Read his outline in Chapter 11 or on your online resources.)

Indirect Methods

indirect methods assessing audiences by observation or secondhand sources

Indirect methods are less straightforward. Personally observe your classmates before, during, and after class. Listen carefully to their in-class contributions for clues about their beliefs and attitudes. For an outside group, consult secondhand sources by talking to people who are familiar with the group or by getting printed brochures or material from group-related websites. The commencement speaker mentioned earlier went to the university's website, read its mission statement, looked at online editions of the campus newspaper, and talked to alumni to get a feel for the makeup, reputation, and ethos of the place.

In summary, knowing your audience's psychological profile can help you better focus your speech. For instance, Terah's topic was organ donation, but questionnaire responses showed that her classmates already knew about organ donors and they had positive attitudes about becoming one. However, they hadn't registered yet, so she focused on two things: (1) how easy it was to sign up and (2) why they should actually complete the process soon (Figure 6.2 shows a sample combination questionnaire.).

A Combination Questionnaire

Name (optional) _____

Age _____   Sex _____   Major _____

How do you define civility?

Have you ever posted an uncivil comment on the Internet?

_____ Yes

_____ No

_____ I'm not sure

Rank these typical online remarks in order from least civil (ranked 1) to most civil (ranked 4):

_____ RepubliCONS are as bad as DemocRATS.

_____ You deserve to die, you troll scumbag.

_____ Are you a liar or are you just ignorant?

_____ Talk about First World problems!

Respond to this idea: Anonymous posts should not be allowed on the Internet.

_____ Strongly agree

_____ Agree

_____ Neutral

_____ Disagree

_____ Strongly disagree

Figure 6.2
A Combination Questionnaire on the topic of Internet civility.

Stop and Check

Assess the Situation

After you consider your listeners' demographic categories and their psychological profiles, take into account situational features such as time and the environment that can affect an audience.

Consider the Time

Three aspects of time affect public speaking: the time of day, cultural time norms, and the timeliness of the topic. First, consider the hour your speech takes place. Ask yourself what problems listeners might face in an early morning session. What about an audience just before lunch when everyone is hungry? Or just after lunch when they're sleepy? What challenges does an evening session pose? Adapt your talk appropriately. For instance, you might be more animated or use more visual support if listeners are sleepy, or you might shorten your speech when it's very late.

Also, consider the *cultural* time system. In the United States, time is commonly considered a commodity that we can save, spend, or give. We have "free" time and "full" schedules. We divide our time into segments, each lasting a specific duration, with distinct activities assigned to each segment.[24] Take your speech class, for example. You chose it partly because it filled a time slot available in your schedule. The clock tells you when class starts and when it ends. In this setting, both the date and length of your speech are important. It matters that you appear on an assigned date with a speech of an assigned length, partly because timing is important in work situations. If your job requires you to give a 10-minute briefing at an 11:00 meeting on a Wednesday in mid-March, you could

In US classrooms and organizations across the country, timing matters. You need to perform on the due date and conform to the assigned speech length.

get a lower appraisal or lose your job if you show up on a Friday prepared with an hour speech—even if the speech is great.

Online courses let students be more flexible in their participation, although instructors typically set general boundaries for speech length and for times to upload speeches, view others' videos, and comment in various forums.

In contrast, listeners from a culture or co-culture with a more relaxed view of time focus less on starting precisely on time or on finishing within a rigid time frame. For example, Professor Robert Levine, a native of fast-paced Brooklyn, taught in slower-paced Brazil where his psychology class was scheduled from 10:00 A.M. to noon.[25] Taking along his cultural expectations, he assumed the class would begin at 10:00 and end at 12:00. To his surprise, students unapologetically strolled in as late as 11:00. At noon he was finished, but most students stayed, asking questions. By 12:15 Levine was fidgety. At 12:30 he ended the class and left, although the students seemed willing to stay even longer.

Third, consider how cultural or social events might affect the audience's response to various topics. For example, a speech about snow is probably a better choice in December than, say, mid-April. Topics such as bullying often follow nationally televised coverage of a situation that got out of hand with disastrous consequences. And topics related to politics may be more interesting and relevant during election years.

Consider the Environment

Room design and equipment can create a pleasant or unpleasant setting for a speech. Instructors tell stories about challenging rooms:

- One class was held in a basement classroom with no windows and three large drain pipes that segmented the room in such a way that not all the students could see one another.
- Another room was wider than it was deep. A grand piano sat in the center, and the blackboards were covered with five-lined staffs for musical notations.
- In online courses, students sometimes gather an audience and videotape their speech in a living room, a cramped workspace, or another improvised setting.

Rooms such as these can all affect your audience, whether or not they realize it. If you can change the location or the seating pattern, do so. But when things are out of your control, make sure everyone can see and hear you.

Other environmental considerations such as the temperature inside (too hot, too cold), the weather outside (sunny and beautiful, stormy and icy), or noise (a rattling air conditioner or radiator) can also affect audience comfort or distract their attention. Recognize potential environmental effects on your audience, and do what you can to make your listeners comfortable and focused on your speech.

Consider Your Audience's Perception of You

credibility listeners' impressions of your character, intentions, and abilities that make you more or less believable

Analysis goes two ways. While you are forming impressions of your listeners, they are forming perceptions about your **credibility**. They make judgments about your knowledge and intelligence regarding the topic as well as your motivations and intentions regarding them. Their evaluations begin before your speech, they're modified while you speak, and they lead to a lasting impression after you finish.[26]

Be Aware of Prior Credibility

If a famous historian comes to campus, you expect her to be an expert on the era and characters she writes about. In the workplace, if two employees report on a project they've worked on for six months, you assume they know what they are talking about. This type of credibility—the speakers' reputation or expertise that makes them believable even before they say a word—is called **prior** or **extrinsic credibility**. Practically speaking, you will lack prior credibility in your classroom, unless for some reason your classmates know something about you that links you to the topic. Consequently, establish a connection between yourself and your topic in the introduction. (The Diversity in Practice box provides some cross-cultural information on prior credibility.)

prior or **extrinsic credibility** credibility that speakers bring to the speech because of their experience and reputation

Credibility in Other Cultures

DIVERSITY IN PRACTICE

Cultures vary in their perceptions of prior credibility. Age and gender are factors in some Native American cultures. When "saying a few words" is necessary, younger men and women seek out older men to speak for them. Tribal elders scolded one young woman for not knowing how to act; she broke tribal traditions by speaking for herself and her husband on a public occasion.[27]

In Kenya, credibility is linked to wealth, social status, education, age, and ethnicity. Wealth comes in the form of wives, children, cattle, or money, but wealth in itself is not the only criterion for respect. The more credible speakers are people who have used their wealth to help others. Furthermore, unmarried men or men with few children or no sons lack authority, especially in rural areas. In a country made up of forty distinct groups, members of certain ethnic groups have higher overall credibility.[28]

Age can also affect audience views of credibility. In the United States, youth and fresh ideas are celebrated. In contrast, listeners in cultures that respect the wisdom and experience that come with age pay less attention to youth and more attention to their elders. Be aware of potential differences whenever you adapt to a culturally diverse audience.

Demonstrate Credibility in Your Speech

Demonstrated or **intrinsic credibility** becomes evident as you give your speech. Think back to the historian. If she seemed unsure about a detail that you even know, you'd probably decide she was not as expert her reputation suggested. Or consider what would happen if those employees were unable to answer questions about the material in their reports. Their overall credibility would suffer.

demonstrated or **intrinsic credibility** obvious knowledge the speaker shows during the speech

When an audience evaluates your credibility, they look for evidence that you are knowledgeable about your subject. Consequently, it is important to do careful research and cite your sources. Define unfamiliar terminology, give examples, tell your personal experiences with the subject, and otherwise show your thorough understanding of the subject. Finally, be prepared to answer questions afterward.

Listeners also expect you to be calm and poised. Think of it this way: If you're agitated during a classroom presentation, your audience will wonder why you cannot control yourself. In contrast, if you appear confident, they will perceive you more favorably.

Take Terminal Credibility into Account

terminal credibility final impression listeners have of a speaker

The overall impression you leave after your speech is over is your **terminal credibility**— a balance between the reputation you brought to your speech, the expertise you demonstrated as you spoke, and the overall information your audience has or might learn about you or your topic. For instance, if your listeners eventually discover that some of your information was incorrect or slanted or that you don't act in ways that support your ideas, they will lose confidence in you and your terminal credibility is damaged. A good example is a high-profile member of the clergy or of the business community who once had great audiences until he or she was uncovered as a fraud.

Summary

You and your audiences are involved in an interactive process in which you form impressions of one another around a topic you've chosen for a specific time and place. You assess your listeners' motivations as well as their demographic characteristics; however, you also realize that characteristics such as age, religion, or ethnicity are salient only at specific times and in specific circumstances.

Just as focus group leaders analyze a group's psychological profile, you can analyze your audience's opinions about your topic. What do they already know or believe? How do they feel about your subject? What attitudes and underlying values influence their interest? Developing a questionnaire with various types of questions is a direct method of identifying listener responses to specific aspects of your subject. Indirectly, you can observe them, looking for clues that suggest their attitudes.

Finally, situational characteristics affect your audience. The time of day, the length of your speech, and the noise level or temperature in the room all influence an audience's interest and attention. Do what you can to minimize environmental distractions.

In turn, your listeners actively evaluate you. Before your speech, they assess your reputation. During your speech, they form impressions of your credibility and your overall trustworthiness based on cultural criteria such as sound evidence, source citation, overall knowledge, and composure. After you've finished, your listeners continue to assess your credibility, either positively or negatively.

This is one of the most important chapters in this text. As good speakers everywhere know, sensitivity to a specific audience is not optional. It is essential to good speech-making.

Reflect on what you've learned.

STUDY AND REVIEW

Public Speaking: Concepts and Skills for a Diverse Society offers a broad range of resources that will help you better understand the material in this chapter, complete assignments, and succeed on tests. Your MindTap resources feature the following:

• Speech videos with viewing questions, speech outlines, and transcripts
• Activities to help you check your understanding and to apply what you've learned to your own life
• Stop and Check and Critical Thinking exercises
• Outline Builder

- Web Links related to chapter content
- Study and review tools such as self-quizzes and an interactive glossary

You can access your online resources for *Public Speaking: Concepts and Skills for a Diverse Society* at cengagebrain.com using the access code that came with your book or that you purchased online.

KEY TERMS

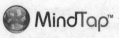

The terms below are defined in the margins throughout this chapter.

Review your **Flashcards**.

absent audience 69	pandering 70
attitude 73	passive audience 69
audience analysis 68	prior or extrinsic credibility 77
belief 73	psychological profile 73
closed question 73	race 71
credibility 76	random audience 68
demographic analysis 69	ranked questions 74
demonstrated or intrinsic	salient 71
credibility 77	scaled questions 73
direct methods 73	self-selected audience 69
ethnicity 71	sex 71
gender 71	social category 71
homogeneous audience 69	spinning 70
hostile audience 69	terminal credibility 78
indirect methods 74	unmotivated audience 68
listening speaker 68	values 74
motivated audience 69	
open question 73	

CRITICAL THINKING QUESTIONS

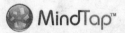

1. Identify times when you have been a member of each type of audience: unmotivated, random, passive, motivated, self-selected, homogeneous, hostile, and absent. Select one situation and describe how your motivation affected the way you listened.
2. What occupation(s) most interest(s) you? What opportunities might you have to address each type of audience listed in Exercise 1 within your chosen occupational field? Which type of audience is most common in that occupation? Which is least common?
3. How would a demographer describe you? Write a self-analysis using the demographic categories listed in this chapter. From what you observe about your classmates, how are you like others in the class? How are you different?
4. Next, identify which aspect(s) of your identity, if any, would be most salient if you were listening to a speech with the following central ideas. What should a speaker do to make the topic appeal to you?

   - To inform my audience about the Feast of the Epiphany, how different cultures celebrate it, and the Mexican tradition of eating rosca de reyes as part of the celebration.
   - To make my audience understand the global impact of rap by looking at rappers from Brazil, South Africa, France, and Korea.
   - To persuade my audience that states should install apps in cars to track the amount of miles they drive and tax drivers by mileage, not per gallon purchased.
   - To convince my audience that the $10.5 billion allotted to NASA is essential.

5. To understand race and ethnicity better, read the first-person account of racial and ethnic identity, available on your online resources. Identify the various labels the author has been tagged with. What conclusions has she drawn?

6. In 1981 *Washington Post* reporter Joel Garreau wrote *The Nine Nations of North America*. You can find a summary of his ideas on Garreau's website. Follow the link to your region and see if you agree with his description of the area in which you live. Then link to another region. Do you think the regions have changed in the last thirty-plus years? If so, how? How might a speaker from your region adapt to an audience in the second region?

7. Song lyrics are written with audiences in mind. Analyze the lyrics to Reba McEntire's 1994 song "She Thinks His Name Was John." You can find them online, or you can watch Ms. McEntire perform this song on YouTube. Who is her target audience? What is her goal? The song came out in 1994. How have audiences changed and/or stayed the same since then?[29]

8. Select a topic that you might use for a speech and then try to see yourself as your classmates might see you speaking on that subject. At this point in the term, what credibility would you bring to this speech? How could you demonstrate credibility in the speech? How do you think your audience would see you after you're finished?

APPLICATION EXERCISES

1. Experienced speakers always try to check out the physical setting for a speech in advance. Work with a group of your classmates to develop a checklist of what to look for in any physical setting and then discuss how specific obstacles might be handled.

2. Choose one of the following topics and talk with a small group of your classmates about the different ways you would use demographic factors in your audience to develop a speech for each of the following groups or audiences.

Topic: Your school's administrators are discussing a policy that will abolish all competitive sports on campus.

Audiences
- Your classmates
- A group of prospective students
- Alumni who are consistent donors to the school
- Basketball team members

Topic: The United States should double its foreign aid budget.

Audiences
- Senior citizens
- A high school government class
- The local chapter of the League of Women Voters
- Your classmates

3. With a small group of students list the physical characteristics of your classroom. Include size, acoustics, lighting, temperature, ambient noise, placement of seats, and distance between speaker and listeners. Then discuss how these physical characteristics might affect the audience's ability to listen effectively. What can you do as a speaker to overcome potential barriers to listening in your classroom setting?

4. To further your understanding of prior credibility, work with several classmates to identify a campus event such as a commencement ceremony, an alcohol abuse workshop for dormitory residents, or a sports recognition banquet for athletes and their parents. Then identify a local, regional, or nationally known figure who would make a good speaker for the event, given his or her credibility on the topic.

THIS CHAPTER WILL
HELP YOU

• Plan your research

• Locate and gather
materials from a
variety of sources

• Critically evaluate
your sources

• Record your informa-
tion in a way that suits
your learning style and
avoids plagiarism

Diana Ong/SuperStock

Researching Your
Speech in the Digital Age

YOU HAVE YOUR TOPIC, your goal, and your audience in mind. Now it's
time to gather speech materials. The amounts and kinds of library holdings,
communication technologies (ICT), and other resources put a wide variety of
available documents at your fingertips within seconds. However, this can be
a mixed blessing. It's easy to rely on Internet search engines, which can lead
to literally billions of often questionable data to sift through.[1] Consequently,
you face the task of analyzing and synthesizing the information you find into
high-quality, manageable speech materials.[2]

As Chapter 2 explained, principles for gathering effective supporting
materials are found in the canon the Romans called *invention*. Choosing the

best material combines several skills that increase your competence in speech-making and contribute to academic and workplace success. They include the ability to

- Formulate a research plan
- Locate the data you need to support your ideas
- Critically evaluate sources and choose the best materials available
- Record your findings in a systematic way that avoids plagiarism

The goal of this chapter is to help you effectively accomplish these major tasks.

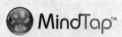

Read, *highlight, and take notes online.*

Develop a Research Plan

Planning a search strategy at the outset will help you focus your research and save time in the long run. The following tips have worked for many students.[3]

First, analyze your topic to decide exactly what you need. Return to your speech goals from Chapter 5 and consider the type of materials you need to engage your specific audience. For example, ask yourself questions such as: Does the audience need big picture information? Definitions? Background information? Identifying these questions at the start can help focus your research.

Let your topic guide your choice of sources. Some subjects, such as scientific topics, require scientific books or articles written by experts. Other subjects may call for personal experiences, historical facts, surveys, or statistics. Current issues need up-to-date research, usually found in news reports.

Budget enough time into your schedule. Although studies reveal that 80 percent of students wait until the last day or two to start working on 80 percent of their papers,[4] good research is time-consuming, so don't expect to get appropriate high-quality, usable information by spending an hour online or in the library the night before the speech. Plan more than one research session, and if you need a book or article through interlibrary loan, factor in the time it will take to get it.[5]

Planning your research makes the process easier and saves time overall.

© wavebreakmedia/Shutterstock.com

Use your librarians' expertise. Tuition dollars pay for library services, so tap into your librarians' extensive knowledge of the research process. Your library's or learning center's website provides informative materials librarians have prepared such as research tips, links to databases, subject-specific, topic-specific, or course-specific guides. Look for "Ask-A-Librarian" features or for contact information so a librarian can answer your specific questions.[6] Two types of librarians are especially helpful. **Reference librarians** are the "go-to" people at the reference desk who are specifically trained to help you find information, whether in hard copy or online.[7] In large academic libraries, **subject librarians** have an advanced degree in a specialized discipline as well as a library degree. Despite their availability, a recent study showed that only two in ten students consulted a librarian in their research.[8] But who knows your library better than the people who work there daily?

Identify key terms for your search. Your library's **Online Public Access Catalog (OPAC)**[9] lets you search for books by title, subject, author, and keyword. If a subject search fails to produce usable titles, try a keyword search instead. Although librarians are revising OPAC's subject terms to become "more like Google,"[10] the terms are still less flexible than Internet search terms. In addition, Internet search engines, unlike OPACs, suggest alternative spellings and adjust to abbreviations.

Keep a running list of all sources as you search. This way, you can easily assemble your final bibliography and return to a source when necessary. If you use the Internet, bookmark each site you search. Carefully keeping track of each source also helps you avoid plagiarism and credit your sources appropriately.

Make critical evaluation a part of your plan. So many resources are available that you might think you're drowning in data—some are highly credible, others are very questionable. Find out as much as you can about every source you use, whether it be a book, article, website, or personal interview. Then compare sources. Some will be OK, some pretty good, and some excellent. Choose the best.

This is not an exhaustive list, but these tips will help you focus your search more effectively.

reference librarian librarian at the reference desk who is specifically trained to help people find information

subject librarian librarian who also has an advanced degree in a particular subject such as law or medicine

online public access catalog (OPAC) digital catalog to help you locate books and materials in your library's holdings

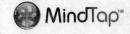 MindTap™

Locate the Data You Need

After you have a general plan, your next step is to actually locate credible written sources such as books, magazines, opinion pieces, and news reports, and nonwritten materials such as information from personal experience, interviews, lectures, performances, and media channels.

Use Written Materials

Written materials traditionally found in hard copy in traditional libraries and news-stands are still there, but today they're also in electronic databases and at Internet sites. Consequently, research continues to change rapidly in the digital age; however, libraries are still campus centers for information—sometimes renamed as "information commons" or "learning centers." Regardless of terminology, they continue to provide carefully selected printed matter plus pictures, maps, and video and audio recordings in various formats. Library materials have academic credibility because they undergo many screenings by editors, librarians, and professors before they are acquired. In contrast, Internet resources require more scrutiny because screened and unscreened materials coexist there.

Regardless of whether you access library or Internet sources, look for books, journals, reference works, news reports, and opinion pieces.

Books

scholarly book book based on research that advances knowledge in an academic field

trade book book aimed at a general audience

Experts write **scholarly books** based on research to advance knowledge in a field aimed at specialized audiences of professionals and researchers. Peer reviewers check them for accuracy before publication. Reference books and works of literature also count as scholarly books. **Trade books**, the kind aimed at a general audience, such as best-selling novels or cookbooks are more common in public libraries than in academic libraries.

You can find many free full-text books online through sources such as Project Gutenberg (45,000 titles), especially classics or books in the public domain. In addition, campus libraries currently provide access to thousands of digitized e-books through sources such as Ebrary (85,000 digital titles), EBL (E-Book Library with 16,000+ titles), EBSCO Academic Books, and PsycBooks (50,000 chapters from academic books, plus 1,600 historic books). It's convenient to download these books or chapters to your personal files and then highlight usable materials.

Reference Materials

specialized encyclopedia text that summarizes information in a specific subject area

Hundreds of reference works provide specific information, such as definitions, dates, and statistics. You're familiar with general encyclopedias that review and summarize information on thousands of topics, but you may be less familiar with the hundreds of **specialized encyclopedias** that provide information about more narrowed subjects. For example, there's an encyclopedia of adoption, one for pacifism, another for Title IX and sports—the variety is great. Many encyclopedias are available online, some for a fee; however, libraries often pay the fees so that you can freely access the information through your library's website.

Dictionaries provide definitions, pronunciations, historical sources, synonyms, and antonyms for words. Also, specialized dictionaries are devoted to individual subjects that might surprise you. There's one for pianists, another for agriculture, even one for sexist quotations. Search your library holdings for "dictionary of" to see the wide range of specialized dictionaries; the Internet also provides specialized dictionaries, some from off-the-wall .com sources but many associated with more reliable .gov or .edu sources.

Campus learning centers provide access to millions of documents in both hard copy and digital formats.

© Ermolaev Alexander/Shutterstock.com

For statistics, the *Statistical Abstract of the United States*, a government document, provides numbers on a wide variety of topics, including US population, health, education, crime, employment, elections, the environment, and defense. Almanacs, such as the *World Almanac*, also provide statistical data. Online, look for reputable sources such as FedStats, which provides data from more than 100 agencies.

What about Wikipedia? Although the advice, in general, is to avoid this online reference site for academic work, it gets more than 8 million views per hour,[11] and truth be told, typical students consult it at some point. In fact, surveys find that 85 percent of students check out it for "big picture" information,[12] much like former generations skimmed encyclopedia articles for an overview of their topics.[13] Is using Wikipedia justified? Some educators say yes.[14] It offers more than 17 million user-generated entries in 270 languages,[15] and "netizens" add about 370,000 articles annually.[16] Moreover, it provides links to other articles, along with notes, references, and external links. However, anyone, even you, can create or edit (or vandalize) an entry, and that's the problem. You're not guaranteed that the group-generated material is reliable, although a study comparing its articles with *Encyclopedia Britannica*'s found a similar number of errors in each.[17] Over the years, some contributors have demonstrated their ability to contribute objectively and accurately; others are banned from editing. Some entries (Chuck Norris is one) are locked because of vandalism. Others, such as George W. Bush, Barack Obama, Jesus, and Islam, are semiprotected—open only to trustworthy Wikipedians.[18] Users must be careful, but the same is true about many online sources.[19]

Periodicals

Libraries subscribe to general interest periodicals like *U.S. News & World Report* or *Sports Illustrated* and more specialized magazines such as *Hiker's World* or *Vital Speeches of the Day*. They also house **trade journals**, which contain topics related to specific occupations such as nursing or architecture, and **academic journals**, such as *Communication Studies*, which publish research findings of scholars writing in academic areas. One good source for complex issues is *Congressional Digest: The Pro-and-Con Monthly*. For example, March 2014 examines federal funding for early childhood education. It provides a history, analysis of current programs, impact studies, and pro and con arguments. It's both in the library and online.

trade journal journal that pertains to a specific occupation

academic journals journals that pertain to a specific area of academic research

Your library makes available databases such as Academic Search Premier (full text from thousands of peer-reviewed journals) or CQ Researcher (in-depth reports on today's issues). In addition, most major trade magazines such as *Time*, *National Review*, and *The Atlantic Monthly* are available on the Internet, as are links to many scholarly journals, although some, such as JSTOR, ask you to register and pay a fee to download materials.

News Sources

Journalism is changing rapidly from print sources delivered to your doorstep to video-only sources available exclusively online. Their value is in their ability to cover current and breaking events. Traditional or **legacy journalism**[20] includes your local town newspapers as well as the *New York Times*, the *Washington Post*, and the *Los Angeles Times*, which are considered "elite media" because of their reputation for high-quality, detailed reporting and because many smaller papers reprint their articles. Diversity in Practice: International and Ethnic Presses also explains news sources targeted to co-cultural and ethnic groups. These, as well as traditional television broadcasts, are available online— some for a subscription fee—along with thousands of local, national, and international news sources.

legacy journalism traditional news sources such as local and national newspapers

native digital news news outlets on the Internet that hire trained journalists and editors

Native digital news outlets—globally, nationally, and internationally—have taken journalism to the Internet where trained journalists and editors bring their skills to new platforms. Currently, 30 major sites such as Vice, BuzzFeed, and Huffington Post exist alongside more than 400 minor or targeted outlets such as Charlottesville Tomorrow.[21] In addition, more video-only news sources are appearing. One example is Newsy, which aggregates content from credible news broadcasts around the globe and combines it into a single piece with links to the original videos.[22] Although various outlets may have a clear bias, the writers and editors are generally professionals.

DIVERSITY IN PRACTICE

International and Ethnic Presses

Foreign news outlets, found both in libraries and online, allow you to gain different perspectives and to hear voices other than those found in mainstream sources. Check out *World Press Review* for original articles and excerpts from international presses. Also look for diverse perspectives within the United States—such as news from labor unions, African Americans, gays and lesbians, Catholics, and Muslims, which all produce news from their perspectives.

Opinion Sources

If you want various opinions on issues, look in the editorial section of reputable news outlets where commentators have been screened for their ability to discuss issues in an intelligent manner. For example, the *Washington Post* [online] provides a Columnist Index, and the *New York Times* offers a variety of viewpoints on its Opinion Pages (in hard copy and online sources).

The quality and trustworthiness of other opinion sources is less assured. For instance, veteran blogger Andrew Sullivan[23] explains that anyone with access to a computer—expert or not—can log their spontaneous thoughts in writing and post them on personal weblogs (blogs). This results in instant and global self-publishing. Because bloggers often respond quickly to breaking events, their risk of error is greater because they may not get all the facts right or have time to process them thoughtfully. Furthermore, once the blog is posted, only minor revisions are allowed. Consequently, their use in academic work is more questionable.

In summary, many materials that were once available only in hard copy are now available online. Table 7.1 shows the advantages and disadvantages of these kinds of materials.

Take Advantage of Nonprint Sources

Often, nonprint sources such as personal experiences, interviews, and lectures or performances can provide excellent information.

Personal Experiences

You probably chose your topic because it somehow relates to your interests and experiences, and you can often use personal experiences in your speeches. For subjects such as demonstrations or how-to speeches, personal expertise is almost essential. Wouldn't you think it weird if a speaker, who never took a photograph, described photography

TABLE 7.1

Library Resources Compared to Internet Sources

Library Materials	Internet Materials
Monitored: knowledgeable people select and track the material	Not Monitored: anyone can post anything, experts and con artists alike
Reviewed: most materials undergo a systematic editorial review process	Not reviewed: most materials lack a systematic review process
Organized: holdings are systematically classified (OPACs, Dewey Decimal System)	Unorganized: no system classifies content, even Google changes algorithms
Non-commercial: materials are not chosen for commercial reasons	Often commercial: factual information competes with commercials and ads
Guidelines: librarians provide explicit guides for evaluating materials	No standardized guidelines: No explicit guidelines to evaluate the content
Limited amount: the number of documents, although vast, has limits	Unlimited amount: billions of documents are available, with more added daily

techniques? Personal experiences with subjects such as preparing a budget or living with diabetes increase the speaker's credibility.

Interviews

If you don't have experience with a topic, you can interview someone who does. Go in person, use email, phone, or Skype to ask for information or get clarification about confusing ideas. Or watch or read a transcript from a show—such as NBC's *Meet the Press* or CNN's *Reliable Sources*—that regularly interviews guests. **Experts** know their subjects because of their studies and occupations. I interviewed two expert librarians when I wrote this chapter. **Laypeople** or **peers** have opinions and insights learned through ordinary living. I interviewed several students for practical tips about their research strategies.

expert people whose knowledge is based on research, experience, or occupation

laypeople or **peers** ordinary people whose knowledge comes from everyday experiences

Because most people have full schedules, keep the following interview tips in mind:

- *Prepare in advance.* Do research about the topic beforehand so you don't waste time going over basic information. In addition, learn about the persons and (in the case of experts) the organizations they represent to better understand their perspectives. Then write out questions to help you remember everything you want to ask and to keep the interview on track. Give these questions to your interviewees beforehand—especially if they are not native English speakers—so they have time to prepare thoughtful answers.
- *Listen carefully.* During the interview, take notes and then read them back to the interviewee, who can then make corrections or additions. Ask questions such as "Is this what you mean?" or "Did I understand this correctly … ?" If you plan to record the interview, ask permission in advance, and place the recorder in full view.
- *Aim to understand your topic from your interviewees' perspective.* If their ideas and actions clash with yours, practice civility. Listen politely, and try to understand how they came to their viewpoints. Remember that they did you a favor by agreeing to an interview.
- *Be time conscious.* Schedule the interview at the other person's convenience, not yours. When you make the appointment, estimate how long it will take and then respect

those limits. Confirm the appointment a few days beforehand. On appointment day be early, even if your interviewee is late. If you must break an appointment for any reason, give the person as much advanced notice as possible.

Yale Undergraduate Career Services[24] gives additional pointers such as making sure you have the person's correct name and title and following up with a thank-you note.

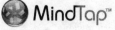

Stop and Check

Lectures and Performances

Performances of various kinds are widely available, live and recorded. Check your library's holdings for recordings of lectures and performances. Universities often make significant campus events available through podcasts. Important political speeches and eulogies for significant public speakers are both televised and online; C-SPAN broadcasts live deliberations from the House of Representatives as well as a variety of speakers on topics of national concern. Internet sites such as TED feature "riveting talks by remarkable people, free to the world"[25] categorized by speaker and by topic. TED also provides transcripts of the speeches.

DIVERSITY IN PRACTICE

Research in Kenya

Although you are expected to research your speech topic, different cultural groups have different research traditions. For instance, a study compared the public speaking norms in Kenya to the guidelines commonly taught in US colleges and universities. Three Kenyan students described typical speech preparation in their culture:

- "Audiences in the African context do not expect researched and memorized speeches, but speeches compiled spontaneously and using the speaker's wisdom."
- "Public speaking in Africa is not … something that someone will spend a week researching."
- "In the African context there are less rules to follow, or at least the emphasis is not as much as it is in the West."[26]

Kenyan students, however, admitted that research and preparation is becoming more common in their country.

The type of research described in this chapter is required for many, but not all speeches, even in the United States. For example, the special occasion speeches described in Chapter 18 are exceptions.

Think Critically about the Material

Educational Testing Service researchers found that although students may be digital natives, a majority of them "do not currently have the skills to analyze and synthesize information into something manageable and useful for their needs."[27] To help remedy this lack, librarians at Ohio State University developed a **MAPit** technique students can use to ask questions about the data and sources they find.[28] *MAP* is an acronym that stands for M (message), A (author or source), and P (purpose).

MAPit strategy developed by librarians that evaluates material according to message, author, and purpose

M = Message

Rate the message or content based on the following tips:[29]

1. *Is the material biased?* Does it emphasize a particular perspective, or is it relatively objective? Is it free of stereotyping? Does the source have an established position on the topic? For example, many news sources have a bias. The leanings of reporters and commentators on Fox News compared to MSNBC are well known. Materials on topics such as environmental or social issues often promote one side or another.

2. *Is the language loaded or neutral?* Do the words used portray one side of an issue more positively or negatively than another perspective?[30]

3. *Is it up-to-date?* Is the information (especially factual or statistical data) current? What's the date of publication of a book or magazine? Are the Internet pages maintained regularly? Look for the most updated sources unless you are doing historical research.

4. *Is it accurate?* Does the material match what you find in other credible sources? Would reputable sources accept the ideas as plausible and accurate? On the Internet, look for links. Do linked sites appear reputable? Does the document list a bibliography drawn from reputable sources? Do the cited studies or polls include the methodology, subjects, and questions asked?

5. *Is it original?* The Internet makes it especially easy to cut-and-paste material from other sources, which makes it difficult to find the originators. For example, identical information about the composer Frédéric Chopin appears on many .com sites, which present the material as if they originated it.

6. *Is it organized well?* If you must decide among documents that appear to be equal in accuracy and quality of information, choose the one that is better organized and easier to use.

A = Author (or Source)

Learn as much as you can about the author or source of the data. Critically evaluate the source as primary, secondary, or tertiary, and look for the domain of Internet sites to figure out the source's perspective.

Primary, Secondary, or Tertiary Sources[31]

Ask yourself the source's relationship to the material. Is it firsthand or derived from other sources?

- **Primary sources**, materials created by individuals and groups who are directly involved in events as they take place, fall into several categories. **Original documents** are items such as diaries, emails, news footage, autobiographies, and minutes of meetings. **Creative works** include books, paintings, poems, and dance performances. **Relics** or **artifacts** are cultural objects such as jewelry, tools, clothing, and other created items.
- Nonparticipants who summarize or interpret original events are **secondary sources**. Some, such as movie reviewers, create their works when the events occur; others, such as biographers, historians, or other authors, create articles, books, textbooks, and so on at the time or months, decades, even centuries later.
- **Tertiary sources** distill primary and secondary sources into collections. Dictionaries, almanacs, and encyclopedias fall into this category.

The source types can overlap. For example, an audio recording of the NASA control room made during the *Phoenix* Mars Lander's final touchdown and a photograph the spacecraft sent from Mars are primary sources, but a news article about the landing is a secondary source that summarizes the events and what led up to them. However, the news article *could* be a primary source if your topic were media coverage of the *Phoenix*

primary source information from a person actually involved in the event

original document evidence recorded by a primary source such as a letter or autobiography

creative work poem, dance, painting, writing, or other aesthetic creation

relic or **artifact** culturally significant creation such as a building, jewelry, or a tool

secondary source summary or interpretation of an event or a person provided by a nonparticipant

tertiary source condenses primary and secondary materials into collections such as encyclopedias

TABLE 7.2

Primary, Secondary, and Tertiary Sources

Primary	Secondary	Tertiary
A letter from Jane Austen to her sister, Cassandra	A magazine article about Jane's correspondence	An encyclopedia entry about Cassandra Austen
An actual Navajo rug	A trade book about Navajo weaving	A website selling Native American weavings
An audio recording of Robert Frost reading his poetry	A scholarly article about the impact of Robert Frost on later generations of poets	A website with quotations taken from Frost's poems

Mars Mission. Encyclopedia entries about the spacecraft are tertiary sources. Table 7.2 provides examples of each source.

Internet Domains[32]

domain the type of site such as .com, .edu, or .org that tells the site's purpose and tax status

Before you even open an Internet document, look for the **domain** suffix, which indicates the provider's primary purpose and tax status. The most common are educational (.edu), commercial (.com), government (.gov), military (.mil), nonprofit organization (.org), and foreign (.ca for Canada, .jp for Japan, and so on). Ask who or what entity published the page. Is it from an educational institution (.edu) or one set up to make money (.com)? Is it from a government agency (.gov) or a noprofit (.org) with an agenda and a need for donations? Choose those that seem the most appropriate, given your topic. Use .com sites with caution and recognize that an .edu document can actually be a student paper, submitted for an assignment.

Once you're on the site, look for information about the author, institution, organization, or agency that accepts responsibility for the material. If this is not immediately apparent, look for a home page or follow links such as "about us," "philosophy," or "background" to learn more about the site's creators. Distinguish between expert or peer sources as well as primary, secondary, and tertiary sources.

P = Purpose

Apply what you remember about the four general purposes from Chapter 2. Is material intended to provide information? To convince of an idea or to motivate to action? To entertain? To celebrate a person, a cultural value, an event, or an achievement of some kind? Authors and sources intentionally create material for a reason.

The mission statement of an organization is one way to discern the perspectives and purposes for the material. For example, Newsy: Multisource Video News says, "It's the only video news service that allows users to compare news sources from around the world to see how a story unfolds. It's a broader view in a concise format."[33] MSNBC offers "news, video, and progressive community"[34] in contrast to National Review, which offers "up-to-the minute conservative commentary on politics, news, and culture."[35]

Record Your Information

Plan ways to record your findings, avoid plagiarism, and cite sources properly. Then, when you sit down to organize your speech, you will have the necessary information at your fingertips, and you can easily classify your ideas into themes and patterns.

Two methods are common for recording information: taking notes (pen and paper) or downloading and marking up materials. Choose the one that matches your learning style or your topic.

Pen and Paper Notes

With all the technology available to download, copy, and print materials, why would anyone use pen and paper to take notes? New research on students who wrote out their notes found that they recorded less overall information than note takers who used laptops, but they did more summarizing and paraphrasing. In the long run, they performed better on tests that required higher-order thinking skills such as understanding concepts, making inferences, and integrating ideas. This study suggests that writing out notes helps you be more mindful about the overall framework and the crucial information in an article.[36] Better yet, writing out information can help you avoid cut-and-paste plagiarism because it's easier to jot down key ideas and summarize the material than to copy long paragraphs. A structured method is to use two types of three-by-five-inch note cards: source cards and information cards.

- Make a separate **source card** for each reference, using a standard bibliographic format. Include the author, date, article or chapter title, book or periodical title, place of publication (for books), followed by the page number(s). For online information, add the website title, sponsoring organization, date you retrieved the material, and the site's URL. Make source cards for materials gathered from nonprint material as well. It is helpful to **annotate** this bibliography, meaning that you write a brief description of the information you found in the source. See Figure 7.1 for an example.

  Next, use a separate **information card** for each idea, statistic, quotation, example, and so on you find. Use quotation marks around direct quotations and each uniquely worded phrase, and write down the page number for each piece of information. This practice will help you avoid plagiarism. On the top of each card, create a heading that classifies the information into a category you might later use as a main point. Also, label

source card card used to record bibliographic information

annotate to summarize a book or article's contents on a source card

information card card for recording and categorizing important data

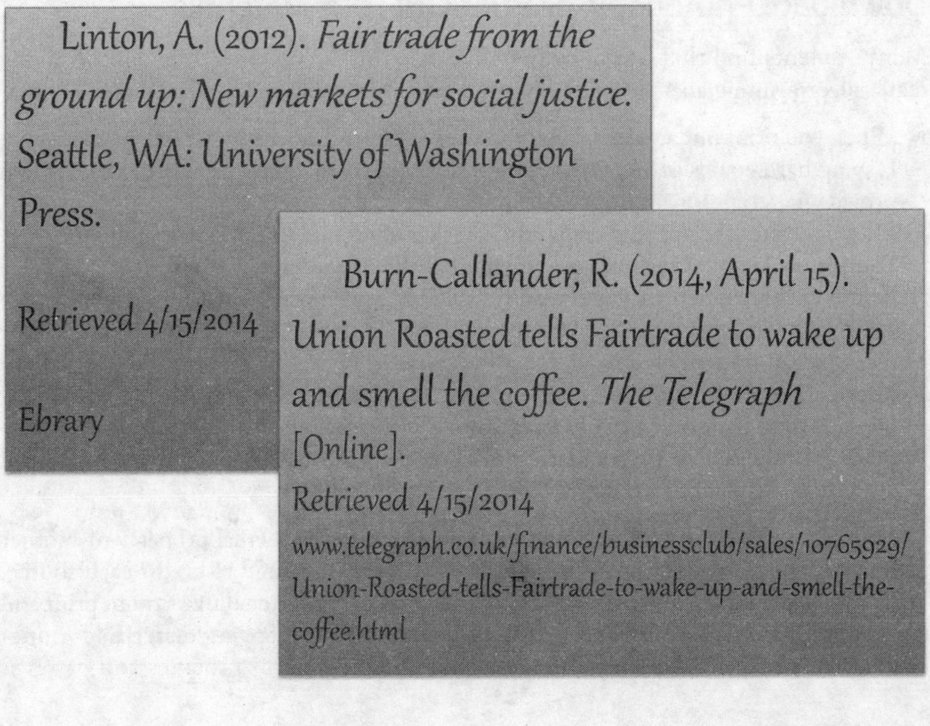

Linton, A. (2012). *Fair trade from the ground up: New markets for social justice.* Seattle, WA: University of Washington Press.

Retrieved 4/15/2014

Ebrary

Burn-Callander, R. (2014, April 15). Union Roasted tells Fairtrade to wake up and smell the coffee. *The Telegraph* [Online].
Retrieved 4/15/2014
www.telegraph.co.uk/finance/businessclub/sales/10765929/Union-Roasted-tells-Fairtrade-to-wake-up-and-smell-the-coffee.html

Figure 7.1
Source Cards Source cards contain bibliographic information. Annotated cards also include a brief summary of the material found in the source.

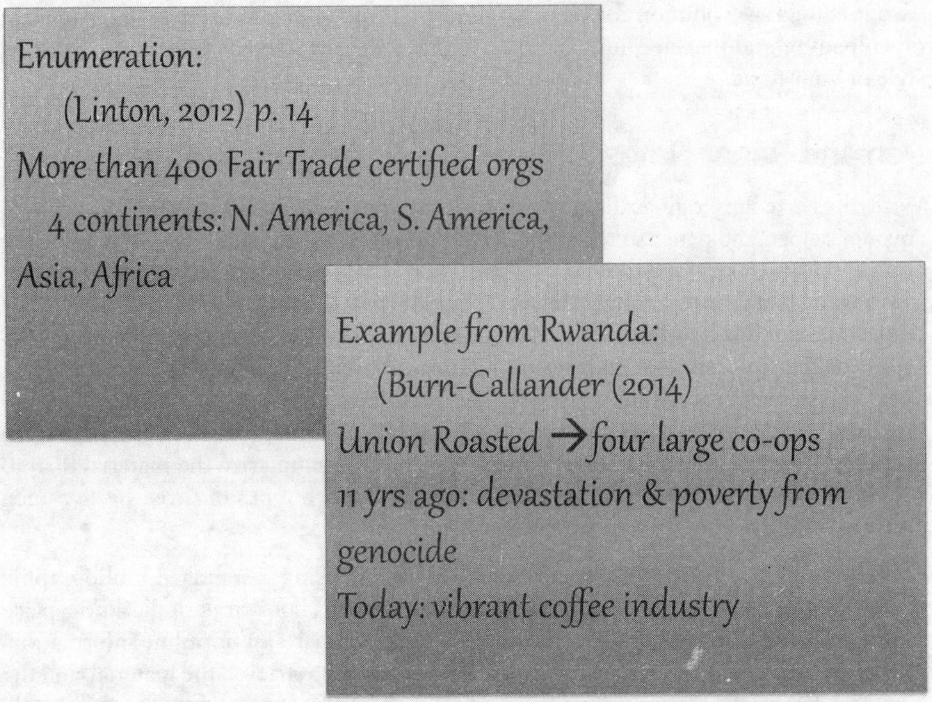

Figure 7.2

Information Cards Use a different information card for each source, and classify each card according to the major idea the information supports. Include an abbreviated source citation, including the page number, on each card.

Enumeration:

(Linton, 2012) p. 14

More than 400 Fair Trade certified orgs

4 continents: N. America, S. America, Asia, Africa

Example from Rwanda:

(Burn-Callander (2014)

Union Roasted → four large co-ops

11 yrs ago: devastation & poverty from genocide

Today: vibrant coffee industry

the card with an abbreviated source citation so that when you use the material in the speech, you can cite its source. Figure 7.2 shows examples of information cards.

The advantage of note cards is that you can separate them into piles and move them around, placing your major point at the top and arranging your supporting information below. You can easily change the order of your points and your relevant supporting materials before creating your outline.

Download, Photocopy, or Print Out Your Materials

Many students find that downloading an article into a computer file, photocopying material, or printing an article directly from the Internet has many advantages.

- When you print out an article, you can more easily avoid cut-and-paste plagiarism.
- Having hard copies of your research can protect you against plagiarism charges and provide materials for future research.
- Many websites are updated daily, and what you find one day might be gone the next. Your printed copy is the only proof you have that it was ever there.[37]
- Your copies are quick, easy, and readily available, and you can have the entire resource in front of you when you sit down to write your outline.
- A download into an electronic file allows you to highlight major ideas and salient information.
- Downloaded materials usually have source information on the printout—but also make sure the source (in standard bibliographic form) is on your photocopies. And write the date you retrieved it.

fair use provision the provision in the federal Copyright Act that allows free use of materials for educational and research purposes

Because copying materials means you are using the intellectual property of another person who has a right to profit from its use, you are obligated to credit each source. Fortunately, the **fair use provision** in the federal Copyright Act allows you to print and use materials for nonprofit educational purposes, so photocopying materials for one-time speech research is within your legal rights as a student.[38]

Use a Standard Format for Source Citation

To avoid plagiarism and build and maintain credibility, list each source in a bibliography at the end of your outline. Alphabetize your sources, and use the standard bibliographic format found in the style or publication manual your instructor recommends. Because so many formats are available, this text does not provide specific examples of the various styles. The basic elements of any source citation include the author(s), date, title, publisher or source, and place of publication or location in a database or on an Internet site.

A few tips can help you cite sources correctly:

- The most common style manuals are available online; in addition, check your campus writing center's or library's website for citation guidelines.
- Some library database or academic articles tell you how to cite the material in a variety of styles.
- Finally, easy-to-use programs such as Citation Machine or EasyBib are available online. A search for "online source citation program" should provide several links.

Whichever style you use, remember two additional rules: (1) use the style your instructor recommends, and (2) use it consistently.

Many online resources now have a **digital object identifier (DOI)**, which locates intellectual property online.[39] This series of numbers and letters comes at the end of the reference. If an online source lacks the DOI, write out the URL where it was located. Here's an example (in APA style, with no end punctuation):[40]

digital object identifier (DOI) series of numbers and letters that locate intellectual property online

Elder, S. D., Lister, J., & Dauvergne, P. (2014, January). Big retail and sustainable coffee: A new development studies research agenda. *Progress in Development Studies, 14*(1), 77–90. doi: 10.1177/1464993413504354

In summary, a vital aspect of research is recording the information so that it is readily available when you need it. If you prefer a structured, linear method, writing out notes on note cards may be your best choice. If you approach the research task holistically, you might download or photocopy your materials and use highlighters to identify important information. Whichever method you choose, always use a standard bibliographic format to list your sources alphabetically.

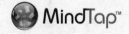 MindTap™

Summary

Part of your competence in speechmaking is your ability to gather information. To be more effective, set aside plenty of time to explore your topic, and use a research plan that is appropriate for the subject.

Look for written materials in hard copy or digital books and reference materials, in periodicals, in both legacy and native digital news sources, and in opinion pieces from credible sources. Consider also nonprint sources such as personal experience, interviews, or lectures and performances. Throughout your research, seek out diverse perspectives from a variety of viewpoints.

Think critically about your materials using the MAPit strategy—a combination of M (message) plus A (author or source) plus P (purpose). Discern whether or not the message is biased, up-to-date, accurate, original, and organized. Ask if the source is primary, secondary, or tertiary. Check the Internet domain for further information about the entity that accepts responsibility for the material. Then decide if the purpose is informative, persuasive, entertaining, or commemorative. An online organization's mission statement can provide clues to its reason for being.

Finally, consistently record your findings using a method that meets your learning style preferences, such as source and information cards or downloading or printing out and marking up. Whatever your method, avoid plagiarism by crediting your sources in your notes and on the bibliography that accompanies your outline. Choose a standard source citation format and then use it correctly and consistently throughout your work.

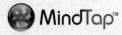

Reflect on what you've learned.

STUDY AND REVIEW

Public Speaking: Concepts and Skills for a Diverse Society offers a broad range of resources that will help you better understand the material in this chapter, complete assignments, and succeed on tests. Your MindTap resources feature the following:

- Speech videos with viewing questions, speech outlines, and transcripts
- Activities to help you check your understanding and to apply what you've learned to your own life
- Stop and Check and Critical Thinking exercises
- Outline Builder
- Web Links related to chapter content
- Study and review tools such as self-quizzes and an interactive glossary

You can access your online resources for *Public Speaking: Concepts and Skills for a Diverse Society* at cengagebrain.com using the access code that came with your book or that you purchased online.

Review your Flashcards.

KEY TERMS

The terms below are defined in the margins throughout this chapter.

academic journals 85
annotate 91
creative work 89
digital object identifier
   (DOI) 93
domain 90
expert 87
fair use provision 92
information card 91
laypeople or peers 87
legacy journalism 85
MAPit 88
native digital news 86
online public access catalog
   (OPAC) 83

original document 89
primary source 89
reference librarian 83
relic or artifact 89
scholarly book 84
secondary source 89
source card 91
specialized encyclopedia 84
subject librarian 83
tertiary source 89
trade book 84
trade journal 85

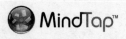

CRITICAL THINKING EXERCISES

1. Read the cover story from a current news source like *Time* magazine. Make a list of all the experts and laypeople quoted in the article. Compare and contrast the type of information given by each type of source—primary, secondary, or tertiary.
2. Discover the international, ethnic, and alternative newspapers and magazines in your library by making a list of available sources that provide diverse perspectives. Or do an online search for "alternative news sources." Read and take notes on an article in at least one of the resources.
3. Do you use Wikipedia? Why or why not? If so, when and how do you use it?

a. Find a Wikipedia article on a very familiar subject such as "George Washington." Skim through the article, and check out the references, sources, or external links at the end.

b. Go to the "view history" link at the top of the page. Describe the kinds of changes that have been made.

c. Then link to some of the Wikipedians who have edited the page. See what you can discover about their credibility.

d. What do you conclude about Wikipedia's overall usefulness?

4. Browse several weblogs on a subject related to your topic. Assess the quality and bias of each blog. Why or when might you use a blog as a source? Why or when might you avoid them?

APPLICATION QUESTIONS

1. To understand the variety and number of specialized encyclopedias and dictionaries online, do a search for "encyclopedia of" and "dictionary of" online or in your library's databases, and list at least ten titles in each category that may someday be useful to you. Note the source of each. Are they from .com or .edu or another domain's sites? Why does this matter? Bring your lists to class and discuss your findings with a small group of your classmates.

2. Have you heard of the "Mozart effect" (the idea that babies who listen to Mozart are smarter)? Do an Internet search for this topic. How many links do you get? What kind of domains (.com, .edu, for example) sponsor the sites? Look beyond the first page of links and use note cards to summarize the information from at least three domains: .org, .com, and .edu. (Try to find a blog and a news report.) Afterward, search for the topic in your campus online databases. How many articles come up there? Bring your findings to class and discuss how you would compare what you find on the Internet with what you find in the library databases. Overall, what would you tell a friend who was playing Mozart to her baby in order to improve the child's IQ?

3. As a class, research a current event or an issue. Go to the library, find and photocopy a print article, or download information from a website. If possible, interview an expert or layperson. Assign some students to consult mainstream sources and others to seek out diverse perspectives. Bring your information to the next class meeting, and discuss and evaluate the various sources and data by determining the purpose, the source bias, the timeliness, the accuracy, and the organization of the material.

4. Set aside an hour to explore news outlets on the Internet. Beforehand, work with your classmates to select an interesting, significant current event, and then surf around, clicking on relevant news links. Take notes. Check Google news for information about current events, noting the variety of papers and television news sources linked there. Afterward, discuss in class the value as well as the drawbacks of using the Internet to do research into current events.

5. Of the two ways to record information presented in this chapter, which method— handwritten pen and paper notes or copied or downloaded material—will you most likely use? Which are you least likely to use? When might you combine methods? Discuss your research style with a classmate.

CHAPTER 8

THIS CHAPTER WILL HELP YOU

- Identify types of facts and learn how to test factual data

- Select numerical data carefully

- Use examples effectively

- Quote authoritative sources

- Use comparison and contrast

- Select appropriate visual evidence

Diana Ong/SuperStock

Choosing Supporting Materials

THINK ABOUT a current controversy such as climate change. Why do intelligent, well-meaning people form such different conclusions that they polarize into opposing camps? Although a majority might believe that weather patterns are changing, people disagree greatly about the causes or effects of these changes. Some argue that nations and individuals must act quickly to save the environment or human-created global warming will devastate the planet.[1] They cite data from seemingly reputable sources such as the National Academy of Sciences, computer models, and the Intergovernmental Panel on Climate Change as well as visual images of melting polar ice. In contrast, others, including scientists and statisticians who've studied the issue in depth, agree

MindT

Review th
chapter
Learning
Objective
and **Start**
with a qu
warm-up
activity.

that change is happening, but they argue that "eco-fundamentalists" overstate the problem, propose ineffective solutions, and neglect more pressing issues such as the global need for safe drinking water.[2] This example shows how reliance on different evidence can lead to very different conclusions about important topics.

Each culture has rules for what counts as credible evidence; consequently, we follow cultural standards for weighing evidence, accepting some information as valid and rejecting other data as inaccurate, inadequate, or irrelevant. This chapter examines six types of evidence that speakers in the United States commonly use: facts, numerical data, examples, quotations, comparisons, and visual evidence. Throughout the chapter you'll find guidelines for thinking critically about the quality of the data or evidence, both when you select materials for your own speeches and when you listen to other speakers.

Provide Facts

Much of your information will be factual because audiences typically need facts before they form their conclusions. **Empirical facts** are verifiable by observation, and **established facts** are those that are consistently validated by many observers. We judge facts as being true or false, accurate or inaccurate, and we derive them from a variety of sources, as these examples show:

- Alicia Keys passed up a full scholarship to Columbia University to pursue her musical career.[3] [source: Biography.com]
- Children with special needs find joy and help through horses in equine therapy. [source: newspaper article]
- Autism develops from specific brain cells that fail to mature during pregnancy.[4] [source: *New England Journal of Medicine*]

Facts differ from personal *opinion*—either yours or that of other people. Opinion adds a subjective interpretation that is open to question. For example, "Alicia Keys should have taken the scholarship instead" is an opinion, not a fact. Generally accepted definitions and descriptions count as facts.

Use Definitions

We look in dictionaries and thesauruses for definitions—the meanings of terms we generally accept in common usage. However, culturally accepted definitions also derive from traditions, philosophers, poets, and so on. For example, *Merriam-Webster* defines a "scholar" as "an intelligent and well-educated person who knows a particular subject very well";[5] In a speech celebrating scholarship, a physics professor defined *scholar* in three additional ways. First was his personal definition:[6]

> What does it mean to be a scholar? I think it means to think deeply about a subject, to grasp it entirely, to make it your own, to make it part of yourself. Being a scholar is different from being a student, or even a teacher. Being a scholar means being willing to approach a subject with informed curiosity, to delve deeply, and to devote yourself to its mastery—beyond grades, beyond credit hours, beyond graduation, for the sake of knowledge itself.

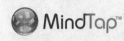

MindTap™

Read, highlight, and take notes online.

empirical facts information verifiable by observation

established fact information verified consistently by many observers

He then added a story about an anonymous monk whose poem to his white cat reflected the monk's definition of scholarship:

You rejoice when your jaws entrap a mouse.

I rejoice when my mind fathoms a problem.

He continued from the Book of Proverbs:

Buy the truth and sell it not; also wisdom, and instruction, and understanding.

This combination of support developed the concept in more detail.

Provide Vivid Descriptions

Descriptions provide details about a subject, such as its size, shape, sound, and color. These details of a mudslide in the state of Washington came from a news story:[7]

Massive debris, which is scattered over a square mile, is 30 to 40 feet deep in places. Septic tanks, fallen trees, and shards of smashed houses lie in the rain-slickened mud beside twisted vehicles and scattered household items. Quicksand-like muck and ice make it difficult for rescue workers to navigate.

The details (septic tanks, fallen trees, muck) give facts; the choice of words (*debris, shards, scattered*) makes these facts easy to visualize.

On a cautionary note, it is easy to pass along unverified or inaccurate facts. If something looks suspicious, double-check it. For example, hundreds of inaccuracies are passed along as "fact," including the following:

• In 1997, Kurt Vonnegut gave a commencement address at MIT that began, "Wear sunscreen. If I were to offer you only one tip for the future this would be it."[8] [Reality: It was not a speech. Vonnegut did not give it. It was not at MIT. A columnist at the *Chicago Tribune* wrote it as her ideal graduation speech, and someone posted it to the Internet, with Vonnegut's name attached.]

- Republican presidents over the last fifty years have lower average IQs than their Democratic counterparts.[9] [Reality: Two campaign workers supporting a Republican's opponent created a list of presidential IQs as a joke. They framed it as a "scientific study" and widely circulated it as factual on the Internet.]
- You should drink eight glasses of water a day.[10] [Reality: The origin of this number is unclear. We should take in as much water as we lose, but that amount varies with factors such as age, activity level, and climate. Food also contains water.]

With the current explosion of available information, especially in electronically stored data, verifying facts is now more important than ever.

Think Critically about Facts

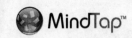

To avoid passing along misinformation, apply the following three tests:

1. *Check for accuracy or validity.* Are the facts actually true and verifiable? Has more than one reputable source reported on them? How were the facts derived?
2. *Are the facts up-to-date?* Perhaps something was true in the past, but do the same conditions hold today? Or have changes over time invalidated the data?
3. *Consider the source.* As Chapter 7 emphasized, use only material from reputable sources, and check for source bias that casts doubt on the data.

In short, test facts by asking three questions: Is this true and verifiable? Is it timely? Who says so?

Use Statistics Carefully

In the United States, we measure and count from preschool on because we like numbers and statistical information. In fact, we typically think of numbers and measurements as "hard facts" that help us understand the extent of an issue or predict the probability of some future happening. Consequently, numerical support used well can increase your credibility and cause you to appear more competent and knowledgeable.

Although useful, numerical data have unique drawbacks. In general, statistics don't tap into emotions, and too many can bore your audience. In fact, good speakers typically balance statistics with examples to both clarify and personalize a topic. Finally, numerical information is often misleading, and if listeners think you are twisting numbers, they will distrust you. So take care to use numerical data both accurately and sparingly.

Provide a Count

Enumeration means counting. A count helps your listeners understand the extent of a problem or issue such as the number of prisoners who have mental health issues in federal prisons (78,800), in state prisons (705,600) and in local jails (479,900),[11] the number of miles of US bridges that are obsolete or structurally deficient (about 70,000),[12] and so on. Two tips will help you use enumeration more effectively.

enumeration a count

1. *Round your numbers up or down.* It can be difficult to remember exact numbers; furthermore, numbers related to people's behaviors can change rapidly. By the time they're published, they may be outdated. Consequently, Twitter won't say "We have 654,753,221 active registered users" because 135,000 sign up daily, so a figure from one week could be outdated by over half a million the next (if the signups continue at a similar rate).[13]

In this culture, we think of numbers as hard data that tell us how extensive a problem is and how things relate to one another.

© iStockphoto.com/rook76

2. *Make numbers come alive by comparing them to something already in your listeners' experience.* We often hear big numbers such as $17.5 trillion, our national debt, but what does that really mean? Many online sources try to help you visualize it. For example, stack of $1 bills would reach past Uranus.[14] And if your salary were $40,000 a year, it would take you 25 million years to earn $1 trillion. If you live to be eighty, you would have to save $34 million every day of your life to have $1 trillion. Multiply that by 17.5.[15]

Think Critically about Statistics

mean average of a group of numbers

median middle number in a set of numbers arranged in a ranked order

mode most frequently occurring number

percentage figure that shows the relationship of the part to the whole, which is represented by the number 100

rates of increase or decrease percentage that uses an earlier baseline figure to compare growth or decline

Common statistics include the mean, median, mode, percentages, and ratios.

The **mean** is the *average* of a group of numbers. To calculate it, add up the individual items and divide by the total number of units measured. The mean is skewed when extreme figures at either end of the range make the comparison less useful. Just average one billionaire's income and the annual incomes of nine people who work for minimum wages to understand the limitations of the mean.

The **median** is the middle number in a set of numbers that have been arranged into a ranked order: half the numbers are above and half below. For example, home prices in a particular area are typically stated as a median, which balances the very expensive mansions against the less expensive fixer-uppers.

The **mode** is the number that appears most commonly. For instance, on some college campuses, a few first-year students may be 16 years old, more are 17, some are in their twenties, thirties, or forties, but most are 18—the mode.

Percentages show the relationship of a part to the whole, which is represented by the number 100. You'll often see percentages stated as **rates of increase or decrease**, which compare growth or decline during a specific period of time to a baseline figure from an earlier period. Treat these rates cautiously, for unless you know the baseline number, the rate of increase or decrease is almost meaningless. Think of it this way: A company that employs two people in the year 2014 and adds an additional employee in 2015 increases its hiring at a rate of 50 percent. However, a company that employs 100 people in 2014 and adds one additional employee in 2015 increases hiring by 1 percent. The actual number of additional employees is the same in each company, but the rates of increase are dramatically different. The reverse is also true: A two-person company that loses one employee decreases by half or 50 percent; there's barely a blip when a larger company loses one worker. As you can see, when baseline numbers are initially very low, the rate of increase is potentially astounding.

Relationships between numbers are often shown as a **ratio**, instead of a percentage because *10 percent* and *1 in 10* are interchangeable; similarly, you could state *60 percent* as *3 out of 5*. Ratios are especially helpful when the percentage is very small; for example, 0.000018 percent equals 18 cases per 100,000. You can see that it's more effective to say, "The study found that suicide rates were 18 out of 100,000 in rural areas and 13 per 100,000 in urban areas," than to say "thirteen-hundred-thousandth of 1 percent of urban residents."[16]

ratio relationship shown by numbers, such as 1 in 10

Use Visual Aids to Clarify Numerical Data

Because numerical data can be complex, present them in visual form whenever you can. Imagine trying to understand a speaker who simply said:

> The cost of living varies by region. According to CNN Money, what you can buy for $50,000 in Portland, Oregon, would cost $97,700 in Manhattan and $69,200 in San Francisco but only $40,900 in Las Cruces, New Mexico, $39,300 in Des Moines, Iowa, and only $35,200 in Norman, Oklahoma.[17]

Would you remember any of these data? Now, imagine that the speaker provides a visual with Table 8.1 on it. How does the visual help you grasp the material more easily?

Obviously, different types of data call for different types of visuals, but graphs and tables are especially good for projecting numerical data. (Chapter 13 explains how to create and display visual materials.) A table such as this one, comparing living costs in several cities, effectively depicts numerical data in a format that listeners can easily grasp.

Critically Analyze Numerical Data

Because numbers are easy to manipulate, evaluate them carefully with these questions before you use them.

TABLE 8.1

Comparative Cost of Living by Region

Portland, Oregon	$50,000
Manhattan	$94,700*
San Francisco	$69, 200
Las Cruces, New Mexico	$40,900
Des Moines, Iowa	$39,300
Norman, Oklahoma	$35, 200

*numbers are rounded

1. *Are the numbers accurate?* Both proponents and opponents of legalization of marijuana cite a widely circulated statistic saying that 60 percent of profits in the drug war with Mexico come from marijuana. However, the figure, released in 2006 by the federal drug czar's office, is based on "dated" models. Rand Corporation researchers say the figure is closer to 15 to 26 percent.[18]

2. *What is the source of the numbers?* Does the source have an interest such as a possibility of financial gain that would make high or low numbers more desirable? For example, one study says that obesity kills 400,000 Americans a year; another says 65 percent of Americans are overweight or obese. However, both researchers were heavily funded by industries that promote weight-loss remedies.[19] How might that matter?

3. *Are the numbers up-to-date?* Using a count or a percentage that is old is generally not applicable to current conditions. The previously mentioned study enumerating obesity deaths used data from the 1940s and ignored fifty years of improved medical treatments.[20]

4. *Before you use startling rates of increase, look at the baseline figures of the percentages.* Note any other relevant factors that might affect this rate. For example, one source said the rate of US children and teens killed by gunfire is 120 percent higher than in the other twenty-five industrialized countries combined.[21] Any deaths are lamentable, but what if the other countries only have 10 such deaths? What if they have 20,000?

5. *Be careful of combined statistics.* The same source said that males experience violent crime at rates 28 percent greater than females; however, females are raped and sexually assaulted at 7.5 times the rate of males. Why might the authors report the figure relating to males as a percentage but the figure relating to females as a multiple? How could you state "7.5 times the rate" as a percentage?

Use Examples

If you're typical, your interest probably increases when a speaker uses an example that illustrates how the topic affects real people. Examples attract and maintain attention, and we listen for them because they make abstract concepts and ideas more concrete and relevant.[22] Illustrations also help audiences identify emotionally with the subject, and they add to your credibility because listeners can see that you understand real-world experiences and the practical implications of your theories and ideas. Examples can be short or long, real or hypothetical.

Use Real Examples

Because real examples actually happened, they provide concrete, true-life illustrations of your concepts. Consequently, as you gather materials, look for actual events or experiences of real people to illustrate your ideas, and provide names, dates, and places to make your examples more vivid. For instance, to illustrate her speech about obsessive-compulsive disorder (OCD), Noemi gave the following details:[23]

> When my friend was 11, he had to make sure his hands were clean before he could sleep. He'd wash them with soap and water several times before going to bed. Even then, he'd get up every 10–15 minutes because he remembered something he'd done to "dirty" his hands. Once, it took him over two hours of compulsions before he could finally sleep.

She gave additional details about her friend throughout her speech.

Examples from your personal experiences can be very powerful. For example, Carrie spoke on the importance of making a grief support specialist available to students on her campus, based on her own experience. (You can read her speech in Appendix B.) Here's how she began:[24]

> The phone rings. You answer it, and suddenly the world stops. You have just become one of the hundred of thousands of college students experiencing the grief of losing a loved one. September 13, 2006, my life changed forever when it was *my* phone that rang. My dad was gone. I was eighteen.

Personal stories are indispensable in some cultures. Focus group participants in a study of Kenyan public speaking rated personal stories as the *most* convincing type of example. One Kenyan said, "We believe you only really know about something if you've experienced it."[25] In fact, some Kenyans thought personal narratives should be placed in a separate category because their impact is so different from other types of narratives.

Consider Hypothetical Examples for Sensitive Topics

Hypothetical examples do not actually happen, but they seem plausible because they commonly borrow elements from several true-to-life stories woven together to create believable characters and situations. Our cultural value on privacy makes hypothetical examples more appropriate than real ones for sensitive topics like mental illness or sexual behaviors, so speakers whose work involves confidentiality, such as physicians, members of the clergy, therapists, and teachers, often use them. Family counselors who present parenting workshops, for instance, might tell hypothetical stories of bad parenting skills because they would never reveal confidential information about identifiable clients. To distinguish hypothetical examples from true-life events, introduce them something like this: "Let's say there's a 16-year-old girl named Carly; let's put her in a close-knit family in rural Oregon…"

hypothetical example not a real incident or person, but true-to-life

Speakers whose work involves confidentiality, such as counselors, often describe hypothetical characters whose predicaments typify the problems that they encounter.

© iStockphoto.com/MachineHeadz

Another way to attract attention and involve audience members emotionally is to create an imaginary scenario that invites listeners to personalize your topic. Here's an opening illustration for a speech about latchkey children:[26]

> Imagine that you're a latchkey kid. Your parent has told you not to answer the door because the person on the other side might be an escaped prisoner or a salesman who wants all your money. You sit with your brothers and sisters behind double doors, a deadbolt, and a peephole, watching TV and eating microwave pizza.

Although hypothetical examples and imaginary scenarios work well in informative speeches, real examples are generally better for persuasive speeches. Think of it this way: Your listeners are probably more persuaded by something that really *did* happen than by something that *might* happen.

ETHICS IN PRACTICE   # Hypothetical Example or Fabrication?

In *Love and Consequences: A Memoir of Hope and Survival*, Margaret B. Jones told of growing up in Los Angeles foster homes and participating in gangs as a racially mixed adolescent. Turns out, Margaret is not "Jones"; she's Margaret Seltzer, a well-to-do white woman, who was educated in private schools and raised by her biological parents. When confronted, Seltzer admitted her story was hypothetical, based on experiences of people she'd met while working in antigang outreach programs. But, she explained, "For whatever reason, I was really torn, and I thought it was my opportunity to put a voice to people who people don't listen to."[27]

Seltzer is not alone. Not long ago, a law student wrote a letter to the editor of his campus newspaper, describing in great detail how campus police manhandled and harassed him, an African American male, as he walked across campus late at night. He shared his story "to bring attention to the topic of police misconduct."[28] Fellow students were saddened and outraged at the officers, and the university immediately began investigating the charges. Turns out, he made them up.

Questions

1. What's the difference between a hypothetical example and a fabricated story?
2. What, if any, ethical concerns should you have when you use hypothetical examples?

Create Emotional Connections with Extended Examples

Extended examples include many details; each one gives your listeners an opportunity to identify emotionally with the subject of the story. Longer illustrations are especially useful for clarifying, explaining in depth, and motivating your listeners. Look at how each detail in this example makes the story more engaging. The subject is texting and accidents:

> D.J. was excited after the first day of her senior year in high school. The year ahead promised to be challenging as well as fun for the blonde teen—a popular student with a good reputation and good grades. She eased her minivan out of the parking lot and headed home, passing familiar landmarks in her small town. A few miles out of town,

she took her eyes off the road for a few seconds and pulled out her cell phone to text a message. Looking up, she saw with horror that the bus she was following had stopped, and a child was getting off. With brakes screeching, her minivan rammed into the back of the bus, shearing the van's roof halfway off and trapping her in the driver's seat. D.J.'s first day was also her last.[29]

Listeners can identify with one or more of the details showing everyday experiences of school and driving. So the tragic result of texting-while-driving has a real person attached. Because extended examples provide multiple points that engage listeners, they are generally more compelling. In fact, narratives or well-developed stories can function as the entire speech.

Combine Brief Examples

Short illustrations are also effective. However, a single, brief example is easily missed, so it's better to string two or three together. Layering them one upon another gives your listeners a number of images they can use to visualize and personalize your subject. The following mentions of people who gain from encounters with equine therapy could be used effectively to introduce the topic of horses and healing:

> Normally quiet as an Asperger's child, Levi shows real excitement as he works with his brother to brush and clean "his" therapy horse. Jessie, who was repeatedly raped in the military, is building trust and relational skills through her interactions with other veterans in a "horses for veterans" program. Caleb was born with mental challenges. His horse is teaching him to stay safe by being aware of his surroundings at all times.[30]

Think Critically about Examples

To evaluate the usefulness of examples, ask yourself the following questions:

- *Is this example representative or typical?* That is, does the example represent a typical person? Or does it seem like an extreme case? Does D.J. seem typical of teens who text and drive? Do the examples of therapy horses represent typical clients? This test relates to the probability of occurrence.
- *Do you have a sufficient number of examples?* Are enough cases presented to support the major idea adequately? Your listeners should be able to see that a significant number of people are affected. Is one 11-year-old boy typical of obsessive-compulsive children?
- *Is the example true?* Did it actually happen? How often? For a hypothetical character, does the experience ring true with what you know about the world and how it operates?

Quote Culturally Acceptable Authorities

Whatever your subject, think of your audience as asking, "Who says so?" Then support your ideas by citing sources your audience will respect and believe, given your topic and purpose. Each culture and co-culture recognizes authorities, which vary across groups. Authoritative sources differ in degree (some have little credibility, others have a lot), and their sphere of influence varies (an authority in one subject may be uninformed in another).[31]

Citing culturally accepted sources is especially valuable when your personal expertise on the topic is limited. Integrating the ideas of experts or credible laypeople into your speeches shows that knowledgeable, experienced people support your conclusions. But quoting authorities bolsters your ideas if, and only if your audience views them as credible on the topic. Therefore, it's up to you to provide pertinent information about the authorities you cite, why you believe their testimony, and why your audience should accept their conclusions.

Quote Culturally Accepted Experts

As Chapter 7 pointed out, we look to people whose occupational or educational expertise, career success, and reputation in their field make them experts. Thus, testimony from scholars, elected officials, scientists, and so on generally provides good supporting materials, if you keep in mind that these experts are often biased. In fact, as their expertise increases, their bias may increase. Think of political figures; the longer they're in office, the more partisan they may be.

Here are examples of expert testimony that would fit well in a speech about therapy horses:[32]

- "Research has proven that equine-assisted therapy helps with balance, posture, coordination, motor skills, and concentration." [Peggy Bass, PhD in special education, thirty years of experience]
- Working with horses helps improve balance and eye movements as well as sensory and social interactions. [Drew Coman, university researcher and doctorate fellow in psychology]

The first example directly quotes the expert, but the second one paraphrases or summarizes the person's main point. Because most listeners are unfamiliar with both sources, the speaker should explain each person's credentials.

We commonly expect people to agree, in general, with others who are similar to them in some notable way. However, people sometimes hold surprising opinions. For example, some well-known conservatives support gay marriage or legalization of drugs, and some well-known liberals take pro-life or pro-nuclear energy positions. Using unexpected testimony like this can be especially powerful in persuasive speeches. Why? Because your listeners will reason that people willing to go against their peers have probably thought through their opinions carefully.

Quote Credible Peers or Laypeople

Often "regular people" who have firsthand knowledge about a subject provide good supporting information. These peer or lay sources may not know scientific facts and related theories, but they can tell you how it feels to be involved as a participant. What do laypeople report about equine therapy? For that, you need a participant's perspective:[33]

- "[My son's] balance has improved, his legs are stronger, and he is much more focused. It has also helped his self-esteem as he is very proud of his progress." [Andrea Fuentes, parent of a son with autism, cerebral palsy, and an almost useless right hand]
- "When Sarah is on Goldie, the horse,...I see a calmness in her." [Sheila Ramer, mother of a 28-year-old autistic daughter]

Each participant's perspective fleshes out details about how the horses are used in therapy.

Proverbs in African Cultures[34]

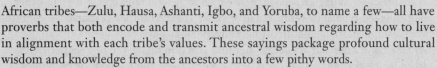

Yoruba Proverb

Ogbon ologbon ni a nfi sogbon, ìmoràn ęnì kan kò jo boro

Literally: We become wiser or smarter through learning from others; one person's understanding or perspective does not amount to much in terms of knowledge.

African tribes—Zulu, Hausa, Ashanti, Igbo, and Yoruba, to name a few—all have proverbs that both encode and transmit ancestral wisdom regarding how to live in alignment with each tribe's values. These sayings package profound cultural wisdom and knowledge from the ancestors into a few pithy words.

Wise conversationalists invariably use proverbs effectively, and every functioning adult in the village community learned to use them properly during childhood. Competent users understand each proverb's meaning and discern the situations in which a specific proverb fits. For example, an apt saying can help resolve land disputes, lead to consensus over an issue that affects the village, negotiate a bride price, and so on.

Proverbs are most effective when a senior person shares with one who is the junior in age, social status, or office. Social etiquette forbids children from using proverbs in the presence of an elder. A young person who puts forth an apt proverb must first show homage to his elders or be thought pompous, poorly brought up, or uneducated.

Look at the Yoruba proverb above.[35] Although it may not be from your cultural heritage, what does it say to you?

Quote Sayings, Proverbs, and Words of Wisdom

Every culture provides a store of sayings, proverbs, phrases, and other wise words that encapsulates culturally important ideas, beliefs, and values. They come from literary and oral traditions, from well-known and anonymous sources, and from philosophical and political treatises. Here are a few examples:

* Selfishness must always be forgiven you know, because there is no hope of a cure. (Jane Austen)
* Examine what is said, not the one who speaks. (Arab proverb)
* Judge not, that you be not judged. (Biblical quotation)
* I am a part of everything that I have read. (Theodore Roosevelt)
* Scars give you character. (Lamar Odom, "my grandmother used to say")[36]

Religious writings can provide rich sources of material when the audience accepts the text as valid. The pope, for example, uses the Bible and Catholic teachings in his speeches; by doing so he affirms his faith's authoritative sources. However, listeners who are not Christians, or Christians who are not Catholics, might question one or both of these sources.

You can access many sayings, proverbs, and wise words on your online component of this program. Diversity in Practice: Proverbs in African Cultures also provides additional details about the importance of proverbs in some African cultures.

Think Critically about Quoting Authorities

Look back at the quotations from experts and laypeople relating to therapy horses, and ask yourself these questions about each source.

1. *What is the person's expertise?* For example, what is Peggy Bass's or Drew Coman's expertise? Is it relevant to the subject under discussion?
2. *Is the person recognized as an expert by others?* How could you determine the reputation of each person?
3. *Is the layperson stating an opinion commonly held by others like him or her?* In other words, is it a typical or representative view? Is each mother's experience common? Or is one or more of the situations extreme?
4. *Are the words taken out of context?* Because you don't have the newspaper article from which the quotations came, you cannot assess the context for each quotation. However, whenever possible, ask if the words fairly represent the speaker's intended meaning. Words out of context can be distorted.
5. *Is the quotation accurate?* Commonly, you'll hear "Pride goes before a fall"; however, Proverbs 16:18 actually says, "Pride goes before destruction and a haughty spirit before a fall." If you have serious doubts about the accuracy or origin of a quotation, check the Quote Investigator online.

For more information, do an Internet search for the exact words "taken out of context" and read several links to identify the effect of misleading quotations.

Find Compelling Comparisons

analogies state similarities between two things

literal analogies compare two actual things that are alike in important ways

Comparisons, also called **analogies**, point out similarities between things. We understand new information or unfamiliar ideas better when we find points of comparison to something that's already in our experience. Comparisons can be literal or figurative.

Literal analogies compare actual things that are similar in important ways. For example, Pakistani speaker Liaquat Ali Khan,[37] addressing the US Senate, pointed out similarities between his country and ours and helped senators understand why Muslims broke away from India's majority Hindu population to create Pakistan:

> Pakistan was founded so that millions of Muslims should be enabled to live according to their opinions and to worship God in freedom....Like some of the earlier founders of your great country, these Muslims, though not Pilgrims, nevertheless embarked upon an undertaking, which, in aim and achievement, represented the triumph of an idea. That idea was the idea of liberty, which has had its ardent followers in all climates and all countries. When our time came, its call summoned us, too, and we could not hold back.

Figurative analogies or metaphors connect less familiar images to well-known images by highlighting similarities between otherwise *dissimilar* things. Consequently, they require your listeners to apply their imagination and integrate likenesses between two otherwise different things or ideas. For instance, this student compared highways to a familiar food:

> Looking at a road is essentially like looking at a cake. The top layer of frosting is essentially a tar seal that is flexible and resists water infiltration. Once the "frosting" wears off—the road's worst nightmare—water is allowed into the more porous second layer of the road. When it freezes it expands, causing the road to break apart on a micro level. So once the frosting is gone, the rest of the cake deteriorates very fast.[38]

Comparing life to a game is a common metaphor, but in her speech to the graduating class one speaker rejected this comparison:

> It is not a sport. Life does not have rules designed to keep the competition fair. There are not a lot of men and women running around in black and white striped shirts blowing the whistle on infractions against humanity. Would that there were.[39]

This example shows that pointing out *differences*, or showing contrasts between a new concept and a more familiar one, can also be a good strategy.

Think Critically about Analogies

Evaluate your use of comparisons and contrasts. To test literal analogies, make sure the items are alike in essential details. For instance, you could mislead your audience by comparing the work of a police officer in Houston, Texas, with one in Sioux Falls, South Dakota. Although their duties may be similar, the differences are significant. A Houston officer is more like officers in large cities such as Los Angeles or Miami with diverse populations. Sioux Falls officers, on the other hand, have more in common with police officers in smaller cities in Michigan or Washington State.

To test figurative analogies, be sure the comparison is clear and makes sense. Can your listeners make the necessary connection of ideas?

Use Visual Evidence

In a culture where visuals are everywhere, we commonly rely on evidence portrayed in pictures, images, and symbols to support ideas. Images can tell a story or put forth an analysis of a topic—or both. In short, visuals give us information and let us "see reasons."[40] How bad is the disaster's damage? Why should I donate to that organization? A photograph of people in need who benefit from your gift provides a reason.

Literal images show the actual subject under discussion[41] and help you fulfill your cognitive, affective, and behavioral speech goals. In her classroom speech on the

figurative analogy states similarities between two otherwise dissimilar things; requires an imaginative connection

literal images show the actual subject

A photograph of a child who is obviously thrilled by being in contact with a horse helps explain the concept of equine therapy.

© iStockphoto.com/carlofornitano

importance of sanitary procedures for body piercings, Katrina displayed graphic pictures of piercings-gone-wrong to support her goals of increasing her listeners' understanding ("I see what you mean!"), getting them emotionally engaged ("That's repulsive!"), and motivating them to act ("I will never get a piercing under unsanitary conditions!").

metaphorical image
implies the subject

Metaphorical images are common in advertising,[42] where fluffy kittens pose beside a box of tissues to imply "softness" or where a flower beside a deodorant implies "pleasant smell." Speakers sometimes use them in talks on subjects such as diversity, where metaphorical images in rainbow colors suggest the variety of beliefs and behaviors in a group.

Margaret LaWare[43] examined the messages conveyed in Chicano/a murals in Chicago. She says these murals make statements or arguments about ethnic pride, community activism, and cultural revitalization. Their images combine to define identity, reflect people's needs, and celebrate their histories. LaWare believes "the murals argue that Mexican American people need not assimilate or give up their culture to survive in an urban center that is both geographically and socially distant from Mexico and from the Southwest."[44]

Think Critically about Visual Evidence

Images tell a story, but not necessarily the whole story, and sometimes they tell a misleading story to promote a particular point of view. For example, a photographer with a negative attitude toward an issue might take a wide shot of a sparse crowd at a rally to indicate how few attended; however, another photographer with a positive attitude might choose a close-up of a single, intensely involved participant to emphasize the importance of the topic.

Analyze the photographs on your college or university's website. Your school uses them to imply messages such as "you will make lifelong friendships if you come here," or "professors are accessible to students," or "the campus is lovely." Typically, the photographs, while technically "true," fail to tell the entire story. Compare the photographs to your personal experiences by answering the following questions:

- What kind of weather is shown in the photographs? Is that weather typical of the climate where your school is located?
- What students are most typical of the student body? What students are shown in the photographs? What types are missing from the promotional materials?
- Which buildings or interiors, if any, are shown? Why do you think they were selected?
- What's left out? Why?

Summary

It is vital to support your ideas with evidence that listeners understand and accept so they can see reasons for your major ideas. Select facts, definitions, and descriptions that you can verify in a number of sources. In addition, select up-to-date facts and take care to not pass along distorted or incorrect information.

In a society that tends to place value on quantification, the judicious use of enumeration and statistics can increase your audience's acceptance of your ideas. However, be sure your numerical support is understandable, up-to-date, and used in ways that do not create misleading impressions. Visual aids are often helpful in clarifying complex numerical data.

Almost all listeners respond to examples, and using specific incidents as supporting material helps make abstract concepts more concrete and relevant. Whether real or hypothetical, brief or extended, illustrations also help listeners identify emotionally with your topic. To be effective, examples should be representative, sufficient in number, and plausible.

The use of quotations or testimony also enhances your credibility. Directly quote or paraphrase the opinions of experts and lay or peer sources. In addition, use cultural proverbs, written texts, and even words of wisdom from relatively unknown sources that your audience will accept as credible.

Comparisons or analogies are an additional means of support. Literal analogies compare or contrast two actual things; figurative analogies compare two things that are generally considered different but share one likeness. Both types add vividness to your speeches.

Finally, visual evidence in the form of pictures, images, or symbols can help your audience "see reasons," which can lead to increased understandings and engaged emotions and can provide a motivation for behaviors.

As you interweave facts, numbers, examples, quotations, comparisons, and visuals, you give your listeners more reasons to accept the conclusions you present.

STUDY AND REVIEW

Reflect on what you've learned.

Public Speaking: Concepts and Skills for a Diverse Society offers a broad range of resources that will help you better understand the material in this chapter, complete assignments, and succeed on tests. Your MindTap resources feature the following:

- Speech videos with viewing questions, speech outlines, and transcripts
- Activities to help you check your understanding and to apply what you've learned to your own life
- Stop and Check and Critical Thinking exercises
- Outline Builder
- Web Links related to chapter content
- Study and review tools such as self-quizzes and an interactive glossary

You can access your online resources for *Public Speaking: Concepts and Skills for a Diverse Society* at cengagebrain.com using the access code that came with your book or that you purchased online.

Review your *Flashcards*.

KEY TERMS

The terms below are defined in the margins throughout this chapter.

analogies 108

empirical facts 97

enumeration 99

established fact 97

figurative analogy 109

hypothetical example 103

literal analogies 108

literal images 109

mean 100

median 100

metaphorical image 110

mode 100

percentage 100

rate of increase or
    decrease 100

ratio 101

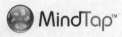

CRITICAL THINKING EXERCISES

1. What facts do you personally believe about global warming or climate change? Why? What actual research have you done on the subject? What kind of information would you trust on an issue such as this? When you find conflicting data on a topic, how do you judge which makes more sense? How would you go about forming a reasoned opinion on this topic? Does it matter if you do? Why or why not?
2. Construct a hypothetical example that would be appropriate on a controversial topic of your choice. Come to class prepared to share your example and explain why you chose the details in it.
3. Go to the online edition of a newsmagazine such as *Time* or *U.S. News & World Report*. Read one of the featured stories and find examples of a fact, example, visual, expert and peer testimony, statistic, and comparison. Be prepared to discuss how each type of evidence functions to make a more complete story.

APPLICATION QUESTIONS

1. Stalin is alleged to have said, "A million deaths is a statistic; a single death is a tragedy." Examples are the primary tool for eliciting emotional identification with the story. They add drama, emotion, and vividness to any topic. Statistics appeal to the mind; examples appeal to the heart. Be prepared to discuss the differences and how to use each in speeches.
2. Bring to class a news source—whether online or in print. With your classmates, choose a topic from the headlines. Collect and display information by dividing the board into five sections, one for each kind of evidence: facts, examples, quotations, numerical data, and analogies. Contribute information from your news source, cooperating with your classmates to fill the board. Evaluate the evidence using the tests presented in this chapter.
3. Discuss with your classmates the criteria that determine whether or not someone is an expert on a particular topic. Can students be experts on their speech subjects? How can they communicate their expertise to their classmates?
4. Make a list of topics that almost require visual evidence. (For example: *feng shui*.) Discuss your list with a group of your classmates and explain why a visual is essential.

THIS CHAPTER WILL
HELP YOU

- Organize your main points

- Identify and use traditional patterns, including chronological, spatial, causal, problem–solution, pro–con, and topical

- Develop and support your main points

- Link the parts of the speech to one another through skillful use of connectives such as signposts, transitions, internal previews, and internal summaries

- Identify and use alternative patterns— including the wave, the spiral, and the star—when they are appropriate

Diana Ong/SuperStock

Organizing Your Main Points

ELISIA CHOI MOVED to a new city and began work as an intern in a major public relations firm. Her first project update to a group of clients clearly explained the proposed design and demonstrated her ability to organize and present complex ideas. Shortly thereafter she was hired to a full-time position in the company. When asked why she spends so much time planning her speeches, she replied,

> A well-organized speech is easy to understand, follow, and remember.
> Someone who organizes her speech well is often viewed as an organized
> thinker and worker. It is important to always portray myself positively as a

MindTap

ew the
ter
rning
ectives
Start
a quick
m-up
vity.

Eric Chan

As Elisia Choi recognized, a well-organized speech is a major plus in most work environments.

valuable asset to the company and team. I never know who may be listening, taking note of my abilities, and considering me for future projects and opportunities.[1]

As Elisia noted, good organization is vital. One student put it this way, "I think of organization as being kind to your audience as well as yourself."

Guidelines for arranging your main points and your speech materials fall into the *canon of disposition*, which was introduced in Chapter 2. This chapter begins with general tips for identifying and organizing main points, moves on to explain several common organizational patterns, describes ways to develop, support, and connect main points, and concludes with alternative methods of arranging the body of your speech.

Read, highlight, and take notes online.

Organize Your Main Points

Although the body is the middle part of your speech, plan it first. Your research has probably turned up several subcategories of information such as a sequence of events or the causes and effects of a problem. Identifying basic patterns can help you organize your main points and your underlying supporting material using a few general organizational tips: limit your points, know some major patterns, and choose the best pattern.

Build Your Outline

Use a Limited Number of Points

Cognitive psychologists say we learn better when we "chunk" information into just a few major units.[2] In other words, listeners will remember your speech better if you limit the number of your main points. Two to five points are common; the key is to keep your structure simple.

To decide on your main points, return to your specific purpose and the central idea you developed in Chapter 5. If you've created them thoughtfully, you should have a pretty good idea about how to cover the material.[3] Keeping in mind your goal and the general direction of your speech, you can start fleshing out your content.

Consider Traditional Patterns

Over centuries of speechmaking, speakers have developed several traditional patterns to fit specific topics and purposes. Some work especially well for presenting information, while others are better for persuasive messages. Here, you'll find six widely used organizational patterns: chronological, spatial, cause–effect or causal, problem–solution, pro–con, and topical. (Chapter 17 describes several additional persuasive patterns.)

Chronological Organization

chronological pattern presents points in a sequential or time order

The **chronological pattern** develops a sequence of events in a given order. Historical topics or biographical speeches describe events that unfold across a period of years.

Process speeches, in which several steps, stages, or cycles follow one another in fairly predictable sequences, almost automatically fall into a chronological pattern. Typically, chronological speeches are informative. Here are the main points in a biographical speech followed by a process speech:

process speech describes a sequence of steps or stages that follow one another in a fairly predictable pattern

Specific Purpose: To inform my audience about the beginning, the evolution, and the breakup of the Beatles.

Central Idea: The Beatles began as the Quarrymen, evolved from the Silver Beetles to the Beatles, became the most famous band in the world, and finally broke up.

I. John Lennon formed the Quarrymen when he was 16.
II. A few years later they became the Silver Beetles and finally the Beatles.
III. They gained their reputation in Europe before storming the United States.
IV. After a dozen successful years, they went their individual ways.

Specific Purpose: To inform my audience about the cycle of domestic violence.
Central Idea: The cycle of domestic violence typically has three stages.[4]

I. Phase one: Tension builds.
II. Phase two: The abuse takes place.
III. Phase three: The batterer promises to change in the honeymoon period.

The key is that events *must* occur in a sequence and follow a clear "first, next, finally" pattern. Occasionally, speakers vary the pattern by beginning with the final point before showing the events that led up to it. For instance, a speaker could first describe the Beatles' breakup and then go back to describe the band's history.

Spatial Organization

A less common way to organize points is to use the **spatial pattern** and organize by location. This pattern is useful for informative speeches about places or things made up of levels or layers. You could move top-to-bottom, east-to-west, region-to-region, floor-to-floor of a building, and so on. Here is an example of spatial organization:

spatial pattern presents points by place or location

Spatial patterns are useful for topics that can be organized by space such as information about various wings of a hospital.

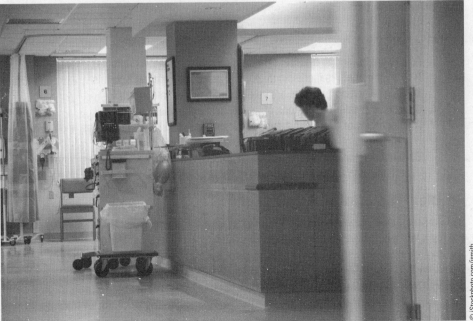

© iStockphoto.com/jsmith

Specific Purpose: To inform my audience about the global impact of hip-hop.
Central Idea: Hip-hop is a phenomenon on many continents.[5]

I.   Brazil's hip-hop scene developed out of favela street parties in the 1980s.
II. France is one of the world's great producers and consumers of hip-hop.
III. Hip-hop hit it big in South Africa about a decade ago with Miss Nthabi.
IV. Korea is just one of the Asian countries with a flourishing hip-hop scene.

Something done in layers (such as creating a parfait) should be discussed in order—bottom-to-top; however, other topics are more flexible. A speech describing a city, for instance, could be organized by direction (north, south, east, west), by population density (most to least populated areas, or vice versa), by income level, and so on, depending on the goal.

Cause–Effect or Causal Organization

When you want to shed light on a problem, a **cause–effect or causal pattern** works well. Here, you examine the reasons underlying a problem (the causes) and the implications of the problem for individuals or for society at large (the effects). You can use either a cause-to-effect or an effect-to-cause pattern. This cause–effect speech was on campaign ads:

Specific Purpose: To inform my audience of the reason people use negative campaign ads and their negative influence on politics.
Central Idea: Campaigns use negative ads in political campaigns for a variety of reasons, but their effect on the electorate is negative.[6]

I.   Campaigns use them for several reasons (causes).
     A. Candidates cast suspicion on their opponents.
     B. Negative ads are memorable.
II. Negative ads affect the electorate.
     A. They are linked to decreased voter turnout.
     B. Voters lose trust in politics and politicians.

Some topics are more effectively presented by using an effects-to-cause pattern—first looking at a problem's effects on an individual or group before exploring its causes.

Specific Purpose: To inform my audience that many Asians are turning to surgeries and cosmetics to change their appearance because of Western media influences.
Central Idea: Many Asians are increasingly trying to modify their appearance because of influences from Western media.[7]

I.   Asians are turning to unnecessary surgeries and cosmetics (effects).
     A. Eyelid surgery is increasingly popular, especially among Koreans.
     B. Skin bleaching products are sold throughout Asian countries.
II. Critics say Western depictions of beauty cause this dissatisfaction.
     A. Ideologies of beauty portrayed in Western media include large eyes, blonde hair, smooth complexions, and skinny or toned bodies.
     B. Multinational companies use standardized advertising that includes computer-enhanced Western models, even in Asian countries.

Problem–Solution Organization

As Chapter 1 pointed out, one core US belief is that life presents challenges we can solve through knowledge and effort. Consequently, we often approach global, national, local, and personal issues as problems that require solutions. A **problem–solution pattern** works well for both informative and persuasive speeches. Not surprisingly, this pattern requires you to look at the problem—sometimes examining its causes and effects—and then propose a solution. Here is an outline for a persuasive speech about taxing mileage, not gasoline:

Specific Purpose: To persuade my audience that a mileage tax should replace the gas tax.

Central Idea: States are not getting enough tax revenues to repair roads and infrastructure, so we should tax miles driven instead of gasoline.

I. Gasoline tax revenues are inadequate for infrastructure repair.
    A. All users put wear-and-tear on highways, but some pay less for their use.
    B. Taxing one type of vehicle more than another is unfair.
II. Taxing mileage instead of gasoline would help solve the problem.
    A. It would bring in revenue based on usage.
    B. It would solve the fairness issue.

Given the same topic, if your purpose were to inform, you'd describe the revenue problem and then introduce your listeners to a variety of solutions, not just one.

pro–con pattern presents arguments in favor of and arguments against an issue

Pro–Con Organization

When you need to explore both sides of a controversial issue, the **pro–con pattern** is very useful. Classify all the arguments in favor of the issue under the *pro* label, and then list the arguments against it under the *con* label. Here is an example of pro–con organization on the topic of linking attendance to grades in college classes.[8]

Specific Purpose: To inform my audience of the arguments for and against mandatory attendance policies.

Central Idea: The policy of linking class attendance to grades has both positive and negative arguments.

I. Proponents make a number of arguments in favor of mandatory attendance.[9]
    A. Better attendance is linked to better grades.
    B. Establishing good participation habits helps in life after college.
    C. Attendance is important for others in the class.
II. Critics give many reasons for discontinuing mandatory attendance.
    A. A captive audience is not ideal for learning.
    B. Students should be able to choose.
    C. The professor is paid regardless of attendance.

This organizational pattern is best when your goal is to explain the nature of an issue in an investigative report. It lets your listeners weigh the evidence and evaluate the arguments for themselves. If your purpose is to advocate for one set of arguments over another, choose a different overall pattern.

Should Division I college athletes be paid? This is just one of many issues where some say yes; others say no. A pro–con speech gives listeners both sides so they can make up their own minds.

© iStockphoto.com/filo

Topical Organization

If your material doesn't really fit into any of these patterns, use the most common pattern—the **topical pattern**. Here, you classify the major points into subdivisions, each of which is part of the whole. Although every point contributes to an overall

topical pattern divides a subject into subtopics, each of which is part of the whole

understanding of the subject, the points themselves can be ordered in different ways. For instance, Daisy used these points:[10]

Specific Purpose: To inform my audience of three stereotypical portrayals of Latinas in the media.

Central Idea: Latinas in media are typically stereotyped as cantina girls, suffering senoritas, or vamps.

I. Cantina girls are teasing, dancing entertainers of easy virtue.
II. Suffering senoritas start well, usually go bad, and end up sacrificing themselves to protect an endangered lover.
III. Vamps deviously use their wiles to gain desired ends, often at the expense of men.

She could easily change the order of these points.

Choose the Best Pattern

A single topic can be organized in a number of ways, so determine which pattern works best given your purposes, supporting materials, audience, and assignment. For instance, you could effectively develop a speech on hip-hop using any one of these three patterns:

Chronological: Hip-hop developed over several decades.

I. Although its roots are much older, rap as we know it dates back to the 1970s.
II. It became very controversial in the late 1980s and 1990s with gangsta rap.
III. Rap continues to evolve with contributions from new talent and new places.

Spatial: In the 1990s US rappers were in two general regions.

I. East Coast rappers were generally based in New York.
II. California was the base for most West Coast rappers.

Topical: Although men dominate in hip-hop, women make their mark.

I. Nicki Minaj is well known.
II. Gift Uh Gab has quality lyrics.
III. Rapsody has been around for a while.

Use these patterns to organize your speech as a whole or combine patterns to organize the points within your speech. For instance, a speech on the history of gambling in the United States could have the main points ordered chronologically with subpoints organized topically. Table 9.1 summarizes these basic patterns.

TABLE 9.1
Summary of Traditional Organizational Patterns

Chronological	Puts points in a sequential or time order
Spatial	Arranges points by place or location
Cause–Effect	Explains reasons for (causes) and implications (effects) of a subject
Problem–Solution	Describes a harmful problem and tells possible ways to solve it
Pro–Con	Reports on the arguments both for and against an issue
Topical	Makes each point a subtopic of the subject

Develop Your Main Points

After you have decided on major points, make them distinct and parallel. Then develop each one by adding supporting materials and connecting your ideas into a smooth flow.

Make Points Distinct

Each point should be clear and separate from the others. For example, one student's speech on CPR was so disorganized that her audience had trouble telling her main points from her supporting material. Here are the main points she presented:

I.   Once you have training in CPR, you also have responsibilities.
II. Rules of CPR for an adult.
III. Signs: Something to look for. [Under this point she explained the steps of CPR.]
IV. Statistics from the American Heart Association.

If she had used one of the traditional patterns, her points would be easier to support and her audience could better follow her train of thought. Here's how a problem–solution pattern would work:

I.   [problem] Every year, thousands of people experience sudden cardiac arrest outside the hospital.
   A. This condition has several causes.
   B. The effects show up in specific symptoms.
II. [solution] More lives could be saved if more people had CPR training.
   A. The American Heart Association teaches people the steps of CPR.
   B. Trained and certified responders have specific responsibilities in crisis situations.

Rhyming or alliterating main ideas are additional strategies that can make points distinct and memorable as these examples show:

Obesity: what dieters don't need, heed, or read.[11]
Advergaming is evaluative, efficient, effective, and engaging.

Make Points Parallel

Next, make your points **parallel**, meaning they are similar in kind and in length. Don't write some as declarative sentences and others as questions. Avoid mixing phrases and complete sentences, and don't put two sentences in a single point, all of which this student did in her first draft:

I.   What is multiple sclerosis (MS)? [*a sentence in question form*]
II. The Big Mystery! [*a sentence fragment or phrase*]
III. Who? [*a single word in question form*]
IV. Effects . . . Symptoms of MS. [*an incomplete sentence*]
V.   Three prominent medications are now being used to treat MS. These are talked about in the magazine *Inside MS*. [*two declarative sentences*]

parallel points points that are similar in kind and length

She should reorganize and rewrite her points as declarative sentences, as shown here:

I.   Multiple sclerosis (MS) is a disease of the central nervous system.
   A. The causes remain a mystery.
   B. Sufferers tend to share age, gender, and regional characteristics.
   C. The condition affects eyesight and bodily coordination.
II. Most physicians prescribe one of three major medications.

Finally, as she looks at these points, she can see that they logically fall into a problem–solution pattern, which becomes her final outline:

I. Multiple sclerosis (MS) is a disease of the central nervous system.
   A. Sufferers tend to share age, gender, and regional characteristics.
   B. The causes remain a mystery.
   C. MS affects eyesight and bodily coordination.
II. Most physicians prescribe one of three major medications.

Support Points with Evidence

Once you've established your main points, return to your research and begin to arrange your materials under the ideas they support. Of course, your time limits will help you decide how much to include, and your audience's previous knowledge of your topic will help you decide what specific information to include and what to leave out.

Here's how Jordan organized his first section on the topic of e-waste.[14] The assignment was a civic awareness speech, which first reported on a problem and then described an organization set up to combat that problem.[15] An audience survey revealed that his classmates all had electronic devices, and most intended to replace at least one

DIVERSITY IN PRACTICE

Some African Organizational Patterns

In many areas of the world, patterns differ markedly from those presented in this text. Two such examples come from Africa.

Madagascar

Elders in the Merina tribe use a four-part organizational pattern when they speak:[12]

1. First is a period of excuses in which the speaker expresses humility and reluctance to speak. He uses standard phrases such as "I am a child, a younger brother." He sometimes relates well-known stories and proverbs.
2. Next, he thanks the authorities for letting him speak at all. He uses a formula that thanks God, the president of the republic, government ministers, the village headman, major elders, and finally the people in the audience.
3. In the third section, he uses proverbs, illustrations, and short poems as he makes his proposal.
4. He closes by thanking and blessing his listeners.

Kenya

The body of a Kenyan speech is often organized in a circular pattern, somewhat like a bicycle wheel. The hub or center is the single main point that links the entire speech. The speaker then wanders out repeatedly from the central point, telling stories and providing other supporting materials and stories that tie back to the main idea. To an outsider, the speech might seem illogical, but Kenyan listeners can easily follow the logical connections among points.[13]

item within the year. Some knew the term *e-waste*; all knew that disposal of electronics could harm the environment, but they were less aware of its extent. Everyone wanted to learn responsible ways to dispose of outdated electronic devices. So as he developed the "problem" section of the speech, he selected definitions, examples, statistics, and other evidence with his audience in mind:

I. [main point] First, let's look at the problem of e-waste.
   A. [definition] A Swiss government agency, the EMPA, defines *e-waste* as any out-of-date or otherwise discarded equipment that uses electricity.
      1. [synonym] *Tech waste* is another term.
      2. [example] E-waste includes computers, cell phones, or household appliances.
      3. [explanation] If you can plug it in and you throw it out, it's e-waste.
   B. [fact] Over the past few decades, the amount of e-waste in the United States has grown steadily.
      1. [statistic] Elizabeth Royte, writing in the *Smithsonian Magazine*, estimated that at least 60 million PCs were buried in US landfills.
         a. [fact] That article was from 2005.
         b. [fact] E-waste has only gotten worse since then.
      2. [statistic] A 2008 EPA report said that 80 to 85 percent of discarded electronics were sent to landfills between 2003 and 2005 and placed e-waste as one of the agency's top priorities.

Jordan similarly supported his next points—specific hazards of electronic wastes and how it affects people—with information his audience was less likely to know. (You can find his entire outline in Appendix B.)

Connect Your Ideas

Connectives are words, phrases, and sentences that lead from one idea to another and unify the various elements of your speech. They function somewhat like bridges that link your points to each other or to the whole. With them, you can emphasize significant points and help your listeners keep their place as you talk. The most common connectives are signposts and transitions, internal previews, and internal summaries.

Connective word, phrase, or sentence used to lead from idea to idea and tie the parts of the speech together smoothly

Signposts are like highway signs because they help the audience know what to expect next in your speech.

© iStockphoto.com/frender

Signposts and Transitions

Signposts signal the audience about what's ahead in the speech. They include words such as *first*, *next*, and *finally* that introduce new points and help your listeners identify the flow of your ideas. Other words and phrases such as *in addition*, *for example*, *therefore*, and *as a result* connect one idea to another. Phrases such as *the main thing to remember* or *most importantly* highlight ideas you want to emphasize. Here are two examples of signposts from Jordan's outline:

* *First*, let's look at the problem of e-waste.
* *More importantly*, electronics contain a bevy of harmful chemicals.

   Transitions summarize what you've covered and where you'll go next in the speech. You can use them both between points and within one of your points. Here is a simple transition between Zitong's major points:[16]

> Now that we've seen how Chinese couples prepare for a traditional wedding [where we've been], let's look at their actual wedding day [where we're going].

   Her second major point was, "Three main events take place on the wedding day: welcoming the bride, performing the ceremony, and pranking the bridal chamber." After she describes the first two causes, she can transition to the final one by saying:

> After the bride is welcomed and the ceremony performed [first and second subpoint], friends and relatives gather in the bridal chamber to "prank" the couple [third subpoint].

Internal Previews and Internal Summaries

Internal previews occur within the body of your speech when you briefly tell the subpoints you will develop under one of your major points. For instance, this internal preview, "Epiphany celebrations vary in Louisiana, Argentina, and Mexico," shows that Cheyenne will use a spatial pattern to develop one of her main points.[17]

   Summarizing a point or points after you've made them is an **internal summary**. Thus, this sentence summarizes the causes before moving on to the effects of amusement park accidents:

> In short, we have seen that equipment failure, operator failure, and rider behavior combine to create thousands of tragedies annually.

   In summary, connectives are the words, phrases, and sentences used to weave your ideas together and enhance the flow of your speech as a whole. As Table 9.2 shows, they serve to introduce your points, show the relationship of one point to another, preview and summarize points within the speech, and overall help your listeners keep their place in your speech.

TABLE 9.2
Connectives

Signposts	Words such as *first* and *next* introduce points; phrases such as *for example* and *as a result* connect ideas
Transitions	Summarize where you've been and where you're going in the speech
Internal Preview	Brief statement of the subpoints you'll develop under a main point
Internal Summary	Brief summary of the point or points you just made in the speech

Alternative Patterns

Some speakers, because of their cultural backgrounds or personal inclinations, prefer a less linear pattern. A more **organic pattern**, visualized as a wave, a spiral, or a star, can provide a clear speech structure in a less linear form.[18]

The **wave pattern**, illustrated in Figure 9.1, repeats and varies themes and ideas. The crests of the waves are the main points, which are developed with a variety of examples leading up to another crest. Conclusions wind down and lead the audience gradually from the topic; or they rebuild, so that the final statement is a dramatic peak. Women and members of various ethnic groups often choose this pattern,[19] which is especially useful for eulogies and ceremonial speaking.

Perhaps the most familiar wave pattern speech is Dr. Martin Luther King Jr.'s "I Have a Dream."[20] Throughout, he uses a number of "crests" including "One hundred years later . . .," "Now is the time . . .," and "I have a dream. . . ." He follows each repetition of the phrase with examples that develop the idea. His conclusion dramatically emerges from the final wave in the speech—the repetition and variation of the phrase "Let freedom ring."

The **spiral pattern** (Figure 9.2) shows points that increase in magnitude or effect. For example, a speech on food waste could move from personal (e.g., food waste at home) to institutional (e.g., waste at the university) to community levels (e.g., waste at restaurants and other institutions in the area), each point spiraling in magnitude. Because each major scenario has greater effects than the preceding one, the audience would see the issue in different contexts.

The spiral pattern is useful for speeches on subjects that build in levels of dramatic intensity such as bullying. Each scene builds in tension, with the most intense scenario reserved for the final spiral.

The **star pattern** is a third visual form. Each point (see Figure 9.3), is more or less equally weighted within a unifying theme. This pattern is useful for speakers

organic pattern alternative pattern that provides a clear speech structure in a less linear form

© iStockphoto.com/Jamie Farrant

Figure 9.1
The Wave Pattern

wave pattern repetitive pattern that presents variations of themes and ideas, with major points presented at the crests

spiral pattern repetitive pattern with a series of points that increase in drama or intensity

star pattern presents relatively equally weighted speech points within a thematic circle that binds them together; order of points may vary

© 3d_kot/Shutterstock.com

© beboy/Shutterstock.com

Figure 9.2
The Spiral Pattern

Figure 9.3
The Star Pattern

who present a similar speech to different audiences. By visualizing the major points as a star, they can choose where to start and what to emphasize, depending on the audience. For example, a speaker might begin with a point the audience understands or accepts and then move to points that challenge their understanding and agreement. For inattentive audiences, starting with the most dramatic point can gain attention from the outset. For hostile audiences, begin with the most conciliatory point. This gives the advantage of quickly making audience adaptations and still covering the points effectively.

The final element is the thematic circle that links the points. By the conclusion, listeners should feel that the theme is fulfilled. This pattern is common during election years. The underlying theme is "Vote for me!" However, instead of giving an identical "stump speech" to every group, the candidate rearranges the issues and targets specific points toward specific audiences.

Repetition patterns are probably best seen in songwriting. Each verse develops the song's theme, while the chorus lyrics are repeated.[21] Although alternative patterns might appear to be easy to create, they still require organizational planning.

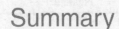

Summary

After you've gathered speech materials, you must organize them into a pattern. Begin with the body of the speech, and choose a limited number of points from among several traditional patterns. Common organizational frameworks include chronological, spatial, cause–effect or causal, problem–solution, pro–con, and topical patterns. These patterns are appropriate for many types of speeches; cause–effect or causal and pro–con are especially good for informative purposes. Problem–solution works especially well for persuasive speeches. Most topics can be organized several ways depending on the purpose and the audience.

After you decide on your points, evaluate them to make sure each one is distinct and they are constructed in parallel form. Support each point with evidence that fits your purpose, the assignment, and the audience. Then weave your ideas together with connectives that link your points and subpoints into a coherent whole.

Although linear patterns are common in the United States, nonlinear arrangements are typical in diverse settings, as the examples from Madagascar and Kenya and the alternative patterns show. Some speakers prefer organic patterns such as the repetitive wave, which is especially suited to ceremonial speaking. In the spiral pattern, the points increase in dramatic intensity. Finally, speakers who want flexible points within a major theme can visualize their ideas in the form of a star. Regardless of the pattern, traditional or alternative, you must carefully identify your main points and then develop them with appropriate supporting materials.

Reflect on what you've learned.

STUDY AND REVIEW

Public Speaking: Concepts and Skills for a Diverse Society offers a broad range of resources that will help you better understand the material in this chapter, complete assignments, and succeed on tests. Your MindTap resources feature the following:

- Speech videos with viewing questions, speech outlines, and transcripts
- Activities to help you check your understanding and to apply what you've learned to your own life
- Stop and Check and Critical Thinking exercises
- Outline Builder

- Web Links related to chapter content
- Study and review tools such as self-quizzes and an interactive glossary

You can access your online resources for *Public Speaking: Concepts and Skills for a Diverse Society* at cengagebrain.com using the access code that came with your book or that you purchased online.

KEY TERMS

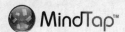

Review your Flashcards.

The terms below are defined in the margins throughout this chapter.

cause–effect or causal pattern 116
chronological pattern 114
connective 121
internal preview 122
internal summary 122
organic pattern 123
parallel points 119
problem–solution pattern 116

process speech 114
pro–con pattern 117
signpost 122
spatial pattern 115
spiral pattern 123
star pattern 123
topical pattern 117
transition 122
wave pattern 123

CRITICAL THINKING EXERCISES

1. Outline one of the speeches available on your online resources. (Don't use a Speech of Introduction; they usually have a slightly different organizational pattern.) Is the organizational pattern easy to discern? What suggestions, if any, could you give the speaker about arranging the points of the speech?
2. Read or watch Dr. Martin Luther King Jr.'s Nobel Prize acceptance speech, which is available online. Try to draw an "outline" of his speech using the star pattern. Identify his main points as well as the thematic circle. Identify, also, the places where he uses the wave pattern.

APPLICATION QUESTIONS

1. Work with a group of your classmates to make a list of ways that speech organization helps speakers be more effective.
2. With a small group of your classmates, take a topic such as credit cards, divorce, alcohol on campus, or immigration, and identify and organize major points in as many of the following patterns as you can: topical, chronological, spatial, cause–effect or causal, problem–solution, pro–con, and spiral.
3. Using one of the basic outlines you created in the previous question, take each major point and, underneath it, identify ways you could use evidence (statistics, facts, testimony, definitions, examples, and so on) to support that point.
4. Using one of the basic outlines created above, write connectives such as signposts and transition statements for each point.
5. Take the theme of creativity or the theme of perseverance. Then work with two or three classmates and discuss how you might create a speech organized around the wave, the spiral, or the star pattern. For example, think of three famous people who persevered—each one in a more dramatic way. Or use examples from your school's sports teams, your personal lives, lives of entertainers, and so on.

CHAPTER 10

THIS CHAPTER WILL HELP YOU

- Develop an introduction that gains attention, motivates the audience to listen, establishes your credibility, and previews your speech

- Develop a conclusion that signals the end, summarizes, provides psychological closure, and ends with impact

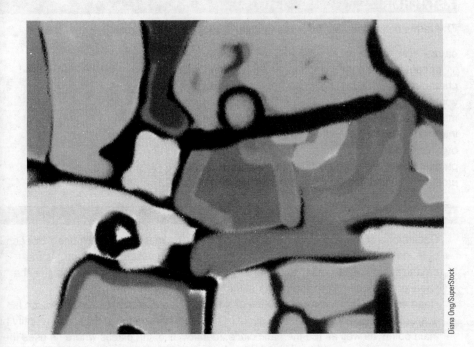

Diana Ong/SuperStock

Introductions and Conclusions

"YOU RARELY GET a second chance to make a positive first impression." This cultural saying is true about speechmaking. When you begin poorly, you have trouble regaining the audience's attention and confidence. On the other hand, when you start strong, you're more likely to be forgiven for minor slips later. Also, an otherwise good speech that trails off or loses focus at the end prevents you from memorably driving home your point. Consequently, to be effective, carefully research, plan, and practice both your introductions and conclusions. Principles in this chapter will guide you in drawing your listeners into your subject and, at the end, concluding in a way that summarizes your thoughts and leaves a memorable impression.

MindT
Review th
chapter
Learning
Objective
and **Start**
with a qu
warm-up
activity.

Plan Your Introduction

Chapter 2 points out that the Roman educator Quintilian identified four purposes for an introduction:[1]

1. To draw your listeners' attention to the topic
2. To motivate your audience to listen
3. To establish yourself as knowledgeable about the topic
4. To preview the major ideas of your speech

Here, you can also provide definitions or background information that your listeners need. These four elements of an introduction serve to answer four basic audience questions: What's this all about? Why should I listen? Why should I listen to you? What will you cover? Figure 10.1 depicts these four introductory functions.

Gain Attention

Gaining attention is the first step in the listening process, so it's important to answer immediately your audience's question, *What's this speech about?* True, saying, "My speech is about...[and then announcing your subject]" introduces your topic, but less effectively than one of the several attention-gaining strategies that follow.

Ask a Question

Both **rhetorical questions**, those that listeners answer mentally, and **participatory questions**, those that ask for an overt response, such as a show of hands, work well. For his speech on the psychology of resilience, this speaker referred to a major flood in the area and then asked a series of rhetorical questions:[2]

Read, *highlight, and take notes online.*

rhetorical question question that listeners answer in their minds

participatory question question that listeners answer overtly

Figure 10.1
Four Audience Questions
Your introduction functions to answer these four questions.

© 2014 Cengage Learning®/Microsoft Image

Who can forget the images of fifty thousand people being evacuated out of Grand Forks? Who can forget the images of flames engulfing eleven buildings and sixty apartment units before being extinguished? What about those hundreds of volunteers who descended into the Red River Valley filling sand bags, trying to hold back the torrent of water which…eventually caused 3.5 billion dollars of damage?

For a participatory question, alert the audience to the response you want. For instance, ask for a show of hands or call on a member of the audience to answer a specific question you pose. Here's how Lindsey opened her persuasive speech about Walt Disney:[3]

Raise your hand if you've been to a Disney park. Which one did you go to? [She specifically calls on several who raised their hands to name the park or parks.]

Good rhetorical and participatory questions can help establish dialogue between you and your listeners at the very outset of the speech because they invite audience responses, whether mental or physical.

Provide a Vivid Description

Describe a scene—either real or imaginary—vividly enough that your listeners can easily visualize it. This opening for a classroom speech on ACL (knee) injuries in female athletes is a good example:[4]

One jump was all it took. It was the beginning of August and Kristina was already at volleyball camp preparing for her second season on the school's volleyball team. She jumped up to hit a ball during a game when she heard a "pop" in her knee. She had torn her ACL, which meant she could not participate in volleyball that year.

Begin with a Quotation

A quotation or a familiar cultural proverb, either *about* a subject or, for a biographical speech, *by* the subject, is a good way to gain attention. Choose a short saying that captures your overall theme—preferably a quotation that is familiar or from a familiar source—and cite that source. International student Zhen Li began his speech on exercising with this quotation from a famous American president:[5]

John F. Kennedy said, "Physical fitness is not only one of the most important keys to a healthy body, it is the basis of dynamic and creative intellectual activity."

Consider song lyrics, poems, scriptural or literary texts, family sayings, or words by a coach or teacher as sources for memorable quotations. You can access thousands of quotations on sites found on your online resources for this text.

Use an Audio or Visual Aid

Photographs, charts, short audio or video clips, and other visual and audio materials also successfully draw attention to your topic. Students have used visuals to gain attention in the following ways:

- Abby played harp music in the background as she introduced her subject, music thanatology—the practice of using music as part of end-of-life care. You can read her outline in Appendix B.
- Alex led into her subject of sleep deprivation with a short video clip of a student sleeping during a class.[6]
- Tessa brought her actual English riding saddle and pointed out the difference between that saddle and the more familiar Western saddle to gain attention to her topic of show jumping.[7]
- Josue began his speech on pay for Division I athletes by drawing attention to his tee shirt; he turned around to show images of Division I football games on the back. Although he had paid good money for the shirt, the athletes who were pictured did not receive one cent.[8]

Begin with an Example

As Chapter 8 pointed out, examples spark attention and help your listeners become emotionally involved with your topic. Use real stories of real people, or scenarios that could be, but are not necessarily, factual. Katie's opening for a speech on power naps began this way:[9]

> It's two in the afternoon, and you've already had three classes. Staying up last night until 3 a.m. writing that paper is starting to take a toll, no matter how many cups of coffee you guzzle down. Now, standing over your warm, cozy bed, it's never looked so inviting. You're faced with a decision: Climb in and sleep for a few hours, but what if you won't be able to sleep later? Or drink more coffee and fight to stay awake until bedtime? A third option is available: Take a power nap.

A Navajo (Diné) Speech Introduction

DIVERSITY IN PRACTICE

© iStockphoto.com/westphalia

Not every cultural group assumes speakers will gain attention first, relate to audience interests next, and establish credibility following that. Audiences at Diné College (formerly Navajo Community College) expect speakers to first answer the question, "Who are you and what is your clan affiliation?" Upon first meeting, members of Diné (Navajo) culture exchange information—first, about their mother's clan; next, their father's clan; followed by their maternal grandfather's clan; and finally, their paternal grandfather's clan.[10] This discloses the roots of the speakers' identity and helps establish their relationship with others in the audience. Only after these personal, identifying facts are shared do speakers and listeners feel comfortable discussing a topic.[11]

Start with Startling Numbers

Numbers and statistics can be dry; however, they can also capture and hold listeners' attention if they are shocking enough or if you put them into an understandable context, as this example illustrates:

> Globally, water-related deaths are responsible for 2.2 million deaths annually.[12] That's equivalent to the population of Paris, France. Every year. In Africa, unsafe water and sanitation cause an average of 115 deaths every minute. Speech classes on campus are limited to 24 students. Imagine an equivalent of almost five speech classes disappearing. Every minute. Of every day.

Refer to a Current Event

Another way to identify with your listeners and establish common ground is to begin with well-known current happenings—airplane crashes, campus controversies, weather disasters, well-publicized trials, elections, and the like. Referring to media events is one way to introduce a disaster-preparedness speech:

> Both the *Zombie Apocalypse* movie and *The Walking Dead* series show the struggles of survivors who must stay alive in a devastated world. Now the chances are low that a zombie plague will wipe out 90 percent of the world; however, in community after community across the nation and world, survivors of large quakes, hurricanes, floods, and other disasters face huge challenges in rebuilding their devastated communities. The government's Centers for Disease Control and Prevention is using the theme "How to Survive a Zombie Apocalypse" to promote disaster preparedness.[13]

Involve the Audience Physically

Some topics lend themselves well to physical actions by the audience. For instance, Hannah chose this strategy to begin her speech on the pros and cons of yoga:[14]

> Please relax and close your eyes. Breathe in through your nose [pause]…and out through your mouth [pause]…in through your nose [pause]…out through your mouth [pause]….Do it one more time [longer pause]….Now open your eyes. So did any of you feel more relaxed or a little less tense after doing that? [pause for feedback]. That's a simple example of the effect yoga can have on you.

Use Humor

If the audience, the occasion, and the topic seem appropriate, and if you have good comedic skills, you might try using humor to gain attention and create a more informal atmosphere. Consider telling a joke or riddle, relating a funny story, displaying a relevant cartoon, or showing a humorous video clip.

Humor has its risks, however. You can embarrass yourself and make your listeners uncomfortable if the joke flops, and you'll create an overall negative image if your joke is offensive. And of course, many subjects are not joking matters. To avoid humiliation, test your attempt at humor in advance on some friends, and let them decide if it's really funny or appropriate. Also, make sure the joke relates to your topic. Otherwise, you might gain attention, but it won't focus on your subject.

Although this is not an exhaustive list of successful opening strategies, these are common approaches used by speakers in a variety of settings. Remember that your opening should not simply gain attention; it must also draw attention to your topic. Furthermore, these strategies are good for maintaining or regaining attention throughout your speech.

Give Your Audience a Reason to Listen

After you have their attention, answer your listeners' second question, *Why should I listen to this speech?* You may think your topic is important and interesting, but your listeners may not. An audience mostly made up of 20-year-olds might initially think a speech on the "hidden poverty" of elderly poor people and the need for retirement planning was irrelevant, but almost everyone has friends and relatives over 65, and someday they will find themselves as the "old-timers." So the topic relates to people they know and care about.

You can also frame a specific topic within a larger issue. Few people will ever bake a rosca de reyes cake for Epiphany, but almost everyone has a favorite holiday food. Few people will ever participate in the sport of dressage (training horses to participate in competitive tasks); however, everyone is familiar with sports in general, and some have trained animals to respond to commands.

Two important human characteristics are curiosity and the ability to learn new things, so some topics simply increase your audience's knowledge or satisfy their curiosity. For example, dueling is no longer the way men establish their honor, but it has a long history in the United States, so John chose this way to relate: [15]

> You may not realize that dueling was once quite a common practice in the United States. In fact, the person on the $10 bill, Alexander Hamilton, was killed in a duel.

Many issues that don't seem to directly concern your listeners may actually affect their wallets, whether or not they know it. National issues that rely on tax dollars for support are in this category; funding for the arts, agricultural research, and weapons development are just a few examples. Chapter 16 provides more details about needs, wants, emotions, and values that motivate people to listen to speeches.

Establish Your Credibility

A third introductory task is to link yourself to your subject and answer the question, *Why should I listen to you?* Typically, you'll describe subject-related experiences, interests,

Brendan McKeon

Audiences relate to some topics easily. But it takes more creativity to link other subjects to your listeners' lives and interests. The cost in time or money, the impact of national or international issues on their lives and future, and an appeal to curiosity are just a few strategies you can use to make connections.

and research findings that show your interest and expertise. If relevant, you can mention your major, courses you have taken, a movie that sparked your interest in the topic, and so on. Here are some examples:

Topic: Safe drinking water. As a nursing major, I know how vital water is to the body, so I wanted to research how unsafe drinking water affects people globally.[16]

Topic: Musical frisson. As a musician and pianist, I have always been engrossed by how music affects us physically and emotionally.[17]

Topic: Retirement Planning. My grandparents are 80 years old. My grandmother still works two jobs, and my grandpa was working until dementia forced him to sell his business. Their social security benefits just don't cut it for them. If they had planned for retirement better, they wouldn't struggle so. Concern for them led me to do research on ways to prevent poverty in retirement.[18]

Of course, explicitly stating your credibility is optional when another person introduces you and connects you with the subject or when your expertise on the topic is well established.

Preview Your Ideas

You may have heard the old saying "Tell them what you're going to say; say it; then tell them what you said." The preview statement, as described in Chapter 5, serves the first of these functions and provides the transition between the introduction and the body of your speech. In the preview, answer the audience question, *What will you cover?*, by stating some form of your central idea and indicating how you will develop it.

When appropriate, a creative approach, such as alliterating or rhyming your points, is more memorable. Here are three previews:

Straightforward and clear. I will first speak about water's function in the body followed by diseases caused by dirty water; then I will explain how water affects the economic success of a community and conclude by highlighting an organization dedicated to bringing clean water to impoverished areas.[19]

Alliteration. In 1990, when Photoshop was first released, the doors opened for a whole new level of media manipulation—creating a perception of beauty that is *un*healthy, *un*ethical, and *un*recognized.[20]

Using a metaphor. Today, I'll retell the story of the boy who cried "wolf," with a few character changes. The boy who cries "wolf" is the American government, and the wolf we are to fear is industrial hemp.[21]

In summary, a good introduction draws attention to your topic, relates the subject to your listeners, links you to the subject, and previews your major ideas.

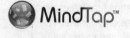

Conclude with Impact

Your conclusion leaves your listeners with their final impression of both you and your subject. Appearing disorganized at the end takes away some of the positive impressions you've built up during the speech. And failure to restate your thesis and review your main points is a missed opportunity to reinforce your speech goals.

Like the introduction, the conclusion has several important functions: to signal the end, to summarize the main points, to provide psychological closure (often by a reference to the introduction), and to end with impact.

Signal the Ending

Just as your preview provides a transition to the speech body, your ending signal provides a transition to your conclusion. Both beginning speakers and professionals use common phrases such as *in conclusion* or *finally*. However, the following signal is more creative:

> I hope my information about safe water has given you a new respect for your own drinking water and an awareness that others around the globe aren't as lucky as we are.[22] [Here, she transitions to the conclusion and restates her speech goal.]

You can also use nonverbal actions to signal that you're nearing the end. For instance, pause and shift your posture, or take a step back from the podium. A combination of verbal and nonverbal elements generally works well.

Review Your Main Ideas

To fulfill the "Tell them what you said" axiom, briefly summarize or recap your main ideas, but the key word is *brief*. The audience has already heard your speech, so don't repeat or add new supporting material. The following example is an effective review:

> I have explained how lack of safe water is detrimental to the human body as well as to communities, and how the nonprofit organization, Living Water, is combatting this problem.

One common strategy is to combine your signal with your summary, as this example shows:

> In conclusion, [phrase signaling the end] hovercraft are low-friction machines, but noise pollution, steering problems, and their inability to climb hills keep them from being street legal[23] [restatement of major points].

Provide Psychological Closure

Linking your conclusion to something from your introduction brings the speech full circle and provides your audience with a sense of psychological closure. Consequently, look in your introduction for something that you could repeat at the end. For instance, if you began with an example, you might return to it in the conclusion. Or you could refer to startling statistics or to quotations you presented in the opening. Here's how Bonita began and ended her speech:[24]

> *Opening.* On July 3, 2003, a man and his family are driving their van down the road as it is getting light. An oncoming driver has been driving since midnight; he tries to pass a bus but fails to see the van coming toward him. Because he is tired, the would-be passer cannot react quickly enough to slide back into his own lane, and his car collides head-on with the van, killing the woman in the passenger seat.

> *Ending.* I myself will avoid driving while tired because the woman who was killed in the van that July morning was my mom. Next time you drive, consider those in the cars around you and think of whose friend, mother, sister, or brother they are. Do you really want others to go through pain and suffering simply so you can get to your destination a little earlier?

You can access the entire text of this speech on your online resources and also watch her deliver the speech as well.

A good introduction and conclusion are like bookends that hold the main points of the speech together.[25]

© Studio DMM Photography, Designs & Art /Shutterstock.com

End Memorably

Plan your final statement carefully so that you leave a positive and memorable impression. Here are a few guidelines:

- Many of the strategies for gaining audience attention—such as rhetorical questions, use of quotations or examples, and use of humor—are similarly effective for concluding with impact.
- Consider using parallel construction. That is, if you began with a story, end with a story; if you began with a rhetorical question, end with a rhetorical question, and so on. Not only is this effective, but it is another way to provide psychological closure.
- In persuasive speeches, it's common to issue a challenge and call people to action.
- Commemorative speakers typically conclude by reinforcing a larger cultural theme or value.

Elisia Choi (see Chapter 9) emphasizes the importance of the ending statement:[26]

> I spend a significant amount of time thinking about my concluding statement. Many speakers often don't think about what their last sentence will be and as a result, end their speeches abruptly. I try to set myself apart by making sure my last sentence is powerful, memorable, and impactful.

These three examples show effective conclusions for an informative, persuasive, and commemorative speech:

Informative purpose. Homelessness affects thousands of people in Portland, and Nightstrike is an organization that deals with this issue in the way their motto states: Loving People Because People Matter.[27]

Persuasive purpose. Our media daily bombards us with perceptions of beauty that is unhealthy, unethical, and unrecognizably deceitful—not to mention unattainable. If a picture is worth a thousand words, let's not allow media to fill our minds with thousands of far-fetched lies. Instead, let's be conscious consumers of media who expose media images for what they truly are and who value the beauty of everyday people.[28]

Commemorative purpose [university convocation].[29] In Shel Silverstein's *The Giving Tree*, we are told that by the end the tree had given the boy everything and had been reduced to just a stump. We are also told five times in the short book that the tree was happy; we are never told the boy was happy. The moral of the story is a simple one. If you want to be happy, be the tree.

In summary, a good conclusion provides a transition, summarizes your major points, gains psychological closure, and closes with a thought-provoking statement. Study some of the speeches and outlines in Appendix B and your online resources and notice the different and creative ways that students memorably end their speeches.

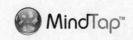

Summary

After you've organized the body of your speech, plan an introduction that will take your listeners from their various internal worlds and move them into the world of your speech. Do this by gaining their attention, relating your topic to their concerns, establishing your credibility on the subject, and previewing your main points. Finally, plan a conclusion that provides a transition from the body, summarizes your major points, gives a sense of closure by referring back to the introduction, and leaves your listeners with a challenge or a memorable thought.

STUDY AND REVIEW

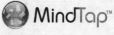

Reflect on what you've learned.

Public Speaking: Concepts and Skills for a Diverse Society offers a broad range of resources that will help you better understand the material in this chapter, complete assignments, and succeed on tests. Your MindTap resources feature the following:

- Speech videos with viewing questions, speech outlines, and transcripts
- Activities to help you check your understanding and to apply what you've learned to your own life
- Stop and Check and Critical Thinking exercises
- Outline Builder
- Web Links related to chapter content
- Study and review tools such as self-quizzes and an interactive glossary

You can access your online resources for *Public Speaking: Concepts and Skills for a Diverse Society* at cengagebrain.com using the access code that came with your book or that you purchased online.

KEY TERMS

Review your Flashcards.

The terms below are defined in the margins throughout this chapter.

participatory question 127
rhetorical question 127

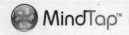

CRITICAL THINKING QUESTIONS

1. Outline a speech given by one of your classmates. Evaluate the effectiveness of the introduction and conclusion. What suggestions, if any, would you give the speaker to improve the beginning or the ending?

2. Review the section on credibility—what your audience thinks of you—in Chapter 6. How and why do a good introduction and conclusion affect your audience's perception of your credibility? How and why do a poor start or finish influence their perception?

3. Read the introductions and conclusions of some speeches you find on your online resources. Evaluate them using the criteria in the text. Does the introduction gain attention, link to the audience, establish credibility, and preview the major points? Does the speaker provide a transition to the conclusion? Review the major points? Provide psychological closure? End memorably? What improvements, if any, would you suggest?

4. Search the Internet for the exact phrase "introductions and conclusions." You should find many sites that were created by both writing and speech instructors. Go to a site for writers, and compare and contrast the guidelines there with the guidelines for speakers that you find in this text. What are the similarities? The differences? How do you account for the differences?

APPLICATION QUESTIONS

1. Before your next speech, partner with someone in your class. Trade outlines and, using the guidelines in this chapter, evaluate each other's introduction and conclusion. Advise your partner on what you think is effective and what could be improved. When you get your own outline and suggestions back, make adjustments that would improve these sections of your speech.

2. Work with a small group of your classmates and create several ways to gain attention for one of the following topics: The most student-friendly restaurants in your town, student loan debt, prescription drug overdose, or ocean pollution.

3. With a small group of students, plan a way to gain attention, relate to the audience, and establish your credibility on one of these topics: the drawbacks of competitive sports for children, eating disorders, vaccinations, how to write a résumé.

THIS CHAPTER WILL HELP YOU

- Outline your speech content in a linear form

- Create a heading that summarizes what you plan to accomplish in your speech

- Use standard outlining features including coordination, subordination, indentation, alternation, and full sentences

- Prepare note cards or a speaking outline

- Know how to record your ideas using an alternative pattern

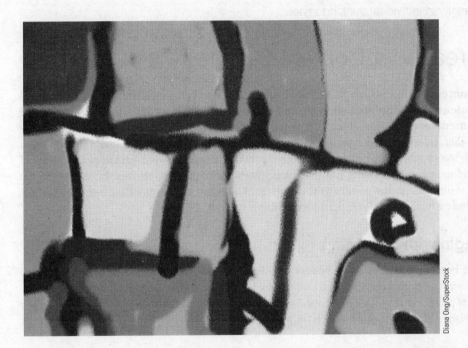

Diana Ong/SuperStock

Outlining Your Speech

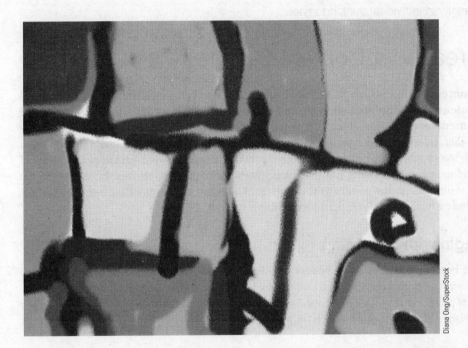

MindTap
Review the chapter learning Objectives and Start with a quick warm-up activity.

ALTHOUGH YOU may wonder, "Why should I write an outline. I'm preparing a speech, not writing an essay," your instructor has good reasons for requiring you to write out your ideas and their relationship to one another. As one student put it in a semester after she'd taken the class:

> The organizational skills I learned in communication class have been valuable tools in several areas. Not only did learning how to outline allow me to develop clear, focused speeches, but it also helps in organizing and focusing papers and presentations in all my classes.

Although this chapter presents tips for creating full-sentence content outlines and speaking notes, experienced speakers know there's no single way to outline a speech correctly, and there's no set length for an outline. Many factors go into shaping your final product, including the type of speech, the circumstances, and the time limitations. The more speeches you give, the more you'll work out your own method for ordering your ideas, given your individual learning preferences. This chapter explains some foundational outlining principles, followed by a description of how to prepare speaking notes. It concludes with ideas for alternative, more visual methods of recording your ideas that take into account diversity in individual thinking styles.

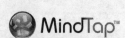

Read, *highlight, and take notes online.*

content outline formal record of your major ideas and their relationship to one another in your speech

structural elements a speech's introduction, body, and conclusion

logical elements a speech's major ideas with supporting materials and their relationship

script the written text containing every word of the speech

Creating a Content Outline

A **content outline** accomplishes two major purposes: (1) it shows the speech's **structural elements**—the introduction, body, and conclusion, and (2) it shows the speech's **logical elements**—the major ideas, the supporting materials, and their relationship to one another. In contrast to a **script** where you write out every word you say, it's more like a skeleton or a blueprint of your ideas that provides the framework for the points you will develop as you talk. Using full sentences instead of fragments ensures that all your ideas are visible and helps you learn the content. Common elements of outline preparation include a heading and standard formatting features.

Begin with a Heading

The heading provides a brief overview of your entire speech. Include the *title*, *general purpose*, *specific purpose*, finalized *central idea* or *thesis statement*, *preview*, and the *organizational pattern* that you've developed using principles found in Chapters 5 and 9. Here is Chelsea's heading for her speech on political campaigns:[1]

Topic:	Political campaigns
General Purpose:	To inform
Specific Purpose:	To inform my audience about four major elements in a political campaign and give examples for each.
Central Idea/Thesis:	Political campaigns typically incorporate four major elements designed to win a political office.
Preview:	The four main parts of a campaign involve money, endorsements, debates, and physical campaigning.
Organizational Pattern:	Topical

Use Standard Formatting

Four features—*alternation* and *indentation* combined with *coordination* and *subordination*—make visible your speech's structural and logical interrelationships.

Alternation and Indentation

alternation varying numbers and letters in a consistent pattern for different levels of points

indentation formatting by spacing various levels of points toward the right

Alternation means you vary numbers and letters, using a consistent pattern. Use Roman numeral (I, II, III,...) for your main points, a capital letter (A, B, C,...) for first-level supporting points, Arabic numerals (1, 2, 3,...) for second-level support, lowercase letters (a, b, c,...) for third-level supporting points, and so on. Also use **indentation** to space various levels of supporting points toward the right and additionally show interrelationships among materials. That is, begin your I- and II-level points at the left margin, but indent

Credit © Tim Timmerman

An outline is like a skeleton that provides a framework for you to flesh out your ideas.

your A and B headings to the right. Then space your third-level supporting points even further right, and so on. This partial outline shows alternation and indentation:

I. US ideologies of beauty are affecting the world.[2]
   A. Many Asian women seek out a surgery called blepharoplasty.
      1. Almost half of all eastern Asians are born with no eyelid crease.
         a. Many Asian women desire a crease.
            1. They think it is more attractive.
            2. A crease makes it easier to apply eye makeup.
         b. However, 25-year-old Tina Quak states, "I think it's a Western idea" (Yee, 2008).
      2. A one-hour surgery can create a crease.
   B. Skin bleaching products are also common.
II. One major cause is standardization of advertising across media....

(*Note:* Some instructors prefer that you use Roman numerals to label your introduction, body, and conclusion and then adjust the labeling of points accordingly.)

Coordination and Subordination

Coordination means that you give each major point the same basic value or weight, you weigh second-level and third-level points similarly, and so on. The word **subordination** has two Latin roots: *sub* (under) and *ordinare* (to place in order). All first-level points go *under* the major points they support; all second-level points go *under* the first-level points they support, and so on. The following outline shows two major points: problem and solution. Subordinated underneath them are the first-level points, causes and effects, which are coordinated approximately equally. (For purposes of illustration, this outline shows third-level points under the first cause only.)

coordination arranging points into levels, giving the points on a specific level the same basic value or weight

subordination placement of supporting points under major points

I. Problem
  A. Causes
    1. First Cause
    2. Second Cause

I. Individuals who are mentally ill don't always get the care they need.[3]
  A. There are several causes for this.
    1. Psychiatric institutions have closed.
    2. Other treatments lack funding.

B. Effects

    1. First Effect

    2. Second Effect

       a. Support

       b. Support

II. Solution

  A. First Solution

  B. Second Solution

B. Many people with mental illness end up on the streets.

    1. They cause on-the-street disturbances.

    2. They often land in costlier jails.

       a. This costs $300–400 per day.

       b. Case workers would be cheaper.

II. Solutions are both national and personal.

  A. Increasing community support for individuals with mental illness would solve some problems.

  B. Personally, we can become aware and support mental health funding with votes.

In summary, during your speech preparation, create an outline that begins with a heading and uses a standard format that includes coordinated points with subordinated supporting materials, arranged by alternating letters and numbers and by indenting material in a way that shows the relationship of ideas to one another.

Leif's complete content outline, shown below with commentary, pulls all these elements together and provides a model and an explanation of his strategies. As you study his outline, notice that it does not read like a speech script. Instead of putting in each word he'll say, he writes out a sentence that summarizes the contents of each point. He also cites the author and date of specific supporting information in the outline itself; at the end, he lists his references in the format required by his instructor.

Student Speech Outline with Commentary

NO-WHEELED CAR OR DRY BOAT?[4]

By Leif Nordstrom

Topic:	Hovercraft
General Purpose:	To inform
Specific Purpose:	As a result of my speech, my audience will understand how a hovercraft works, tell some advantages and drawbacks, and know why these vehicles are not street legal.
Central Idea/Thesis:	Although hovercraft are environmentally friendly all-terrain vehicles with many uses, their drawbacks keep them from being street legal.
Preview:	I will discuss how a hovercraft works, describe some positive aspects, and explain why they are not street legal.
Organizational Pattern:	Topical

By writing out the heading, Leif makes sure his speech focus is clear and that his outline will accomplish his stated purposes.

Introduction

I. According to my survey, 72% of you say you've never seen a hovercraft.

II. You may think of this [display image of the *Jetsons'* spacecraft] when you hear "hovercraft" and you think they fly in the air.

  A. Here's a clip of a real hovercraft [10-second clip].

  B. They're classified as watercraft, although they're all-terrain vehicles.

Identify your speech introduction, body, and conclusion. This introduction gains attention, relates to the audience, establishes credibility, and previews major points.

III. My senior year of high school, I personally built a hovercraft [two photos] because I wanted to experiment with the engineering.

IV. I will discuss how these vehicles work, some positive aspects about them, and what keeps them from being street legal.

Body

I. Hovercrafts are a physicist's dream.
  A. [I will draw a diagram and explain the base, skirt, ground, housing for the propeller, the propeller itself and the duct.]
    1. A common misconception is that a propeller on the ground creates lift.
    2. Instead, a single propeller on the top pushes air into a duct that enters the base area, builds up air pressure, and creates a cushion of air.
    3. This air cushion overcomes the craft's weight.
  B. Physicists love hovercraft because there's minimal friction on the ground.

II. Hovercrafts have many positive features.
  A. They are unique all-terrain vehicles [display photo].
    1. They are mostly used on water.
    2. They can also go on sand, ice, grass, dirt, or relatively flat pavement.
  B. According to discoverhover.org. (2004), most hovercraft are used as rescue vehicles, especially over thin ice and hazardous terrain.
    1. They exert minimal pressure on the surface, which keeps the rescue crew out of the water (Fitzgerald, 2004).
    2. The ice in this photo [display ice rescue photo] is so thin that the weight of another vehicle would crack it.
  C. Hovercraft have environmental benefits.
    1. Their small engines use less fuel; many of you said you value fuel-efficiency.
    2. They exert only 0.33 pound per square inch of pressure, which makes them easy on the environment.
      a. This is 1/30 of a human's footprint pressure (Fitzgerald, 2004).
      b. Just standing on a beach, the average person exerts 3 pounds per square inch (Ernst, n.d.).
      c. During walking, the average jumps to 25 pounds per square inch (Ernst, n.d.).
      d. Hovercraft could drive over you and not hurt you.
  D. Hovercraft are very safe.
    1. I know from experience that, in a collision, they generally bounce off obstacles and inflict no damage to the ground (Borough, 2012).
    2. Finally, Borough (2012) says there is not a single recorded injury in the United States in over 40 years.
Transition: Now that you know a little bit about hovercraft and their benefits, let's discuss three reasons why they are not street legal.

III. Three factors keep hovercraft from being street legal.
  A. They create noise pollution.
    1. During one experience, I couldn't hear my own voice over the engine.
    2. The noise comes from turbulence off the propeller blades (think: helicopter noise), but newer technology is helping somewhat (Hover-Gen, 2010).
  B. They are extremely hard to control.
    1. You cannot turn them.
      a. On the show *Top Gear* the quote was, "If you can see it, you're too late to turn" (BBC, Australia, n.d.).
      b. Because it has no grip, you must deal with airflow by power sliding every corner and swinging the back around.
    2. Another problem is stopping; most have no braking system.
      a. You have to turn the vehicle around against its own inertia.

Point IV is his preview, the transition between the speech introduction and body. It tells the audience to listen for topically organized information.

Leif labels the body of his speech, and he uses the principle of coordination. Points I, II, and III are first-level points that are made up of second-, third-, and fourth-level supporting materials. Second- and third-level supporting points are subordinated by indentation and alternating numbers and letters.

All points are phrased as declarative sentences, one sentence per point.

He cites the author or source and date beside the material it supports.

Subpoints A through D are first-level points, 1 and 2 are second-level supporting points, and a and b are third-level supporting points.

This is the separation point leading to his final point, so Leif writes out a transition.

b. Another way is to shut down the engine and grind the bottom, which I do but don't recommend.

c. Companies like neoteric have figured out a braking system, but brakes are not common (Neoteric, 2012).

3. Most importantly, they are not street legal because they can't climb hills—which goes back to physics.

  a. You have an incline [draw on whiteboard].

    i. The lack of friction increases the amount of force needed to go up an incline, force they don't have.

    ii. In contrast, the cars we drive have grips on the tires plus momentum to keep them on the road.

  b. Finally, roads are raised slightly in the center [illustrate with hand] to let the water run off to the side.

    i. A hovercraft going down a paved road would have to angle toward the center all the way.

    ii. That would be hard to do.

By setting apart the conclusion, he makes sure that he's crafted a memorable ending that summarizes the speech and is both purposeful and brief.

Conclusion

I. In conclusion...

II. Hovercraft are low-friction machines with several advantages, but noise pollution, steering and brake problems, and hills keep them from being street legal.

III. The next time you hear the term *all-terrain vehicle*, you can talk about the "real" ATV.

IV. It's not from the *Jetsons*, but it is, in fact, a real-live hovercraft.

Leif formats his references in the American Psychological Association (APA) style. Ask your instructor which format he or she prefers, but always list the references you consulted during your speech preparation.

Sources:

BBC Australia. (2010). Hovercraft van, part 4. *Top Gear*, Season 20, Episode 2. Retrieved from http://www.topgear.com/au/videos/2002-7

Borough, P. (2010). 10 common questions about hovercraft. Retrieved from http://www.peterboroughhovercraft.com/ARTICLE10questions.htm

Instead of writing his notes on index cards, Leif could take advantage of the "click to add notes" feature on PowerPoint. He sees the notes; the audience does not.

My Hovercraft

Source: Leif Nordstrom

Positive features

    unique ATVs   mostly water

Also   sand   ice   grass   dirt   flat pavement

Ernst, M. (2010). Hovercraft: Material to accompany activity. Graduate Fellows Program, University of North Carolina at Wilmington. Retrieved from http://uncw.edu/smec/gk_fellows/Documents/HovercraftReference.pdf

Fitzgerald, C. (2004). About hovercraft: Hovercraft faq. Retrieved from http://www.discoverhover.org/abouthovercraft/faq.htm

Hamilton, B. (2012, February 21). Personal interview.

Hover-Gen. (2010). Hovercraft and the environment. Retrieved from http://www.hover-gen.com/hovercraft-and-the-environment/

hovpod. (Producer). (2006). Hovercraft [Web video]. Retrieved from http://www.youtube.com/watch?v=zp9q_2uIk-M

Janovich, A. (2011, June 8). WV senior crafts his future plans. *Yakima Herald-Republic*. Retrieved from http://www.yakima-herald.com/stories/2011/06/08/wv-senior-crafts-his-future-plans/print

Kemp, P. (Ed.). (2006). Hovercraft. In *Oxford Companion to Ships and the Sea*. Retrieved from http://www.encyclopedia.com

Neoteric. (2012). The history of Neoteric, Hovercraft, Inc. Retrieved from http://www.neoterichovercraft.com/about_neoteric/company_history_2010-2019.htm

Creating Speaking Notes

Your content outline provides a permanent written record that you can file away after you speak. It's also useful during rehearsal to run through and get your speech firmly in mind. However, content outlines differ from **speaking notes**—what you actually use when you deliver the speech. Create these notes by using **key words**, including just enough phrases or words to jog your memory as you speak. Use full sentences only for transition statements, direct quotations, and complicated statistics. This section describes two major formats for speaking notes: notes and speaking outlines.

speaking notes the notes you use to deliver your speech

key words important words and phrases that will jog the speaker's memory

Speaking Notes

Earlier editions of this text described written notes on index cards. Small note cards are not outdated; however, today's speakers also write notes on their cell phones or on small tablet computers. Some use presentation software such as Prezi or PowerPoint as their notes. (PowerPoint has space under each slide for your notes.) Here are some general tips for speaking notes:

- Delete nonessential words—use only key, or significant, words and short phrases.
- Highlight important concepts or words you want to emphasize during delivery.
- Include source information so that you can cite those sources as you speak.
- Add delivery advice such as *pause* or *slow down*.
- Practice in front of a mirror using your notes. Revise them if they are not as helpful as you would like.

    Tips specifically for note cards include:

- Write legibly.
- Number your cards so you can quickly put them in place if they get out of order.
- Write on only one side because turning cards over can be distracting.
- Use no more than five or six lines per card, and space your lines so that you can easily keep your place.
- For longer speeches, use more cards instead of crowding additional information onto a few cards.
- During your speech, use your cards unobtrusively. Place them on the lectern if one is available, and never wave them.
- Don't read from your cards unless you are reading a direct quotation or giving complicated statistics; then hold up a card and look at it frequently to show your audience that you are being as accurate as possible.[5]

    Figure 11.1 shows two note cards for Leif's speech on hovercraft.

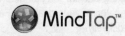

Figure 11.1
Speaking Note Cards Your note cards are a highly individualized set of key term cards that will jog *your* memory.

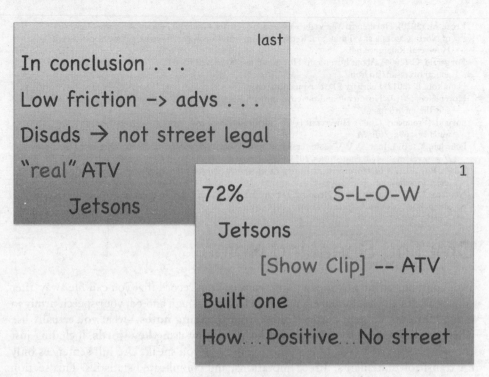

last

In conclusion . . .

Low friction -> advs . . .

Disads → not street legal

"real" ATV

Jetsons

1

72%   S-L-O-W

Jetsons

[Show Clip] -- ATV

Built one

How...Positive...No street

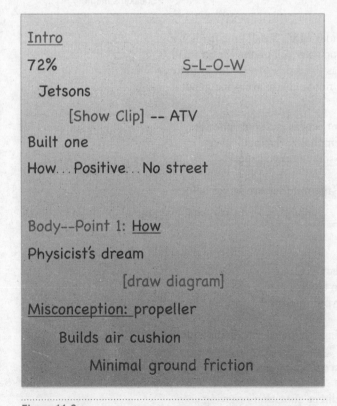

Intro

72%   S-L-O-W

Jetsons

[Show Clip] -- ATV

Built one

How...Positive...No street

Body--Point 1: How

Physicist's dream

[draw diagram]

Misconception: propeller

Builds air cushion

Minimal ground friction

Figure 11.2
Speaking Outline On standard-sized paper, write key words to remind you of your ideas plus "advice" words to remind you of your delivery.

Speaking Outlines

Another strategy is to write key terms from your outline on a standard sheet of paper. Figure 11.2 shows the first page of a speaking outline. Many of the tips for creating note cards apply to this format, but there are some minor differences:

- Use plenty of space to distinguish between the various sections of your speech.
- Use highlighter pens to distinguish the sections easily. For example, you might underline signposts and transition statements in orange and use yellow to emphasize the introduction, the body, and the conclusion.
- Use different font sizes and formatting features to break up visual monotony and to direct your eyes to specific places as you go along. For example, you might use indentation, color, or alternated lower-case and capitalized words.
- If you have several sheets of notes, spread them across the lectern in such a way that you can still see the side edges of the lower pages. Then when you move from one page to another, slip the top sheet off unobtrusively and tuck it at the bottom of the pile.
- If no lectern is available, you can place your pages in a dark-colored notebook or folder that you hold with one hand while gesturing with the other. (Angle the notebook so your audience won't see your pages.)

Speaking outlines help you maintain eye contact with the audience, secure in the knowledge that if you lose your train of thought, you can glance at your notes to regain your place.

To understand the different functions of these outlines, study this section excerpted from Leif's content outline, his speaking notes, and the speech itself. Each format includes source citations:

From his content outline:

    D. Hovercraft are very safe.
        1. I know from experience that, in a collision, they generally bounce off obstacles and inflict no damage to the ground (Borough, 2012).
        2. Finally, Borough (2012), a small company, says there is not a single recorded injury in the United States in over 40 years.

From his speaking notes:

> **Finally** ... safety
> ... bounce ... <u>no ground damage</u>
> <u>describe personal experience</u>
>   **ZERO injuries** in 40 years (Borough 2012)

From the speech itself: (*Note:* In extemporaneous delivery, wording will vary somewhat each time.)

> Hovercraft are also very safe because they're not hitting on the ground at all. If you have a collision, generally you'll bounce off of whatever you hit. [slight pause] I hit a few things on my hovercraft and I wasn't strapped in—there was no strap—so I flipped forward a little bit, but the hovercraft itself wasn't damaged. According to Borough, a small hovercraft company, there have been no recorded injuries in the United States for forty years due to hovercraft, which speaks to its safety record.

Individual Cognitive Preferences

DIVERSITY
IN PRACTICE

Diversity takes into account differences in **cognitive preferences** or thinking styles. Because each of us has a distinctive thinking style, every classroom contains "a diverse population of learners."[6] Your thinking style comprises the ways you typically prefer to perceive, reason, remember, and solve problems. Culture and technology influence cognitive styles to an extent, but the way you process information is unique to you.[7]

Research into brain hemispheric dominance discovered that our right brains process information more globally, intuitively, and artistically, whereas our left-brain processes are more linear, analytic, logical, and computational.[8] We have "intelligence preferences," our inborn predispositions to prefer particular ways of thinking, including analytical (schoolhouse type), practical (street-smart, contextual), and creative (imaginative, problem solving).[9] Cognitive researchers recognize the value of a whole brain approach that gravitates toward our preferences but flexes as the situation demands.[10]

This is not a cognitive science text; however, diversity of cognitive preferences and the fact that they reflect both a personal and a cultural orientation fit the emphasis of this book.

(continued)

cognitive preferences the way you prefer to perceive, reason, remember, and solve problems; it's culturally influenced but unique to you

Why include this topic in an outlining chapter? Because the linear pattern described here and in most public speaking texts is a more left-brained, analytical way to frame a speech, which may or may not match your intellectual preferences. Although you may be assigned such an outline, your personal style may be more holistic or creative; consequently, when you organize speeches in other contexts, you may prefer alternative, more visual ways of showing your points. Either way, the key is to ensure that your speeches are structured and your ideas have a logical connection.

How to Create an Alternative Pattern

Diversity in Practice: Individual Cognitive Preferences points out that your cognitive preferences may lean toward more visual or imagistic thinking. Consequently, you might prefer an alternative pattern, such as the wave, spiral, or star, described in Chapter 9. If so, your depiction of your speech's content will be less conventional, but you can still design an appropriate representation of your ideas and their relationship to one another by using the tips provided here:[11]

* First, select an appropriate pattern and sketch the diagram.
* With your pattern in mind, write out your main points.
* Next, indicate what you'll use for developmental material and subordinate this material under the main point it supports.
* Indicate how you plan to begin and end your speech, and then write out key transition statements.
* Use standard indentation and numbering only if it's helpful.

Mark Antony's dramatic speech from Shakespeare's play, *Julius Caesar*, features a wave pattern. Figure 11.3 shows how to format it. Antony used a recurring theme, "The

Figure 11.3
Using an Alternate Pattern
This figure depicts the points in Mark Antony's speech visualized in a wave format.

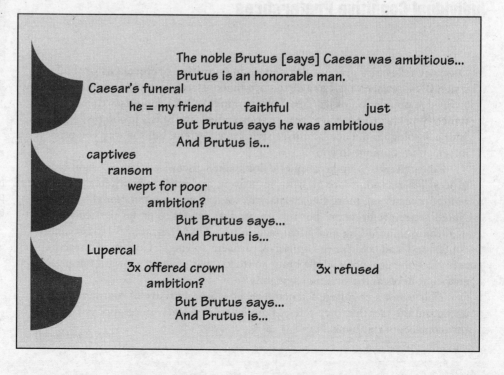

The noble Brutus [says] Caesar was ambitious...
Brutus is an honorable man.
Caesar's funeral
he = my friend   faithful   just
But Brutus says he was ambitious
And Brutus is...
captives
ransom
wept for poor
ambition?
But Brutus says...
And Brutus is...
Lupercal
3x offered crown   3x refused
ambition?
But Brutus says...
And Brutus is...

noble Brutus says Caesar was ambitious…Brutus is an honorable man." (You can watch this speech on YouTube by searching for "Mark Antony's Speech." Watch the 1953 version starring Marlon Brando.)

Summary

As part of the speech-making process, it's important to understand and show the ways that your points and subpoints relate to one another. Consequently, instructors typically ask you to show your ideas in a linear outline that alternates letters and numbers and uses indentation for subpoints. These features coordinate your main points and subordinate your supporting materials under them. Write your content outline in full sentences, and include a list of references at the end.

However, don't read your content outline when you speak. Instead, use note cards or a key word outline to help you remember your main points but prevent you from reading your speech verbatim. Content outlines differ from speaking notes or speaking outlines and from what you actually say in the speech.

A linear outline is not the only way to record your ideas; in fact, one way to recognize diversity is to admit that people with various learning styles may actually benefit from using an alternative, more visual way to record speech content. If you have the opportunity to choose an alternative pattern, first sketch out a simple diagram and then arrange your major ideas and supporting materials around it.

STUDY AND REVIEW

Reflect on what you've learned.

Public Speaking: Concepts and Skills for a Diverse Society offers a broad range of resources that will help you better understand the material in this chapter, complete assignments, and succeed on tests. Your MindTap resources feature the following:

- Speech videos with viewing questions, speech outlines, and transcripts
- Activities to help you check your understanding and to apply what you've learned to your own life
- Stop and Check and Critical Thinking exercises
- Outline Builder
- Web Links related to chapter content
- Study and review tools such as self-quizzes and an interactive glossary

You can access your online resources for *Public Speaking: Concepts and Skills for a Diverse Society* at cengagebrain.com using the access code that came with your book or that you purchased online.

KEY TERMS

*Review your **Flashcards**.*

The terms below are defined in the margins throughout this chapter.

alternation 138
cognitive preferences 145
content outline 138
coordination 139
indentation 138
key words 143

logical elements 138
script 138
speaking notes 143
structural elements 138
subordination 139

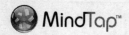

CRITICAL THINKING EXERCISES

1. To understand how to adapt outlines for situations outside the classroom, visit the online resources. This online guide to public speaking and presentation skills that shows the general framework for outlines could be used in a scientific conference talk, a community association meeting, and a business proposal to investors. How are these outlines similar to and different from the content outlines described in this chapter? Why do you think this is so?

2. Go to your online resources to watch and critique two student speeches of your choice. Your online resources include the transcript, outline, and video of each speech. Evaluate how the speaker uses speaking notes.

APPLICATION EXERCISES

1. Outline a speech while one of your classmates delivers it. After the speech, give the outline to the speaker, and ask him or her to check its contents for completeness and faithfulness to the intended structure and contents.

2. Using the same outline, ask another student to evaluate your formatting—use of indentation, alternating numbers and letters, complete sentences, and the like.

3. Work with another person in your class and create speaking notes for one of the speeches or outlines in Appendix B.

4. Before you give your next speech, work from your content outline to prepare a speaking outline. Let a classmate evaluate both outlines and make revisions that would improve either one or both.

5. Experienced speakers do not always prepare a content outline like Leif Nordstrom's, complete with heading and references. Ask your instructor to describe how she or he outlines lectures, informal talks, and speeches to groups outside the classroom.

Diana Ong/SuperStock

THIS CHAPTER WILL
HELP YOU

• Explain how words are linked to culture and meaning

• Understand the denotative meaning of words including jargon

• Define connotative meanings of words including epithets and euphemisms

• Distinguish between the oral and written style in language

• Choose language that is concise, familiar, concrete, repetitive, vivid, powerful, and appropriate

• Use ethical language that is inclusive and positive about groups and individuals

• Give guidelines for listening and speaking in linguistically diverse contexts

Choosing Effective Language

MindTap
iew the
oter
rning
ectives
Start
a quick
m-up
ity.

LANGUAGE CONVEYS MORE than just ideas. The words you use also provide clues about your region of origin, age, educational level, income level, sex, ethnicity, and occupation—even if you're all speaking "American." For example:

• *Regional diversity:* A "dust bunny" can be a "dust kitty" (in the Northeast), a "woolie" (in areas of Pennsylvania), or "house moss" (in the South). *The Dictionary of American Regional English* identified 174 terms for those little wads of dust under your furniture.[1]

• *Occupational diversity:* Lawyers write, "This agreement to arbitrate is not a prerequisite to healthcare or treatment."[1] However, a caseworker would more likely say, "You don't have to sign this to get treatment."[2]

- *Cultural and gender diversity:* Across many cultures, women use more polite and precise forms of speech than men do. In some languages, such as Japanese, women and men use different words for some of the same objects.[3]

In the study of rhetoric, language falls within the *canon of style*, which is the focus of this chapter. First, it looks at ways our vocabularies both reveal and express cultural assumptions. Next, it provides tips for effective language choices in public speeches. Finally, it discusses language issues in linguistically diverse settings.

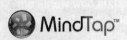

Read, *highlight, and take notes online.*

language verbal code consisting of symbols that a speech community uses for communication

word verbal symbol that stands for or represents an idea

Languages and Culture

Languages are systems of verbal symbols that members of a speech community use to share ideas. Some symbols are visual; for instance, a country's flag stands for that country. But more commonly we use verbal symbols or **words** to express cultural ideas. Co-cultures often use both the larger culture's vocabulary and terminology that is unique to their group.

Words and Meaning

Think of words as the names we give our "cultural memories." They serve as "markers of cultural attention"[4] or of shared experiences we consider significant enough to name. The theorist Kenneth Burke explains that when we learn to "name," we assume a perspective on the world[5] because our labels form our social realities.

For example, English has many time-related words such as *hours, minutes, milliseconds, tomorrow,* and *eternity*; in contrast, the Hopi language has no word that means *later*.[6] This suggests that English-speaking cultures are much more time conscious than Hopi culture.

Cultural changes bring about linguistic changes. The *Oxford English Dictionary* updates four times a year and recently added or revised 900 words including *bestie* and *bookaholic*.[7] In the last few decades *gridlock, serial killer, microchip,* and *junk food* reflected cultural changes. In basketball, *slam dunk* and *air ball* became common terms.[8] When your grandparents were growing up, microchips or slam dunks or junk food didn't exist or weren't important enough to name.[9] Languages also change over time, as you notice every time you read a Shakespearean play. Without footnotes, the archaic words are difficult to understand.

Because both the words *range* and *open* are ambiguous, they each have several meanings. Substituting one meaning for another can be humorous.

Denotative Meanings

The **denotative meaning**—the meaning you find in a dictionary—is what the word names or identifies. **Ambiguous words**, by definition, have more than one meaning, For instance, the word *range* could denote many things:

- A vocal *range*
- A mountain *range*
- A shooting *range*
- An electric *range* for cooking

- A *range* of activities
- Home on the *range*[10]

denotative meaning what a word names or identifies

The word's context helps you discern the meaning. As you plan language for your speech, choose the correct word for the correct context to denote your intended meaning. Consult a dictionary or thesaurus if you are unsure.

ambiguous words identify more than one object or idea; its meaning depends on the context

Increasing your vocabulary and discriminating among shades of meaning between words are valuable skills, because a larger vocabulary enables you to communicate your thoughts more precisely. Check your vocabulary prowess by searching the Internet for the list of 100 words that every high school graduate should know. (It's challenging!)

Jargon denotes specialized, technical language that serves special groups (doctors, lawyers), interests (feminism, education), activities (football, gardening), and so on. For example, football has specialized meanings for *drive*, *down*, and *safety*. When everyone in your audience knows the meaning of the jargon, it's appropriate to use it. However, when you're communicating with nonspecialists, you should define and clarify technical terms to include all your listeners.

jargon a specialized, technical vocabulary that serves the interests and activities of a particular group

Connotative Meanings

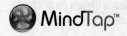

Connotative meanings are the emotional overtones the words carry. That is, words represent feelings and associations related to the ideas they denote. For instance, *chocolate* is not just a food produced from cacao seeds (denotative meaning); it can connote romance or dietary temptation, depending on the individual. Because language is often emotionally charged, people sometimes choose negatively loaded words to demean persons or ideas, or they substitute neutral or positive terms to talk about unpopular ideas.

connotative meanings emotional overtones, related feelings, and associations that cluster around a word

Epithets are words or phrases, often with negative connotations, that describe some quality of a person or a group. For example, politicians use terms such as *flip-flopper* or *corporate welfare* because opinion polls show that voters respond negatively to those terms. Words like *Bible-thumper*, *tree hugger*, or *nerd* are negative epithets used to frame perceptions about these groups. Calling anti-abortion advocates *anti-choice* creates a negative image, whereas the group's self-chosen title, *pro-life*, has positive connotations.

epithet word or phrase with a powerful negative connotation, used to describe some quality of a person or group

Groups or individuals targeted with an epithet sometimes try to lessen the negative effect by accepting and using the term themselves. For example, opponents of the Affordable Care Act labeled it *Obamacare*, hoping to create negative associations. However, President Obama confronted this term directly, "I have no problem with people saying 'Obama cares.' I do care."[11]

Euphemisms, in contrast, substitute an agreeable or inoffensive term for a more embarrassing, unpleasant, or offensive word. We commonly use them for things we hesitate to speak about such as bodily functions (*nature is calling*), religion (*the Man Upstairs*), death (*kick the bucket*), or weight (*big-boned*). Euphemisms also mask unpleasant situations such as corporate layoffs. It's supposedly easier to be given a *career change opportunity* or be *outplaced* rather than *fired*.

euphemism word or phrase that substitutes an inoffensive term for a potentially offensive, embarrassing, or unpleasant thing

Public speakers, especially politicians, often use euphemisms for controversial actions, ideas, and policies. Planned tax increases become *membership fees* or *revenue enhancements*. *Enhanced interrogation techniques* is military-speak for torture. Similarly, *shell shock* (World War I) became *combat fatigue* (World War II), which became *post-traumatic stress syndrome* (Vietnam War). Each subsequent term further removes the condition from its cause.[12] Be alert for connotative language. By carefully chosen words, speakers hope to create a desired spin or interpretation. (Learn more about this subject by searching the Internet for the word *euphemisms* or *doublespeak*.)

In summary, languages are systems of symbols—words that denote or stand for ideas and evoke feelings or connotative meanings that differ from person to person.

Carefully choose the correct word for the context. Pay attention to connotative meanings, either positive or negative, that listeners might attach to your words. And adapt your dialect and your jargon to your audience and the occasion. As you do this, you take into account the cultural implications of your language choices.

DIVERSITY IN PRACTICE

dialect a variant form of a language

Standard English the English dialect most commonly used in public speaking and in US institutions

code switching changing from one dialect to another

Dialects

A **dialect** is a variant form of a language that differs in pronunciation, vocabulary, and/or grammar. English dialects include international English, British English, Black English (sometimes called ebonics or African American English—AAE), and a variety of regional and ethnic variations.[13] **Standard English** is most common in education and business in the United States; it is the language of journalists and textbook authors.

If you speak a dialect, you may choose to be bidialectical—using Standard English in public contexts and your dialect around family and friends. This is called **code switching**. For example, Martin Luther King Jr. adapted to various settings, as an excerpt from a biography explains:

> King was … a code switcher who switched in and out of idioms as he moved between black and white audiences. But he also made such moves *within* his black talk and his white talk. … [He was] a man who blended all sorts of oppositions. The key crossings were not just between black and white but between raw and refined, sacred and secular, prophetic and pragmatic. This mixing suggests … a "postethnic" man.[14]

Use Language Effectively

Give your speech in an oral style that fits the context, purpose, subject matter of the speech, and your personality. This section first describes elements of an oral style and then explains several principles in the canon of style that will help you choose language more effectively. It closes by discussing ethical aspects of appropriate language.

Use an Oral Style

James Winans, author of an early speech textbook, cautioned his students, "A speech is not an essay on its hind legs."[15] Written texts are more static; writers choose words carefully and they use more complex words and greater diversity in vocabulary because readers can take their time, stop, look up words, pause to think, read, and reread.[16] A speech, in contrast, is dynamic; it exists in a specific time frame, and words, once uttered, are gone. However, speakers have the advantage of engaging the audience by using gestures, vocal stress, and other nonverbal cues to communicate their ideas.[17] **Oral style** is less formal and more personalized. (Figure 12.1 shows some differences between oral and written style.)

oral style characteristics of spoken language compared to written language

This excerpt from a speech given at the Los Angeles Film Festival by an entertainment CEO showcases oral style. He is developing his first main point: Rule One: Make Smarter Movies![18]

Oral Style	Written Style
Dynamic and interactive	Static
Short, simple, concrete but vivid words	More complex words, greater vocabulary variety
Shorter sentences; fragments acceptable	Longer, more complex and complete sentences
Less formal, more personalized language	More formal, precise language
Repetition of words and ideas	Less repetition; readers can stop, ponder, reread, and look up words
More engaging; speaker adds nonverbal emphasis	Not able to emphasize meanings nonverbally

Figure 12.1
Oral and Written Style[18]

When I started [my company], I told people I wanted to make movies I'd pay to see twice.... Give me movies with stories and ideas that people care about.

You say, yeah, but kids today expect special effects. Well, my kids are 9 and 13. My daughter has watched *Twilight* seven times. It has the worst special effects in the world. The ridiculous way that guy runs looks like the track star with blurry legs in that TV commercial. But does she really care that the special effects in the next *Twilight* movie will be any better?

As if.

What she cares about is that Robert Pattinson fights off the werewolf guy for Kristin Stewart.

This excerpt contains several elements of oral style.[19] The speaker uses fairly short sentences—even fragments, and one sentence starts with *but*. His vocabulary is familiar and concrete and his words paint vivid pictures. He uses personalized language (*you, I*) and repetition. The following section describes several basic principles of effective oral language: be concise, choose familiar words, be concrete, build in repetition, use vivid language, and select an appropriate form.

Be Concise

It's easy to clutter a speech with **verbiage**—nonessential or "filler" words such as *just* and *like* ("Teens need *like* about nine hours of sleep." "All of a sudden it was *just*, *like* quiet.") The phrase *what you want to do* is especially common in demonstration speeches, as this excerpt from a cooking show on television illustrates:

verbiage nonessential language

The cake chef said: "*What you want to do* next is *you want to* take the coffee and pour it over the cake."

He could more concisely say: "Next, pour the coffee over the cake."

Although brevity or conciseness is valued in the United States, many other cultures value flowery language. Consequently, what we may consider verbiage, other groups may regard as essential elements of eloquence. [20]

Use Familiar Words

The purpose of public speaking is to clarify ideas, not make them more confusing. So short, familiar words are part of the oral style. Avoid jargon when you can, but because many topics involve technical terms, you will have to translate jargon terms into understandable English.

For her speech on stem-cell research, Ciara used a variety of simpler words to explain technical terms:[21]

- *Stem cells* (compared to something familiar—a "blank" cell)
- *Blastocyst* (defined five to seven days after conception)
- *Embryonic stem cells* (defined as a cell from a blastocyte's inner mass of cells)
- Pluripotent stem cells (defined as cells that can develop into many types of cells)
- Adult stem cells (defined as derived after birth, including placenta and umbilical cord cells)

It helped to write out the words and display a diagram so listeners could see as well as hear the complex jargon terms.

Be Concrete

concrete word specific, rather than general or abstract, term

Another way to help your listeners form precise understandings is to choose **concrete words** that are specific rather than abstract, particular rather than general. Words range along a scale of abstraction such as this:

abstract/general	animal
	vertebrate
	mammal
	dog
concrete/particular	greyhound

When you say "I adopted a greyhound" your ideas are much more concrete than when you say "I adopted a dog." But that is more concrete than "I adopted an animal."

Specifying greyhound adoption is much more concrete than pet adoption in general.

Clella Jaffe

The more distinct your word choices, the more vivid your images, and the more precise your meanings.

This excerpt from British author Doris Lessing's lecture to the Nobel Peace Prize Committee[22] is exceptional for its use of concrete language:

> [I'm in] northwest Zimbabwe early in the eighties, and I am visiting a friend who was a teacher in a school in London.... [H]is school ... consists of four large brick rooms side by side, put straight into the dust, one two three four, with a half room at one end, which is the library.... [T]here is no atlas, or globe in the school, no textbooks, no exercise books, or biros [ballpoint pens], in the library are no books of the kind the pupils would like to read: they are tomes from American universities, ... rejects from white libraries, detective stories, or with titles like *Weekend in Paris* or *Felicity Finds Love*.

Each carefully chosen word presents concrete sensory imagery that helps you place yourself into the sights and the emotions of the setting.

In contrast, **vague words** are imprecise, with indefinite boundaries. For example, what is *large*? *Small*? Compared to what? A large glass of orange juice is not on the same scale as a large barn. One way to minimize your use of vague words is to choose details that specify or illustrate what you mean. For instance, if you talk about a small inheritance, give a dollar figure that shows how you're defining small. One listener may think $500 is small whereas another has $50,000 in mind.

Build in Repetition

Repetition is common in an oral style. One strategy is to repeat the same word or phrase at the beginning of clauses or sentences. For example, President Reagan's tribute[23] to the space shuttle *Challenger* astronauts included these repetitive phrases: "We will cherish each of their stories, stories of triumph and bravery, stories of true American heroes." Another type of repetition restates the same phrase at the end of a clause or a sentence. Lincoln's famous phrase "government of the people, by the people, for the people" is an example. This excerpt from a commencement address is full of repetition. You can imagine the speaker gesturing, varying his voice, and using effective pauses to drive home his points:[24]

> I came in the house one day when my younger son Asa was playing the piano. Extraordinary piano player. Playing this Rachmaninoff piece. And I stood at— we had this little small house, big grand piano, took up the whole living room. And I stood in the back door. Couldn't see Asa, he was on the other side of the wall. But the whole house was, like, reverberating like this, just reverberating. And I realized as I stood there that the house was not reverberating with the piano. The house was not reverberating with Rachmaninoff. The house was reverberating with Asa. Asa was filling the house. That piano just sits there. Rachmaninoff is just little dots on a piece of paper until he puts his hands on that keyboard and then the music happens.

Speakers often repeat words, but reverse them in a second phrase. (The technical term for this is **antimetabole**.) Some examples include:[25]

The absence of evidence is not *the evidence of absence*. (Carl Sagan, scientist)

I don't throw darts at balloons; I throw balloons at darts. (Joe Montana, quarterback)

Eat to live, not live to eat. (Socrates, philosopher)

President Kennedy's inaugural address, printed in Appendix B, includes several famous examples of antimetabole including, "Ask not what your country can do for you; ask what you can do for your country."

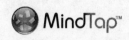
MindTap™

vague word imprecise term that has indefinite boundaries

antimetabole saying words in one phrase, and reversing them in the next phrase

Use Vivid Language

Colorful, vivid language helps keep listeners' attention and interest. Vivid linguistic devices include alliteration, rhyming, metaphors and similes, and personification.

alliteration word with a recurring initial sound

Alliteration is the use of words with the same recurring initial sounds. It can occur within a sentence: one activist wondered what "*t*raits, *t*enacity, and *t*alents" make a good environmentalist?[26] Alliteration is also a good way to help listeners remember main points. This speaker alliterated both the title and the main points in his speech, "What's Promised, What's Possible":[27]

> I'd like to tell you about the five C's of healthcare.... Two of these five C's you already know—cost and coverage. These are the issues we hear about all the time.... And while everyone is talking about the costs of health care and the lack of coverage, meaningful change will only come when we address other issues.

> These are the other 3 C's—the issues we're not hearing about: consistency, complexity, and chronic illness.

rhymes words that end in the same sound

Rhymes—whether single words, longer phrases, or entire lines—are defined as words that end in the same sounds. Although rap artists rhyme their entire presentations, most people use rhymes in more limited ways. In his speech about electronic drums, Bob rhymed three words within one sentence: "What or who would you rather have in your band, a *mean* and *clean* drum *machine* or a stereotypical rock drummer?"

Rhymes are also effective for wording your main points to make them more memorable. Here are two examples:

> We are faced with two choices: retreat or compete.

> Workplaces typically have three generations of employees: boomers, bloomers, and zoomers.[28]

metaphor comparison of two dissimilar things

A **metaphor** compares two dissimilar things without using the words *like* or *as*. To Professor Michael Osborn,[29] speech students are *builders* who frame and craft their speeches, or they're *weavers* who intertwine verbal and nonverbal elements into a successful performance, or they are *climbers* who scramble over barriers or obstacles such as speech anxiety on their way to a successful speech. Each metaphor lends a different perspective to the subject. Which comparison best describes you as a speech student? Can you come up with a better metaphor for speech making?

mixed metaphor combining metaphors from two or more sources, starting with one comparison and ending with another

One hazard in using metaphors is the possibility of creating a **mixed metaphor**, beginning with one comparison and ending with another. To illustrate, one panelist on a news program said, "We must solve the root problem, or the line will be drawn in the sand, and we'll be back in the soup again." Unfortunately, he combined three images, which left his listeners with no clear image of the problem. Should they dig out the root, avoid the line, or stay out of the kitchen?

simile short comparison that uses the word *like* or *as* to compare two items that are alike in one essential detail

Similes, like metaphors, compare two different things that are alike in one essential detail; however, they use *like* or *as* to explicitly state the connection. Here are two examples:

> When we harbor resentment, it's like drinking poison and hoping the other person dies.[30]

> There was a time when our people covered the land as the waves of a wind-ruffled sea cover its shell-paved floor, but that time long since passed away with the greatness of tribes that are now but a mournful memory. (Chief Seattle)[31]

Many metaphors and similes arise from our experiences of being human, and people the world over understand them. For instance, all human groups experience

Archetypal symbols—such as natural phenomena, journeys, sickness and health, and parents and children—are widely used as metaphors by people all over the globe Chief Seattle referred to prairies, storms, rain, and seas in his speeches.

day and night, sickness and health, seasonal changes, natural phenomena, and family relationships. These form the basis for our most fundamental **archetypal symbols**.[32] We refer to the dawn of civilization and to sunset years, to a cancer that destroys our economy and to a healthy marriage. Other common comparisons relate to cultural modes of transportation (the ship of state) to sports (the game of life), and, as the culture changes, to electronic technology (experiencing static, feeling wired).

archetypal symbol recurring metaphor and simile that arises from shared human and natural experiences

Personification means giving human characteristics to nonhuman entities such as animals, countries, natural objects and processes, and social processes. Chief Seattle used personification in an 1853 speech, given before the governor of the Washington Territory:[33]

personification giving human characteristics to nonhuman entities

> Yonder sky that has wept tears of compassion upon my people for centuries untold, and which to us appears changeless and eternal, may change.

Use Appropriate Forms

Generally, language in public settings is more formal, with fewer slang expressions, compared to private settings; however, your audience and the situation should have the final influence over your linguistic choices. For example, the language in a lecture differs from the language in a eulogy. Similarly, you'd use different words and different levels of formality when speaking to teenagers gathered in a park than when addressing members of an alumni association at a formal banquet, even for the same topic.

Use of dialect can be appropriate for some speakers, but not for others. An African American, for instance, might use African American English (AAE) when it's expected and appropriate; however, a Euro-American or an Asian American who used AAE, even in the same setting, would almost certainly be out of line.

Choose Powerful Language[34]

Powerful language is straightforward, direct, and to the point without a lot of hesitations. You want your audience to think you are sure of yourself and sure of your information! However, powerless language can give the impression that you lack confidence in yourself or what you are saying.[35] Here are a few of the most common forms of powerless language in student speeches:

hedges words such as *kinda* or *I think* that can lead listeners to distrust your competence or your knowledge of your topic

- **Hedges** Words called **hedges**, such as *sort of*, *kinda*, *I guess*, or *maybe*, make you seem less sure of yourself.

  - I had a story that I *kinda* wanted to talk about. Last year with my track team, we really had *I guess* one event that didn't go well. (speaker seems unsure of herself)
  - *I think maybe* he went to Yale as a young man. (speaker seems unsure of his material)

tag question short question tagged onto the end of a sentence; some can be helpful but others are annoying

- **Tag Questions** Short questions at the end of a sentence, or **tag questions** (such as *isn't it?* Or *doesn't it?*), invite the audience to agree with your conclusions. They are not always bad, but try to avoid two annoying repetions: *OK?* And *you know?*

disclaimer word or phrase that leads the audience to doubt your competence or expertise

- **Disclaimers** Audiences use **disclaimers** to form doubts about your credibility or your competence on a topic.

  - *I'm no expert on this but …*
  - *This may sound crazy but …*
  - *I don't really know, but I'm guessing that …*

Be sure of your information, and avoid powerless forms of language.

In summary, effective language incorporates an oral style that differs from written language in several important ways. You'll be more effective if you use concise, familiar wording, incorporate repetition and vivid vocabulary, and make sure your language is powerful and appropriate to your personality and the audience, topic, and situation.

Use Language Ethically

Because words and phrases can include or exclude, affirm or dismiss individuals or entire groups, language choices have ethical implications.[36] Emory University's Statement on Inclusive Language recommends, "A recognition of the full humanity of all peoples should prompt an attempt to speak and think in ways which include all human beings and degrade none."[37] **Inclusive language** is not only ethical, it's practical because it can increase your credibility. One study[38] found that speakers who put down persons with disabilities or focus on the disability rather than on the individual lose credibility, likability, and persuasiveness. Inclusive terminology and positive presentations of groups or individuals are elements of ethical language.

inclusive language ethical terminology that affirms and includes, rather than excludes, persons or groups of people

Choose Inclusive Terminology

Racist language privileges one racial or ethnic group and degrades or devalues others. **Ageist language** portrays older people in ways that demean or devalue their age. Phrases like *over the hill* or *look ten years younger* subtly reinforce the notion that youth is better than age. Finally, **sexist language** gives priority to males, their activities, and their interests.

Nonparallel language is a specific form of sexist language that speaks differently about men and women. It's nonparallel to designate a female by adding a suffix to a male term, as in *actor-actress* or *steward–stewardess*. It's also nonparallel to mark job titles, as in a *female judge*. (Would you ever say a *male judge*?) Similarly, couples may be termed *man and wife* but not *woman and husband*. (*Husband and wife* is parallel because both terms designate roles.)

Use of the "generic *he*" or the use of the suffix *–man* makes women invisible. So substitute inclusive labels such as *chair* for *chairman*, *mail carrier* for *mailman*, and

racist language language that privileges one racial or ethnic group over another

ageist language language that negatively influences the way listeners think about older people

sexist language language that privileges males and their activities and interests

nonparallel language language that does not treat the two sexes equally

firefighter for *fireman*. Other language that excludes assumes that relationships are all heterosexual or that *Americans* are synonymous with *US residents*. (Canadians, Brazilians, and Guatemalans are also Americans.)

Present People and Groups Positively

Phrases such as *just a secretary*, *white trash*, or *dumb blonde* are put-downs or **dismissive language** applied to people in ways that discounts their ideas. Epithets frame negative perceptions of people or groups. Examples of slurs include *sissy*, *dumb jock*, *computer nerd*, and *little old lady*. In contrast, terms such as *computer genius*, *athlete*, or *retiree* create more positive or more neutral images.

> **dismissive language** put-downs; language that discounts the importance of someone's viewpoint

Mention differences only when they matter in the context of the speech. For instance, say "*my professor*" unless it is somehow important to say "my *Latina* professor." Don't mention someone's competency as if it were unusual for that group: Instead of "an *intelligent* welfare recipient," simply say, "a welfare recipient." Don't describe people with disabilities as pitiable, helpless victims, but don't suggest they are more heroic, courageous, patient, or special than others, and avoid contrasting them to *normal* people.[39]

ETHICS IN PRACTICE

Ban Bossy?

In early 2014, female leaders from business, politics, nonprofit organizations, and entertainment banded together to create a "Ban Bossy" campaign.[40] They contended that words like *pushy* or *stubborn* or *bossy* or the other *b*-word are often attached to girls and women who take leadership roles. In contrast, a boy or young man who makes decisions and tells others what to do is a leader. They argued that *bossy* is unequally applied to women more than men. One supporter, Beyoncé, says women should instead say, "I'm not bossy; I'm the boss."

Pushback was swift—even by women. Detractors chalked the campaign up to feminism gone awry in attempt to control what we could or should say. Others accused the founders of banning bossy by being bossy. Parodies sprang up on the Internet as men and women began to talk about the language used to describe women. Overall, the campaign drew attention to the language used to describe women.

Questions

1. Do you think the word *bossy* is demeaning to girls? To women?
2. Does negative speech ever violate someone's human rights?
3. Read some of the comments online about the Ban Bossy campaign. What do you think the organizers were trying to do?
4. List some negative words used to describe girls or women. If a boy or man acted in a similar way, what words might describe him?

In short, terminology is not neutral. Your word choices can influence audience perceptions regarding issues as well as individuals and groups. The fact that some language choices demean others raises ethical questions and colors your listeners' impressions about you. Choosing inclusive, positive language shows respect for diversity and enhances your credibility as well.

Language and Pluralistic Audiences

Students enter classrooms across the country with many types of linguistic diversity:

- Monolingual (speaking one language only)
- Bilingual (speaking two languages or dialects)
- Multilingual or multidialectical (speaking three or more languages or dialects)

Communicating in a linguistically diverse setting is often complicated and frustrating, but you can plan ways to benefit everyone involved. A few simple strategies can help you speak more effectively in multicultural settings. Many of these suggestions are elements of the oral style:

- As you prepare, try to "hear" the terminology and jargon related to your topic in the way a nonnative speaker of English might hear it, and make plans to define difficult words and jargon during your speech.
- Whenever possible, choose simple words that most people understand, but don't talk down to your audience.
- Identify words that might be confusing and display them on visual aids.
- Build in repetition and redundancy by saying the same idea in a number of different ways. This way, if listeners are unclear about a concept the first time around, they may grasp it when it's expressed another way.

Listening to a speaker whose first language differs from yours calls for a more-than-normal effort. These tips can help you listen more effectively:[41]

- Approach the speech with a positive attitude, expecting to understand.
- Listen all the way through. Make special efforts to keep your mind from wandering in the middle of the speech. It may help to take notes, and concentrate on the main points rather than on each specific word.
- Give appropriate nonverbal feedback to demonstrate your interest, patience, and support for the speaker.
- Control your negative emotional responses. Let's face it, linguistic barriers are challenging, and it's easy to get frustrated or bored when faced with language differences.

Many public speaking settings have both speakers and listeners who are not native speakers of the language they must use in their speech. In these situations, remember that the goal is to communicate ideas, not every detail.

Image Source/SuperStock

- Don't laugh, even if the speakers laugh nervously at their language skills.
- Use patience and **perspective taking** by putting yourself in the speaker's shoes and imagining what it would be like to give a speech in a foreign language to native speakers of that language.

Remember that the major goal of any speech is communication of ideas, not perfection of language skills. Also, remember that nonfluency is linked to inexperience in English, not to a lack of intelligence or education.[42]

perspective taking trying to imagine something from another person's point of view

Summary

Language is a tool that humans use to communicate with one another and build complex societies. We create words to name our cultural memories, meaning that we label those things we notice and need to know in order to survive. Passing on these labels perpetuates our cultural ideas in new generations. Languages are dynamic, and words are added, borrowed, and discontinued in response to social changes.

Words denote or stand for objects, actions, and ideas; jargon, a technical vocabulary common to members of an occupation, can confuse outsiders who don't know its meaning. More importantly, words have connotative meanings that consist of the feelings and associations that they imply. Epithets generally carry negative connotations, whereas euphemisms put negative things more positively.

Oral style contrasts with written language in several ways. It is dynamic, interactive, and engaging because speakers can use nonverbal cues to add emphasis. This style is less formal and more personalized than written language. It uses simpler, more concrete words, shorter sentences—even fragments. Repetition is a hallmark of oral style.

Your speaking effectiveness depends on how well you can put your ideas into words. Thus, there are several guidelines for using language effectively. Be concise, choose familiar words, be concrete, build in repetition, use vivid language, and select a form that's appropriate to you, the topic, the audience, and the context.

In recent years, people have become concerned about the power of words—especially those used in discriminatory ways—and have worked to create inclusive language that affirms individuals and groups and presents them in a positive light.

Finally, you may someday be in a public speaking situation where you either speak in a second language, requiring the use of an interpreter, or, more likely, where you listen to a speaker who is not a native speaker of English. In these situations, it is most important to communicate ideas rather than expect linguistic precision. When you listen to a speaker from another linguistic background, take the responsibility of listening with an open mind in a supportive manner.

STUDY AND REVIEW

Public Speaking: Concepts and Skills for a Diverse Society offers a broad range of resources that will help you better understand the material in this chapter, complete assignments, and succeed on tests. Your MindTap resources feature the following:

- Speech videos with viewing questions, speech outlines, and transcripts
- Activities to help you check your understanding and to apply what you've learned to your own life
- Stop and Check and Critical Thinking exercises
- Outline Builder
- Web Links related to chapter content
- Study and review tools such as self-quizzes and an interactive glossary

Reflect on what you've learned.

You can access your online resources for *Public Speaking: Concepts and Skills for a Diverse Society* at cengagebrain.com using the access code that came with your book or that you purchased online.

Review your Flashcards.

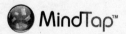

CRITICAL THINKING EXERCISES

1. A webpage titled "Incredible Facts" claims that the English word with the most dictionary meanings is *set*. (You can access this information on your online resources.) First, come up with all the meanings of *set* that you can, and then use a dictionary to look it up. Do you agree with the author, or can you prove him wrong? Then thumb through a print edition instead of an online dictionary, and look for other ambiguous words with more than ten meanings.

2. Your online speech archives give you the opportunity to listen to the greatest words ever spoken in the English language. Link to "Top 100 Speeches" and you'll find Lou Gehrig's 1939 farewell to baseball, General Douglas McArthur's farewell to Congress, Margaret Chase Smith's "Declaration of Conscience," and ninety-seven more. Listen to a speech of your choice and then write a paragraph explaining how the language choices contribute to the effectiveness of the speech.

3. Find a speech by a speaker who represents a culture different than your own on your online resources. Locate the metaphors and similes in the speech. Note the similarities and differences between the metaphors of that culture and your own.

4. Interview a member of an occupation that interests you, and make a list of jargon terms associated with the job (for example, carpenters, musicians, foresters, pharmacists, truckers, bankers). How many terms do you know? Which terms are unfamiliar? If you were listening to a speaker from that occupation, what would you want the speaker to do so that you would better understand the speech?

5. Watch Dr. Martin Luther King Jr. delivering his "I Have a Dream" speech or JFK delivering his inaugural address, focusing especially on the vivid language choices. The links are available on your online resources.

APPLICATION EXERCISES

1. Outside of class, search the Internet for the word *ebonics* or African American English (AAE). (Look for .edu sources.) Print out at least two articles and bring them to class. In a small group, discuss one of the following questions; then share your group's conclusions with the entire class.
   - Identify some ways that AAE (ebonics) differs from Standard English.
   - What controversies swirl around AAE? Why do you think the dialect is controversial?
   - What do linguists say about the dialect?
2. Access the *Oxford English Dictionary* for recent updates. Go to its website, www.public. oed.com/whats-new, and make a list of six new words you know and six that are unfamiliar to you. Bring the list to class and share it.
3. A speech can be informative without being interesting. Make a list of not-so-interesting topics and, working with a small group of your classmates, choose one and then think of alliteration, rhyming, repetition, metaphors, similes, or personification that could make the topic more interesting.
4. Work with your classmates to make a list of the car models owned by class members (Fiesta, Explorer, Mustang, and so on). Within a small group, identify the denotative meaning of each word. Then discuss the connotative associations that manufacturers hope will sell the car.

CHAPTER 13

THIS CHAPTER WILL HELP YOU

- Explain the purpose of presentation aids

- Create a plan for visual, audio, and multimedia aids

- Choose specific presentation aids, including three-dimensional and two-dimensional visuals and audio resources

- Determine the advantages and disadvantages of using various presentation technologies

- Apply principles of visual design

- Follow guidelines for using visual aids

Diana Ong/SuperStock

Presentation Aids

IN HER SPEECHES, Edith Widder, founder of the Ocean Research & Conservation Association, takes her listeners "on a trip to an alien world"— not to a distant planet, but to the delicate ecosystems of the deepest oceans where glowing animals live in "the weird, wonderful world of bioluminescence."[1] Because words alone are "totally inadequate" to convey her ideas, she incorporates photographs, video clips, cartoons, and a live demonstration to show sea creatures that light up when danger approaches. You can access her speech on your online resources.

As you plan your **presentation aids**, keep in mind that the word *aid* means to help, assist, or give support. Consequently, your visual, audio, or multimedia choices are not just decorative additions to your speech. Used well, they are a powerful means of support that help your audience engage, understand,

Mind
Review th
chapter
Learning
Objective
and **Start**
with a qu
warm-up
activity.

and remember information. Used poorly, and audiences think you either lack skill or didn't take the time to create and rehearse them well.[2]

This chapter discusses the purpose, planning, and principles for designing and using visual, audio, and multimedia support. Most of the chapter focuses on visual support, but it also suggests ways to use audio and multimedia resources as well.

Purposes for Presentation Aids

Presentation aids exist for the audience, and their major purpose is to help listeners process your information through more than one modality. By providing sensory support for those who learn best by seeing, hearing, or doing, you are adapting to audience diversity.[3]

The **dual coding theory (DCT)**, developed by cognitive scientists, says our brains process material through two separate but parallel and interconnected pathways or codes—imagery and language—that we can use separately or together. That is, you can create meanings through hearing words alone or seeing images alone, or you can understand a concept through **dual processing**—hearing words while seeing images.[4] (See Figure 13.1.) Researchers have found that spoken words supported by relevant images (such as a graph during a speech about grade inflation) makes learning easier and creates better retention than hearing spoken words accompanied by decorative images (such as unrelated photographs chosen simply for their attractiveness[5]) or by text-heavy visuals (which are hard to read while someone is speaking).[6]

The right visual or audio support is essential for information that is difficult to express in words alone.[7] Topics about artists or composers are in this category. For instance, images of Jackson Pollock's paintings are essential for a speech about Pollock's career, and clips from Hector Berlioz's symphonies help an audience understand his "eerie" music. In addition, many complex or technical topics require visual support. In fact, one author says, "Much of modern science can no longer be communicated in print."[8] Leif's speech about hovercraft in Chapter 11 is understandable because of his visuals, and it's easier to explain an ACL injury by showing a diagram of the knee joint. Demonstrations, similarly, are best understood with visuals. How well could you explain the process of folding a flag in words alone?

Visuals plus words can also emphasize or reinforce important concepts when the visual is relevant to the topic, not merely decorative.[9] The mullet hairstyle, for example, is familiar enough that a speaker could probably get by just describing it; however, drawings of mullets throughout history would add to the presentation. Consider also, where a visual might emphasize or reinforce an idea, show your speech structure, support your concepts, or show relationships between your ideas.[10] Kelsey used a list to preview the four aspects of advergaming she would explain.

Finally, well-placed aids can relieve the monotony of words alone and help maintain audience attention. So look for places where attention might lag and supporting materials could draw listeners' focus back onto the speech. Kelsey included photographs of several advergames as she discussed them; later in her speech, she showed a photograph of an expert she was quoting.

In summary, identify the purpose of each visual by asking: Which learning preferences do these visuals support? Is it necessary? Is it interesting but not essential? Is the image relevant to the words, or is it merely decoration? Will it help maintain attention? In each instance, make sure the intellectual content of the visual is challenging.[11]

presentation aids visual, audio, and multimedia support that helps audiences understand and remember information

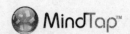

dual coding theory (DCT) theory that our brains process material two ways: through language and through images

dual processing combining words and images to create meanings

Dual Coding	
Language system	Visual system
words	images
More left brain	More right brain
Together → Dual Processing	

Figure 13.1
Dual Coding Theory.

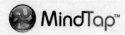

Planning Your Presentation Aids

After you have identified the concepts that need support, your next step is to plan which aids to use, taking into account your topic and purpose, the occasion, your audience, and the availability of presentation technology. The key is to choose the *best* support, not just the easiest to create. This section will discuss three basic types of aids: three-dimensional visuals, two-dimensional visuals, and audio or video resources that you can use separately or integrate into multimedia packages.

Three-Dimensional Visuals

Three-dimensional visuals in the form of objects, models, or people are helpful when listeners need to experience a subject or see it demonstrated.

Objects

What coach would even try to convey the finer points of shooting free throws without using a basketball? What camp counselor would explain a craft without using actual materials? For some subjects, three-dimensional objects are essential, especially in informative speeches that demonstrate a process.

Your topic and the setting determine whether or not an object is realistic. For example, what object could you use for a speech about mortgages? Pandemic preparedness? Grief counseling on campus? However, a little creative thinking applied to many topics can come up with objects that add touch, smell, or taste to a speech. Here are a few examples:

- An old Beatles album for a speech about that famous band
- Samples of sushi offered at the end of a speech explaining that food
- A small rug for the topic of Navajo weaving
- A small quadcopter to illustrate how tiny some unmanned aerial vehicles (AEVs, or drones) can be

Models are good visuals when actual objects are unavailable.

Some objects are inappropriate or even prohibited. For instance, firearms are illegal in classrooms, and it's unwise to use live animals. Furthermore, some objects are impractical because they're too expensive or too hard to get. Marko couldn't bring his motorcycle into the classroom. (Fortunately, his classmates were willing to walk to a nearby parking lot where he spoke from the seat of his bike.) Bottom line: objects must be legal, accessible, and practical. If they should be large enough for everyone to see, individual listeners should each have an object.

Models

When an object is impractical, a **model** can substitute. Scaled-down models depict large objects such as buildings, dinosaurs, or drones; enlarged models depict small objects such as atoms, ants, or eyeballs. Science teachers often use models such as an enlarged human cell or a scaled-down solar system to illustrate scientific concepts. Architects present scale models to decision makers who decide whether or not to fund a proposed building.

To acquire a model, you might be able to borrow one from a professional, or you might make your own. For instance, one student spoke about his summer job as a pyro-technician (a fireworks display technician). Because federal regulations and common sense prevented him from bringing explosives into the classroom, he made a model of the spherical explosive device, complete with a fuse. He supplemented the model with several objects: the actual cylinder into which he dropped lit explosives while on the job and the jumpsuit and safety helmet he wore at work.

model a facsimile of an object you can't easily bring to the speech

People

Friends, volunteers from the audience, even your own body are often good ways to demonstrate a concept. For example, Jacinda, an Alaskan of Eskimo origin, used two volunteers from the audience to demonstrate the "stick pull," a native sport. She also wore a T-shirt with the letters W-E-I-O, which stands for "World Eskimo-Indian Olympics." You might incorporate the audience as a whole by asking them to participate in some sort of exercise.

In summary, three-dimensional objects, models, or people are indispensable in certain types of speeches, especially demonstration speeches. However, when it's unrealistic to use them, many other types of two-dimensional visuals are available.

Two-Dimensional Visuals

In many cases, two-dimensional visuals are more practical and appropriate than actual objects or models. These visuals fall into two categories: text-based and image-based visuals.

Text-Based Visuals

Text-based visuals, such as lists, rely on written words, although you can incorporate art in a minor way. Without the art the message still comes through, but without the words it does not. Lists are popular for chronological speeches because stages or steps lend themselves to listing. Listing key words or phrases can also summarize the main points of topically arranged speeches. For example, Chelsea used a list, plus relevant art, to preview her main points, as shown in Figure 13.2 on the following page.

A recent study asked students what they thought was the most difficult thing about creating text-based slides and what they disliked about text-based visuals. Typical challenges included, "To put in the most important points in a concise manner." Typical dislikes were "too much text" and "too many lines."[12] Students also disliked having the presenter read directly from the slides.

Text-based visuals are most effective when you keep them simple and frame the ideas in words, phrases, or short sentences instead of sentences or paragraphs. Although

text-based visuals carries meaning in the written words rather than in visual images

Figure 13.2
This word list shows the structure of the speech. The art is appropriate, but nonessential to the message.

Political Campaigns

- Money
- Endorsements
- Debates
- Physical Campaigning

six-by-six rule limit information to six lines, six words per line

research does not prove the **six-by-six rule**,[13] many experts recommend that you use no more than six lines, no more than six words per line. In addition, always discuss every point on your visual.

Image-Based Visuals

image-based visuals carry meaning in visual images; written words are secondary

Image-based visuals rely on some sort of figure or picture to convey meaning. They include charts, drawings, diagrams, maps, graphs, and photographs.

flowcharts shows the order or directional flow in which processes occur; may simply be a series of labeled shapes and arrows

Charts **Flowcharts** show the order in which processes occur by using arrows to indicate directional movement. Flowcharts can include drawings (pictorial flowcharts), or they may simply be a series of labeled shapes and arrows. Casey used a pictorial flowchart showing how an underwater breathing apparatus takes oxygen from the water to create "artificial gills." See the flowchart in his video on your online resources. **Organizational charts** show hierarchies and relationships. A family tree, for example, depicts relationships among family members.

organizational charts shows hierarchies and relationships

diagrams drawing or design that explains, rather than realistically depicts, an object or process

Diagrams, Drawings, and Maps **Diagrams** are line drawings or graphic designs that explain, rather than realistically depict, an object or a process. Drawings or diagrams can stand alone or be added to lists or other visuals as supplementary support. Substitute them for illegal firearms, inaccessible motorcycles, buildings that are too large or insects that are too small to bring into your classroom. Use diagrams to illustrate processes such as the acid rain cycle or the circulatory system. Consider showing a cartoon that perfectly illustrates your point and adds humor to your talk, but make sure you read the caption to the audience.

Maps visually represent spaces such as the heavens, the earth, or the weather. There are several kinds of maps:

political maps shows current borders for states and nations; can be outdated in a fast-changing world

- **Political maps** show borders between nations and states. They become outdated with changing political developments. For example, any map of Africa dated before

2011 has obsolete sections because a new country, South Sudan, was added in July of that year.

- **Geographic maps** show mountains, deserts, lowlands, and other natural features. They are updated only when remote or previously unexplored territories, such as areas of the ocean floor, are mapped.
- Other maps include building blueprints and floor plans, maps of routes between two points, city maps, and campus maps.

geographic maps shows mountains, deserts, and other natural features; not easily outdated

Photographs The old saying "A picture is worth a thousand words" is not necessarily true. Pictures are of little value if they are merely decorative or if your audience cannot see them. However, many students successfully use photographs. Shane showed pictures of drones, and Zitong showed snapshots from Chinese weddings. For his speech on aqualungs, Casey projected a large, high-resolution photograph of a beetle that scientists used as a model for aqualung development.

To use photographs successfully, choose only high-resolution images. Also find a way to display your photos so that everyone can see them. Avoid passing a photo around; only the person closest to you sees the picture as you explain it, but the last person sees it long after you've described it. Put the source of the photo on the visual and in your list of references.

Graphs As Chapter 8 pointed out, speeches full of numerical data are often boring, difficult to follow, and impossible to remember without some sort of visual. Depicting your material in one of four types of graphs allows your listeners to see how your numbers relate to one another.

1. **Line graphs** present information in linear form; they are best for showing variables that fluctuate over time, such as changes in tuition over two decades. They are also good for showing the relationship of two or more variables, such as a comparison of state and private school averages during the same period. (Figure 13.3a on the following page shows fluctuation in the funding of three projects over a fifteen-year period.)
2. **Bar graphs** compare data from several groups such as the salaries of men and women with differing educational levels. (See Figure 13.3b.)
3. **Pie graphs** are especially good for showing divisions of a population or parts of the whole. The pie graph in Figure 13.3c depicts ways typical Americans get to work.
4. **Picture graphs** or **pictographs**, the least common of the four types, are especially effective for data related to objects or people. Each picture represents a certain number of individual cases, as Figure 13.3d demonstrates.

line graph displays in a linear form one or more variables that fluctuate over a time period

bar graph compares data from several groups by using bands of various lengths

pie graph represents parts of the whole or divisions of a population by circles divided into portions

picture graph or **pictograph** presents data in pictures, each representing a certain number of individual cases

In summary, three-dimensional objects and text- or image-based visuals are useful in visually oriented cultures. However, in some cases, recordings of sounds or images are even more effective support.

Video and Audio Support

Audio and video support requires extra preparation and planning, but these resources can help you better convey certain types of information.

Audio Resources

Audio support is particularly important with music- or sound-related topics. Your audience can hear the sounds you are explaining, whether your topic is a musical style, a specific instrument, or a particular composer's works. Although less common, you can

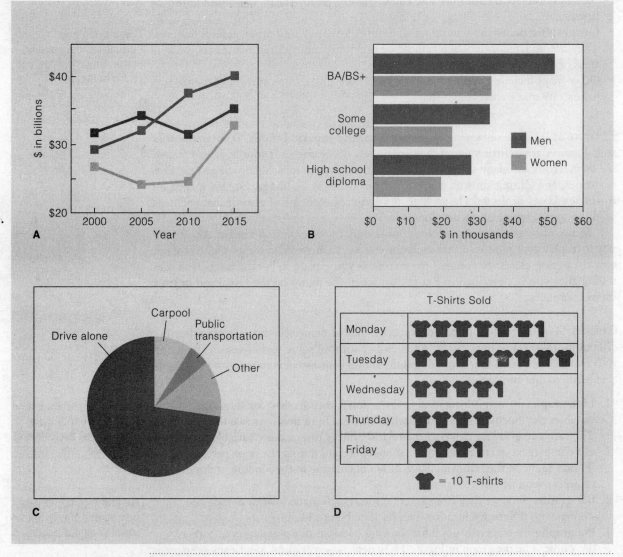

Figure 13.3

Graphs Four major types include (a) a line graph, (b) a bar graph, (c) a pie graph, and (d) a pictograph.

effectively use sounds other than music. Before her speech on whales, for instance, Mary Beth played a recording of a whale song and asked her listeners to identify the source of the sound.

Video Resources

The Internet has endless video resources, including clips from television shows, feature films, advertisements, and home videos. By carefully selecting short segments to illustrate your points, you can clarify ideas dramatically and memorably, as these examples demonstrate:

- Lisa made the *Guinness World Records* for being part of the largest tap dancing group ever assembled at one time for a performance. As she explained ways to get listed in the famous record book, she used a 15-second video clip that her mother had recorded.

- Bralee showed two clips from *Friends* to illustrate product placement.
- Chelsea played a short campaign ad to support her point about getting endorsements for a candidate.

These students succeeded because they preplanned carefully. Their short clips illustrated their concepts; they selected the scene in advance; and they planned exactly when to start and stop the visual.

In summary, skillful construction and use of visuals distinguish good speakers from adequate ones, and as you learn to work with visuals, your competence will increase. Presentation aids are especially useful with diverse audiences, as Diversity in Practice: Visual Aids and Culture shows.

Visual Aids and Culture

DIVERSITY IN PRACTICE

Although technology has changed across the millennia, visual aids have a long history. In oral cultures, speakers used objects to clarify ideas, help listeners better understand abstract concepts, and dramatize words. For instance, in the sixth century BCE, the Hebrew prophet Ezekiel created a model of the city of Jerusalem and then used a toy army and siege machines to destroy it, symbolizing its future destruction.[14] In the days of the Roman republic, noted orators such as Cicero used statues and other landmarks in the Forum as visual aids.[15]

Today, communicators in pluralistic settings, such as international marketers[16] and presenters who must speak in a second language, know the value of visual support. In the classroom, visual aids help nonnative speakers of English understand and be understood in the following ways:

- Nonnative speakers of English often worry that their English is not clear enough or that they will make mistakes when they speak. By putting key words on visuals, listeners can see as well as hear their ideas.
- Visual aids put the focus—at least part of the time—on the visual rather than the speaker. This may lessen a nonnative speaker's anxiety.
- Visuals, such as words on a list or figures on a graph, can function as cue cards to remind speakers of their main points—another strategy for minimizing the fear of forgetting.
- Key words, diagrams, and other visuals can help nonnative speakers in the audience. If they are unfamiliar with specific terms, they can understand the diagrams and visuals and jot down the important words to study later.

In our image-saturated culture, many audiences now expect visual support. Consequently, a good presentation aid package that skillfully uses available technology is culturally appropriate in a diverse society.

Planning the Presentation Technology

The technology for displaying visuals is big business; in fact, giant corporations exist solely to provide machines and materials for creating and displaying visual support. This section covers a number of common ways to display visual aids, along with their advantages and disadvantages. Many of these presentation technologies are common in classrooms; other forms are more common in workplaces and other settings. (*Note:* Students taking this course online should check with their instructors about incorporating presentation technology into their video speeches.)

Presentation Software and Projectors

A variety of projectors (LCD or DLP, for example) connect directly to computers and project what appears on the monitor onto a screen. If you create visuals using a **presentation software program** such as PowerPoint or Prezi, you'll need a data projector. This technology has many advantages. Visuals are easy to create and edit. You can insert hyperlinks to add audio and video support. Prezi lets you zoom in and out as you move between points. During your speech, you simply launch your presentation and move from visual to visual with a click of the mouse.

> **presentation software program** computer software to create a package of lists, tables, graphs, and clip art

Unfortunately, software programs are often used poorly. For example, millions of speakers turn out trillions of slides annually.[17] However, many slides are so ineffective that they detract from the message—but the problem lies in the creators, not the technology.[18] Think of presentations you've seen. How many were well done or memorable compared to the number that were boring and poorly designed? Avoid pitfalls by following these guidelines:[19]

* Beforehand, plan the package as a whole. Write out the words you'll use for text-based visuals, and sketch in the visual-based images. Mentally identify the purpose for everything you include.
* Then go back and edit out every nonessential word or image.
* Choose only high-resolution images that will display clearly.
* Create text-based slides in black and white at first and then add color sparingly to emphasize significant ideas.
* Rehearse at least once without the slides to make sure that they don't substitute for your message.

Document Cameras and Overhead Projectors

> **document cameras** high-resolution cameras that display documents and three-dimensional objects

Document cameras (also known as visual presenters) have been called "the 21st-century overhead projector"[20] because they are like a scanner, microscope, whiteboard, computer, and projector rolled into one. Some units are compact enough to fold into a notebook-sized carrying case. These high-resolution cameras let you project photographs, slides, three-dimensional objects, a document you've created, and so on. You can zoom in on a painting or enlarge a small model so that tiny details are visible.[21]

Just a few years ago, overhead projectors were everywhere, and they're still around in some places. Their advantages? Transparencies are simple and inexpensive to make; they are easy to store and transport. You can draw freehand or photocopy a printed image directly onto one, or you can print on one directly from your computer. However, you cannot create multimedia links, and the transparencies, once made, are not easily revised.

The following guidelines apply to both document cameras and overhead projectors:

* Before you begin speaking, turn on the machine and adjust the focus. Then turn it off until you're ready to display your visual.
* To draw attention to some part of your visual, point on the visual, not the screen. Place a pointed object where you want listeners to focus and then move your hand away from the image.

© Brian A Jackson/Shutterstock.com

Today's technology provides many ways to display visuals in a variety of situations.

- If you use a text-based visual repeatedly but want to highlight material each time, place a blank transparency over the material and underline, mark, or write on the blank, using wet erase markers. This keeps your original clean, and you can easily clean your markings off the top sheet.

Chalkboards or Whiteboards

Chalkboards or whiteboards are standard equipment in most educational settings because of their many advantages. They're great for explaining unfolding processes, such as math problems. They also encourage informality, which is appropriate in some contexts. Finally, they are useful in settings that include speaker–audience interactions such as brainstorming sessions.[22]

Unfortunately, boards have three major drawbacks. (1) You can't prepare your visual beforehand, and unprepared visuals create additional anxiety if you prefer to have things ready in advance. (2) Most people don't write well on boards, so the visuals look unprofessional. (3) You turn your back on your audience while you write on the board. This is probably the major drawback of boards in general.

Boards continue to evolve. **Interactive whiteboards** can connect to a document camera or a computer with markup software. You can then use "electronic markers" or even your finger to overwrite material on the board. Finally, you can save your markups to files and later retrieve, email, or print out.[23]

interactive whiteboards connects to other technology; you can overwrite material and then save your markups

Posters and Flip Charts

For convenience and economy, poster board is a low-tech option. Because it's readily available in a variety of weights and colors at campus bookstores and art supply stores, posters are widely used—even by members of Congress. In the workplace, people who give the same speech over and over, such as financial planners, often use professionally prepared posters. They are effective with relatively small audiences, but at greater distances posters are difficult to see, and small details don't show up. In addition, you need an easel to hold them. These tips will help you make more professional-looking posters:

- Use rulers or yardsticks to ensure straight lines and avoid a "loving-hands-at-home" look.
- Use more than one color to attract and hold interest.
- For a more professional look, use computer-created text or adhesive letters.
- To protect posters from becoming bent or soiled, carry them in a portfolio, or cover them with plastic when you transport them.

flip chart tablet you prepare in advance or create on the spot; turn to a new page or tear off and display pages as you finish them

Flip charts are oversized tablets, lined or unlined; they are common in businesses and other organizations but rare in college classrooms. Their name reflects the fact that you can turn the pages. They're made of paper that varies from tablet thickness to stiffer weights. Larger charts work well in conference rooms; smaller ones work well for presentations to just a few listeners.

Flip charts can function like a chalkboard or whiteboard, especially in brainstorming situations where you interact with your audience. Used this way, you must overcome disadvantages similar to those of a whiteboard. Your writing may be messy, and writing on the chart causes you to turn your back on the audience. Some presenters ask a second person to do the writing.

If you repeat the same presentation for different audiences, prepare your visuals on heavier-weight flip chart and use them much as you would use a series of posters, exposing each new visual as you discuss it. The separate visuals will stay in order. In addition, because the cover is stiff, the tablet can stand alone on a table, which makes it a useful display method when other equipment is unavailable.[24]

Handouts

Brochures, pamphlets, photocopies, or other handouts free audiences from having to take extensive notes and give them details they can study later.[25] Handouts can also provide supplementary information you don't have time to cover in your speech. At the end of his health-related speech, one student distributed brochures from his campus health services; another distributed a photocopied diagram illustrating an origami project. Handouts are common in business settings; for example, sales representatives commonly give brochures to potential customers.

Your primary challenge is for the handout to supplement, but not replace your message so that your audience listens to you instead of just reading the handout. The following tips apply:

- Distribute handouts, face down, before you begin speaking; then, when you discuss the material on them, ask your listeners to turn them over.
- Mark the points you want to emphasize with a letter or number so you can easily direct listeners to specific places on the handout. For example, a speaker who distributes a map could highlight one area with an *A*, a second area with a *B*, and a third with a *C* and then draw the listeners' attention to each place as she discusses it.
- Put identical material on a slide and project it as you speak. Highlight the information you want them to find on their handout.
- If the handout provides only supplementary information, distribute it at the end of the speech.

In summary, today's presentation technologies range from high-tech projectors and computer-generated slides to low-tech handwritten flip charts and posters, providing a range of options for displaying visual materials. Effective speakers know how to select and use the types that work best, given their topic and the situation.

Can a Visual Be Unethical?

Speakers have an ethical responsibility to do their listeners no harm. This includes any behavior that could place listeners at risk for physical or psychological injury or harm. Read the following true examples from classroom speeches and then discuss with your classmates some ethical questions they raise:

- One student killed, skinned, and cleaned a live fish in front of her stunned classmates.[26]
- Another opened his speech on terrorism creatively and dramatically with a role-play scenario. He arranged with a couple of his friends to dress in fatigues, carry realistic but fake automatic weapons, burst into the classroom, and order everyone to hit the floor. He didn't anticipate the reactions: Students screamed and cried. One person, an immigrant from a country where terrorist incidents were common, hyperventilated. Someone called 9-1-1, and she ended up in the emergency room. Class ended immediately.
- Students have displayed visuals of aborted fetuses.
- One student showed pornographic photographs to illustrate her speech about pornography.

Questions

1. Does any example fail to meet the standard of doing no harm, whether physically or psychologically? If so, which one(s)? Why?
2. Try to think from the speakers' point of view. Why might each speaker have chosen that particular aid?
3. What presentation aids could each speaker have substituted?
4. How persuasive do you find shocking or offensive visual aids that stir negative emotions?

   If you have questions about the appropriateness or safety of any material you intend to use, consult your instructor in advance of your speech.

Apply Proven Design Principles

Because of the prevalence of presentation aids, researchers are studying the effects of specific design features on audiences. Not surprisingly, they have found that certain fonts and background color combinations can distract audiences; in addition, sound effects and small letters interfere with audience comprehension.[27] To avoid negative effects on your listeners, pay attention to design, fonts, and colors as you prepare your visuals.

Design Your Slides

Many books and online resources describe ways to create professional looking, aesthetically pleasing visuals. Excellent guidance on designing and using presentation aids is accessible on your online resources. These four principles are common:

1. *Simplicity:*[28] Professionals such as Garr Reynolds of Presentation Zen put simplicity at the top of their list. Limit yourself to one idea per visual and eliminate everything that does not contribute to the message. Minimize bullet points and text. Use plain transitions and animation.

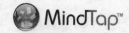 MindTap™

2. *Repetition*:[29] Select a theme and use the same elements (fonts, colors, and so on) throughout your visuals. Use one font for all your titles. Do likewise for the subtitle and text fonts. And limit yourself to a couple of complementary fonts such as Candara and Candara bold.[30]

3. *Contrast*: Add visual interest by adding color or formatting for contrast. For instance, centering the title, underlining the subtitle, and bulleting the points can help your audience better see the relationships among ideas. Using boldfaced formatting makes letters show up better on slides. And attributes such as italicizing can highlight and emphasize specific ideas, but use these features sparingly, or the impact will be lost.

4. *Spacing*: Balance your material across the entire visual, but leave plenty of negative (unfilled) space. Many designers recommend the "rule of thirds." Divide your visual into thirds horizontally and then vertically. You'll end up with nine areas of the same size. Place important elements along the lines or on the places where they intersect. For additional information and many excellent examples, do an Internet search for "rule of thirds PowerPoint."

Choose a Readable Font

Whether you create your visuals on poster board or use a computer program, *readability* should be your primary concern, so choose a font your audience can read easily. Here are some ideas to help you choose among the hundreds of available fonts:

1. Use title case (Capitalize the First Letter of Major Words) or sentence case (Capitalize only the words you'd capitalize in a sentence), and avoid all capital letters.

2. One type of font is not necessarily better than another, but research shows that readers prefer **serif fonts** (with cross lines at the top and bottom of letters) for handouts[31] and that **sans serif fonts** (with no cross lines) work well on slides.

3. It goes without saying that letters should be large enough to be visible and that titles and first-level material should be larger than second-level material.

serif fonts a font with cross lines at the top and bottom of letters

sans serif fonts a simple font with no cross lines on each letter

For more information, search the Internet for "personality of fonts." For example, fonts are seen as stable (Arial), polite (Cambria), rigid (impact), and so on.[32] A British psychologist called the font Georgia "individual, sophisticated, with a curviness that suggests a little bit of rocker chick."[33] Fonts with rounded O's and tails are "friendly" but more angular fonts are "cold." Cities, celebrities, and politicians select fonts. For instance, both the city of Seattle and President Obama chose Gotham as their signature font.[34]

Evaluate the effectiveness of each of these student-designed slides. Figure 13.4 is for a speech on the history of art therapy, Figure 13.5 is on traditional Chinese weddings, and Figure 13.6 is on nuclear fusion. What suggestions, if any, would you give each student?

Use Color for Emphasis

Color adds interest and emphasis and attracts and holds attention. However, carefully plan your color scheme because colors have cultural connotations. For example: red can be a good emphasis color, but it is "culturally loaded." In the United States it symbolizes anger ("seeing red") or danger (being "in the red"); in China, it symbolizes luck and celebration; in India, it is associated with purity. Red is the most common color found on national flags. Blue may be the "safest" global color. In the United States, it symbolizes stability ("true blue"). In China, it connotes immortality; the Jewish faith associates it with holiness.[35]

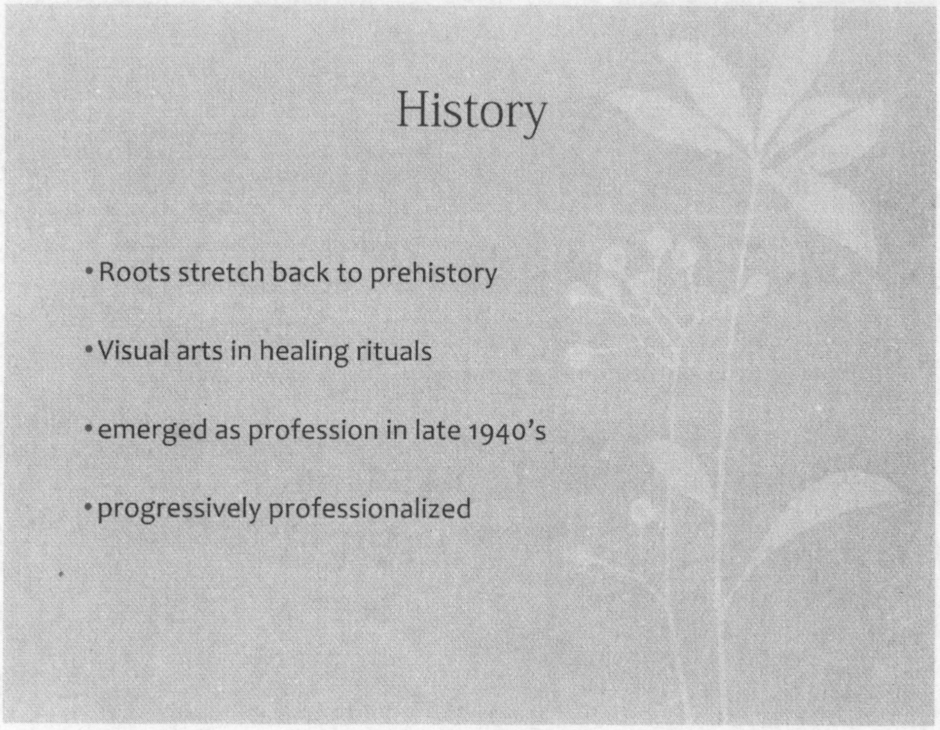

History

- Roots stretch back to prehistory

- Visual arts in healing rituals

- emerged as profession in late 1940's

- progressively professionalized

Figure 13.4
PowerPoint slide for a speech on the history of art therapy. What is done well? What might you change? Why?

Traditional Chinese Bride & Groom

© zhaoyan/Shutterstock.com

Figure 13.5
PowerPoint slide on traditional Chinese weddings. What feedback would you give to this speaker about this visual?

For words and images, choose colors that contrast dramatically with the background color. White or ivory-colored posters and slide backgrounds or clear transparencies are generally best, with text material in high-contrasting black or dark blue. Always consider the room lighting and setup, especially when your technology requires dimmed lights;

Figure 13.6
PowerPoint slide on nuclear fusion. How would you evaluate this text-based visual?

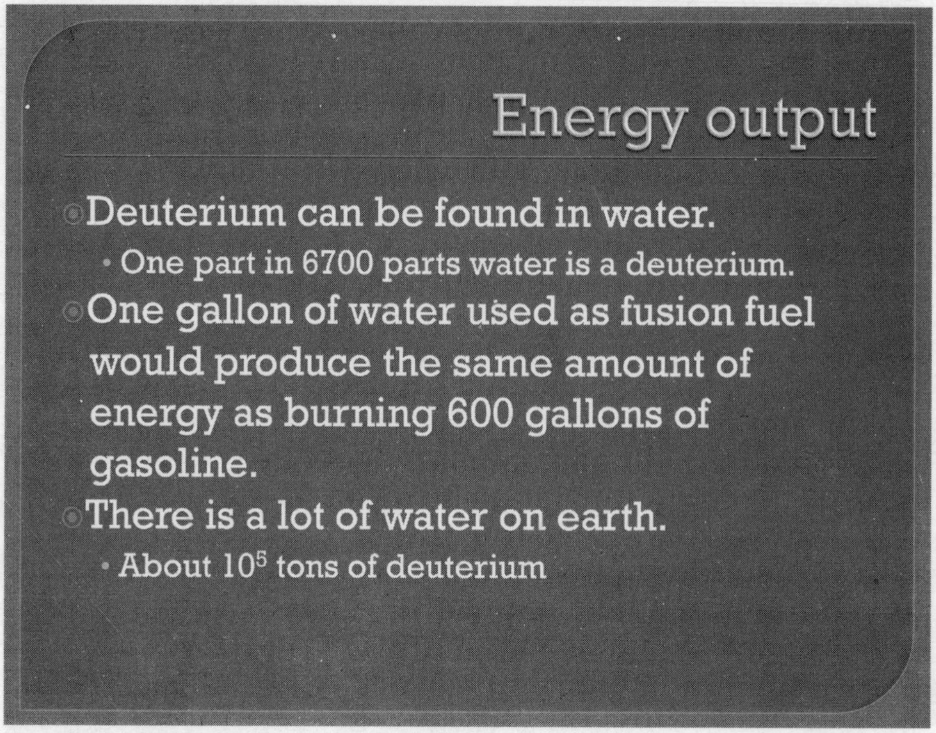

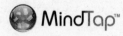

Energy output

- Deuterium can be found in water.
  - One part in 6700 parts water is a deuterium.
- One gallon of water used as fusion fuel would produce the same amount of energy as burning 600 gallons of gasoline.
- There is a lot of water on earth.
  - About 10^5 tons of deuterium

© 2014 Cengage Learning®/Microsoft Image

the colors that are bright on your computer will look faded on the screen. Experiment until you come up with a combination that works in the specific context. To avoid a cluttered look, use a maximum of three colors on all of your visuals.[36]

The most pleasing visuals follow principles of good design. They should be simple and balanced with fonts that create readability and repeated colors that emphasize important points. Overall, remember that your aids are just that—aids. They aren't your message, and they aren't a display of your personal artistic or computer skills.

General Guidelines for Using Presentation Aids

As noted throughout this chapter, each type of presentation aid comes with specific guidelines, but the following general principles apply pretty much across the board:

- Whatever type of aid you choose, make sure everyone can hear or see it.
- Display visuals only when you discuss them. For example, use a cover sheet on posters when they're not in use, or press the "B" key on your computer to bring up a blank screen between slides.
- Talk to your audience, not to your visual.
- Rehearse using your aids. If you can't use the actual equipment, at least visualize yourself using it—think about where you'll stand, how you'll point out specific features, what you'll do when you're not discussing content on the visual.
- Whenever machines are involved, have a Plan B. What will you do if the equipment fails? An alternate plan, often in the form of a handout, can save your speech. In the big picture, demonstrating your composure in case of equipment failure enhances your credibility.[37]

Now that you have read the chapter, return to the introduction. From the information provided, how effective do you think Edith Widder's visuals were overall? Give a reason for your answer.

Summary

As a speaker in a media-saturated culture, it is to your advantage to use visual and audio support to illustrate your ideas, keep your audience's focus, and make abstract ideas more concrete. By dual coding, your listeners better comprehend and retain information. Before you make a single visual, sit down with your outline and determine where support is essential, where it would be useful, where variety is needed, and where audio or visual aids would accommodate for a variety of learning styles. If you can state the purpose for every item of support you use, you will have a meaningful package.

Use three-dimensional objects, models, and people when they are legal, practical, and accessible. Or use two-dimensional objects that can be displayed in a variety of ways. These include lists, charts, graphs, photographs, drawings, diagrams, and maps. Finally, don't overlook the potential of audio or video recordings that will help your listeners get your message. They are especially helpful for helping nonnative speakers of English understand and be understood.

Choose a means of display that suits your topic and the room in which you will speak. Various projectors—LCD or DLP, document cameras, and overhead projectors—chalkboards or whiteboards, and interactive boards combine with poster boards, flip charts, and handouts as high-tech and low-tech ways to present visual aids. All have advantages and disadvantages, but have a Plan B in case the equipment fails somehow.

Emerging technologies have produced sophisticated presentation programs that allow you to create professional-appearing visuals and multimedia presentations for enhancing (not replacing) your speech. Use proven principles of design, including simplicity, repetition, contrast, and spacing. Choose readable fonts and color that emphasizes ideas. And follow a few rules: Display visuals only when you are discussing them, and talk to the audience, not to the visuals. Make sure your aids are visible and audible to everyone. Rehearse your presentation in advance of your speech.

Remember that competent use of visual materials enhances your credibility. Professional-looking resources create more positive impressions than those that appear to be scribbled out just minutes before your presentation. Further, a disastrous incident of equipment failure may actually increase your credibility if your listeners see you handle the stressful situation with composure. And you can demonstrate good sense and ethical awareness by selecting and presenting only visual support that does not violate your listeners' expectations.

STUDY AND REVIEW

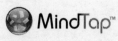

Reflect on what you've learned.

Public Speaking: Concepts and Skills for a Diverse Society offers a broad range of resources that will help you better understand the material in this chapter, complete assignments, and succeed on tests. Your MindTap resources feature the following:

- Speech videos with critical viewing questions, speech outlines, and transcripts
- Interactive versions of this chapter's Stop and Check activities, as well as Critical Thinking Exercises and Application Exercises
- Speech Builder Express
- Weblinks related to chapter content
- Study and review tools such as self-quizzes and an interactive glossary

You can access your online resources for *Public Speaking: Concepts and Skills for a Diverse Society* at cengagebrain.com using the access code that came with your book or that you purchased online.

Review your Flashcards.

KEY TERMS

The terms below are defined in the margins throughout this chapter.

bar graph 169
diagram 168
document camera 172
dual coding theory (DCT) 165
dual processing 165
flip chart 174
flowchart 168
geographic map 169
image-based visual 168
interactive whiteboard 173
line graph 169
model 167

organizational chart 168
picture graph or
    pictograph 169
pie graph 169
political map 168
presentation aid 165
presentation software
    program 172
sans serif font 176
serif font 176
six-by-six rule 168
text-based visual 167

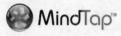

CRITICAL THINKING EXERCISES

1. Think about public speakers you know who use visuals. What kinds of visual support are most common? Which do you see used least? Which presentation technologies are most common? Least common? Do most speakers use visual aids well, or should they follow some tips in this chapter? Explain.
2. Which technology for displaying visuals will you probably use for your classroom speeches? Which would you not consider? If you are taking this course online, what is available to you? In your future employment, what equipment do you think you'll use the most? The least? Why?
3. Make a visual package using a presentation software program such as PowerPoint. First, draw your slides on paper, spacing the information across the slide and cutting every unnecessary word or image. Then go to your computer and make the slides. Experiment with layout, fonts, and colors. Use the slide show function to look at the overall balance of the visual; adjust line spacing and font size as necessary.
4. Browse the Internet using your favorite search engine for material about visual aids. Analyze the credibility of several sites. Does the URL contain an .edu or a .com? Why might that make a difference? Who wrote the materials? When? What links are there? With this information, assess the overall usefulness of each site.
5. Explain what kinds of visuals you think would work most appropriately for a speech on each of the following topics. Describe more than one, if possible. Which would be best? Which could be Plan B?
   - The cloud cycle
   - The physical effects on the lungs of smoking
   - The Oregon Trail
   - Ozone depletion
   - Changes in mortgage interest rates over two decades

APPLICATION EXERCISES

1. With a group of classmates, do an equipment assessment of the room where you'll speak. What technology is available? Is there an Internet connection? Where are the electrical outlets? Can you dim the lights? If you need equipment, how do you order it?

2. Discuss with a group of classmates the visuals you've seen used during the last week. When would visuals have made it easier for you to understand the material? When would visual or audio support have helped you pay better attention? Which support, if any, was best for your learning style preferences?

3. Discuss with a small group of your classmates how to best display a drawing in (1) a large auditorium, (2) a classroom, (3) a speech given outdoors, (4) a presentation in someone's living room, and (5) a video that you plan to post to the Internet. (Several ways may be appropriate.)

4. Working in a small group, choose a sample outline or speech from Appendix B and design at least three visual aids for it. Show your designs to the rest of the class and explain your choices.

5. PowerPoint turned 25 in 2012. You can access the website of Robert Gaskins, one of its originators, on your online resources. There find the PRESS stories along the right side of the web page. Read at least two and make a list of negative and of positive aspects of PowerPoint. Come to class prepared to discuss your list.

6. With some classmates, compare PowerPoint to Prezi. (If you are unfamiliar with Prezi, go to YouTube and watch a video introducing it.)

CHAPTER 14

THIS CHAPTER WILL
HELP YOU

• List four methods of
delivery and explain
when and how to use
each

• Describe ways to maxi-
mize your personal
appearance, clothing,
and accessories

• Plan ways to gesture
effectively

• Build eye contact skills

• Vary your voice effec-
tively in presentations

Diana Ong/SuperStock

Delivering Your Speech

A RECENT TOP TEN list of good speakers placed Michelle Obama as number one. Other notables included Florida senator Marco Rubio, Olympic gold medalist Missy Franklin, Yahoo CEO Melissa Meyer, and, of course, Bill Clinton. The bottom ten included Vice President Joe Biden, Zynga's CEO Mark Pincus, and Olympic gold medalist Ryan Lotche. Top ten speakers combine credible messages with passion and energy to connect with audiences. Those in the lowest ten had distracting mannerisms; one smiled too often and inappropriately, another spoke in monotones with "ums" and "uhs," and still another appeared unlikable and unrelatable. Content is important, but delivery sets some speakers apart.[1]

    Delivery—how you perform your speech—is the topic of this chapter. It first elaborates on the four major types of delivery introduced in Chapter 2,

MindTo

*Review the
chapter
Learning
Objectives
and Start
with a qui
warm-up
activity.*

giving tips for developing skills in each one. Next it describes nonverbal elements—personal appearance, movements or mannerisms, and vocal variations—that can enhance or detract from your words. The goal throughout is to help you present your speech skillfully and appropriately.

> **delivery** the verbal and nonverbal behaviors you use to perform your speech

Select the Appropriate Type of Delivery

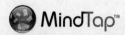

Read, highlight, and take notes online.

Chapter 2 introduced the four major types of delivery: manuscript, memorized, impromptu, and extemporaneous. Each has its place, and each comes with suggestions for effective use.

Manuscript Delivery

Manuscript delivery—writing out the entire speech and reading it—is especially useful in formal situations, where precise wording matters or the speech is significant. You'll hear it for ceremonial speeches such as eulogies, awards, or important political speeches. Manuscripts are also good for radio or television speeches where exact timing is essential. Finally, speakers who suffer severe speech anxiety often find that a manuscript minimizes their fears.

> **manuscript delivery** reading a speech

Although written speeches can be information rich, they can be boring if read in a way that does not engage the audience. Most classroom and workplace situations recommend a more engaging method.[2]

For competent manuscript delivery,[3] first write out the speech word for word in an oral style, using short sentences and fragments and incorporating personalized language and rhetorical questions that connect with the audience.

Rehearse by reading each sentence aloud several times, absorbing the meaning of each phrase. Next, read the entire manuscript aloud and highlight or underline ideas that need emphasis. Use slashes to show pauses. Finally, read the manuscript again, emphasizing words, pausing, and looking up as much as possible. Go back and change any wording that does not sound conversational.[4] Because most people don't like speeches that sound "read," practice until you can give the speech in a natural manner. Type your final script in a large boldfaced font (20 points), using double or triple spacing and numbering each page.[5]

When you are totally familiar with your text, plan how you'll use the manuscript. With a podium, place your sheets of paper high enough on it so that you can see the words without lowering your head too much.[6] When you deliver the speech, keep two pages visible (like an open book). Read from the page on the right, and when you finish it, slide the page on the left over it and continue without a break. If you don't have a podium, put the manuscript in a dark folder or clipboard or write it out on your digital tablet.

Your online resources for this book include several sites that show manuscript delivery. Barbara Jordan's keynote address at the 1976 Democratic National Convention, Barbara Bush's address at Wellesley College, and every important presidential address you find there features manuscript delivery.

Memorized Delivery

Web Link

Memorized delivery was the norm in classical Rome, where orators learned their speeches word for word. Orators in oral cultures still memorize their tribe's stories and legends, a tradition that ensures that the exact stories are preserved throughout

> **memorized delivery** learning the speech by heart, then reciting it

succeeding generations. Memorized speeches are uncommon in today's classrooms or workplaces, although professional speakers who repeatedly give the same talk eventually know it by heart. Students on speech teams often memorize the speeches they deliver dozens of times in competitive tournaments.

Some students believe that memorizing their speeches will help them overcome their fears. Unfortunately, the opposite often happens. Standing in front of an audience, a beginning speaker's mind can easily go blank. I once met an older woman who vividly remembered her college speech class. She said she was scared to death to give her speech on the topic of spanking, so she decided to memorize it. Unfortunately, memory failed her, and her resulting embarrassment followed her for more than fifty years.

Another drawback is that memorized speeches can sound "recited," not natural or conversational. Instead of engaging the audience, the speaker appears to focus on the speech. If you ever give the same speech repeatedly, the key is to treat each audience and occasion as unique, so that you don't just recite words.

If for some reason you must memorize a speech, here are some tips:[7] Write out your talk using oral style. Vivid language, such as alliterated main points or parallel wording, can aid your memory.[8] Learn your speech line by line first and then chunk by chunk, all the time thinking about the meaning. Practice speaking conversationally—as if you are talking to each audience member individually. Finally, put key terms on note cards in case you find yourself stumbling.

Impromptu Delivery

impromptu delivery speaking with little advanced preparation

Impromptu speeches are given with little advanced notice; consequently, this mode takes the least amount of preparation and rehearsal. However, your life, your knowledge, or your experiences usually prepare you to make the speech. In fact, people are rarely, if ever, asked to talk about totally unfamiliar subjects. For example, you may suddenly decide to say a few words at a farewell party. You don't have time to write out a speech and practice it. Instead, you quickly think of something relevant to say about the person who's leaving.

Today's speakers can write out their speeches or notes on a digital tablet or cell phone and use them instead of sheets of paper or cards when they deliver their speeches.

You may shudder at the thought of speaking without preparation and rehearsal, especially if a reward or punishment such as a grade or a job evaluation is at stake. However, business consultant Steve Kaye says this type of speaking is so common in the workplace that "business leaders are eventually going to be asked to give an impromptu speech at some point in their careers,"[9] and top leaders can count on a 99.9 percent chance that they'll be asked to say a few words at banquets, company picnics, farewells, and so on. (Of course, "winging it" is a bad strategy if you've been assigned to give a carefully prepared speech.)

If the situation arises, don't panic.[10] In fact, expect to be called on when you are in a key position of some sort (a child of parents celebrating an anniversary, a friend of a graduate, a project manager, and so on). Listen carefully to what other speakers say at the occasion, and make mental notes of points they omit. If you have a few minutes of advance warning, apply what you know about speech structure (gain attention, make a few points, support each one briefly, make an ending statement). Think of a couple of points to develop briefly, and jot down key words when possible. Or decide on one good story. When possible, tie into things others have said. Finally, conclude with a memorable statement and then sit down instead of rambling on and on.

Martin Luther King Jr.'s "I Have a Dream" speech is a good example of a speech that begins with manuscript delivery but ends with impromptu speaking. In the final section, he departs from his script and draws from his vast knowledge of the Bible, of song lyrics, of previous sermons, and so on to deliver some of his most inspirational lines.[11]

Extemporaneous Delivery

Most speeches are not read, not memorized, and not given spur of the moment. Instead, they are delivered extemporaneously. Lectures, briefings, sales presentations, class reports, you name it—most good speakers prepare their ideas carefully in advance but use speaking notes when they talk. Although they lose some precision in language, this method frees them to speak conversationally and to make eye contact with listeners. Learning **extemporaneous delivery** is important for both school and career success.[12]

extemporaneous delivery preparing a speech carefully in advance but choosing the exact wording during the speech itself

Create speaking notes, as described in Chapter 11, that will help you remember the order of your points and important supporting material. (To avoid reading, don't put too many words in your notes. Then you'll have nothing to read.)

Give yourself plenty of time to learn your material. The key is to memorize the thought patterns, not every word.[13] Try dividing the content into sections and then working on each one separately. Or concentrate on one element at a time; for example, in one run-through, focus on your visual aids, in another, on the content, on signposts, or on smooth transitions.[14] Time yourself and make adjustments. Conclude with at least two full rehearsals: one to find your errors, the second to correct them.[15] Challenge yourself to practice enough to be really good, not just adequate.[16]

On speech day, review your outline, go over your notes, and head off to the speech with the confidence and security that comes from thorough preparation.[17] If you happen to make a mistake during delivery, don't say "I'm sorry." Just pause slightly, regain your place, and continue as if nothing happened.

Each of the four types of delivery—manuscript, memorized, impromptu, and extemporaneous—is common in the United States (Table 14.1). Each has strengths and weaknesses. The key throughout is to think about your listeners, not your delivery. The noted orator Sir Winston Churchill, Britain's prime minister during World War II, always kept his audience in mind. Once when he was rehearsing in the bathtub, his valet heard him through the door and asked, "Were you speaking to me, sir?" Churchill replied, "No, I was addressing the House of Commons."[18]

TABLE 14.1
Types of Delivery

Manuscript	Write the speech out word for word and deliver it by reading the text
Memorized	Learn the speech by heart and recite it conversationally from memory
Impromptu	Prepare the speech on the spot, using information you know about the topic
Extemporaneous	Prepare and outline the speech in advance; rehearse; use note cards with the major points and key words but select the exact wording as you speak

Maximize Your Personal Appearance

Part of successful delivery includes coordinating your physical appearance, your clothing, and your accessories to give your audience a good impression of you.

Physical Appearance

Images of physically perfect bodies pervade our media, and by comparison, most people have at least one flaw. Features like less-than-perfect skin, crooked teeth, visible birthmarks, above- or below-average weight or height, or use of a wheelchair can cause reluctance to speak publicly; you may feel as if you're in the limelight, being scrutinized.[19] However, don't worry too much; audiences don't see just your physical characteristics; they form an overall impression based on essentials you can control such as cleanliness and grooming.[20]

Clothing

Clothing can create positive or negative impression. Whatever the context, you can look like you take the assignment seriously. A good general rule is to select attire that doesn't draw attention to itself and is appropriate to the situation. In the classroom slightly more conservative and simple clothing generally works best. Visualize the impression you're creating from the audience's point of view. Would a top with a "busy" pattern or a message T-shirt distract from your talk? One student who normally wore a black T-shirt decorated with the image of a creature whose fangs dripped blood, changed to a simple black shirt on speech days.

In other contexts, check out clothing expectations, given the group and the occasion. For instance, a student who was invited to speak at a university staff retreat dressed as if she were going to a job interview, not realizing the retreat was located in the woods and participants would wear casual clothes. She later confessed, "I was overdressed!" If she had asked before going, she would have known.

Accessories

Make your accessories matter. These are the objects you add to your clothing such as eyeglasses, jewelry, hats, and scarves. They are also the things you carry such as briefcases or folders. Professional-looking clipboards or folders for your speaking outlines

A combination of clothing, accessories, facial expressions, and posture make this speaker appear confident and natural.

can make you look prepared and competent. Avoid accessories that distract or draw attention to themselves. Simple is generally best.

In summary, don't worry about aspects of your appearance that you can't fix. Instead, be well groomed and choose clothing and accessories that make you look your best.

ETHICS IN PRACTICE
Managing Impressions

There are ethical implications in trying to create an impression of yourself. When you try to be authentic or when you try to deceive your audience to one degree or another, you are making ethical choices. Presenting verbal and nonverbal messages that you actually believe is **sincere**. In contrast, intentionally choosing to create false or misleading impressions is **cynical**, because you don't believe your own messages.[21]

You can probably think of public personalities who try to appear genuinely interested in people because they want their money, time, or votes. Lawyers hire consultants to advise and coach their clients in selecting clothing, mannerisms, and nonverbal techniques to create an impression of innocence in jury members' minds. Ivy League–educated politicians wear flannel shirts or hard hats to "connect" with the working class. The list goes on.

Using the following questions, discuss with a small group of your classmates the ethical appropriateness of these and similar actions.

sincere speakers presenting verbal and nonverbal messages they themselves believe

cynical speakers presenting verbal or nonverbal messages they don't believe in an attempt to create a false image

Questions

1. Is it wrong to imply that a politician, an Ivy League graduate from a wealthy family, is similar to blue-collar listeners? Why or why not?
2. Are lawyers and consultants acting ethically if they try to create an image of innocence for clients they believe are guilty?
3. What if they believe in their clients' innocence?
4. How do sincere lawyers and politicians contribute to the judicial or political process?
5. How do cynical lawyers and politicians contribute to the judicial or political process?

Develop Effective Mannerisms

Although some aspects of your appearance are relatively fixed, to a significant degree you can control your mannerisms. Gestures, posture, and eye contact are especially important in this culture.

Control Your Gestures

Gestures are the movements you perform unwittingly during speech as part of your expressive effort.[22] They range from large motions such as posture, walking, and gesturing to very small movements such as raising one eyebrow. Bodily movements function to supplement your words, display emotions, help audiences understand the structure of your speech, and, in some cases, betray nervousness.[23]

Supplementing with Gestures

It's common to use gestures to emphasize an idea or to add to your words. For example, you might say "It's about this wide" and extend your hands to show the distance. Pointing out something, such as an area on a map, is also common. A *Harvard Business Newsletter* article says speakers can alert their audiences to the speech's high points and transitions because listeners want cues that help them listen better.[24] So consider using posture and movements to emphasize your speech structure.

Here are a few ways to use bodily movements to add to your speech:

- Make your gestures purposeful by planning where you'll use them. It's easy to wave your arms about randomly or to repeat an annoying or distracting gesture.
- To emphasize structure, students on speech teams learn to "walk their points." They begin the introduction in one place and then take a couple of steps to the right to develop their first point, a few steps to the left signal the next point, and so on. The conclusion is given from the starting position. It may seem awkward to walk *every* point, but consider where and how movement could supplement your verbal transitions and signposts.

Audiences look at facial expressions, eye contact, and posture, and they listen for vocal qualities that disclose a speaker's attitude toward them and the topic.

© Lisa A/Shutterstock.com

- Step back slightly or drop your hands from the podium to signal a transition.
- During one rehearsal, focus on your gestures and practice them until they seem natural. Avoid holding your elbows close to your body as you gesture.
- When possible, video a rehearsal and watch yourself with the sound turned off. Analyze when and how you use your hands and arms to make effective points, and when and how your movements are meaningless. Practice what to do with your hands when you are not gesturing.

Displaying Emotion

Facial expressions are especially useful in conveying feelings such as disgust and contempt (appropriate for a topic such as the blood diamond industry) or humor and delight (appropriate for an awards speech). Posture can show confidence and pride or sadness and defeat (just look at the winning and losing benches on a sports team). Here are some tips for showing emotion:

- Maintain pleasant facial expressions. You don't have to smile all the time, but it's important to show a friendly attitude toward your audience.
- Even if you don't feel confident, you can look and act it. Stand tall; relax; hold your head erect and look directly at the audience.
- Put yourself into the right emotional attitude toward your material and the occasion. For example, if you want your audience to get excited about an idea, you get excited about it. If you want them to be disgusted, you be disgusted. On a ceremonial occasion, be happy; in a serious problem-solving meeting, be serious.

Avoiding Nervous Mannerisms

Bodily movements can betray your nervousness or stress. You might be tempted to fidget with your hair, bite your lip, or scratch your face. Or you might twist your ring or tap your note cards against the podium. Finally, you might use a gesture in a way that cuts you off from your audience—like folding your arms across your chest during intense questioning. These gestures suggest you are subconsciously protecting yourself against the perceived psychological threat of the questioner. To minimize nervous gestures:

- Watch a video of yourself rehearsing, noting any nervous mannerism you use and then plan specific ways to avoid them. Or rehearse in front of some friends and ask them to list your movements that betray a lack of confidence. Discuss with them ways to improve.
- On speech day, eliminate the temptation to fidget. For example, if you typically twirl a pen, don't take one to the podium with you. If you constantly flip your hair out of your eyes, secure it somehow.
- On your speaking outline, write cues such as DON'T SCRATCH, if that is your habit.
- Be especially aware of your body language, especially during a question-and-answer period. Work to maintain an open body position, and avoid crossing your arms defensively, even if the questioning becomes pointed.

Make Eye Contact

In the United States, the phrase "Look me in the eye and say that" is partly premised on the cultural notion that people won't lie if they're looking at you. Here, **eye contact** communicates that you are friendly, honest, dynamic, extroverted, and approachable; purposely avoiding another's gaze generally signals a lack of interest.[25] This concept transfers to public speaking where the audience forms impressions of you based on your eye contact. Eye contact also helps you know if your audience is confused or bored, so you can adjust your speech accordingly.

eye contact looking audiences in the eye; communicates friendliness in the United States

Making eye contact can be difficult at first. It is tempting to look at your notes, the floor in front of you, the back wall, or out the window—all gazes that communicate discomfort. Here are some tips for developing effective eye contact:

- Look in at least three general directions: at the listeners directly in front of you, those to the left, and those to the right. Because of your peripheral vision, you can generally keep most listeners within your vision as your gaze changes direction.
- If your audience is sitting in a rectangular shape, mentally divide the group into a tic-tac-toe–like grid, and make eye contact with a friendly face in each grid.[26] This will help you look at various people within the room, not just at one or two.
- Hold your gaze with an individual for three to five seconds; finish a thought or idea before you look at someone else.[27]
- Resist the urge to make more eye contact with listeners you perceive as more powerful. In the classroom, don't just zero in on your instructor; in the workplace, don't focus on your boss's reactions at the expense of other listeners.
- Keep in mind that some people don't like to be looked at, perhaps out of shyness; perhaps for cultural reasons, they've been taught to avoid direct eye contact. If you sense your gaze makes someone uncomfortable, just scan in the general direction, but don't focus on that person's eyes.[28]

Expectations common in the United States are not universally applicable. For instance, Japanese speakers use less direct eye contact, and it is not unusual to see listeners with downcast or closed eyes at a meeting or a conference because this demonstrates attentiveness and agreement rather than rejection, disinterest, or disagreement.[29]

Vary Your Vocal Behaviors

vocalics or **paralinguistics** all aspects of spoken language except the words

Vocalics, also known as **paralinguistics**, deals with all aspects of spoken language except the words themselves—including things such as voice quality, pitch variation, and speech rate. Because of vocal cues, whenever you hear a voice on the radio, you can easily tell whether the speaker is young or old, male or female, a southerner or northerner, a native or nonnative speaker of English. Often you can detect moods such as boredom, hostility, or enthusiasm. This section discusses two major aspects of vocalics related to public speaking: pronunciation and vocal variation.

Work on Clear Pronunciation

articulation the way you enunciate or say specific sounds, an element of pronunciation

stress accenting syllables or words

Pronunciation, the way you actually say words, includes articulation and stress. **Articulation** is the way you say individual sounds, such as *th*ese or *z*ese, b*ir*d or b*oi*d. Some speakers reverse sounds, saying *aks* instead of *ask*, for example, or *nuculer* for *nuclear*. **Stress** is the way you accent syllables within words—poe-LEESE (police) or POE-*leese*. Some people alter both articulation and stress; for instance, the word *comparable* can be pronounced two ways: COM-*purr-uh-bul* or come-PARE-*uh-bul*.

Your articulation often discloses your region of origin, ethnicity, and social status. For instance, regional differences include the drawn-out vowels typical of the "southern drawl" and the *r* added by many Bostonians to the end of words. Ethnic dialects such as Appalachian English or African American English have distinctive articulation and stress patterns. And the accents of nonnative English speakers reflect patterns from their first language. Links between social status and pronunciation form the premise for the classic movie *My Fair Lady*. Although Eliza Doolittle says the same words as Professor Higgins, her pronunciation marks her as a member of the lower class. By changing her pronunciation (as well as her dress and grooming), she eventually passes as a Hungarian princess.

© RTimages/Shutterstock.com

Everyone has a unique voiceprint. Let your distinctive voice work for you by making sure you articulate and stress words properly and by varying your pitch, rate, and volume to enhance your speeches.

In a multilingual world and in pluralistic classrooms and workplaces, accents are everywhere, and as travel, immigration, and technology continue to shrink the world, you'll hear even more in the future. Unfortunately, we tend to judge one another on the basis of accents that indicate social class, ethnic group membership, or status as a nonnative speaker of English;[30] however, Diversity in Practice: Culture and Delivery presents a good argument for affirming a variety of accents.

Because clear expression is essential to understanding, here are some tips for improving your pronunciation and articulation:

- When you're unsure of a word's pronunciation, consult a dictionary. Most online dictionaries now provide an audio feature, so you can hear the word pronounced. Some words, such as *status*, have two acceptable pronunciations—STAY-*tuhs* or STATT-*uhs*. When the dictionary provides two variations, the first is preferable.
- Work on sounds or words that cause you difficulty. Winston Churchill had a lisp, so he carefully rehearsed words that began with /s/.[31] Ralph had trouble saying the word *probably*, so he broke it into syllables—PRAW-*buh-blee*—and articulated each one slowly and clearly.
- During rehearsals, slow down and articulate your words clearly.
- In the speech itself, speak slowly enough to avoid slurring your words together or dropping the endings.
- If you have a serious articulation problem, consult a professional speech therapist.

Culture and Delivery

DIVERSITY IN PRACTICE

This chapter presents norms in the United States, but different cultures have different standards for good delivery, and understanding and adapting to these differences will make you a more culturally sensitive communicator. Arabs and Latin Americans tend to use direct eye contact, as advised in the chapter, but

(continued)

Nigerian, Chinese, Puerto Rican, and Pakistani communicators tend to gaze less directly.[32]

Arabs, Italians, and African Americans tend to speak louder and more intensely than Native Americans and East Asians. North Americans tend to be uncomfortable with long pauses, but Japanese, Navajos, and speakers in India use pauses for reflection and for gathering of one's thoughts.[33]

Many immigrants take classes to improve their pronunciation, but YanHong Krompacky, herself an immigrant, tells them not to waste their money as long as their English is comprehensible and fluent. She argues, "This country is built on accents. Accent is one of the most conspicuous symbols of what makes America the free and prosperous land its own people are proud of and other people long to live in."[34]

Use Vocal Variation

vocal variations changes in volume, rate, and pitch that combine to create impressions of the speaker

Aristotle's classic text on rhetoric[35] discussed three important **vocal variations**: volume, pitch, and rate (which he called rhythm).

> It is not enough to know what we ought to say; we must also say it as we ought....It is, essentially, a matter of the right management of the voice to express the various emotions—of speaking loudly, softly, or between the two; of high, low, or intermediate pitch; of the various rhythms that suit various subjects. These are the three things—volume of sound, modulation of pitch, and rhythm—that a speaker bears in mind.

What kinds of impressions do vocal variations create? If you speak in a soft monotone instead of varying your pitch, you'll sound bored or sick; a louder monotone sounds angry. And several studies[36] conclude that audiences typically associate vocal rate and volume with the following personality traits:

Loud and fast speakers: self-sufficient, resourceful, dynamic

Loud and slow speakers: aggressive, competitive, confident

Soft and fast speakers: enthusiastic, adventuresome, confident, composed

Soft and slow speakers: competitive, enthusiastic, benevolent

Is there a relationship between your rate of speech and your credibility? Research shows that audiences associate rapid speech with intelligence and objectivity. They link a moderate rate to composure, honesty, an orientation toward people, and compassion.[37] To make vocal variations work for you, follow some of these rehearsal suggestions:

- One professional trainer suggests you babble during one rehearsal. That is, give your speech in nonsense syllables but use the vocalics, gestures, and body movements that express its emotional content.[38]
- Record your speech and listen to your voice. Notice whether or not your tone of voice, rising or falling inflection, and stress on specific words create the meanings you want. Take notes on specific things you do well and things to improve. Rehearse the parts that could use more energy.

During your actual performance, remember these suggestions:

- The most important rule is to speak loudly enough to be heard throughout the entire room.[39]

- Intentionally relax your throat before you speak and whenever you feel tense as you speak.[40]
- Use the lower range of your voice; higher pitches make you sound younger and more excitable.
- Speak naturally and conversationally. Don't force enthusiasm.
- Change vocal inflections when your audience appears to be losing interest; add pitch variation and slightly increased volume and rate to communicate enthusiasm; **vary your volume and rate to add impact.**[41]

Pause for Effect

Pauses can be effective or embarrassing to both you and your listeners. Effective pauses are intentional—ones purposely used between major ideas or to give your audience a few seconds to contemplate a difficult concept. In a speech to corporate executives, Judith Humphrey[42] advised:

> [C]onsider this: when does the audience think? Not while you're speaking, because they can't think about an idea until it's delivered. They think during the pauses. But if there are no pauses, they won't think. They won't be moved. They won't act upon what you say. The degree to which you want to involve the audience is reflected in the length of your pauses.

In contrast, ineffective pauses or hesitations disrupt your fluency and signal that you've lost your train of thought or you're searching for words. **Unfilled pauses** are silent; **filled** or **vocalized pauses** include *uh* or *um*, *like*, *OK*, and *you know*. Many professionals, as well as beginning public speakers, use *um*s. However, too many can be distracting, so work to minimize them. To use pauses effectively:

unfilled pause silent pause

filled or **vocalized pause** saying *um* or *uh* or other sounds during a pause

- Find places in your manuscript or outline where your audience needs you to pause so they can absorb what you just said. Use double slash marks // to mark these places. Then rehearse these intentional pauses. What may seem like a very long pause to you may be about right for your listeners.
- During a rehearsal, ask a friend to count the number of vocalized pauses you make and then give the speech again, and eliminate as many *um*s or *uh*s as you can.

Everett Collection, Inc.

In the movie *Meet Joe Black*, William Parrish addressed the board of Parrish Communications. Watch the clip of this movie online. Notice how his initial *um*s and nervous mannerisms give way to meaningful pauses, gestures, and movements that add emphasis to his words. (You can access this link through your online resources.)

- Use pauses as punctuation marks. For example, at the end of the body of the speech, try pausing, moving one step backward, and then saying, "In conclusion…" Your pause functions as a period that signals a separation in your thoughts.

A number of movies listed on your online resources under "Movie Speeches" provide excellent models of good speakers who aren't afraid of pauses. Queen Gorgo's speech to the Spartan Council in the movie *300* and Coach Gary Gaines's speech on "Being Perfect" in the movie *Friday Night Lights* are just two examples.

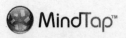

communicative competence the ability to communicate in a personally effective and socially appropriate manner

confident style a way of speaking characterized by effective vocal variety, fluency, gestures, and eye contact

conversational style speaking that's comparatively calmer, slower, and less intense, but maintains good eye contact and gestures

Put It All Together

Communicative competence is defined as the ability to communicate in a personally effective and socially appropriate manner.[43] The key to a competent performance is to find the delivery that works best in a given situation. A **confident style** incorporates vocal variety, fluency, good use of gestures, and eye contact to create an impression of dynamism as well as credibility. If you're naturally outgoing, this style may best fit your personality. However, in some situations—somber occasions, for example—you should choose a more **conversational style** that's calmer, slower, softer, and less intense, but still maintains good eye contact and gestures.[44] Listeners associate this style with trustworthiness, honesty, sociability, likableness, and professionalism, and it may actually fit you better if your personality is more laid back. But more conversational speakers can adapt for an occasion, such as a rally, where excitement runs high and people expect a more enthusiastic delivery. Both styles are persuasive.

Don't worry if you are not yet dynamic or confident. Instead, begin to develop your personal delivery style, using your appearance, mannerisms, and vocal variations to your advantage.

Think Critically about Delivery

Political candidates often illustrate the link between delivery and effectiveness. For example, President Reagan was called the "Great Communicator," and Barack Obama's speaking skills are praised globally. In contrast, many politicians fail the "charismatic challenge." One presidential candidate's voice was described as "somewhere between that of a dentist's drill and the hum of a refrigerator."[45] Another's delivery was wooden, earnest, solemn, uptight, and focused more on content than on delivery. Enter the consultants. Some handlers spun their bland candidate as "authentic." Others sat beside their candidates, watching and rewatching videos of speeches, analyzing volume, rate, gestures, and facial expressions. Their overall advice was to loosen up—leave the podium, gesture widely, smile. Politicians know that no matter how wonderful their ideas, their message will be lost if their delivery annoys the audience or puts them to sleep.

In small groups, discuss the following questions:

1. What qualities are important in a president? How does presidential image matter? What do you think of the handlers' decision to spin unremarkable delivery as "authentic"?
2. Should a candidate undergo a makeover or "be herself," regardless?
3. President William Taft (1909–1914) weighed around 300 pounds. Could he be elected president today? Why or why not? Is this good or bad?
4. Women candidates often claim that media coverage is sexist. Words like *shrill*, *strident*, and *giggle* appeared in stories about them, but not about their male

opponents.[46] Women are critiqued on their wardrobes, hairstyles, and accessories; men rarely are. In your opinion, does this constitute sexism? Why or why not?

5. Could Abraham Lincoln—with his looks and awkward mannerisms—be elected in this television-dominated society? Why or why not?

Videotaping Your Speech[47]

If you are taking this course online and must record and upload your speeches, some additional considerations apply. You might be asked to assemble a live audience; if not, know that whoever sees your video can watch, rewind, stop, and fast-forward your speech. Ask your instructor if you should make eye contact with your live audience or with the online audience. Preparation includes:

- **Place**. Film in a quiet space with a simple background that will not distract the audience.
- **Lighting**. To make sure the space is lit well, open curtains and turn on lights in the room. Then do a test video to see how well the camera picks up the room's lighting.
- **Camera**. If possible, set the camera on a tripod about 5 to 8 feet from where you'll speak. Set up your visuals (if you use them) and plan where you'll stand in relationship to them. Then look through the frame to identify the area it will record. If you plan to move around, note how much room you'll have to stay in the frame. Test the microphone and see if it picks up your sound adequately.
- **Speaking Notes**. Put a dark cover sheet behind your speaking notes so that the camera doesn't pick up a lot of white. Or write your notes on a digital tablet or cell phone.
- **Clothing**. Avoid clothing with very small patterns or pin stripes that can create an optical illusion of movement on video.[48]
- **Taping**. Ideally, find someone else to operate the camera—starting a few seconds before you begin and leaving it on a few seconds after you're through.

Overall, don't be distracted by the setting, the audience, or the technology. Deliver the speech as naturally as possible by focusing on your message and your purpose for speaking.

Summary

Of the four major types of delivery, memorization is common in oral cultures and in competitive speech tournaments, but it is less frequently used elsewhere. You may speak spontaneously in the impromptu style, or you may read from a manuscript. But more commonly, you'll join the ranks of extemporaneous speakers—preparing in advance but choosing your exact wording as you actually speak. Each type of delivery has its place, and each comprises a number of skills that you can develop through practice.

Because delivery involves nonverbal elements, you can create a more positive impression of yourself by managing your body and voice to affect listeners' impressions of you. The study of body language and public speaking is at least as old as Aristotle— and he surely didn't invent the idea. Modern scholars continue to explore specific aspects of appearance, mannerisms, and vocal variations that create positive or negative impressions in audiences.

Your clothing, your grooming, and your accessories communicate your competence. Your mannerisms—gestures, eye contact, and vocal variation—are also important in creating impressions of dynamism, honesty, and other characteristics of credibility.

As your nonverbal skills increase, your competence in public speaking increases correspondingly.

As with all attempts to influence others, the attempt to manage impressions has ethical implications. Speakers who believe in both the verbal and nonverbal messages they are sending are said to be sincere, but those who try to create false or misleading impressions are termed cynical.

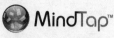

Reflect on what you've learned.

STUDY AND REVIEW

Public Speaking: Concepts and Skills for a Diverse Society offers a broad range of resources that will help you better understand the material in this chapter, complete assignments, and succeed on tests. Your MindTap resources feature the following:

- Speech videos with critical viewing questions, speech outlines, and transcripts
- Interactive versions of this chapter's Stop and Check activities, as well as and Critical Thinking Exercises and Application Exercises
- Speech Builder Express
- Weblinks related to chapter content
- Study and review tools such as self-quizzes and an interactive glossary

You can access your online resources for *Public Speaking: Concepts and Skills for a Diverse Society* at cengagebrain.com using the access code that came with your book or that you purchased online.

Review your **Flashcards**.

KEY TERMS

The terms below are defined in the margins throughout this chapter.

articulation 190	filled or vocalized pause 193
communicative	impromptu delivery 184
competence 194	manuscript delivery 183
confident style 194	memorized delivery 183
conversational style 194	vocalics or paralinguistics 190
cynical 187	sincere 187
delivery 183	stress 190
extemporaneous delivery 185	unfilled pause 193
eye contact 189	vocal variations 192

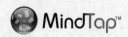

CRITICAL THINKING EXERCISES

1. Make a video of one of your rehearsals or speeches and then watch it. Specifically pay attention to your gestures, noting your use of purposeful movements and of movements that betray nervousness. Plan strategies to improve your gestures, eliminating those that create negative impressions and strengthening those that produce favorable impressions.
2. Watch the recording again. This time, evaluate your eye contact. Throughout your speech, notice the way you use your voice. Check for appropriate rate and volume; be alert for pauses, and count the number of *um*s you use, if any. Write a plan to improve these nonverbal aspects of delivery.

APPLICATION QUESTIONS

1. With a small group of your classmates, make a set of guidelines for delivery that is appropriate to your classroom's unique culture. For example, would you change the advice about clothing or accessories presented in this chapter? What might you add that is not covered here?

2. In his book *The Presentation of Self in Everyday Life* Erving Goffman says the combination of environment, appearance, and mannerisms forms a "front."[49] Whether intentional or unwitting, this front influences the way observers define and interpret the situation. With this in mind, identify some public speakers who effectively live out their front.[50] Then discuss why some public speakers appear to be something they're not. That is, why do they present themselves as competent or trustworthy, and you later discover they aren't? What are some ethical implications of fronts?

3. Create a worksheet that identifies the elements of delivery mentioned in the chapter. Give it to a classmate just before your speech, and have him or her note nonverbal aspects of your delivery; afterward, discuss with that person strategies you can use to improve problem areas.

4. Write a script for an ad selling one of these products:
   a. Used car
   b. Perfume
   c. Vacation to South America
   d. Brand of cola

   Bring your script to class and exchange it with a classmate. Demonstrate the type of vocal variation you would use if you were delivering the ad.

SPEECH VIDEO

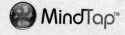

Log on to your online resources to watch and critique examples of memorized, extemporaneous, manuscript, and impromptu speeches.

CHAPTER 15

**THIS CHAPTER WILL
HELP YOU**

- Analyze your audi-
  ence's knowledge
  of your subject

- Create several
  types of informative
  speeches, including
  demonstrations
  and instructions,
  descriptions, reports,
  and explanations

- Follow guidelines that
  make your informative
  speeches more
  effective

Diana Ong/SuperStock

Informative Speaking

OBVIOUSLY, THE WORLD is awash in information, and vast amounts of data
are cheaply and quickly distributed globally. Most people are happy to have
information distributed through so many channels, but are we better informed
as a result?[1] Think about it. How much of the information you hear affects you
personally? What's vital to know, and what's trivial? What information helps
you live better, and what's simply interesting or distracting? It's easy to feel
overwhelmed unless someone relates the material to our lives and helps us
integrate new information with old. Then we can make sense of our world and
use our knowledge to make wise decisions.[2]

Informative speakers can fulfill an important cultural role by sorting through
facts and data to create speeches that help audiences know more or understand
a subject better. Here are a few examples:

Mind
Review th
chapter
Learning
Objective
and *Start*
with a qui
warm-up
activity.

- A representative of a nonprofit organization provides information on how to host a bead party to raise funds for female-owned businesses in a developing country.
- A counselor informs recent college grads on ways to pay down their loans.
- Public health educators in central Africa empower women with facts they need to protect themselves against sexually transmitted diseases.

This chapter first distinguishes four levels of audience knowledge you should analyze before you speak. Next, it describes several types of speeches, including demonstrations and instructions, descriptions, reports, and explanations—with several skeletal outlines of speeches in these categories. General guidelines for informative speaking conclude the chapter.

Analyze Your Audience's Current Knowledge

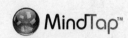

Read, highlight, and take notes online.

Listeners fall into four general categories: those who (a) know nothing about your topic, (b) have minimal information, (c) have forgotten or outdated information, or (d) have misinformation. Each level of understanding calls for different strategies.[3] To be effective, analyze what the audience already knows and believes about your topic so that you can adjust your speech accordingly.[4] This can be challenging because a single audience often contains listeners from more than one category.

Presenting New Information

When your audience is unfamiliar with your subject, your task is to provide a basic overview of the topic. For instance, what do you know about Dong Nguyen (creator of the Floppy Bird game)? Mochi pounding? Chinese wedding customs? Most people are unfamiliar with them, so any information will be novel. For unfamiliar topics, follow these guidelines:

- Provide basic, introductory facts—who, what, when, where, and how information.
- Clearly define new terminology and jargon.
- Give detailed, vivid explanations and descriptions.
- Make links to your audience's knowledge by using literal and figurative analogies and by comparing and contrasting the concept with something familiar.
- Help listeners understand why the topic is relevant.

Presenting Supplemental Information

The great inventor Thomas Edison said, "We don't know a millionth of one percent about anything."[5] This means that listeners who are somewhat familiar with your topic will have gaps in their knowledge.

At the outset, think about what your audience already knows about your topic. Is it totally unfamiliar to them? Do they have outdated information or misconceptions? What do they need to hear? Answering these questions helps you design a speech that makes the information more useful to your listeners.

They need supplemental information, not a rehash of basic facts. An audience that knows about sleep deprivation, for example, will be more impressed if you provide little-known facts about this health risk. Use these guidelines with audiences whose information is limited:

- Dig into your research sources to discover less common details and facts.
- Go beyond the obvious and add in-depth descriptions, details, and explanations.
- Narrow a broad topic and provide interesting and novel information about just one aspect of it. For example, instead of another broad overview, focus on the relationship between sleep deprivation and obesity or heart disease.

Presenting Review or Updated Information

Sometimes listeners were once familiar with your subject, but they've forgotten some or most of what they learned, or they lack current, updated information. Here, speak to refresh their memories, reinforce their knowledge, and keep their information current. Reviews and updates are common in schools or workplace settings. For instance, upper division courses briefly review basic concepts before going into depth on new materials. In workplaces, employees may have learned about privacy laws a decade ago, but a workshop on new regulations keeps them updated. To review or update information, use these guidelines:

- Review material by approaching the subject from different angles and different perspectives.
- Be creative; use vivid supporting materials that capture and hold attention.
- Use humor if appropriate, and strive to make the material interesting.
- Present the most recent available information. Because of the current proliferation of information generated by technology, data can quickly become outdated, and people who want to stay current must be lifelong learners.

Countering Misinformation

A third type of audience has misconceptions or misunderstandings that you can clarify by providing definitions and facts and by countering misinformation. For instance, students from different ethnic or religious backgrounds often find themselves countering misconceptions about their cultures or beliefs, and politicians typically clarify policy positions that their opponents have distorted. When you counter misunderstandings, your material may be inconsistent or contradictory to what listeners "know," so consider the following:

- To prepare for emotional responses—often negative—present the most credible facts you can find, and tone down the emotional aspect.
- Look for information derived from scientific studies, especially quantification, when statistical or numerical support would be best.
- Define terminology carefully. Explaining the origin of specific words or ideas is often a good strategy.
- Counter negative prejudices against and stereotypes about a topic (such as a particular culture or religion) by highlighting positive aspects of the subject.

In summary, the amount of information your audience brings to your speech should make a difference in the way you select and present meaningful information, and various listeners can have differing levels of understanding. By assessing listeners' knowledge about your subject in advance, you can more effectively prepare a speech that meets their need to know.

The Global Importance of Information

© iStockphoto.com/art12321

Article 19 of the Universal Declaration of Human Rights (1948) states:

> Everyone has the right to freedom of opinion and expression; this right
> includes freedom to hold opinions without interference and to seek
> and impart information and ideas through any media and regardless
> of frontiers.[6]

This Article recognizes the potential dangers of an **information imbalance**, where some individuals and groups have overwhelming amounts of information and others have very little and thus lack fundamental understandings of the world. (The entire UN declaration can be accessed on your online resources.)

In the light of this value, the United Nations News Centre commends areas around the world where information is making a difference. For example, Afghanistan released voting information, which the UN hopes will enable fraud complaints to be processed thoroughly.[7] In seven countries in West Africa, health workers used culturally sensitive informative strategies to disseminate information about the deadly Ebola virus. Some people had never heard of it before; others had unfounded fears based on rumors; but all needed "information blasts" to know how to protect themselves.[8]

information imbalance some people or groups having very little access to information while others have it in abundance

Types of Informative Speeches

Informative speeches fall into several categories. Demonstrations and instructions, descriptions, reports, and explanations are common in classrooms and careers. Two basic methods are useful for organizing and explaining information: division and classification. **Division** involves breaking the whole into parts and discussing each part individually. For example, Kylie divided the topic of Asperger syndrome into causes, symptoms, and

division a method for presenting information by breaking the whole into parts and explaining each one

classification a method of presenting information by explaining things that are put into categories according to a principle

treatments. She then developed each subtopic in more detail. **Classification** also divides a topic into categories, but it then uses a common standard to rate or rank the groups. For instance, because languages are classified by how hard they are to learn, a speaker might explain why Spanish is classified as a Level I language, Hindi as Level II, Zulu as Level III, and Chinese as Level IV.[9]

Doing Demonstrations and Providing Instructions

Instructions answer the question, "How do you do that?" Nate Berkus is famous for showing how to create an interior design; Dave Ramsey tells people how to put their finances in order. They're just two of thousands of teachers, coaches, and salespeople who both show (demonstrate) and tell (give instructions) how to do a procedure, how to use a specific object, or how to complete a task. Several general principles apply:[10]

1. First, use the principle of division and break the topic into required stages or steps. Then ask: What's absolutely essential? What comes first? Which step is easiest? Which is hardest? What does the audience already know how to do? Where will the audience most likely be confused? Which step takes the most time? Organize the steps sequentially.
2. Next, concentrate on clarifying and simplifying difficult or confusing steps. Carefully preplan the environment to facilitate learning—you might have your audience move their chairs or stand up and spread out around the room. Or you may need to furnish supplies for them to do the project along with you.
3. Plan your visual support. If actual objects are practical, use them; if not, plan videos, diagrams, or other visuals. Then practice working with your props so you can use them and still maintain rapport with your audience.[11] Knowing that she could not simply describe how to draw a hand in words alone, Beth led her listeners through the process by actually drawing on a whiteboard as shown in the photographs.[12]

Specific Purpose: To inform my audience about six steps in drawing a hand.
Central Idea: It's easy to draw a hand if you follow six steps.

    I. Step 1: Block out the outline using simple, geometric shapes.
    II. Step 2: Identify the bone structure, including all the knuckles.

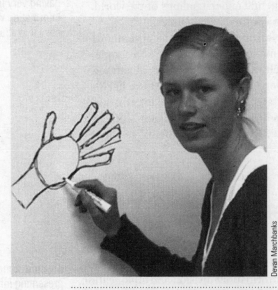

For her how-to speech on drawing a hand, Beth drew on the board as she explained the process. Her audience drew along, following her step-by-step instructions.

III. Step 3: Draw around the basic outline in Step 1.
IV. Step 4: Add details of knuckles, fingernails, creases, rings, and so on.
V. Step 5: Shade, using dark, medium, or light shades.
VI. Step 6: Erase excess lines.

In her introduction, she made sure each student had a pencil and a blank sheet of paper. Then, as she spoke, each student completed the step she described.

4. Time the entire process. If the process is too long, then just demonstrate it and provide handouts with step-by-step instructions for listeners to do later. (One student could not teach her classmates to fold an origami crane in a seven-minute speech; twenty-two minutes later, everyone had half-folded cranes when the class ended.) For a lengthy process, another strategy is to prepare several versions, stopping each at a different point. Cooking and art instructors commonly do this. A cook, for example, begins a complicated dish, but instead of waiting twenty minutes for it to bake, he sets aside the partly finished pan, reaches for a second pan that contains a baked version of the dish, and then adds finishing touches. Similarly, a sculptor shows an essential step in creating a pot; then she leaves it to dry and takes up a pot prepared in advance for the next step.

Not all "how-to" speeches require a demonstration. You can give tips on topics like resolving conflict, listening more effectively, or managing time wisely. In these cases, you focus on instructions or pointers that provide information listeners need to accomplish the goal.

Giving Descriptions

Descriptions answer the question, "What's it like?" Before you can describe an object, place, or event to someone else, again use the principles of division or classification to analyze it. For instance, to describe a painting, divide it into sections and point out details of color, form, and texture that listeners might miss at first glance. Or classify several paintings according to era or style and compare and contrast the details. Descriptions of places, objects, and events range from personal to global. Because listeners are generally more interested in topics close to their daily lives in location, time, and relevance, explicitly relate each topic to their perceived interests and needs.

Describing Places

People often want information about places such as a college campus or a tourist site. Consequently, college guides describe campus sites as they show prospective students around. And travel authors or park rangers are just two types of professionals who describe places. In fact, Rick Steves is famous for his descriptions of tourist destinations.

In descriptive speeches, provide vivid, precise imagery. Use visual aids including maps, drawings, slides, brochures, or enlarged photographs, and consider spatial or topical organizational patterns. International topics such as the Gobi desert or Vatican City make good topics. For his speech about *Ha Noi*,[13] Namky showed photos and described four attractions: Sword Lake, The Temple of Literature, Ho Chi Minh's Mausoleum, and the One Pillar Pagoda.

Describing Objects

Descriptions of objects, including natural objects (glaciers), human constructions (the Vietnam War Memorial), huge things (the planet Jupiter), or microscopic matter (carbohydrates), are common. Students have described inanimate (wind generators) or animate (brown recluse spiders) objects by providing information such as their origin, how they are made, their identifying characteristics, how they work, how they're used, and so on.

Topic choices range from personal to international. Personal topics include physical features such as skin or fingernails. Campus objects include a historical tree or a memorial plaque, and cultural artifacts include the Golden Gate Bridge and guitars. International topics have included the Great Wall of China and London's Big Ben.

Describing Events

Events range from personal (birthday customs), community (local festivals), national (holidays), to international (the bombing of Hiroshima). In Appendix B, you'll find Lishan's explanation of the Chinese holiday that corresponds to St. Valentine's Day. Chronological or narrative patterns work well for step-by-step events such as the bombing of Hiroshima. The topical pattern is useful for happenings that consist of several different components. Here is an example of major subtopics for a speech describing a city event.

> **Specific Purpose:** To inform my audience about the Portland Rose Festival.
> **Central Idea:** The Rose Festival in Portland, Oregon, features something for everyone.

> I. The Queen's Coronation features court members from each city high school.
> II. The Junior Parade involves children.
> III. People from all over the region participate in the Grand Floral Parade.
> IV. City Fair on the waterfront features performers, carnival rides, and other attractions.
> V. The Rose Show is for flower lovers.

When you describe events in concrete detail and vivid language, your listeners can place themselves at the happening, and your speech lets them participate vicariously.

Presenting Reports

Reports answer the question, "What have we learned about this subject?" Investigative reporters search for answers to questions such as, "What are scientists learning about new treatments for melanoma?" Campus reporters pass along conclusions reached by university task forces. In classrooms and workplaces, here and abroad, people give reports. This section discusses two common topic areas: people and issues.

Reporting about People

What individuals have shaped our world? What did they accomplish? How did they live? Answer such questions by providing sketches of influential historical or contemporary characters. Biographical reports can be about thinkers (Plato), military men and women (Mongol warriors, Boudicca), artists (Mary Cassatt), writers (Wole Soyinka), and so on. Villains (Machiavelli) as well as heroes (Harriet Tubman) make good biographical subjects.

Generally, chronological, topical, or narrative patterns best fit a biographical report. Alex divided his subject into two categories: (1) Dong Nguyen's life and (2) his most famous video game. He then used chronological subpoints to develop his first section.

> **Specific Purpose:** To inform my audience of who Dong Nguyen is and how he is related to the game Flappy Bird.
> **Central Idea:** Dong Nguyen, the Vietnamese developer of Flappy Bird, took the game app down because it was too addictive.

  I. Dong Nguyen is a Vietnamese video game developer.
      A. This very shy computer game developer created Flappy Bird.
      B. The game practically ruined his life.
      C. He won't have his photo taken, and he disconnected from the Internet.
 II. Flappy Bird became a very famous game globally.
      A. It earned Nguyen $50,000 a day in advertising revenue.
      B. He took the app down because he thought it was too addictive.
      C. Rumors continue on whether or not it will return.

Speeches about groups such as the Amish, Indigenous Australians, or medieval knights are also interesting. Here, the subject Thuggees is organized topically:

Specific Purpose: To inform my audience about Thuggees, professional assassins, who gave the name to today's thugs.[14]

Central Idea: Historically, Thuggees or Thugs were professional assassins who operated in the region of India for several hundred years.

  I. In more remote areas of India, travelers journeyed on horseback or on foot.
      A. They banded together with strangers for safety and companionship.
      B. Each carried money to buy necessities along the journey.
 II. Organized Thuggees joined these travelers.
      A. The Thugs gained their trust and helped get needed supplies.
      B. When trust was complete, the Thuggees strangled the travelers, buried them, and took their belongings.
III. Today, *thug* means criminal or villain or hooligan.
      A. The original Thugs killed thousands, maybe even millions.
      B. As you can see, today's thugs are not the same as Thuggees.[15]

Today, the word *thug* denotes criminals of many kinds; however, a speech about Thuggees—the group of assassins they're named after—informs listeners that historical Thugs gained trust before they strangled and robbed their victims.

Science & Society Picture Library

As you develop your major points, keep in mind your audience's questions: "How is a speech about this person or group linked to my concerns? What impact has this subject had on society? Answer these questions, and your listeners will better understand the relevance of the person or group. You can access links to biographical information on thousands of individuals, both contemporary and historical on your online resources.

Reporting about Issues

News sources present issues currently being discussed in our communities, our nation, and our world. We deliberate about international, national, local, and campus issues that are complex and controversial. Here are a few examples:

- What have we learned about the effectiveness of alternate energy sources?
- What do we know about measles outbreaks in the United States?
- What issues does each side emphasize as they support or oppose a flat tax?

Think of this speech as an investigative report, where you research the facts surrounding an issue and then present your findings. Your goal is to help people understand and think clearly about a topic—to provide facts listeners can use to formulate their own conclusions. Consequently, do not argue for one position or another, although you may decide to follow up your report with a persuasive speech on the same topic.

Periodical databases or Internet news sites can help you access up-to-date news sources. Look for answers to questions like these: What exactly is the issue? What current beliefs or theories are commonly held about the issue? What is the extent of the problem (how many people does it affect)? How did this situation develop? What solutions are proposed? What are the arguments on both sides of the issue? Generally, pro–con, cause–effect or causal, problem–solution(s), narrative, and topical patterns are most effective for investigative reports.

Specific Purpose: To inform my audience about the pros and cons of wind energy.
Central Idea: There are several arguments both for and against the widespread use of wind energy.

I. There are advantages to using wind turbines to produce electricity worldwide.
   A. Wind is a clean source of renewable energy that emits no greenhouse gases.
   B. Wind power can help minimize dependency on foreign oil.
   C. The technology is constantly being improved so that electricity produced during peak wind hours can be "banked" and used during peak demand hours.
II. There are a number of problems related to wind turbines.
   A. The blade/wind friction of the wind turbines emits noise and a light flicker that disturbs people who live by wind farms.
   B. Many people think wind farms destroy the beauty of the landscape.
   C. Wind farms can interfere with wild bird habitats.
   D. There are environmental impacts during the manufacturing, setup, maintenance, and dismantling of the turbines after they wear out.

Issues can be personal (eating disorders), campus (parking problems), local (potholes), national (ACT versus SAT tests), or global (child labor) in scope. Many global decisions, such as what to do with nuclear waste, have broad implications. Others, although less significant, are related to larger problems. For example, cosmetic surgery on teenaged women is linked to issues of women's rights and stereotypes of female beauty.

ETHICS IN PRACTICE   The Right to Information

Freedom of information is vital in the United States. But are there limits on our rights to know? Even in the United States, not all information is available to just anyone, and cultural values such as privacy or national security allow for "privileged" or "confidential" information in some cases. Reporters have gone to jail rather than name their sources.[16] Politicians or corporations try to protect strategy secrets. The government keeps files on citizens they suspect of posing a danger.

Because free access to information is a recognized right, the US federal government passed the Freedom of Information Act (FOIA) to give citizens access to federal agency records or information (including your personal FBI file, should you have one). However, it excludes records from Congress, the courts, or state and local government agencies.[17]

Every day, citizens put personal information online, but who has the right to this data? In 2013, whistle-blower Edward Snowden leaked top-secret documents revealing how much information the government gathers on citizens: phone calls, emails, the length of conversations, locations, traveling companions, websites visited, and so on.[18] Perhaps less scary, Facebook is just one site that collects personal information plus data on the website browser, the IP address, and the length you're on the site. For example, Facebook collaborated with the Obama campaign to collect digital data on potential voters from Facebook pages.[19] Corporations put cookies in your Internet surfing device to learn your preferences and then target products to you. Google saves all the emails sent through Gmail to index and create models with the goal of targeting ads to you. This data collection apparently does not alarm Americans; we have not demanded laws protecting our privacy, and we like free sites (with ads) rather than paid sites (without ads).

Questions

1. Can you think of instances where withholding information is a good thing?
2. Have you been deprived of information that you thought you needed? If so, describe the situation and tell the results.
3. Is there a difference between "limits on our rights to know" and "censorship"? Explain your answer.
4. What personal information, if any, has been published on the Internet without your consent? Explain.
5. List some ads that pop up when you go on the Internet. Why do you think that ad targeted you?
6. How do you feel about a political campaign working with social media to collect your personal data so they can tailor a political message to you?
7. Edward Snowden is controversial because he fed the media classified documents showing the extent of the government's surveillance both here and abroad. Some consider him a hero; others think he's a villain. Read some news and opinion articles about him and come to class prepared to discuss his intentions and his tactics.

Explaining Concepts

The explanatory or **expository speech** is more simply called the "speech to teach." Expository speakers set forth, disclose, unmask, or explain an idea in detail.[20] Science and history teachers regularly define terms and explain concepts; parents also answer

expository speech the "speech to teach" that explains an idea in detail

the endless "whys" of 4 year olds with explanations. Good expository speakers can identify the hurdles listeners are likely to encounter in their attempt to comprehend the concept. They then plan ways to overcome those barriers and make meanings clear.

Defining Terms

Definitions answer the questions "What is it?" or "What does it mean?" Definition speeches are common in classrooms and workplaces—for example, a literature professor defines genre, a speech professor clarifies the concept of communication climates, and an employer defines sexual harassment for new employees. Inspirational speakers also define words: a minister defines generosity; a commencement speaker describes success; a coach defines perseverance. In short, although people act in ways we might classify as *generous* or as *sexual harassment*, we can neither see nor touch generosity or harassment; defining those terms helps us as a society discriminate between appropriate and inappropriate behaviors.

One effective organizational pattern for a speech of definition[21] presents first the denotative and then the connotative meaning of a word. (Chapter 12 discusses denotation and connotation in detail.)

1. **Denotative Meaning**: Focus on the definition of the word as found in reference books, such as a thesaurus or etymological dictionary. The *Oxford English Dictionary* or another unabridged dictionary provides the most thorough definitions. Books in an academic discipline show how scholars in that field define the term; for example, the definition of *confirmation* found in a dictionary differs from the definition you'd find in a book on interpersonal communication. Develop the denotative point of your speech by selecting some of the following strategies:

   - Provide synonyms and antonyms that are familiar to your audience.
   - Explain the use or function of what you're defining.
   - Give the etymology of the word. What's its historical source? How has the concept developed over time?
   - Compare an unknown concept or item to one your audience already knows.

   For example, an "Allen wrench" might be unfamiliar to some listeners, but a "wrench that looks like a hockey stick" or an "L-shaped wrench" helps them select the specific tool, given a lineup of wrenches.[22]

2. **Connotative Meaning**: Focus on connotative meanings, the emotional associations of words, by using realistic life experiences as creatively as possible. Here, draw from whatever you can think of that will add emotional elements to your explanation.

   - Relate a personal experience that demonstrates the idea.
   - Quote other people telling what the term means to them.
   - Tell a narrative or give a series of short examples that illustrate the concept.
   - Refer to an exemplar—a person or thing that exemplifies the term.
   - Connect the term to a familiar political, social, or moral issue.

For example, in the denotative section of her student speech on destiny, Terez first provided the dictionary definition and then explained the etymology of the word like this:

The Roman saying *Destinatum est mihi* meant "I have made up my mind." In Rome, destiny meant a decision was fixed or determined. Later the word reappeared in both Old and Middle French in the feminine form *destiné*. Finally, from the Middle English word *destinee*, we get the modern form of the word.

Next, a transition led to her connotative section, which consisted of an extended example of a near-fatal car wreck that devastated her family.

However, it isn't the word's etymological history that is meaningful to me. You see, destiny is a depressing reminder of a car accident. . . .

Terez concluded with the following quotation by William Jennings Bryan:

Destiny is not a matter of chance; it is a matter of choice. It is not a thing to be waited for; it is a thing to be achieved.

Including both denotative definitions and connotative associations provided a fuller picture of the concept of destiny.

Giving Explanations

Think of explanations as translations: You take a complex or information-dense concept and put it into common words and images that make it understandable. Explanations commonly answer questions about processes (How does it work?) or about concepts (What's the theory behind that? or Why?).

How was Brunelleschi's Dome in Florence, Italy, constructed? How do honeybees communicate? Why do we yawn? To answer questions like these, you'll describe stages, ordered sequences, or procedures involved in processes, both natural and cultural. You can explain how something is done (training guide dogs for the blind, face transplants), how things work (reverse mortgages, compasses), or how they're made (driverless cars, fire extinguishers). Not surprisingly, chronological patterns are common.

Topics about concepts can be challenging because of their complexity. What is intelligence? What does Main Street mean in American culture? What is a thought? These questions relate to abstractions—the mental principles, theories, and ideas we form to explain both natural and social realities. For instance, politicians routinely

In the 1941 movie *Meet John Doe*, actor Gary Cooper delivers a speech explaining the concept of "John Doe," the average person. You can access his speech on your online resources. Notice the many examples he uses to develop his definition.

refer to "Main Street" in their speeches, but how do ordinary people understand the concept?[23] Here are some guidelines to consider, using the concept of "intelligence" as the topic:

- Simplify complex ideas by dividing them into their component parts. For example, intelligence can be broken down into categories that include social intelligence, spatial intelligence, and musical intelligence.[24]
- Carefully define terminology, avoiding technical jargon. Exactly what falls into the category of spatial intelligence? Use examples that clarify this component of intelligence, or show the items from the tests that measure spatial intelligence.
- Clarify confusing details by using analogies, both figurative and literal, to compare the concept to something that listeners already understand. In this case, you might compare spatial intelligence to running a maze.
- Use detailed examples of concrete situations that illustrate the actions of people who test high in various kinds of intelligence.

Type of Speech	Question(s) It Examines
Demonstration	How do you do that?
Description	What's it like?
Report	What have we learned about this topic?
Explanation	What is it? What does it mean? How does it work? What's the theory behind it?

Figure 15.1
Informative speech types

We often disagree over theories, concepts, and ideas. For instance, exactly what qualifies as a work of art? People's ideas differ. What caused the dinosaurs to become extinct? Theories vary. What constitutes a living wage? Not everyone gives the same answer. The purpose of explanatory speaking is not to argue for one definition or another but to clarify the concept, sometimes by comparing and contrasting differing definitions and theories regarding it. Figure 15.1 summarizes the types of informative speeches and the questions each is designed to answer.

Guidelines for Informative Speaking

A common complaint about informational speaking is that it's boring.[25] Consequently, use some of these tips for keeping your audience's attention and for being both understandable and relevant:[26]

- **Do an "obstacle analysis" of your audience**. Identify the parts of the message they might find hard to understand and then work on specific ways to make those sections clear. Next, identify internal barriers that would prevent listeners from learning your material. You might face psychological resistance if you choose a scientific topic for people who think science is difficult and boring or if you challenge an audience's current misconceptions about a subject they hold dear. Plan ways to deal with each obstacle.[27]
- **Organize your material carefully**. Be kind to your listeners by stating each major point clearly and by building in signposts such as *next* and *in addition* that help them identify the flow of ideas. Use structures such as lists, comparisons–contrasts, or cause–effect patterns. Provide transitions, internal previews, and summaries that show how your material is linked—using words and phrases such as *because*, *therefore*, and *as a result* (see Chapter 9). **Discourse consistency** also helps; for example, you might begin every section with a question or alliterate your main points throughout the entire speech.[28]

discourse consistency
using a repetitive style such as alliteration of main points throughout the speech

- **Personalize your material**. Help listeners see the connection between your topic and their experiences, goals, beliefs, and actions. When they see the information as personally relevant, they're more likely to listen and learn effectively.
- **Compare the known to the unknown**. Start with what your audience knows and build on this foundation, showing similarities and differences between your topic and what listeners already know.
- **Choose your vocabulary carefully**. To avoid bewildering listeners with technical information and incomprehensible jargon, define your terms and explain them in everyday, concrete images. Avoid trigger words with negative connotations that might set off negative reactions in audience members.
- **Build in repetition and redundancy**. **Repetition** means that you say the same thing more than once. **Redundancy** means that you repeat the same idea several times, but you develop it somewhat differently each time. Phrases such as *in other words* or *put simply* are ways to build in redundancy. Repeat and redefine the critical parts of the message to reinforce these crucial points in your listeners' minds.[29]
- **Strive to be interesting**. In your preparation, occasionally try to hear your speech as if someone else were delivering it. Do you find yourself drifting off? If so, where? Search for ways to enliven your factual material. Examples and detailed descriptions, for instance, engage your audience because they invite your listeners to form mental images as you talk.

repetition saying the same thing more than once

redundancy repeating the same idea more than once, but developing it differently each time

If you follow these guidelines, you will increase your listeners' motivation and interest in the topic. And your careful attention to details will help them understand the material more clearly.

Summary

The ability to give and receive information has always been empowering; this is especially so in the Information Age. Those who lack information do not have the basic knowledge they need to perform competently in complex societies. As a result, a variety of people in a variety of settings give informative speeches. Their goals are to present new information, to supplement what's already known, to review or update material, or to correct misinformation.

There are several categories for informative speaking that answer listeners' questions such as "How do you do that?" or "What does that mean?" These include demonstrations and instructions, descriptions, reports, and explanations.

Finally, remember seven keys to informative speaking. Do an obstacle analysis that identifies elements within the topic or within the listeners that might prove to be barriers, and then work to overcome those obstacles. Organize the speech carefully, and provide links that connect the material. Relate your topic to your listeners, and make vocabulary choices that clarify your ideas. Think of creative ways to present your information, and throughout your talk, tie abstract concepts to concrete experiences that are familiar to your listeners. Finally, include repetition and redundancy to reinforce the critical points of the message and, as always, strive to be interesting.

STUDY AND REVIEW

Public Speaking: Concepts and Skills for a Diverse Society offers a broad range of resources that will help you better understand the material in this chapter, complete assignments, and succeed on tests. Your MindTap resources feature the following:

Reflect on what you've learned.

- Speech videos with critical viewing questions, speech outlines, and transcripts
- Interactive versions of this chapter's Stop and Check activities, as well as Critical Thinking Exercises and Application Exercises
- Speech Builder Express
- Weblinks related to chapter content
- Study and review tools such as self-quizzes and an interactive glossary

You can access your online resources for *Public Speaking: Concepts and Skills for a Diverse Society* at cengagebrain.com using the access code that came with your book or that you purchased online.

Review your **Flashcards**.

KEY TERMS

The terms below are defined in the margins throughout this chapter.

classification 202
discourse consistency 210
division 201
expository speech 207

information imbalance 201
redundancy 211
repetition 211

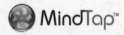

CRITICAL THINKING EXERCISES

1. Make a list of possible topic from the field of communication. Look for information that could help your classmates communicate better. For example, topics such as how to work through conflict, how to become independent from parents, or how to successfully navigate the early stages of a romantic relationship are useful in interpersonal communication. Nonverbal communication topics include different concepts of time or the types of touch. For mass communication, you could explain how camera angles communicate meaning or how other countries regulate the Internet.

2. Descriptions can be speeches in themselves, or good descriptions can be elements of larger speeches. To improve your descriptive skills, identify a place, an object, or an event and then make a list of vivid words that provide information about the look, the feel, the smell, the taste, or the sound of the item or place.

3. Search the Internet for the exact term "informative speaking." Read the material on a site from either a speech team (also called a forensics team) or from a university professor who provides additional information about speaking to inform.

APPLICATION QUESTIONS

1. Within a small group in your classroom, discuss implications of the unequal distribution of information. For example: What if only some societies knew how to make sophisticated weaponry? What if only some individuals or groups knew their cultural history? What if only women had access to health information and men were excluded? What if only people under 35 years of age, with incomes over $80,000 a year, knew how to use computers?

2. Working with a small group, generate a list of speech topics for each category. The audience:

   - Is totally unfamiliar with the topic (examples: biliary atresia, *dun dun* drums).
   - Has some knowledge of the topic, but not all the details (driving while texting, pumpkins).
   - Has studied the topic, but needs a review (the five canons of rhetoric, D-Day).

- Has outdated information (an updated iPhone).
- Has major misconceptions regarding the topic (cheerleading, tarantulas).

Select a subject from two different categories and discuss how you would modify your speech plans to accomplish your general purpose with each topic.

3. In a small group, think of creative ways to present an informative speech that reviews audience knowledge about one of these familiar topics:

- Good nutrition
- What to do in case of a fire
- How to read a textbook

CHAPTER 16

**THIS CHAPTER WILL
HELP YOU**

- Identify ways that
  ethos, or speaker
  credibility, functions
  as an element of
  reasoning

- Explain the role of
  pathos, or emotional
  proofs, in reasoning

- Identify ways that
  reasoning strategies
  vary across cultural
  groups

- Explain four basic
  types of *logos*, or
  rational proofs, and
  know how to test
  each one

- Recognize several
  kinds of fallacious
  reasoning

- Identify elements of
  invitational rhetoric

Diana Ong/SuperStock

Foundations
of Persuasion

SCHOLARS HAVE STUDIED rhetoric—the art of persuasion—for centuries, but during World War II, they began to focus more specifically on the conditions and strategies that could give rise to a leader such as Hitler. Why could he persuade so many otherwise ordinary people to do such horrible things? Why would others resist and heroically rescue Nazi targets? One study of rescuers found that, although they were similar in most ways to nonrescuers, they more often grew up in homes where parents disciplined them through reasoning, explanations, and advice.[1] In other words, their parents used persuasion, not coercion, to help them make wise choices.

MindTo

Review the
chapter
Learning
Objectives
and **Start**
with a quick
warm-up
activity.

Persuasion is defined as the symbolic process in which a communicator creates an **argument** in an attempt to convince others to change their attitudes or behaviors in an atmosphere of free choice. However, persuaders can only raise a need and create a case for change; their audiences must choose whether to change or to resist their appeals.[2]

What makes a message persuasive? Centuries ago, Aristotle identified three modes of persuasion, which he called **artistic proofs** because you, the speaker, must create them:

> The first kind depends on the personal character of the speaker [*ethos*]; the second on putting the audience into a certain frame of mind [*pathos*]; the third on the proof, or apparent proof, provided by the words of the speech itself [*logos*].[3]

Persuasive methods are found in the canon of invention. This chapter describes ethos, pathos, and logos, which work together to form a totality of "good reasons." In other words, emotion is often reasonable; reason has emotional underpinnings; and it is both reasonable and emotionally satisfying to hear a credible speaker. Creating and evaluating arguments by using these three modes will help you be a better speaker and listener. However, "winning" an argument is neither desirable nor possible in many cases, so the chapter concludes with principles and forms of invitational rhetoric.

Develop Ethos or Speaker Credibility

Audiences place their confidence in speakers they see as personally believable, trustworthy, and of good character. Their inner reasoning runs something like this: "She really knows what she's talking about. She also seems to have good intentions, so I trust what she's saying." In contrast, a speakers' credibility can discredit his claims if listeners think, "He's using one-sided material from very extreme sources! He just wants us to buy something. I don't trust his motives, so I don't really trust his information."

These examples illustrate the artistic proof called **ethos**—the proof that comes from your personal qualities. Here, Aristotle explains how ethos is often your most effective mode of persuasion:

> Persuasion is achieved by the speaker's personal character [*ethos*] when the speech is so spoken as to make us think him [or her] credible. We believe good [people] more fully and more readily than others: this is true generally whatever the question is, and absolutely true where exact certainty is impossible and opinions are divided. [4]

Because ethos depends on your listener's perception of you as a speaker, you can shape a positive impression by paying attention to your personal appearance, showing confidence, making eye contact, using appropriate gestures, and avoiding vocalized pauses as described in Chapter 14. Four additional components of ethos include: good character, goodwill, good sense, and dynamism.

persuasion the symbolic process in which a communicator intentionally creates an argument in an attempt to convince others to change their attitudes or behaviors in an atmosphere of free choice

argument an intentional, purposeful set of reasons created to explain disputed beliefs and conclusions

artistic proofs reasons the speaker creates to accept an argument

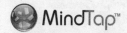 MindTap™

Read, highlight, and take notes online.

ethos personal credibility or character traits that make a speaker believable and worthy of the audience's confidence

Exhibiting Good Character

Remember the Latin phrase introduced in Chapter 1: *Vir bonum, dicendi peritus*—"The good person, skilled in speaking"? Character counts. Your listeners will believe you more readily if they trust you, so demonstrate honesty, integrity, and trustworthiness by documenting your sources and giving facts that square with what they know to be true. Choose topics that matter to you, and stick by your convictions, even when they are unpopular. Politicians get into trouble when they appear to be poll driven and pander to different audiences, flip-flopping from position to position instead of holding to their core beliefs.

ETHICS IN PRACTICE

Developing Good Character

© Scala/Art Resource, NY

Quintilian

As chief educator of Rome, Quintilian distinguished oratory from rhetoric when he wrote about the education of persuasive speakers.[5] Rhetoric, he proclaimed, is amoral; it can lead to both good and bad results. In contrast, oratory is a moral activity; orators defend the innocent, repress crime, support truth over falsehood, persuade listeners toward right actions, and promote positive civic action.

Evil persons cannot be effective orators because their greed, misdeeds, and concerns over being caught in their deceits make them neglect the tools of invention, and audiences will reject them. Instead, virtuous orators should cultivate traits of truth seeking, justice, and honor before they take to the public stage. To form moral and intellectual character, they should study philosophy, seek wisdom, and pursue sincerity and goodness. Only after they have developed character, should they study oratory. Quintilian was realistic enough to recognize that no one could be perfect, but he urged each orator to be both good and sensible.

Questions

1. What is your response to Quintilian's claim: "I do not merely assert that the ideal orator should be a good [person], but I affirm that no [one] can be a good orator unless he [or she] is a good [person]"?[6]
2. Do the same high standards hold for people who give informative speeches? Why or why not?
3. How might our culture be changed if the study of public speaking came during the last semester of every college student's senior year—as the culmination of his or her education—and if all other studies were considered foundational?
4. Imagine that Quintilian were somehow transported into the Internet age. How might he advise digital citizens to prepare for participation in the "public stage" of cyberspace?

Expressing Goodwill

Audiences want to know you have their interests in mind, that you understand their situations and view them positively. You can project **warmth** through behaviors that signal interest and engagement, especially through pleasant facial expressions. Genuine, not faked, smiles show warmth and positive interest in others. Observers feel more connected to someone who appears relaxed and smiles, so they smile in return, promoting a positive feedback loop.[7]

Another component of goodwill is **identification,** or **co-orientation**. Kenneth Burke,[8] one of the twentieth century's most respected rhetoricians, explained that a variety of divisions separate us, but identification helps bring people with diverse beliefs and behaviors together.

How do you identify with your audience? One way is to find areas of **common ground**—to emphasize your similarities. This is obviously easier when you share beliefs, values, attitudes, and behaviors; however, diversity makes identification more challenging, so search for commonalities on which to build. For instance, regardless of differences, you and your audiences need safety and self-esteem. Here's a good example of an Asian American speaker finding common ground with her largely African American audience.

> So I salute you, a cherished ally. . . . We are Japanese, Filipinos, Chinese, Asian Indians, Koreans, Vietnamese, Laos, Thais, Cambodians, Hmongs, Pakistanis, and Indonesians. Each has a distinct beautiful ethnic cultural heritage, but our goals are the same as yours. We want to remove racial barriers, we want equal opportunity for our members, and we want to create greater horizons for those who follow.[9]

Although identification typically relies on commonalities, in some cases differences can make you more credible, depending on the topic. For example, Maysoon Zayid, a Palestinian Muslim advocate and comedian, has cerebral palsy as a result of a birth injury. Her speeches about disability and careers are more persuasive because of her differences. You can watch her TED talk on your online resources.

Demonstrating Good Sense

Good sense is a cluster of characteristics, made up of several components, including:

* **Intelligence:** Have a broad understanding of your subject, complete with up-to-date information of the highest quality. Be able to discuss related historical developments, and link your topic to contemporary national and international issues. Then, listeners will recognize that you're not just bluffing your way through your speech and that you have the discernment to select only the most credible information.
* **Sound reasoning:** Support your claims with trustworthy evidence and logical connections between ideas. Avoid fallacies and unwarranted or excessive appeals to emotions.
* **Composure:** Maintain your poise in a stressful situation. On one hand, if you become overly agitated, your audience may wonder why you can't control yourself. On the other hand, if you remain composed and controlled, they'll perceive you more favorably. However, note the differences in cultural expectations described in Diversity in Practice: Composure in Other Cultures.

Showing Dynamism

Dynamism, or forcefulness, is a fourth trait that influences credibility. It is linked to extroversion, energy, and enthusiasm. (See Chapter 14.) This doesn't mean that introverts can't be credible; however, your visible enjoyment of your topic, your enthusiasm, and your overall liveliness contribute to your ethos. Think of it this way: aren't you more likely to believe someone who states ideas forcefully rather than apologetically?

warmth using behaviors that signal positive interest and engagement, especially through pleasant facial expressions

identification, or **co-orientation** concerns shared among speakers and listeners that help overcome divisions and bring diverse people together

common ground specific areas or concerns that both speaker and audience consider important

MindTap™

DIVERSITY IN PRACTICE

Composure in Other Cultures

Concepts of ethos depend on the cultural context. Thomas Kochman, author of *Black and White Styles in Conflict*, explained that credible speakers in the African American tradition are often forceful and emotional rather than calm and composed.[10] Good speakers are genuinely intense, and sometimes their emotional expressiveness contrasts greatly with the order and procedure common in the Euro-American style of public speaking. For this reason, listeners brought up in the Euro-American culture may consider them loud or aggressive.

Similarly, Janice Walker Anderson[11] found that Arabs traditionally expected effective speakers to show their emotion and to heighten the audience's emotions through the rhythm and sounds of words. In these cultures, overstating a case indicates the speaker's sincerity, not a distortion of facts; in contrast, a soft tone indicates that the speaker is weak or perhaps dishonest.

Include Pathos or Emotional Proofs

Contrast the following situations:

- You're listening to a speaker who seems credible and who supports her claim well. However, you lack enough interest and motivation to be concerned about the issue.
- You're listening to a second speaker (same topic) who also seems credible and supports her claim well. But this one links the subject to your core beliefs, values, personal goals, and emotions. You find yourself caring about it and wanting to believe and act as she proposes.

motivation internal, individualized factor that results when we understand how topics affect our lives in a personal way

pathos appeals or reasons directed toward audience emotions

The second speaker understands that **motivation** is an internal, individualistic, or subjective factor that results when listeners understand how topics affect their lives in a personal way. It's essential to persuasion. In other words, we look for emotional and psychological reasons to support our decisions. And in the end, our subjective reasons can be as influential as our logical ones. This demonstrates the power of emotions in reasoning—the proof Aristotle called **pathos**.

Although you often respond subconsciously to emotional appeals, your conscious thoughts may run something like this: "I feel sorry for the people who lost all their possessions in the disaster; I'm going to donate," or "Going to the career center like the speaker suggests will help me get a better job," or "I've experienced frustration just like the speaker. I can relate!" Pathos relies on appeals to emotions and to needs.

Appealing to Positive Emotions

According to Aristotle, emotions are all the feelings people have that change them in ways that affect their judgment. Modern psychologists say we "approach" pleasurable emotions such as love, peace, pride, approval, hope, generosity, courage, and loyalty. We also feel good about our core beliefs and values, such as freedom and individualism. Appealing to positive feelings and values can motivate listeners to accept and act on your claims.

Narratives and examples are especially effective in highlighting emotional appeals. In this speech excerpt, Remi gives several examples of strategies her university is employing to ensure that food waste has positive outcomes.

> Leftover food such as chicken, vegetables, and pasta is used in soup the following day. Unsold sandwiches and fruit from the snack bar are given away Friday nights in the dining hall. The university donates about 150 meals to Urban Services every Friday. Plant Services is also working on a vermiculture (worm bins) to compost salad leftovers.[12]

These examples help students (who might feel guilty for wasting so much food) feel more hopeful by knowing that their wasteful habits are not entirely destructive. Because she is not condemning their behaviors, her listeners are not defensive, so they can more easily examine their personal eating habits.

Appealing to Negative Emotions

People try to avoid unpleasant emotions such as guilt, shame, hatred, fear, insecurity, anger, and anxiety. However, fear, anger, and guilt can motivate us to avoid real dangers—a fact that the campaign against texting and driving uses effectively. Think of a story you've heard or an ad you've seen that shows crashed cars of teens who "just this once" drove while texting. Don't they make you want to prevent the problem?

Both negative and positive emotions can be powerful motivators in persuasive speeches.

Analogies work well to arouse negative emotions. In this speech excerpt, Hillary Clinton likened the Internet to the Berlin Wall as a way to arouse negative emotions toward censorship and division by showing how they violate core values of free expression and connection.

> As I speak to you today, government censors somewhere are working furiously to erase my words from the records of history. But history itself has already condemned these tactics.... The Berlin Wall symbolized a world divided and it defined an entire era. Today, ... the new iconic infrastructure is the Internet. Instead of division, it stands for connection. But even as networks spread to nations around the globe, virtual walls are cropping up in place of visible walls.

> Some countries have erected electronic barriers that prevent their people from accessing portions of the world's networks. They've expunged words, names, and phrases from search engine results. They have violated the privacy of citizens who engage in non-violent political speech.[13]

Appeals to negative emotions can be forceful, sometimes with disastrous results. Consider how effectively hate groups appeal to listeners' weaknesses, rages, fears, and insecurities. In addition, it's easy to overdo negative appeals, and excessive appeals to guilt or fear may turn off an audience. A famous environmentalist's negative appeals made one listener "go numb." He advised her to evaluate the psychological impact of her appeals to fear and guilt and to present instead a "politics of vision" that connects environmental goals to positive emotions—to what is "generous, joyous, freely given, and noble" in the audience.[14]

Appealing to Needs

One of the most widely cited systems of classifying needs follows the work of Abraham Maslow,[15] who ranked needs into five levels, each building on the others—generally in the same order. Although he described five levels, Maslow himself believed that "most behavior is multi-motivated"[16] and that a combination of levels is active in each situation. Here are the levels and some suggestions for addressing each one:

- **Basic needs:** Link your topic to your listeners' basic survival needs for water, air, food, and shelter.
- **Security and safety:** Explain how to gain peace of mind, job security, safety, comfort, better health, physical safety, and so on.
- **Love and belonging:** Show how your topic helps your listeners be better friends, creates a stronger community, or builds ties between people.
- **Esteem:** Demonstrate respect for your listeners, and mention their accomplishments when appropriate. Find ways to make them feel competent to carry out your proposals. Let them know that their ideas, opinions, and concerns are significant.
- **Self-actualization:** Challenge your listeners to look beyond themselves and reach out to others. Encourage them to dream big dreams and accomplish unique things. As the Army slogan says, "Be all that you can be."

A speech on food waste is built around our basic need for food and our need to create a stronger community. One on America's deteriorating infrastructure appeals to our needs for safety and comfort while we travel. A speech on hovercraft (Chapter 11) shows how engineers think outside the box to create unique inventions.

(To learn more about Maslow's work, search the Internet for "Maslow's hierarchy of needs." Look for additional levels that other scholars have added to his hierarchy.)

Understanding Complex Motivations

As you can see, using pathos is complex because needs, wants, emotions, and values overlap. As you create emotional appeals, keep in mind four important factors that influence motivation.[17]

1. **Sometimes you must choose between two goals or emotions.** Perhaps the choice is between needs—job security or the ability to reach your potential. Or you may have to choose the lesser of two evils—higher gasoline taxes or fewer highway repairs.
2. **Circumstances affect motives.** A person who just ended a significant relationship may worry more about belonging and self-esteem than someone in a long-term relationship. What motivates you is often different from what motivates someone in a different socioeconomic group or in a different age group.
3. **Our responses often reflect mixed motives.** The donor who gives out of loyalty to her institution may also feel pride when a building is named in her honor. An angry blogger may write out of underlying anxiety, fear, and frustration.
4. **Motivations are often group centered.** What we want for ourselves, we want for others, including our family, friends, religious groups, schools, towns, states, society, and world. Consequently, a speech about injustices in other countries can motivate listeners who want security for themselves and their own families, as well as for strangers.

Testing Emotional Appeals

Emotions are not always trustworthy, so it is important to examine them to see if they make sense. For example, if fear is your prime motivator, ask yourself if it is irrational or justified? Excessive use of emotional appeals can cloud logical reasoning.

When you're listening to emotional appeals, ask questions such as these: Why am I feeling guilty? Is my guilt reasonable? Is this speaker trying to manipulate me through my feelings? Although he is causing me to feel angry, is anger my primary emotion? Or could my underlying emotion be fear? Does this challenge to my cherished beliefs create anxiety that I am masking with anger?[18]

Finally, make sure the emotion is used ethically. Generally, it is unethical to appeal to emotions in an attempt to bypass logic. For example, an appeal to national pride may create an argument for going to war in a way that clouds more rational arguments against military involvement. A speaker may use fear to motivate listeners to act for their personal profit rather than for their own good. (See Ethics in Practice: Demagoguery.)

ETHICS IN PRACTICE

Demagoguery

Moviestore collection Ltd/Alamy

Ideally, good speakers blend the three artistic proofs; however, the term **demagogue** refers to speakers who rely on ethos and pathos more than on logical reasoning. A study of Huey P. Long, a controversial politician during the Great Depression, identifies a demagogue as:

> [A self-righteous person who claims] to bring order to chaos, thereby representing strength, resolve, and absolute autonomy . . . [by placing] much more emphasis on the feelings inspired by ethos and pathos, and largely at the expense of logos and reasoned argument.[20]

A demagogue's defining characteristic is "polarizing propaganda that motivates members of an ingroup to hate and scapegoat some outgroup(s)"[21] by promising a coming era of stability and control; the result is an "us" and "them" mentality. Demagogues are often dynamic, dramatic, passionate speakers who inspire devotion among followers. Some characterize themselves as just a common person fighting for the people,[22] but others include opportunists who work for their own gain, politicians who inflame passions to gain or maintain power, and doomsayers who create a heightened sense of crisis in order to reveal their novel solutions.[23]

Was Huey P. Long a demagogue? Critics say yes, but to his credit, he used his persuasive powers to benefit people in the lower economic classes by providing free textbooks in school, new buildings and roads, construction of Louisiana State University (including a great football team), and the redistribution of wealth.[24] He was assassinated at age 42.

Questions

1. Make a list of people you think of as a rabble-rouser or demagogue. (Politicians and media commentators are commonly in this category.) Tell why you label each person this way. Would others agree that your label is appropriate? Why or why not?
2. The word *demagogue* has negative connotations. Why is demagoguery considered to be one of the most unethical forms of speaking?

Demagogues often emerge during times of instability. In the Depression era, Huey P. Long was branded a "champion of the common man"[19] by his supporters and "a demagogue" by his detractors. This colorful character became a fascinating movie subject in both the 1949 and 2006 films titled *All the King's Men*.

demagogue a polarizing speaker who appeals to audiences more on the basis of emotion and personal charisma than on reasoned arguments

Use Logos or Rational Proofs

Logos, often called rational proofs, refers to the verbal arguments you make relating to your subject. These arguments include analogy, inductive, deductive, and causal reasoning.

logos arguments from the words of the speech itself; often called rational proofs

Reasoning by Analogy: Figurative and Literal

analogy comparison of one item that's less familiar or unknown to something concrete and familiar

Chapter 8 defines an **analogy** as a comparison between one item that is unknown or less familiar and something already familiar to the audience. You can reason by using *figurative* (metaphor) or *literal* (parallel case) analogies.

Figurative Analogies (Metaphors)

reasoning by metaphor comparing two things that are generally different but share a recognizable similarity

Reasoning by metaphor figuratively compares two things that are generally different but share a recognizable similarity. This type of reasoning is fundamental and universal, practiced by cultures globally and historically,[25] and typical of African and African American speakers.[26] Aristotle associated metaphor with mental brilliance, as seen in this quotation from *Poetics*.

> [T]he greatest thing by far is to be a master of metaphor. It is the one thing that cannot be learnt from others, and it is also a sign of genius, since a good metaphor implies an intuitive perception of the similarity in dissimilars.[27]

Here are some examples of metaphors taken from speeches given by professionals. What images do they evoke in you?

- Good news is music to our ears; insecurity causes us to play it by ear; when we are getting along, we are in harmony or in tune with one another.[28]
- Graduation speakers are like mixed seasonal vegetables. When you go to a restaurant, you expect them on your plate. But they're not the reason you went there and they're not what you remember about the meal. So I stand before you today, like some forgettable but hopefully tasty mix of broccoli, snow peas, and summer squash.[29]
- The presidency is the most visible thread that runs through the tapestry of the American government.[30]

Metaphors are inherently dialogical because they require your listeners to participate actively and make sensible connections between the two things you compare. In addition, the images inherent in metaphors have emotional overtones. Contrast your feelings about *roadblocks* or *open doors*, a *harvest* of justice or the *moneyed scales* of justice; a *turkey* of a deal or a *gem* of a deal.

Our metaphors guide our actions. For example, what is the role of your college or university in your community? Is it a good neighbor, a partner, a beacon of light? Your metaphor affects how you engage the community. If you choose "partner," your involvement is arguably different than if you think of yourselves as a "beacon of light."

Literal Analogies (Parallel Cases)

parallel case or **literal analogy** comparing likenesses between two similar things; arguing that what happened in a known case will likely happen in a similar case

Whereas metaphors highlight similarities between two different things, reasoning by **parallel case** or **literal analogy** points out likenesses between two similar things. We often use this type of reasoning to formulate policies by asking what another person or group decided to do when faced with a problem similar to our own. Here are some examples.

- How should your campus deal with sexual assaults? Look at case studies of schools similar to yours that instituted an effective program, then infer whether that campus's solution might or might not work for yours.
- How should a business prevent vandalism? Look at prevention strategies installed by similar businesses in similar locations.

In summary, literal analogies use actual cases based on real experiences to formulate policies and make predictions about the future. That is, we predict that what happened in a known case will happen in a similar case that we project.

Testing Analogies

Reasoning by metaphor is not generally considered a "hard" proof. The best test is to make sure your listeners can make a sensible connection between your concept and the comparison so that they better understand your idea.

Test parallel case more directly by considering the following two questions:

1. Are the cases really alike? Or are you "comparing apples to oranges"? The University of Michigan is heralded a model for combatting sexual abuse on campus,[31] but would that model transfer to a workplace situation?
2. Are they alike in essential details? The University of Michigan is a large, public, diverse place with a Greek system. Is it similar enough that its model could be adapted to a small, private, religious institution in a rural area?

Reasoning Inductively

Inductive reasoning begins with specific instances or examples and then formulates a reasonable generalization or conclusion from them. In other words, inductive reasoning moves from the particular to the general; it is a characteristic of women and speakers from a variety of ethnic groups. For example, African American leaders typically tie knowledge to human experiences, human actions, and human interactions. Knowledge does not exist for its own sake or in the abstract. What is relevant is considered relevant because it makes a difference in people's lives.[32] (Diversity in Practice: Reasoning and the Sexes provides additional information on men's and women's use of inductive reasoning.)

inductive reasoning starting with specific instances or examples, then formulating a reasonable conclusion

DIVERSITY IN PRACTICE

Reasoning and the Sexes

© pkchai/Shutterstock.com

Although both men and women reason inductively, some feminist philosophers argue that inductive reasoning is a *major* reasoning strategy for women. They say that women typically begin with specific experiences of real people, such as the wife of an injured veteran, the family trapped in minimum wage jobs, the student who owes more than $100,000 in student loans, and then generalize from these examples. This means that women's reasoning is characteristically grounded in personal experiences that arise out of their interpersonal relationships.[33]

(continued)

Women are commonly stereotyped as reasoning with their hearts rather than their heads—an overgeneralization that may have some basis in fact. Studies of women's patterns of thinking show the importance of emotion in their reasoning process.[34] Although obviously different from "dispassionate investigation," emotions complement logic and intertwine with rational proofs. Feelings are not inferior to reason, and they are not something women must "overcome" in order to think clearly. Instead, emotions can be a source of knowledge, and "truth" or "knowledge" without emotion is distorted.[35]

In contrast, some scholars discount fundamental differences between genders. They say that using evidence, linear thinking, and deductive logic are not inherently masculine, and both men and women reason this way. Furthermore, intuitive and emotional arguments are not inherently feminine; men often reason through experiences, emotions, and empathy.[36] For example, a university[37] study of male and female scientists found no major differences in use of inductive, deductive, or causal reasoning processes. However, they discovered that, given an unexpected finding, men tended to assume they knew the cause, whereas women tracked it down.

Whatever differences there may be, the "difference must be viewed as a resource for—not an impediment to—meaningful dialogue."[38]

Here's how inductive reasoning works in everyday life. You buy a new car and love its features. Your car is one specific example. You talk to other owners who similarly love the same make and model. *Consumer Reports* rates the car highly, based on the features and repair records of cars like yours. The car's reputation becomes established: This make and model is a good buy.

Kimball used these three examples in his speech on ocean acidification to support his conclusion.[39]

- Five years ago in Willapa Bay, Washington, it was discovered that oyster larvae weren't building shells and growing into adults; experts blamed ocean acidification.
- Tests off California's coast show disintegrating seashells and deterioriating shells of mollusks in the waters there.
- Corals from sixty-nine of the reefs comprising the Great Barrier Reef off Australia showed a drop in calcification.

Generalization: Destructive forces are at work in the Pacific Ocean.

Because you can be sure of a conclusion only if you can observe 100 percent of a population, it is ideal, but highly improbable, to look at every example before you form a conclusion. Consequently, select a representative sample, survey the characteristics of that sample, formulate conclusions and then generalize your findings to the larger population it represents. But use caution: If Kimball reported only on Pacific Ocean research, he couldn't necessarily assume that his conclusions applied globally. Other factors may be at work in different waters.

Testing Inductive Reasoning

The three major tests for inductive reasoning are all linked to the tests you used to evaluate examples in Chapter 8.

1. Are enough cases represented to justify the conclusion? Or are you forming a conclusion based on too few cases?
2. Are the cases typical? That is, do they represent the average members of the population to which the generalizations are applied? Or are they extreme cases that may show what could happen, but not what usually happens?
3. Are the examples from the time period under discussion, or are they out of date?

Reasoning Deductively

Inductive reasoning moves from specific examples to conclusions or generalizations, but **deductive reasoning** goes the other direction. It begins with a generalization or principle, called the *premise*, and moves logically to an application in a specific case. (See Figure 16.1 for an example of the relationship between inductive and deductive reasoning.) In formal logic, the deductive reasoning process is often shown in the form of a *syllogism* such as this:

> Major premise: Everyone who goes through a Bar Mitzvah is Jewish.
>
> Minor premise: Aaron just had his Bar Mitzvah.
>
> Conclusion: Therefore, Aaron is Jewish.

When you're sure of the major premise, you can state your conclusion with confidence. Because a Bar Mitzvah is the Jewish coming-of-age ceremony, only young men in that religion go through it. In contrast, many premises are less certain. Although some, such as "all people are mortal," are 100 percent true, others, such as "This make and model of car is good," may not be valid in every case; a specific car might be a "lemon." So it's wise to qualify both your premises and your conclusions. Here is an example about the value of urban debate leagues:

> Major premise: Participation in high school urban debate leagues helps *many* students get better grades.
>
> Minor premise: Yolanda Baylor is a debater at an inner-city high school in the South Bronx.
>
> Conclusion: She has *probably* improved her grades.[40]

When you reason deductively, you rarely state the entire syllogism, so your listeners must fill in the unstated premises. Aristotle called this an **enthymeme**. For example, you might say, "Is Aaron Jewish? Of course. He just had his Bar Mitzvah," and let your audience make the necessary connections. Or (talking with friends about

deductive reasoning starting with a principle (the premise) and applying it to a specific case

enthymeme omitting part of the syllogism in an argument and letting listeners supply what's missing; inherently dialogical

Figure 16.1
Inductive and Deductive Reasoning You observe a number of spaniels and inductively reason that they make good pets. Using that premise, you deduce that Curly, the specific spaniel you've chosen, will be a good family dog.

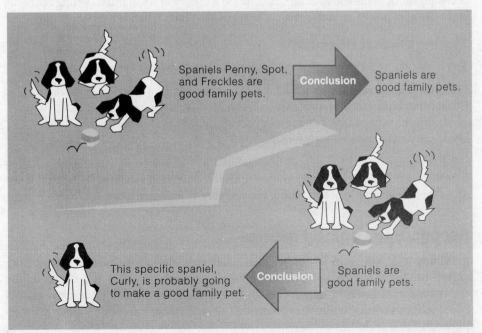

Spaniels Penny, Spot, and Freckles are good family pets.

Conclusion

Spaniels are good family pets.

This specific spaniel, Curly, is probably going to make a good family pet.

Conclusion

Spaniels are good family pets.

buying a new car), "You can't go wrong if you purchase a car like mine." Your friends then use their generalizations about cars and recommendations to make sense of what you've just said.

Using enthymemes is inherently dialogical, for your listeners must form conclusions based on their knowledge of what you *don't* say. However, if they know nothing about your subject (the rules regarding Bar Mitzvahs or the connection between debating and grades, for example), they'll miss your meaning.

Testing Deductive Reasoning

There are two major tests for deductive reasoning:

1. For the conclusion to be valid, the premises must be true or highly probable.
2. To be reasonable, the conclusion must follow from the premise.

Reasoning Causally

causal reasoning linking two factors in such as way that the first occurs before the second and regularly leads to the second as a matter of rule

Causal reasoning links two events or occurrences in such a way that one comes first and regularly leads to the second. For example, the lack of oxygen to the brain (first event) is followed by death (second event)—this link has been demonstrated time after time.

Cause–effect thinking is fundamentally engrained in the Euro-American belief system where we actively seek reasons leading up to a particular phenomenon. Unlike the lack of oxygen→death example, cause-and-effect links are less provable in complex situations where many variables could be linked to an outcome. For example, what causes women to be historically underrepresented in highly paid STEM (science, technology, engineering, and math) careers? Are structures in place that don't attract female students to STEM courses? Do individuals, families, and society fail to provide encouragement and support for young women to choose these careers? Do most women prefer learning styles that mesh better with other majors? Many factors are involved. When reasoning by cause, the key is to produce enough reasons to warrant the connection between the two factors.

Here are just a few of the causal claims currently in the news: Chewing gum for five minutes before a test can improve performance.[41] Ocean acidification inhibits the development of shells and skeletal structures in a variety of sea animals. Sitting for hours every day puts people at greater risk of heart disease and diabetes.[42]

Testing Causal Reasoning

Test causation by asking a series of questions to assess whether the reasoning is valid.

1. Is there a real connection? Does one follow as a result of the first, or do the two events simply exist together in time? (Is it correlation or causation?)
2. Is this the only cause? The most important cause? Or are other factors at play?
3. Is the cause strong enough for the effect?

In summary, you have at your disposal a variety of reasoning strategies, including figurative and literal analogies, inductive and deductive reasoning, and causal links. All of these reasoning types fall under the category of logos, or rational proofs.

Recognizing Logical Fallacies

fallacy failure in logical reasoning that leads to unsound or misleading arguments

A **fallacy** is a failure in logical reasoning that leads to unsound or misleading arguments.[43] Fallacies have been around for thousands of years, as you can tell by the Latin names given to some of them. As a speaker or critical listener, you should examine arguments carefully to avoid using or being taken in by the common fallacies shown in Table 16.1.

Type of Fallacy	Example
Unsupported assertion	Offering a claim without any evidence ("I deserved an A in class; why did you give me a C?")
Ad populum or bandwagon	Literally, "to the people"—an appeal to popular reason instead of offering evidence ("We all agree …" or "Everyone says …")
Ad hominem (personal attack)	Literally, "against the person"—an attack against the source, not the evidence or reasoning ("Of course, a liberal would think that way.")
False analogy	Comparing two things that are not similar enough to warrant the comparison (Although thousands of websites use the analogy, "Animal Auschwitz," mistreatment of animals, is not similar to the Nazis' treatment of their enemies.)
Faulty generalization	Inductive fallacy that extends the conclusion further than the evidence warrants ("I hate that politician; everyone in his political party is corrupt.")
Slippery slope	Stating, without proof, that if one step is taken, a snowball or domino effect will cause other negative results ("If you take away any gun rights, pretty soon hunters won't even be able to keep their shotguns.")
Post hoc (ergo propter hoc)	Fallacy of causation; literally, "after this, therefore because of this"—assumes that, because one thing follows another, the first caused the second ("I took my lucky rabbit's foot to the test with me, and I passed with flying colors.")
False dichotomy	Stating an issue as an either–or choice, overlooking other reasonable possibilities ("Either you get a college degree or end up in a low-paying job.")

Table 16.1
Common Reasoning Fallacies

Fallacious arguments fail to provide evidence or present faulty evidence for the claim. Fallacies also attack the messenger instead of countering the message itself. Fallacies of analogy, causation, induction, and false choice are common. Learning to recognize fallacies will help you think more critically about the arguments you make and those you hear every day.

In conclusion, other cultures may not use Aristotle's terminology to name the proofs of ethos, pathos, and logos, but that does not mean they don't exist in some form. Across the globe, speakers follow cultural ideas about what makes a speaker trustworthy, and they address their listeners' emotional and rational responses, as Diversity in Practice: Cultural Reasoning Preferences explains.

unsupported assertion unsupported claim

ad populum an appeal to popular opinion

ad hominem an attack on the messenger rather than the message

false analogy comparing two things too dissimilar to warrant the conclusion drawn

faulty generalization a fallacy of induction; generalizing too broadly, given the evidence

slippery slope a fallacy of causation; saying one small thing will lead to larger things without offering proof

Cultural Reasoning Preferences

Culture influences our reasoning resources in a number of ways that can easily lead to misunderstandings between cultural groups.[44]

- **Topics considered appropriate to debate vary across cultures**. Chapter 1 pointed out that taboo topics vary across cultures. Some groups, for instance, would not bring up such issues as gay rights, day care, or euthanasia. Openly speaking about sex is unthinkable in some places.

(continued)

DIVERSITY IN PRACTICE

post hoc a fallacy of causation; a false cause

false dichotomy an either–or
fallacy that ignores other
reasonable options

- **Cultures conceptualize issues differently**. In the United States people
  commonly think of issues as problems and solutions we can define, propose,
  test, and then eliminate or enact; other cultures think problems result from
  fate, a bad relationship with the deity or deities, or being out of harmony
  with one another or the universe.[45]
- **The norms for structuring and framing a discussion vary**. Some cultures
  ground their discussions in the historical perspectives of the participants or
  rely on stories to frame their speeches, rather than looking for causes and
  effects or making claims and counterclaims. Also, in the highly individualistic
  culture of the United States, we typically ask, "Who won the argument?" But
  in collectivist cultures, members deplore arguments that present one position
  as superior to another and draw attention to the rhetor.[46] They see themselves as a community of equals who must cooperate to reach consensus.
- **Levels of explicitness differ across cultures**. In the United States, we
  commonly state conclusions explicitly and concretely. However, other
  cultures tolerate much more ambiguity; their speakers exert influence
  through subtlety and indirectness.
- **Forms of proof are often dissimilar**. What's considered rational or
  irrational, what counts as evidence, and what constitutes a good reason
  varies cross-culturally. As Chapter 8 pointed out, facts, statistics, and studies
  by experts are typically used here, but elsewhere, narratives, analogies,
  authoritative texts, and the sayings of wise, experienced elders make sense to
  the listeners.
- **Communication styles vary**. Mainstream US culture is biased toward
  linear, analytical models of reasoning. Other cultural groups reason more
  holistically through drama, intuition, and emotional expressiveness.[47]

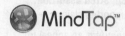

Incorporate Principles and Forms of Invitational Rhetoric

Positions on polarizing issues such as politics, religion, or lifestyles can be so deeply
rooted that presenting your best arguments credibly and sensitively will not be
persuasive. In these circumstances, you may prefer **invitational rhetoric**.[48] It's a form
of sensemaking that invites your audiences to hear your perspectives and then invites
them to present their own views. The point is not to "win the argument." Change may
or may not result, but you might achieve mutual understanding. The scholars behind
this concept identify three principles and associate two forms with invitational rhetoric.

invitational rhetoric
inviting audiences to enter
and understand the rhetor's
world and then share their
own perspectives; focuses
on mutual understanding and
mutual influence, not winning
or change per se

Combining Three Principles

Invitational rhetoric focuses on mutuality of understanding and influence based on the
principles of equality, individual value, and self-determination. It's one way to develop a
dialogical spirit, as described in Chapter 3.

1. **Equality**: Instead of imposing your "superior" views on others who "need" to
   change, you view your listeners as equals. Your strategies aren't aimed at overcoming
   their resistance; however, you do identify possible barriers to understanding and try
   to minimize or neutralize those. In short, you provide your viewpoints and open
   yourselves to theirs.

For example, say it's an election year. Your classroom contains active supporters of three different candidates. You all have formulated good reasons for your choices. As an invitational rhetor, you share the path you've traveled in making your decision, and you invite your classmates to share theirs.

2. **Nonhierarchical value of all**: This means you approach your audience as equaling you in rank; you look for the value in their conclusions as well as your own. You don't attempt to demean their position and point out their deficiencies, and you try to maintain a positive, civil relationship with those who hold differ views.

   Back to the election. By not considering yourself intellectually or morally superior by virtue of your viewpoint, you can respect your classmates' conclusions, because you try hard to see the point of their reasoning. There's no yelling, no put-downs, and no character assassination of one another's candidates.

3. **Self-determination**: Invitational rhetoric may or may not result in change. If listeners change their opinions or their behaviors, it won't be because you shamed or scared them into accepting your views. And you may modify your own positions to incorporate some of their insights. Sometimes, you and your listeners may agree to disagree while remaining mutually respectful.

   You and your classmates eventually split your votes, but regardless of who's elected, you have insights into the reasoning involved in each position, and you have learned more about working effectively in the political climate that will follow the election.

Including Two Forms

How does invitational rhetoric look in real situations? This alternative way of approaching issues typically takes two forms: offering perspectives and creating conditions that result in an atmosphere of respect and equality.

1. **Offering perspectives**: You explain what you currently understand or know, and you show a willingness to yield, examine, or revise your conclusions if someone offers a more satisfying perspective. When confronted with hostile or very divergent viewpoints, **re-sourcement** is one way to respond creatively by framing the issue in a different way.

   re-sourcement creatively framing a divisive issue or viewpoint in a different way that may be less threatening

   If this sounds complicated, consider how Gayle offered her perspective on not spanking children (to listeners most of whom believed in spanking). She related an incident when her young daughter Celeste discovered a prescription pill her grandmother had dropped—one that could cause serious medical problems. Celeste framed this as *ownership* (It's mine! You can't have it!). Because of the danger, Gayle was tempted to swat her daughter; instead, she reframed Celeste's discovery as an *act of heroism*. (Hooray! You saved the dogs from danger. Let's give that pill back to Grandma.) Celeste happily complied. A spanking was avoided.

2. **Creating conditions**: Create conditions in which your audiences feel safe, valued, and free to offer their own perspectives in two ways. First, use **absolute listening**, which means listening without interrupting or inserting yourself into the talk and listening without criticism or counterarguments. Second, use **reversibility of perspectives**. While others are sharing their ideas, try to think from their perspectives instead of your own. The Native American saying "Don't judge people until you've walked a mile in their moccasins" demonstrates perspective taking.

   absolute listening listening without interrupting or inserting oneself into the talk

   reversibility of perspectives an attempt to think from the other's perspective as well as one's own

Invitational rhetoric, a form of reasoning often associated with women, is a model of cooperative, dialogical communication in which you and your audiences generate ideas. Because it is rooted in affirmation and respect, it's arguably an ethical way of coming to conclusions. Further, because you're not intent on controlling the ideas of others, you can disagree without figuratively going to war.

Summary

Whether you are making simple daily decisions or arguing about complex national policy questions, the canon of invention provides you with many resources for making sound decisions. Although it is often impossible to prove a claim beyond any doubt, you can at least interweave a variety of reasoning strategies to support your ideas.

Aristotle presented three kinds of artistic proofs thousands of years ago. They are artistic because you, the speaker, must create them. He considered the first proof, *ethos* or personal credibility, to be the most important. Although elements of credibility vary across cultures, believable speakers should demonstrate good character, goodwill, good sense, and dynamism.

Pathos or emotional proofs involve appeals to your listeners' positive and negative emotions as well as their needs. The chapter presented five basic needs: survival, security, belonging and love, esteem, and self-actualization. Emotions combine to form motivations that are both complex and mixed, and emotional appeals should be tested to see if they make sense.

The final proof, *logos* or rational proof, comes from your words. Analogies, both figurative and literal, involve reasoning by comparison. Inductive reasoning draws generalizations or conclusions from a number of examples. Then, using deductive reasoning, generalizations are applied to particular cases. Finally, causal or cause–effect reasoning links things that exist in time in such a way that the second results from the first. All these methods require the application of specific tests; otherwise, they can lead to fallacious or faulty conclusions.

An alternative way to make sense of complex issues is to practice invitational rhetoric based on equality, individual value, and self-determination rather than on control. You offer your perspectives and create conditions in which others are free to offer theirs. Absolute listening and reversibility of perspectives let you hear and learn from the viewpoints of others. Change may or may not result.

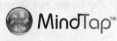

Reflect *on what you've learned.*

STUDY AND REVIEW

Public Speaking: Concepts and Skills for a Diverse Society offers a broad range of resources that will help you better understand the material in this chapter, complete assignments, and succeed on tests. Your MindTap resources feature the following:

- Speech videos with critical viewing questions, speech outlines, and transcripts
- Interactive versions of this chapter's Stop and Check activities, as well as Critical Thinking Exercises and Application Exercises
- Speech Builder Express
- Weblinks related to chapter content
- Study and review tools such as self-quizzes and an interactive glossary

You can access your online resources for *Public Speaking: Concepts and Skills for a Diverse Society* at cengagebrain.com using the access code that came with your book or that you purchased online.

Review your *Flashcards*.

KEY TERMS

The terms below are defined in the margins throughout this chapter.

absolute listening 229
ad hominem 227
ad populum 227
analogy 222
argument 215
artistic proofs 215
causal reasoning 226
common ground 217
deductive reasoning 225
demagogue 221
enthymeme 225
ethos 215
fallacy 226
false analogy 227
false dichotomy 228
faulty generalization 227
identification or
   co-orientation 217

inductive reasoning 223
invitational rhetoric 228
logos 221
motivation 218
parallel case or literal
   analogy 222
pathos 218
persuasion 215
post hoc 228
reasoning by metaphor 222
re-sourcement 229
reversibility of
   perspectives 229
slippery slope 227
unsupported assertion 227
warmth 217

CRITICAL THINKING EXERCISES

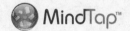

1. Find a political cartoon or an advertisement for a product that interests you. How does it appeal to emotions (both positive and negative)? To needs? To values? How does the source establish credibility? What type of reasoning (logos) does it show?
2. Find a letter to the editor in your local newspaper about a controversial topic, or read a comment that follows an online news article. Identify the types of reasoning the author uses and then evaluate his or her arguments. Do they pass the tests for reasoning given in the text? Assess the overall effectiveness of the argument.
3. Watch the movie *Twelve Angry Men*, or watch clips of some of the movie's speeches found on YouTube. Focus on the persuasiveness of the arguments stemming from logical and emotional appeals and from the credibility of the speaker(s).
4. For more examples of persuasive reasoning, go to your online resources to watch and critique one or more of the following: "Cyber-Bullying," "Grief Counseling on Campus," "Immediate Action," "Cultural Sensitivity and the Peace Corps," or "Spanking" (invitational rhetoric).

APPLICATION EXERCISES

1. With a small group of classmates, make a list of possible speech topics that relate to each of the levels of need in Maslow's hierarchy.
2. Connect to the link to Debatabase: The International Debate Education Association website on your online resources. Under the category "Popular Debates" link to a topic that interests you. Working with a partner and, each one taking a side, read through the major arguments and the supporting materials. Decide which position has the most compelling arguments and why.
3. Read the student speech below. It has good and bad elements. To guide your analysis, stop throughout your reading and answer the questions inserted between points in the text.

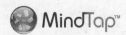

THE BENEFITS OF HUNTING
By Anonymous

Animals, I'm sure, have a place in everyone's heart. No one would like to see animals live pitiful lives and die by the hundreds from overpopulation and starvation. Well, this has happened before, and it could very well happen again if hunting is once again abolished by people who are uneducated about its true benefits.

If the welfare of animals means anything to you, it is essential that you listen closely to the biological facts that support hunting as being beneficial to wildlife, for in order to conserve wildlife, we must preserve hunting.

In the next few minutes, I will tell you about the damages resulting when people's right to hunt in certain areas is taken away. I will inform you of the uneducated ideas of animal activists and, finally, explain the differences between hunters and poachers.

a. *What do you think about the use of the phrases "I'm sure," "everyone," and "no one"? What effect does the use of the term "uneducated" have?*
b. *What is the speaker's purpose here?*

So many people are unaware of the damage that occurs to wildlife when hunting is taken away from a particular area. The best example of this happened in the state of Massachusetts. There, an animal rights group rallied and petitioned against deer hunting. Their efforts led to the banning of hunting in Massachusetts. During the period in which deer hunting was allowed, the deer population was around 100,000. Within the first year after the law was enacted, the population soared to 150,000.

Sounds good? Well, it wasn't! The overabundance of deer created a famine. Deer began to eat forest trees, gardens, and roots. They ate down to the foliage, leaving the plants unable to grow back the next year. Three years after the law went into effect the deer population went from 150,000 to only 9,000. It took the state ten years to return the deer population to normal. Eventually, the hunting ban was reversed, and the deer population has remained at its carrying capacity. I think hunting plays a major role in keeping species from overpopulation.

c. *What kind of reasoning is the speaker using? Does it pass the tests? Do you think her conclusion is obvious? Why or why not?*
d. *She says in her introduction that she will present biological facts about hunting. Does she do so to your satisfaction?*

People often argue that animals were fine before humans invented guns. However, before the Europeans came over here with guns, there weren't sprawling cities like Los Angeles and Portland to take up most of the animals' habitat. In those days, there was far more land for the animals to live on. Today, modernization has pushed the animals into a smaller wildlife area, leaving them less food and less room for breeding. Therefore, it is easier for the animals to overpopulate. Hunting has played a major role in keeping the animal population at a normal number. If hunting is taken away, the animals are sure to overpopulate.

It has been proven that humankind, even in its earliest form, has always hunted animals. Here in North America, before Europeans and guns came over, Indians hunted animals on a consistent basis. They killed hundreds of buffalo by herding them over cliffs every year. They caught school after school of salmon that migrated up the rivers. These hunts have always played a major role in population management, whether or not you choose to label it as a law of nature.

e. *What argument does the speaker attempt to argue against? Does she do so to your satisfaction?*

However, people argue that Indians needed to hunt animals to live, whereas today's North Americans don't need to kill animals to survive. So what if we can survive on fruit and vegetables? Humans are born omnivorous, meaning it is natural for us to eat both meat and plants. What is inhumane about eating an animal for food? Weren't we designed to do so?

f. *Here is the second argument she attempts to counter. How well does she succeed? Explain your answer.*

People also argue that the laws of nature will take care of animals. Hunting has always been a major part of the laws of nature. Without mountain lions to kill rabbits, the rabbit population would be a long-gone species because of overpopulation. Humans as well as mountain lions are animals. Our predation is as important to other animals, such as deer, as the mountain lion's predation is to rabbits.

g. *What is the third argument she attempts to counter? What kind of reasoning does she use?*
h. *Which of the three arguments do you think she did the best job of minimizing? Which argument did she confront the least adequately?*

Animal activists harass hunters all the time. These people have false perceptions of what hunting really is and who hunters really are. At a rally against deer hunting, a woman speaker argued, "Hunters are barbarians who are in it for the kill. Hunters would use machine guns if they could. Plus, the deer are so cute." I think that argument is pathetic and holds absolutely no validity.

Another instance of hunter harassment occurred at Yellowstone National Park. An animal activist was not satisfied with only verbal harassment, so he struck the hunter on the head twice. Are animal activists really the peaceful and humane people they claim to be? And they still believe that hunters are bloodthirsty, crazy, and inhumane!

i. *Do these two examples pass the tests for their use? Are they typical? How does the speaker generalize from them? How might she make her point instead?*
j. *Does calling an argument "pathetic" work well here? Why or why not?*

Many of these misperceptions about hunters come from the association of hunters with poachers. Hunters are not poachers! Poachers are people who kill animals when they want, regardless of laws and regulations that were set to protect the animals. These are the kind of people who hunt elephants for their ivory tusks or kill crocodiles for their skins. Poachers kill deer in areas that are off-limits, during off-limit hunting seasons. These people are criminals who are extremely harmful to wildlife. Hunters would turn in a poacher in an instant if they caught one. Poachers give hunting a bad image in the eyes of the public. It's too bad that the animal activists don't go after the poachers who are extremely harmful to animals and stop pointing a finger at hunters who follow the laws and regulations.

k. *Why does the speaker contrast hunters to poachers? In what ways, if any, is this an effective argument?*

If hunting is banned, just imagine a drive through the mountains on a road covered with emaciated skeletons of cadaverous deer who died of starvation. No longer can you take a picture of Bambi, your favorite deer that you saw every year at Yellowstone National Park. For Bambi and his family were overpopulated, and they slowly wilted away until their final day. Too bad there weren't a few healthy bucks taken by hunting that year to keep Bambi and family at a cozy carrying capacity where there was plenty of delicious food for all of them.

l. *Here, the speaker uses a great deal of pathos. Identify emotional language and images. Is this effective? Why or why not?*

The argument that animal activists use against hunting is fabricated mainly from emotions. If they are personally against killing an animal, I can respect that. But they have no place trying to ban hunting. It is proven by biological facts that hunting is necessary for wildlife management. It provides millions of dollars that fund the construction of programs that help wildlife. It keeps species from overpopulating and starving to death. In order for wildlife to flourish at an optimum population number, hunting must continue to be a major part of wildlife management.

THIS CHAPTER WILL HELP YOU

- Find a subject for a persuasive speech

- Decide on a claim of fact, value, or policy

- Diagram and explain Toulmin's model of reasoning

- Analyze your audience's attitude toward your topic

- Develop a speech to convince

- Create a speech to actuate behaviors

Diana Ong/SuperStock

Persuasive Speaking

FROM ANCIENT ATHENS to today's law courts, governing assemblies, and ceremonial or ritual occasions, rhetoric—the art of finding the available means of persuasion—has enabled democracy to thrive.[1] Because civic engagement and free speech are valued in US culture, you, too, can be a person of influence who attempts to persuade others to believe or to act in ways you find desirable. The role of persuasive speaking varies cross-culturally, as Diversity in Practice: Persuasion in China illustrates.

This chapter provides information about selecting a topic, using a model of reasoning, deciding on a claim, and analyzing your audience's attitude toward that claim. Then it gives guidelines for creating speeches to convince and to motivate listeners to act.

MindTa

*Review the chapter Learning **Objectives** and **Start** with a quic warm-up activity.*

Persuasion in China

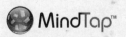

Chinese art symbolizing yin-yang (Tai Chi).

As China rapidly becomes a global superpower, interactions between China and the West highlight some fundamental assumptions about influence and persuasion. Li Liu,[2] a professor at Beijing Normal University, summarizes the Western model of persuasion as a combination of ethos, pathos, and logos by which persuaders hope to sway others. In contrast, Chinese persuasion follows a more collectivist model that is dialogical and interdependent—reflecting Confucian ideals of harmonious relationships that balance *yang* (power, light, masculinity) and *yin* (passivity, darkness, femininity).

In China, a person's sense of self is embedded in family and social relationships; consequently, persuasion is grounded in these associations. Within the family, influence is based in filial piety (respect for parents) and in maintaining family harmony. Outside the family, influence is grounded in *guanxi*, or relationships that operate on reciprocity; obligations that emerge from these relationships become tools of influence.

How do cultural differences work out in practice? Researchers explain that messages are more persuasive when they are tailored to embedded cultural frames, when they include culturally relevant themes, and when the recipients are aware of cultural distinctions. For example, European Americans were more likely to believe that caffeine posed risks and they should alter their behaviors when the message was framed as hurting them personally. However, Asian Americans were more persuaded by messages that focused on their relational obligations.[3]

On **weblink 17.1**, watch the video in which two Chinese people explain the concept of *guanxi*. Then talk with a few classmates about how *guanxi* might affect an American who is doing business in China.

Select Your Persuasive Topic

Choosing a persuasive topic can be challenging. It should be disputable, significant to others, and important to you because it's arguably more ethical to influence others toward a viewpoint or action that you personally believe, care about, and actually practice. So begin your topic search by asking yourself several questions.[4]

- *What do I believe strongly?* What do I accept as true that my audience might dispute? What issues and ideas do I think are false?
- *What arouses my emotions?* What angers me? What are my pet peeves? What arouses my pity? When am I happiest? What do I fear?
- *What social ideals do I support?* What changes would I like to see in society? What current problems or conditions could improve if we were convinced there is a

DIVERSITY IN PRACTICE

MindTap™

Read, *highlight, and take notes online.*

problem, that solutions exist, and that we can be part of those solutions? For which causes would I sign a petition or join a protest?

- *What practices enrich my life?* What have I discovered that makes life more meaningful? What activities expand our horizons? Improve our health? Lead to more fulfilling personal relationships?

Carrie's speech about grief counseling on campus grew out of her experiences following her father's death. (It is available in Appendix B and on your online resources.) Other students spoke to convince listeners that rap music reinforces male dominance, that photoshopped images in ads are unethical, that the audience should attend a ballet or learn another language, and so on.

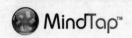

Make a Claim

claim a debatable point or proposal, conclusion, or generalization that some people won't accept without some sort of evidence or backing

After you have chosen a topic, your next step is to identify the major **claim**—a debatable point or proposal, conclusion, or generalization—to support, whether it be fact, value, or policy.

Claims of Fact

factual claims argument about debatable points, causation, or predictions

Factual claims address controversial questions about what, when, where, why, or how something happened or will happen. We use terms such as *true* or *false*, *correct* or *incorrect*, *yes* or *no* to assess their validity. The three general categories regarding facts are debatable points, causal relationships, and predictions.

debatable points disputable statement about facts of existence or history

Debatable points are disputable statements about things that do or do not exist (existence) or things that did or did not happen (history). Here are two examples about which reasonable people disagree:

There is life on other planets.

Lee Harvey Oswald acted alone to assassinate President Kennedy.

causal claim claim about the relationship links between occurrences

correlation two things occur together, but one does not necessarily lead to the other

Causal claims are made about the relationship between occurrences. Often two things regularly occur together (**correlation**). But does that mean they are linked in such a way that the first one leads to the other? In other words, correlation and causation are not synonymous. For example, skipping breakfast and poor grades may occur together in an elementary school (correlation), but does skipping breakfast actually lead to poor grades (causation)? Other factors such as tardiness and absences may have more impact on grades than breakfast.[5] Here are examples of causal claims:

Certain meat marinades reduce carcinogens in grilled chicken.[6]

Too much time spent on Facebook causes depression in young girls.

claims of prediction claim that something will or will not happen in the future

Claims of prediction contend that something will or will not happen in the future. For example,

Almost every country will be able to build or buy armed drones within ten years.[7]

A deadly strain of flu will become a pandemic in the coming year.

In short, debatable points, causal claims, and predictions generate differences of opinion that need evidence or support before audiences accept them. All three types often exist in the same issue. Take climate change, for example. Someone might argue that (1) unnatural climate change *exists*, (2) human activity *caused it*, and (3) if we don't do something, *there will be* dire consequences for the planet. Others might accept the existence of change, but dispute the causes or the proposed solutions.

© kwest/Shutterstock.com

Claims of Value

When you evaluate something using terms such as *right* or *wrong*, *good* or *better* or *best*, *beautiful* or *ugly*, *worthwhile* or *not worthwhile*, you're making a **value claim**. Here are some value claims (with the evaluative term in italics):

> It's *unfair* for giant corporations to avoid paying taxes.

> Boxing is *inhumane*.

> National security is *more important* than personal privacy during airport screenings.

Note that the third claim agrees that national security and personal privacy are both important, but the argument is over which value should take priority in the specific context. Similarly, in the abortion debate, pro-choice people are not anti-life, nor are pro-lifers anti-choice. However, the two sides disagree over which value should have precedence when a woman faces an unwanted pregnancy.

Resolving value conflicts requires agreement on the **criteria** or standards for deciding what is moral or immoral, fair or unfair, humane or inhumane. That's why it's vital to state the criteria you're using to judge. If you can convince listeners to accept your standards, they'll more readily accept your judgment; even if you fail to convince them, they can at least understand the reasoning behind your argument.

Claims of Policy

Policy claims are disputable statements we make about courses of action, whether personal or on a broader basis. To identify them, look for the terms *should* or *would*. There are basically three types of policy claims: policies should change, behaviors should change, and policies (or actions) should remain the same.

value claim argument about right or wrong, moral or immoral, beautiful or ugly

criteria the standards used for making evaluations or judgments

policy claims disputed claim about the need to act or the plan for taking action

status quo Latin phrase that means "the existing state of affairs"

burden of proof responsibility of the speaker who argues against the status quo to make the case for change

Status quo is a Latin phrase that means the existing state of affairs, and arguments against the status quo are arguments for change. When you argue against the status quo, the **burden of proof** is your responsibility because, as the cultural saying puts it, "If it ain't broke, don't fix it." Consequently, it's up to you to prove that there is a significant problem and that it can and should be fixed by the solution you propose. Examples include the following:

Congress should adopt a flat tax system.

Our campus should create a grief support system.

Some policy claims aim at personal behaviors. Here, your goal is to have your audience change their actions, as these examples illustrate:

Every student should get involved in a civic engagement project.

Students should cut up their credit cards.

presumption assumption that change is not necessary until proven otherwise

In contrast, arguments supporting the status quo are in favor of the current situation and against change. These claims have **presumption**, meaning that the status quo is assumed to be workable. (In courts of law, presumption of innocence lies with the defendant. The prosecution must prove guilt beyond a reasonable doubt.) Here are some claims supporting the status quo:

The university should not raise tuition.

You should stay in school instead of dropping out.

Often people agree that there is a problem, and they may even agree on its causes. However, they argue over solutions. For example, educational reformers may agree that education needs improvement, and they may similarly argue against the status quo, but their solutions become debatable. Some argue for smaller classes. Others advocate for alternative schools; still others think vouchers are the way to solve specific problems.

Although we separate claims of fact, value, and policy for analysis, in reality persuasive speeches commonly include a combination of claims. Effective speakers skillfully blend fact, value, and policy claims in order to successfully persuade an audience.

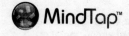 MindTap™

Use Toulmin's Model of Reasoning

argument intentional, purposeful, rational activity created to explain disputed beliefs and conclusions

Toulmin's Model of Reasoning a linear model designed to show six elements of reasoning common in the United States

Some people say they hate to argue because they think of arguments as word fights. However, as Chapter 16 pointed out, in rhetoric, an **argument** provides a set of reasons in support of a disputed idea or action. Put another way, an argument is "an intentional, purposeful activity involving reason and judgment"[8] that you create to explain your beliefs and conclusions to people who don't initially accept them.[9] Professor Stephen Toulmin[10] diagrammed a six-element linear model—**Toulmin's Model of Reasoning**—shown in Figure 17.1, that depicts a type of reasoning common in the United States.

Claims, as noted earlier, are the debatable points or proposals, conclusions, or generalizations that some people won't accept without some sort of evidence or backing.

qualifiers word or phrase that limits the scope of the claim

Qualifiers are words and phrases that limit or narrow the scope of the claim. Instead of saying *always* or *never*, substitute limiting phrases such as *in most cases*, *in males between the ages of 7 and 9*, *usually*, and *among women with a college degree*.

grounds, data, or **evidence** supporting material for claims

unsupported assertion unsupported claim

Grounds, data, or **evidence** are materials used to support your claims as described in Chapter 8. Use facts, examples, statistics, and so on from a variety of reliable sources, and arrange the data in the order your listeners will find most reasonable or most forceful.[11] Without sufficient and credible grounds, your claims are **unsupported assertions**.

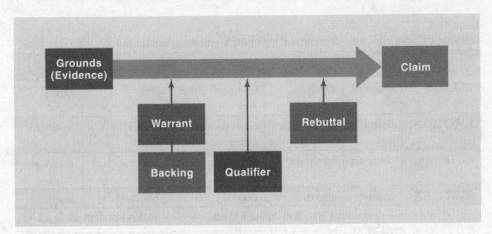

Figure 17.1
Toulmin's Model of
Reasoning

Warrants are the assumptions, justifications, or logical links you and your listeners use to connect your evidence with your claim. Warrants come from cultural traditions and institutional rules, laws, or principles.[12] For example, the Constitution lets police officers search a suspect only after they get a warrant showing sufficient evidence to link the suspect to the crime. If a fingerprint on a gun (evidence) matches the suspect's print (additional evidence), it is logical to conclude that the suspect fired the gun (claim of fact) because our fingerprints are all unique (the warrant that links the evidence to the claim).

In many cases, warrants are implicit. For example, ads for vitamins use words like *perkiness*, *power*, and *energy*. The advertisers assume that buyers want those qualities and will associate them with the product. An audience that disagrees with the warrant won't accept the argument.[13]

Backing gives additional reasons to support or defend a warrant that is not broadly understood or broadly accepted. For example, if blood were found on a defendant's jacket (evidence) but the jury doesn't get the link (warrant) between the blood evidence and the defendant, the prosecution brings in experts who explain the science of DNA (backing) and testify that the blood must belong to the victim (backing). If buyers don't associate "perkiness" with vitamins, the ad makers might bring in scientific evidence or testimonials to strengthen the link.

The **rebuttal** part of the model assumes your listeners have questions that begin with the word *But ...* or the phrase *But what about ... ?* As a "listening speaker," you should try to hear their potential counter arguments and then prepare to deal with them directly. Demonstrating that you've considered arguments both for and against your conclusions and that you still have good reasons for your claim enhances your persuasiveness.

In summary, if you learn to recognize the type of claim you are making, qualify it, provide evidence and backing to warrant it, and then confront potential audience rebuttals, you will be more effective in presenting your ideas to others and having them recognize your views as reasonable.

warrants assumption that justifies or logically links the evidence to the claim

backing additional reasons to support or defend a warrant

rebuttal counterargument the audience might have

Assess Your Audience's Attitude

Much persuasion-related research focuses on attitudes, which Chapter 6 described as positive or negative evaluations of a topic, claims, and goals. Attitudes include both mental (what we believe about it) and emotional (how we feel about it) components, and

Table 17.1
Audience attitudes involve a combination of their beliefs, emotions, and actions regarding your topic.

	strongly	**moderately**	**neutral**	**moderately**	**strongly**
BELIEFS	disagree	disagree	no beliefs either way	agree	agree
EMOTIONS	hostile	negative	no evaluation either way	positive	favorable
ACTIONS	never act	rarely act	unaware of need to act	sometimes act	always act
ATTITUDE	negative	negative	neutral	positive	positive

<------convince first, then motivate to act------> <--reinforce or motivate to act-->
most difficult--easiest

they form the basis for our actions. The Princeton University Cognitive Science website summarizes attitudes as complex mental states "involving beliefs and feelings and values and dispositions to act in certain ways."[14]

Chapter 6 showed an attitude scale ranging from strong agreement or acceptance to strong disagreement or nonacceptance. Table 17.1 illustrates how an audience's attitude can range from strong support to strong opposition to your claim. In between, are neutral listeners—often because they lack information to form an opinion either way or because they are apathetic and lack motivation to care or to do something about the issue. Obviously, it's most difficult to persuade someone who is strongly opposed to the position you are advocating.

In general, the following guidelines will help you plan effective speeches that are sensitive to audience attitudes:

- **When listeners are neutral toward your claim**, ask why. Do they lack information? If so, start by giving relevant information they can use to form an opinion. Follow up with emotional appeals to create either a positive or negative attitude toward your topic. Are they apathetic? Then use emotional appeals by linking the topic to them in as many ways as you can, and appeal to values such as fairness and justice.
- **When differences are mild**, approach your audience directly. Use objective data to make a clear case; present the positive facets of your subject, and make links to personal and community values your audience accepts. This way, although they might still disagree with you, they can understand why you hold your position.
- **When your listeners are negative toward your proposal**, rethink your options. With mildly or moderately negative audiences, try to lessen the negative so they can see positive aspects of your proposal. If they're strongly opposed, you face a hostile audience. So set modest goals and aim for small attitudinal changes. Present your points clearly so that they will at least understand how you came to your conclusions.
- **When audiences reject your proposals**, approach the subject indirectly by establishing common ground. For instance, begin with a statement with which everyone agrees, and explain why there is agreement. Then make a statement that most would accept, and explain why this is so. Move gradually to the disputed point. By this time, they will have seen that they agree with you on many points, and as a result, they may be less negative toward your ideas.[15]
- **When the audience is hostile toward you personally**, it's vital to emphasize common ground between yourself and your listeners—challenging as this is.

Generally, attitudes change incrementally, so expect change to be gradual. Each new encounter with the subject may bring about only a slight alteration in attitude, but eventually, the small changes can add up.

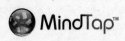

Choose a Specific Purpose

After you better understand your audience's attitude and how that affects your strategies, consider the specific response you want from your listeners. Do you want them to mentally accept your ideas? Do you want to motivate them to act? Each specific purpose requires different strategies.

Persuasive Goal: To Convince

Often, audience members don't believe your claim or accept your value judgment, either because they hold a different viewpoint or because they haven't thought much about the subject. Consequently, when you want mental agreement with your claim—whether it is a claim of fact, value, or policy—you design a speech to **convince**.

> **convince** a persuasive purpose that targets audience beliefs

Convincing about Facts

Some general strategies are effective when your goal is to convince listeners to believe a disputed fact, accept a causal relationship, or agree that your prediction is probable.

- Define important terminology and provide a history of the issue.
- Build your case carefully, using only high-quality evidence that passes the tests for credible supporting material. Research studies show that statistics are particularly useful for this goal.[16]
- Rely more on logical appeals than on emotional appeals.
- Prove your competence by being knowledgeable about the facts and by citing your sources.
- Show respect for your listeners' intelligence and divergent beliefs.

For example, Kelli decided to argue a factual claim of causation: *Playing with fashion dolls leads to poor body images in young girls.* Many audience members disagreed mildly; the females who grew up playing with these dolls didn't feel particularly harmed. The males hadn't thought much about it. So most of her audience was neutral or moderately opposed to her causal claim. Her burden was to prove the link, and her best strategies were logos or rational proofs. Here is how she built her case:[17]

- First, she provided a brief history of the most famous fashion doll of all: Barbie.
- She countered a common myth ("Barbie's body would be bent in half constantly if she were alive because her lower body could not support her upper body") by reporting, "I couldn't find any facts to support this, but I did find a study in *Sex Roles Journal* of 1996 that discussed the proportions of Barbie's body."[18]
- Next, she explained a study reported by developmental psychologists in the journal *Adolescence* that showed the importance of toys in children's development.[19]
- Following this, she reported that a study from the journal *Developmental Psychology*[20] explained that children internalize images from dolls and become aware of their body image at around age 6, and some 6-year-old girls already have body dissatisfaction. The study also compared girls who played with Barbie to girls who played with Emme, a larger-sized fashion doll, and found the former had more negative body images.
- Her final point was a finding that adolescent females believed fashion dolls were images of perfection, and both males and females believed they affected girls' self-image. Most said they were bad role models.[21]

- She concluded by emphasizing her goal: Her purpose was to convince listeners of a link between fashion dolls and body image (causal claim) not to call for a ban on these dolls (policy claim).

Overall, the studies by experts provided Kelli's listeners with good reasons to see the link.

Convincing about Values

Because we don't agree on evaluations of people, objects, policies, and so on, we often try to convince others to share our judgments. Here are two value claims: (1) embryonic stem cell research is wrong; and (2) finding cures for people who are currently alive is more important than preserving an embryo. The first makes a judgment about the issue; the second argues that both values are important, but one supersedes the other in a specific context.

For a variety of reasons, value judgments within a single audience may vary so widely that some judge a topic, such as gay marriage, as unethical whereas others consider it a moral necessity. Furthermore, because values are assumptions about what is good, value questions often generate deep emotional responses. It is nearly impossible to move listeners from judging a topic as unethical to evaluating it as highly ethical because of a single speech, but here are some tips for arguing value claims:

- **Use emotional appeals**. Examples are a good way to help listeners identify with those involved in the issue. Also, link the topic to related values that everyone can agree on, such as fairness or freedom.
- **Appeal to authority** if your audience accepts your source as authoritative. (See Chapter 8.) Some audiences will be moved by appeals to cultural traditions, words of poets, philosophers, scientists, or scriptural texts; others will discount those same authorities.

One useful organizational strategy is the **criteria-satisfaction pattern** in which you first establish the standards you're using to evaluate the topic and then show how

criteria-satisfaction pattern good for value or definition speeches; sets forth standards for judgment or for inclusion in a category and then shows how the proposal meets or exceeds these standards or fits into the category

Value claims often arouse deep emotions, and many people feel horror at the claim that a snake makes a *good* pet. So Helene carefully set up acceptable criteria for good pets and then showed how snakes met those criteria.

© Matt Jeppson/Shutterstock.com

your subject meets those standards. Set audience-centered criteria[22] by answering questions such as these:

- What criteria do we use to make and apply judgments regarding this issue?
- Where do these criteria come from?
- Why should we accept these sources?

Helene faced a hostile or at least moderately negative crowd when she presented her value claim: *Snakes make good pets.* So she first set up some criteria that people commonly look for in a good pet:[23]

- A pet should be interesting.
- Pets should be easy to care for.
- You should be able to read a pet's emotions.
  She then linked each point to snakes.
- She presented several interesting facts about snakes.
- She described how easy they were to care for.
- She explained how to read a snake's emotions.

At the end of her speech, no one was ready to run out and buy a snake, but listeners were more willing to evaluate snakes positively—at least as pets for someone else.

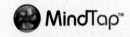

Convincing about Policies

To convince an audience that a policy claim is workable, you must adequately address the **stock issues**, which are defined as the fundamental questions that must be answered if a proposition is to be accepted or rejected. In other words, what questions would a thinking, reasonable person ask and need to have answered to make a reasoned decision about a particular issue?[24]

The four stock issues related to policy claims are harm (or ill), blame, cure, and cost.

- **Harm** is sometimes called ill. Here you define the problem, explain its history, and show that it is significant enough to call for a solution. Develop the *quantitative harms* (the number of people affected) by using statistics or studies that show how widespread it is. Also include *qualitative harms* (how it affects an individual's or group's quality of life) by using examples or testimony from people involved with the problem.
- **Blame** is the "cause" part of the problem where you link a cause or causes to the effects you established in the harm section. What elements of the status quo contribute to the problem or allow it to remain unsolved? Some causes may be *structural*, meaning that laws or organizations are either in place and should be removed, or that structures are lacking, and the problem exists because they are not there. Other causes may be *attitudinal*, meaning that individuals or groups lack the understanding or the will to solve the problem. Either way, support your causal claims by using scientific studies, plausible explanations, and testimony from experts who have investigated the problem in depth.[25]
- **Cure** is the "solution" section of the speech where you provide a plan and describe how it will create **solvency**, an effective solution to the problem. What must happen for the problem to be solved? Who will do it? How? Through what agency? At what price? How will the plan eliminate or bypass the structural or attitudinal causes? Clear and detailed answers to these questions will help convince your listeners that your plan will actually solve the problem.
- **Cost** is the "feasibility" part of the plan in which you do a cost–benefit analysis and weigh the *advantages* against the *disadvantages.* You must show that the plan will actually work. Some plans look good on paper, but they are too costly in time or money to be practical.

stock issues the questions a reasonable person would need to have answered before forming a reasoned decision about a topic

harm the problem in a stock issues case; also called ill

blame the cause of the problem

cure the solution

solvency the proposed plan will actually solve the problem

cost advantages weighed against the disadvantages

In summary, you must convince your audience that a problem exists and that it affects a significant quantity of people and alters their quality of life. You then convince them that it was caused by structures or attitudes that can either be eliminated or circumvented by your proposed plan. Give enough details so that listeners can understand how the plan will work, and provide a cost–benefit analysis so they are convinced that it is practical.

US citizens got a lesson in policy debating when the federal government enacted health care reform called "Obamacare."

- **[Harm]** Almost everyone agreed that problems existed in the status quo and affected great numbers of people in ways that hurt their quality of life. Health costs were high; insurance rates were skyrocketing; not everyone had access to the treatments and medications they needed, and so on.
- **[Blame]** Congress pointed to structural causes including (depending on who you asked) for-profit health insurance companies, too many malpractice lawsuits, the lack of a single-payer government system, and so on. Attitudes also contribute. Too many people demand unnecessary procedures from costly specialists.[26]
- **[Cure]** Congress passed a giant plan that most members did not actually read. Critics disputed details of the plan; some thought it went too far; others thought it didn't go far enough. When it actually rolled out in October 2013, several flaws showed up that required adjustments to the plan.
- **[Cost]** The cost of the overhaul was hotly debated. Cost-saving benefits were touted by supporters and disputed by detractors. Advantages and disadvantages are still being weighed.

Time, energy, and money continue to go into the ongoing task of ensuring that the structural changes in the law will eventually solve for the quantitative and qualitative harms in the previous health care system.

Persuasive Goal: To Actuate

When you want your audience to change their behaviors, your specific purpose is to **actuate**. This requires you to consider their beliefs about your topic, their motivations, and their opinions about whether or not they can and should act as you suggest. This section discusses two theories that explain motivations to act: cognitive dissonance theory and the Theory of Reasoned Action (TRA). It then provides an organizational pattern commonly used to motivate behaviors.

Cognitive Dissonance Theory

Often we behave in ways that are inconsistent with our beliefs or values. Leon Festinger[27] developed the **cognitive dissonance theory** to explain the resulting inconsistency or **dissonance** we experience. He originally studied smokers who continued to smoke even though they knew it harmed their bodies. In this theory, living organisms, including humans, seek balance or equilibrium. When challenged with inconsistency, we try to return to a balanced psychological state. Consequently, if our behaviors fail to match our beliefs, we typically experience discomfort until we either alter our beliefs to match our behaviors or alter our behaviors to match our beliefs.

Inconsistency between action and belief is one of the best motivators for change. For example, it is easier to persuade you to consult an employment counselor if you are stuck in a job you hate than if you love everything about your current workplace. If you strongly support a political party's ideas but do nothing, it's easier to persuade you to vote than if you care nothing about politics. In short, keep this theory in mind when your audience's behaviors don't match up with their beliefs and ideals.

actuate motivate the audience to do something

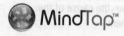

cognitive dissonance theory humans seek stability or equilibrium; when faced with inconsistency they seek psychological balance; this may motivate them to change in order to be consistent

dissonance inconsistency or clash

We are motivated to act when our attitude toward the task is positive, we think other people would support our actions, and we think we can actually do the task. This then reduces dissonance by bringing our behaviors into line with our ideals such as helping others.

The **Theory of Reasoned Action (TRA)** is another good way to think about the process of motivating actions because it adds a social component—what our friends and family think. It assumes that we are rational and will systematically weigh the costs and benefits of acting, given an opportunity to do so.[28] We also act in ways that allow us to meet the expectations of others. In short, our behaviors line up with three things: (1) our attitudes, including both our beliefs and feelings about the topic; (2) our **subjective norms**, which are our perceptions of what people who are important to us think we should do; and (3) our **perceived behavioral control**, our opinion about our ability to accomplish the behavior in question.[29] All three factors influence our intentions to act, although our attitudes generally carry more weight. Interestingly, one study found that people in a collectivist culture scored higher on subjective norms, but this did not necessarily predict their intention to act.[30]

For illustration, let's say a speaker urges listeners to donate blood, and she wants them to understand that they can easily do this. So, in addition to motivational appeals, she includes specific information about where and when to find the bloodmobile on campus. An audience member might reason like this:

> I think I'll donate blood this afternoon (intention) at the bloodmobile on campus (opportunity). I dislike needles and taking time from my studying (negative attitude/ cost), but I like the idea of saving someone's life (positive attitude/benefits). My friends and family donate blood (subjective norms), and they'd admire me for donating (benefits). Therefore, I'll do it.

In contrast, another listener might respond differently:

> I don't intend to donate today or in the near future (intention). I hate needles and can't take time from studies (negative attitude/cost), and I do a lot of other things to help others. None of my friends or family would know or care (subjective norms) whether or not I went. So count me out.

In short, the Theory of Reasoned Behavior adds a social dimension to motivation. People are moved to act, not only by inconsistencies between their behaviors and beliefs,

theory of reasoned action (TRA) links behavioral intentions with attitudes, subjective norms, and perceived behavioral control; assumes we rationally weigh costs and benefits of our actions

subjective norms our perceptions of what significant people think we should do

perceived behavioral control our opinion about our ability to do a behavior

but also by how they think others will perceive their actions and by whether or not they believe they can act successfully.

Monroe's Motivated Sequence

One commonly used pattern is especially effective when you want people to do something. **Monroe's Motivated Sequence** is a modified problem–solution format, named after Alan Monroe, a legendary professor at Purdue University.

Because people need encouragement to do what they know they should do, it's important to provide emotional as well as logical reasons for behaviors. This pattern includes the word *motivated* because it builds in several steps that increase motivational appeals. (*Note:* This pattern is not a formula in the sense that you must include each element. Rather, Monroe suggests various ways to develop your points.) Here are the five easily remembered steps in the sequence, as explained by Monroe himself.[31]

1. **Attention Step:** As with any other speech, begin by gaining the audience's attention and drawing it to your topic.
2. **Need Step:** This step is similar to the problem part of a problem–solution speech. Monroe suggests four elements: (a) *statement*—tell the nature of the problem; (b) *illustration*—give a relevant detailed example or examples; (c) *ramifications*—provide additional support such as statistics or testimony that show the extent of the problem; and (d) *pointing*—show the direct relationship between the audience and the problem.
3. **Satisfaction Step:** Next, propose a solution that will satisfy the need. This step can have as many as five parts: (a) *statement*—briefly state the attitude, belief, or action you want the audience to adopt; (b) *explanation*—make your proposal understandable (visual aids may help at this point); (c) *theoretical demonstration*—show the logical connection between the need and its satisfaction; (d) *practicality*—use facts, figures, and testimony to show that the proposal has worked effectively or that the belief has been proved correct; and (e) *meeting objections*—show that your proposal can overcome your listeners' potential objections.
4. **Visualization Step:** This is the unique step. Here, you ask listeners to imagine the future, both if they enact your proposal and if they fail to do so. (a) *Positive*—describe a positive future if your plan is put into action. Create a realistic scenario showing good outcomes your solution provides. Appeal to emotions such as safety needs, pride, pleasure, and approval. (b) *Negative*—have listeners imagine themselves in an unpleasant situation if they fail to put your solution into effect. (c) *Contrast*—compare the negative results of not enacting your plan with the positive things your plan will produce.
5. **Action Step:** Call for a specific action: (a) *name* the specific, overt action, attitude, or belief you are advocating; (b) *state* your personal intention to act; and (c) *end* with impact.

Terah, a nursing major, wanted to give an organ donor speech, but her survey revealed that her classmates had a lot of information and a good attitude toward donation, so she focused on motivating them to put their good intentions into action by giving specific details they could easily do. Here are her major points:[32]

Attention: My survey showed that you want to be organ donors but have not yet signed up.

I. It's easy and accessible.
II. From my research, I will give you specific steps to take to become an organ donor.

Need: My survey showed that I don't need to convince you of a need for organ donor, and I don't have to clear up misconceptions.

Monroe's Motivated Sequence a call to action in five steps: attention, need, satisfaction, visualization, and action

Satisfaction: My survey revealed that you need how-to information about signing up.

I. For $34 and proof of identity, the Department of Motor Vehicles can mark your driver's license.
II. You can get a free donor card from www.organdonor.gov/donor/index.htm.
III. You can sign up for free at www.donatelifenw.org or on the online donor registry at www.organdonor.gov/donor/registry.shtm.
IV. Be sure to tell your family your wishes because they may have to tell doctors who ask about donating.

Visualization

I. Imagine you sign up, a tragedy happens, and Josh in New Mexico gets your heart, Mary in Colorado has a new kidney, Glen in North Dakota receives your liver, and many more have improved lives from other tissues.
II. Now imagine you don't follow up, a tragedy happens, and several very sick people can't benefit from your organs.
III. Which choice is ideal?

Action

I. Follow one of the easy procedures and sign up to be a donor.
II. I did this last year, and I'm very glad I did.
III. No more procrastination; do it today!

As you might imagine, this pattern is good for sales speeches when your goal is to create a need and motivate people to purchase a product.

Summary

The best subjects for persuasive speeches come from the things that matter most to you personally. For this reason, ask yourself questions such as "What do I believe strongly?" "What arouses my strong feelings?" "What would I like to see changed?" "What enriches my life?" Your answers will generally provide topics that you're willing to defend. Choosing your subject is only the first part of topic selection. You must then decide whether you will focus on developing a claim of fact, value, or policy. Toulmin's Model of Reasoning can help you visualize the elements needed to defend your claim successfully.

Understanding the strength of the audience's attitude—comprised of their beliefs, emotions, and actions regarding your topic—will help you develop specific strategies for audiences who are hostile or somewhat opposed to your ideas, for audiences who are neutral, and for audiences who are generally supportive of your claim.

This chapter explained how to develop speeches around two specific goals: to convince or to actuate behaviors. A speech to convince aims to gain audience agreement with your conclusions, whether they are about facts, value judgments, or the wisdom and feasibility of specific policies. A speech to actuate tries to motivate the audience to act in the ways you propose. According to cognitive dissonance theory, motivation comes when our beliefs and actions don't match up; aligning them helps us regain the desired state of balance or equilibrium. The Theory of Reasoned Action adds a social component. We act when our beliefs and attitudes are favorable toward the behavior in question, when we believe that we can accomplish it, and when we think others are supportive of our actions. One of the most common patterns for motivating people to act is Monroe's Motivated Sequence with its five elements: attention, need, satisfaction, visualization, and action.

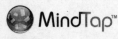

Reflect *on what you've learned.*

STUDY AND REVIEW

Public Speaking: Concepts and Skills for a Diverse Society offers a broad range of resources that will help you better understand the material in this chapter, complete assignments, and succeed on tests. Your MindTap resources feature the following:

- Speech videos with critical viewing questions, speech outlines, and transcripts
- Interactive versions of this chapter's Stop and Check activities, as well as Critical Thinking Exercises and Application Exercises
- Speech Builder Express
- Weblinks related to chapter content
- Study and review tools such as self-quizzes and an interactive glossary

You can access your online resources for *Public Speaking: Concepts and Skills for a Diverse Society* at cengagebrain.com using the access code that came with your book or that you purchased online.

*Review your **Flashcards**.*

KEY TERMS

The terms below are defined in the margins throughout this chapter.

actuate 244
argument 238
backing 239
blame 243
burden of proof 238
causal claim 236
claim 236
claim of prediction 236
cognitive dissonance
   theory 244
cost 243
cure 243
convince 241
correlation 236
criteria 237
criteria-satisfaction pattern 242
debatable point 236
dissonance 244
factual claim 236
grounds, data, or evidence 238

harm 243
Monroe's Motivated
   Sequence 246
perceived behavioral
   control 245
policy claim 237
presumption 238
qualifier 238
rebuttal 239
solvency 243
status quo 238
stock issues 243
subjective norms 245
Theory of Reasoned Action
   (TRA) 245
Toulmin's Model of
   Reasoning 238
unsupported assertion 238
value claim 237
warrant 239

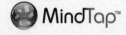

CRITICAL THINKING EXERCISES

1. To review the elements of the Toulmin Model, watch a crime show and identify the types of evidence required to prove the factual claim: *the defendant did the crime.* How does the evidence required for legal cases differ from the evidence you use to support factual claims in the classroom? How is it similar?
2. To better understand Leon Festinger's theory, do an Internet search for "cognitive dissonance theory" and follow a couple of links that have .edu in their URL. How can this theory help you achieve your goals for your classroom speech?
3. To better understand the TRA, search the Internet or your library databases for Theory of Reasoned Action. What elements of this theory (alternatively called the Theory of

Planned Behavior) should you keep in mind to help you achieve your goals for your persuasive speech?

4. Listen to at least one persuasive speech by a professional speaker, taking notes on the speaker's arguments. (C-SPAN or ted.com are good sources for such speeches.) What kinds of claims does the speaker make? How does he or she support the claims? Who are the intended audiences? How effectively does the speaker adapt to audience attitudes? **Weblink 17.2** maintains links to these sites.

5. To explore hostile speaking in greater depth, go to **weblink 17.3**. The author is a professional consultant. Compare his list of ten typical responses to hostile audiences with his six positive alternative strategies. This is a .com website. How credible do you think the author is? Why?

6. Critique Linnea Strandy's speech "Fair Trade Coffee," which is organized according to Monroe's Motivated Sequence. You can find her speech in your online resources. Give at least three reasons why the visualization step is a good motivator.

APPLICATION EXERCISES

1. Scan a current news source and identify at least two news items of the day that address issues in each category: fact, value, and policy. Bring the list to class and discuss it with your classmates.

2. With a small group in your classroom, identify areas in which national attitudes have changed regarding a controversial issue. How did persuasive public speaking contribute to those changes?

3. Working with a partner, use Monroe's Motivated Sequence to outline the points of a speech to motivate your audience to action. Use one of the following categories:

- Sales: Convince listeners to buy a product.
- Public service: Ask the audience to contribute time or money to a worthy cause.

CHAPTER 18

**THIS CHAPTER WILL
HELP YOU**

- **Create introductions
  and farewell speeches**

- **Make announcements**

- **Understand the role
  of special occasion
  speaking in creat-
  ing and maintaining
  cultures**

- **Give award and nomi-
  nation speeches**

- **Create commemorative
  speeches**

- **Compose an inspira-
  tional speech by using
  the exemplum pattern**

Diana Ong/SuperStock

Speaking on Special Occasions

CELEBRATIONS, SOLEMN OCCASIONS, and other events that reaffirm group values are the settings for special occasion speeches. Some of these speeches *celebrate* or honor an event, person, or place. Others *commemorate* or memorialize significant cultural happenings. Still others *inspire* or *entertain*. Special occasion speeches typically have an integrative function that helps connect people to one another and to their shared goals.[1] Overall, they reinforce and maintain the common belief-attitude-value cluster that influences the group's behaviors.

This chapter provides guidelines for introductions and farewells, for announcements, nominations, and awards, for tributes, toasts, and eulogies,

Mind
Review
chapter
Learning
Objectiv
and *Stan*
with a q
warm-up
activity.

and for speeches that inspire, reinforce values, and (often) entertain. In addition, Diversity in Practice: Organizational Culture describes some aspects of organizational culture that affect your speech.

Introductions

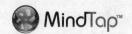

Read, *highlight, and take notes online.*

When strangers first meet, they want to know "Who is this person?" "What do we have in common?" "What brings her here?" Introductions are short informative speeches that provide the facts people need to interact effectively with a newcomer. You might introduce a classmate, a new coworker, or a speaker at a special event. In each situation, keep your introduction brief. Chapter 2 provided guidelines for introducing a classmate. Here are some tips for introducing an unfamiliar person to your school or work environment:

* Provide the newcomer's name and job title, if applicable.
* Give a few details about the person's educational and occupational background as well as personal characteristics or accomplishments that will help the audience know a little more about him or her.
* Close by welcoming the newcomer to the group.

Here is a sample introduction of a new faculty member in an elementary school. Notice that it briefly presents her qualifications and provides the current faculty and staff with enough information about her background and some of her interests that they can interact effectively with her.

This year, we are pleased to welcome a new faculty member, Cornelia Baily-Hunter, who will be joining us as our music specialist.

Cornelia received her BA in Music Education from Indiana University, South Bend, and her Master's of Music Education from Penn State. Her passion for music in a child's life dates back to her elementary school days when a very patient orchestra teacher introduced her to the joys of playing the oboe. She marched in the band in high school, joined the university's orchestra, and earned tuition money by playing in a woodwind quartet that performed at weddings and other social functions. Before moving here to the Southwest to be closer to family, she taught for six years in Pennsylvania.

Cornelia, we're glad you're here. We know you will be a great addition to the faculty.

To introduce a guest speaker, include some information about the occasion that precipitated the invitation as well as about the actual speaker. Here are some elements to include in such speeches:

* Greetings and/or a welcome to the group
* A statement about the occasion
* Announcement of the speaker's name and topic
* A brief account of the speaker's background, education, training, achievements, personality, or any other salient information that relates to the topic or the audience

Be prepared to make a few closing remarks after the talk. Briefly thank the speaker, and make a simple, short reference to the central idea of the speech.

Farewells

Saying good-bye is never easy because departures cause disruptions that affect those left behind to a greater or lesser degree. This is true whether or not the person was well liked. For example, consider the emotions that arise when a popular professor takes a position in another university, a beloved rabbi retires, an unpopular manager joins another company, or the seniors on the football team graduate. Because all these departures signal changes in an organization's social patterns, farewell speeches function to ease the inevitable adjustments that both the departing individual and the group must make.

For these occasions, express emotions—especially appreciation, sadness, affection, and hope for the future. Balance the sadness by speaking about happy times. Telling humorous stories is a good way to do this.

When you are the person leaving, include some or all of these elements in your farewell:

- Remind group members of what they've meant to you personally.
- Identify some lessons you learned from being with them.
- Tell stories that you'll carry with you as happy memories.
- Express both your sadness at leaving and your hopes for the future.
- Encourage them to continue to uphold the organization's mission and values.
- Invite people to write or visit you in your new location.

When you bid farewell to a departing person, you speak not only for yourself but also for your group, so include these elements in your speech:

- Recognize the person's accomplishments in the group.
- Identify positive personal characteristics that you will remember.
- Use humorous anecdotes.
- Express your personal sadness and the group's sense of loss.
- Wish the person well in his or her new location.
- When appropriate, present a gift as a remembrance.

Announcements

Announcements provide facts about upcoming events or developments of interest. In clubs and organizations, businesses and faculty meetings, announcements are an agenda staple because they answer the questions "What's happening?" or "What's new?" Essential to these short speeches are details regarding time, place, cost, and so on, as the following guidelines shows:

- First, draw your listeners' attention to the event.
- Provide such details as who, what, when, and where the event takes place.
- Give both the costs and the benefits of attending.
- End with a brief summary of important information.

Here's a sample announcement:

Have fun and do good at the same time by attending the third annual Oregon Food Bank Benefit, which will be held Tuesday, August 2, from 5:30 to 9:00 P.M. at McMenamins Grand Lodge in Forest Grove. Listen to the Big Band sounds of Swing DC and meet some representatives of the Oregon Food Bank, who will be there to take donations of cash or canned goods. The restaurant will donate half of all food and beverage receipts to the food bank. Children are welcome.

So help stop hunger in Oregon a week from Tuesday, from 5:30 to 9:00 P.M. in Forest Grove. The Internet provides a map and directions to the lodge, or call 503-992-9533 for details.

Organizational Culture

The term *corporate culture* shows that we commonly think of organizations as small cultures within the larger society. Your school or workplace has an ethos or personality—a culture that comes out of its core beliefs, values, attitudes, and behaviors—that you can find in its mission statement. Organizational culture comprises many elements that organizational members know and newcomers must learn. Here are just a few:[2]

- History—the founders, the founding date, the founding mission
- Political system—the way power is distributed, who leads and who follows and when
- Distribution of wealth—pay equity, merit pay, bonuses, stock options, and dues or collections
- Art, music, and dress—logos, songs, or uniforms
- Language—jargon or special in-group terminology
- Rituals—banquets, picnics, award ceremonies, installations
- Folklore—narratives and myths, heroes and villains, described in the stories passed from person to person within the organization[3]

These last two aspects of culture are particularly relevant to public speaking. In *Theory Z: How American Business Can Meet the Japanese Challenge*, W. B. Ouchi[4] explains that organizational symbols, ceremonies, and myths communicate a group's beliefs and values. The stories that are told and retold and passed from one generation to another explain organizational values, beliefs, and memories. Knowing these symbols and stories is important in understanding the organization; using them in public speaking can be a powerful form of proof to members of the organization.

Nominations

Nominations are short persuasive speeches that do two things: (1) introduce your candidate to the group, and (2) present brief arguments explaining why he or she should be elected. The following elements are essential:

- Name the office, and tell its importance to the organization as a whole.
- List the reasons the candidate is right for the office.

statement of reasons pattern pattern that lists reasons and then explains each one

criteria-satisfaction pattern speech pattern that first sets up standards for judging and then shows how the subject meets the standards

Two persuasive organizational patterns are especially effective: (1) a **statement of reasons pattern**, where you list and explain the reasons one by one; and (2) a **criteria-satisfaction pattern**, where you set up criteria for the office and then show how the candidate meets the criteria. In his nomination of Sonia Sotomayor for the Supreme Court, President Obama set the following criteria:[5]

> First and foremost is a rigorous intellect, a mastery of the law, and ability to hone in on the key issues and provide clear answers to complex legal questions. Second is recognition of the limits of the judicial role....Yet these qualities alone are insufficient....It is experience that can give a person a common touch and a sense of compassion and understanding of how the world works and how ordinary people live. And that is why it is a necessary ingredient in the kind of justice we need on the Supreme Court.

He then explained why his nominee met the criteria. After describing her academic and professional background, he noted:

> Walking in the door, she brings more experience on the bench and more varied experience on the bench than anyone currently serving on the US Supreme Court had when they were appointed.

He concluded with details of her life to show that she understood how society functions and how common people live.

Award Speeches

Individualistic cultures recognize meritorious work or character traits that embody the group's ideals. It's common to present recipients with a permanent memento of some sort. When you present an award, emphasize the group's shared beliefs, values, and commitments and include these elements:

- Name the award and describe its significance. What personal traits or accomplishments does it honor? In whose name is it being presented? Why is it given? How often is it awarded? How are the recipients selected?
- Summarize the selection criteria and the reasons this recipient was chosen.
- Relate the appropriateness of the award to the recipient's traits.
- Express good wishes to the recipient.

In contrast, more collectivist cultures rarely single out one individual to praise over others. (New Zealanders, for instance, have the saying "The tall poppy gets mown down.") Consequently, members of these cultures may feel uncomfortable if their personal characteristics are publicly acknowledged. In these situations, honor the entire group rather than a single individual.

Accept an award with a brief speech that reinforces the values the award symbolizes, as these guidelines and sample acceptance speech show:

- Thank those who honored you.
- Acknowledge others who helped you.
- Personalize what it means to you.
- Express appreciation for the honor.

> Thank you, Professor Choi, for those kind words, and thanks to the committee for selecting me as the Outstanding Communication Arts graduate this year. Each member of our honor society is such a high achiever that each one deserves recognition as well. We've spent four years of "quality time" together…and I'll never forget the great times we had at the Northwest Communication Association meetings!
>
> Of course, we all rely on the support of our dedicated faculty—and each professor here is outstanding. You're not only knowledgeable and wise, but you also take a personal interest in the life of each of your advisees and majors. Thanks, too, to my parents for their financial and emotional support through these past four years. I appreciate you all.
>
> Next year I will serve with AmeriCorps and study for the LSATs in preparation for law school after that. Watch for me on social media!
>
> Thank you once again.

Tributes

A tribute (called an *encomium* in Latin) praises the qualities of a person (the Basque artist, Jorge Oteiza), thing (a dog), idea (love), organization (NASA), event (D-Day), or group (members of a legendary sports team). Subjects may or may not be living. A tribute for a living subject should focus on the person's character and achievements; tributes to historical characters should balance the subject's virtues and accomplishments. In 1870, lawyer George Graham Vest gave this tribute to dogs during a lawsuit over a foxhound killed by a sheep farmer.[6]

> Gentlemen of the Jury: The best friend a man has in the world may turn against him and become his enemy. His son or daughter that he has reared with loving care may prove ungrateful….The money that a man has, he may lose….The people who are prone to fall on their knees to do us honor when success is with us, may be the first to throw the stone of malice when failure settles its cloud upon our heads.
>
> The one absolutely unselfish friend that man can have in this selfish world, the one that never deserts him, the one that never proves ungrateful or treacherous is his dog. A man's dog stands by him in prosperity and in poverty, in health and in sickness. He will sleep on the cold ground, where the wintry winds blow and the snow drives fiercely, if only he may be near his master's side. He will kiss the hand that has no food to offer….He guards the sleep of his pauper master as if he were a prince. When all other friends desert, he remains….
>
> If fortune drives the master forth, an outcast in the world, friendless and homeless, the faithful dog asks no higher privilege than that of accompanying him, to guard him against danger, to fight against his enemies. And when the last scene of all comes, and death takes his master in its embrace and his body is laid away in the cold ground, no matter if all other friends pursue their way, there by the graveside will the noble dog be found, his head between his paws, his eyes sad, but open in alert watchfulness, faithful and true even in death.

Toasts are given across the globe to give goodwill wishes to honorees.

Needless to say, Vest won the case. Here are some guidelines for a tribute:

- In the introduction, tell why the subject is significant or worthy of honor.
- Because the intent is to highlight characteristics, ideas, and behaviors that benefit society, at the outset, identify a few ideals the subject represents.
- Consider using a statement of reasons pattern. For example, a student tribute to the baseball great Ted Williams gives three reasons to praise Williams: patriotism, perseverance, and charity.[7]
- Develop each point with illustrations from the person's life.
- This is not primarily an informative speech, although you probably need to include information about the subject.

One of the most famous speeches in this category is President Reagan's Tribute to the *Challenger* Crew which is available online. See also St. Paul's famous tribute to love found in the Bible (I Corinthians 13).

Toasts

Toasts are ritual speeches that honor a person or persons on birthdays or graduation days, at wedding or anniversaries, at reunions or holidays, and so on. Toasts typically come at the end of a meal and involve a ritual drink to express goodwill toward the honoree. The host has the opportunity to offer the first toast. During the toast ritual:

- Make sure all participants have a drink at hand.
- Stand and hold your glass at waist level while you propose the toast.
- Look at the honoree throughout the speech.
- At the end, raise your glass, say a ritual phrase such as "to your happiness," and take a small sip.
- Honorees remain seated and do not drink. After the toast is drunk, they stand, thank the person offering the toast, and often follow up with a toast of their own.

The speech itself should be short but well planned following a few general guidelines:

* If people are unaware of your relationship with the honoree, briefly state it, but keep self-references short; the occasion is not about you.
* State the honoree's name at the beginning and the end of the speech.
* Give reminiscences that show your goodwill for the guest of honor such as how you met or personal traits you appreciate. Avoid embarrassing stories or inside jokes.
* Be brief.
* End with sincere best wishes.

Toasts are common in many cultures. In fact, the Internet gives you phrases to express goodwill wishes in languages from Albanian to Zulu.

Eulogies

Eulogies are perhaps the most difficult speeches to give because they commemorate someone who has died. Don't try to summarize the person's entire life; instead, highlight a few things that celebrate the person's personality and virtues and then share your feelings and experiences to comfort other mourners. For example, here are some lines from Jonah Goldberg's eulogy for his father:[8]

> I think it would be a mistake to think my dad's wisdom and his humor were different facets of his personality. For him, "humor" and "wisdom" were different words for the same thing. After all, a sense of humor is merely the ability to see connections between things we haven't noticed before (while laughter is what we do when we realize that those connections should have been obvious all along). Is wisdom really such a different thing?
>
> Maybe it is, but it never really seemed to be in my dad.
>
> Call it wisdom or humor, my dad saw the world through different lenses....[W]hat was obvious for my dad was often insightful, profound, or hilarious to the rest of us. And, conversely, what was obvious to most people could be a complete mystery to him. To call my dad "handy" or overly burdened with street smarts would be a stretch.

Here are some guidelines for preparing a eulogy:

* Keep in mind your goal, which is to appropriately celebrate the deceased person's life by focusing on positive, memorable characteristics and accomplishments.
* If you're the only one giving a eulogy, consult family members and friends for insights and examples that capture essential characteristics or positive traits. You might ask what information the family prefers you *not* mention.
* Draw from your memories, and share appropriate feelings and experiences.
* Humor, used sensitively, can be appropriate and comforting.
* Consider using the wave pattern and organize your eulogy around a repeated theme like "Harry was an honest, honorable man..." or "John was a devoted friend..." or "Molly had enough energy for three people..." Support each crest of the wave with an example.
* Lines from poetry or the deceased's favorite lyrics often work well.
* Don't worry about delivery. If you break down or otherwise show emotion, your audience will be sympathetic. If you fear you'll lose control, write out and read your eulogy, or arrange beforehand with the person officiating to take over if you simply cannot continue. (For an example of appropriate emotion in a eulogy, watch Cher's

speech at the memorial service for Sonny Bono, her former husband. It's available online.)
- Keep it short. Unless you're told otherwise, limit your remarks to five to ten minutes at the most.

Commemorative Events

Commemorative speeches are common at breakfast, luncheon, and dinner meetings, as well as at conventions and other ceremonies. Although their basic purpose is to inspire and to reinforce beliefs and values, these special occasion speeches are often entertaining as well. Each speech is different; however, the following characteristics are typical:

- **Build the speech around a theme**. Find out in advance if one has already been selected for the occasion; if so, prepare your remarks around it. If not, select your own inspiring theme. Here are some titles of recent commemorative speeches that show the speaker's theme: "If I Were to Sing Tonight"[9] (by an Irish American governor at the American Irish Fund gala); "I Was a Teenage Scientist"[10] (by a university president at a science talent search dinner); and "From Tentative Twig to Mighty Branch"[11] (by a university vice chancellor at a welcoming ceremony for new students and their parents).
- **Inspire listeners**. Positive emotions and values such as hope, courage, respect, perseverance, and generosity are common in inspirational speeches. Notice the many positive emotions and values in this excerpt from the prime minister of Australia Julia Gillard's[12] address to the US Congress:

   For my parents' generation, the defining image of America was the landing at Normandy…risking everything to help free the world. For my own generation, the defining image of America was the landing on the moon. My classmates and I were sent home from school to watch the great moment on television. I'll always remember thinking that day: Americans can do anything. Americans helped free the world of my parents' generation. Americans inspired the world of my own youth….I see the same brave and free people today. I believe you can do anything still. There is a reason the world always looks to America. Your great dream—life, liberty and the pursuit of happiness—inspires us all.

- **Pay special attention to language**. To make your speech both inspiring and memorable, choose vivid, moving, and interesting words and phrases. Describe scenes in detail; select words that are rich in connotative meanings. Some of the most famous inspirational lines come from Martin Luther King Jr.'s speeches (available online) or from John F. Kennedy's inaugural address, which you can read in Appendix B. The following excerpt comes from a commencement address:[13]

   This planet came with a set of instructions, but we seem to have misplaced them. Important rules like…don't let the earth get overcrowded, and don't touch the thermostat have been broken. Buckminster Fuller said that spaceship earth was so ingeniously designed that no one has a clue that we are on one, flying through the universe at a million miles per hour, with no need for seatbelts, lots of room in coach, and really good food—but all that is changing.

The speaker concluded by inspiring students to use their knowledge to restore the planet.

- **When appropriate, use humor**. For certain events, such as after-dinner speeches also called "the speech to entertain," humor is essential. This example comes from the opening of a psychiatrist's[14] address to medical students:

  I want to talk to you, soon-to-be-full-fledged doctors, about mystery, myth and meaning in medicine. But first I'd love to hear you explain to me the mystery, myth, and meaning of choosing a psychiatrist to speak to you at your graduation. What does it say about this class that a psychiatrist, a shrink, is your choice of speaker? ...[W]hat is going to happen now when someone asks you, or your family members and friends who are here today, "Have you ever seen a psychiatrist?" Think about it, you could be in trouble. Let me encourage you all to not be too literal in your answer to that question.

- **Be relatively brief**. These occasions are times to state major themes that reinforce important values and emphasize listeners' ideals, history, and memories.

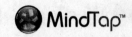

  For further examples, go to your online resources and read the transcripts of commencement addresses from a variety of speakers.

Speech to Inspire

Inspirational speeches take place in settings such as sports banquets, service organization meetings, or religious gathering. Here, the **exemplum** pattern is one that speakers have used for thousands of years.[15] Exemplums are created around a quotation that one or more stories illustrate. The pattern has five elements: a quotation, the source, a paraphrase, one or more narratives that illustrate it, and the application or point. The following brief summary of the main ideas in one student's exemplum speech illustrates each element.[16]

exemplum speech pattern built around a quotation and developed by at least one narrative

1. **State a quotation or proverb**. Grant me the serenity to accept the things I cannot change, the courage to change the things I can, and the wisdom to know the difference.
2. **Identify and explain the author or source of the proverb or the quotation.** Theologian Dr. Reinhold Neibuhr wrote this in a sermon given between World Wars I and II; it was later printed on a card and distributed to soldiers. But it is most famous as the slogan for Alcoholics Anonymous.
3. **Rephrase the proverb in your own words**. In other words, we should improve situations when we can or find ways to live contentedly when we know we cannot change our circumstances.
4. **Tell a story that illustrates the quotation or proverb**. Her story described how she wore hearing aids from age 3 on. Only when she went to school did she realize she was different, and she withdrew until years of speech therapy and training helped her accept her condition and inform others when she didn't understand them. This lessened her stress.
5. **Apply the quotation or proverb to the audience**. Everyone should learn to accept things as they are and to focus on what they have, not on what they lack.

Select your narrative from personal experiences, from historical events, or from episodes in someone else's life. Your story should represent, illustrate, or explain something important to you, perhaps a turning point in your life. Identify a lesson or point to your story and then find a quotation that supports this point. You might use a cultural saying, such as "silence is golden," or you can consult sources of quotations (listed topically and by author) in the reference section of the library or online.

Summary

Special occasion speeches function to integrate the members of the group with one another and with the community in which they exist. You'll hear these talks in a variety of organizations—from clubs and volunteer associations to business, educational, and religious institutions. You may have numerous opportunities to introduce newcomers or bid farewell to a person departing your group, to make announcements or nominations, to present or receive awards, to honor people with tributes, toasts, or eulogies, and to make other speeches that celebrate special events or that inspire audiences on special occasions.

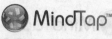

Reflect on what you've learned.

STUDY AND REVIEW

Public Speaking: Concepts and Skills for a Diverse Society offers a broad range of resources that will help you better understand the material in this chapter, complete assignments, and succeed on tests. Your MindTap resources feature the following:

- Speech videos with critical viewing questions, speech outlines, and transcripts
- Interactive versions of this chapter's Stop and Check activities, as well as Critical Thinking Exercises and Application Exercises
- Speech Builder Express
- Weblinks related to chapter content
- Study and review tools such as self-quizzes and an interactive glossary

You can access your online resources for *Public Speaking: Concepts and Skills for a Diverse Society* at cengagebrain.com using the access code that came with your book or that you purchased online.

Review your **Flashcards**.

KEY TERMS

The terms below are defined in the margins throughout this chapter.

statement of reasons pattern 254
criteria-satisfaction pattern 254
exemplum 259

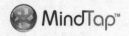

CRITICAL THINKING EXERCISES

1. For an excellent example of an awards acceptance speech, read or listen to Martin Luther King Jr.'s Nobel Peace Prize acceptance speech. You can easily find it online. Jot down at least three "wave" patterns in the speech (see Chapter 9) and list at least two examples of vivid, interesting language.
2. Go to YouTube and search for "wedding toast." (Some speeches there are technically not toasts because no drink is involved.) Evaluate at least two speeches according to the following guidelines: it should be (1) relatively short, (2) focused on the couple not the speaker, and (3) including positive, not embarrassing, details.

APPLICATION EXERCISES

1. Write an announcement about a campus event and deliver it to your class.
2. Create and deliver an exemplum speech around a quotation. Use a personal experience in which you learned a significant lesson that the quotation summarizes.
3. Work with a small group of your classmates to write a speech of introduction, farewell, or award presentation or acceptance.

SPEAKING IN SMALL GROUPS

ACROSS THE GLOBE, the ability to work well in small groups is essential in organizations that regularly accomplish tasks through cooperative teams and groups. In fact, recent college graduates said the ability to work in teams is the most important skill that employers seek.[1] Task-oriented teams often produce excellent results, but they can be frustrating if you are unaware of group dynamics. This appendix first presents some advantages and disadvantages of group work. Next, it gives tips for working in two types of groups: investigative groups and problem-solving groups. It closes with a description of formats commonly used to present the group's final product.

Advantages and Disadvantages of Group Work

You've probably heard the saying "Two heads are better than one." However, when you're trying to accomplish a task with a group plagued by scheduling conflicts, dominating members, or nonparticipants, you may be tempted to work alone. Truth be told, the many advantages of group work must be balanced against the disadvantages.

Advantages of Group Work

The advantages of working in groups and teams gave rise to their popularity:[2]

- **Groups have access to more information and knowledge than an individual working alone.** It's only reasonable that more people equal more experiences and more combined knowledge, and a person who has expertise in one area but lacks it in another needs others to balance those weaknesses. Together, the group can pool resources and generate more information than an individual could produce.
- **Participants bring various viewpoints to the group that can help more creative ideas emerge.** By combining personalities and thinking styles, the group as a whole can respond more creatively to an issue than if the solution relies on only one person's ideas. Diversity within a group also increases the members' understandings of different cultural perspectives that bear upon the issue.
- **Group work provides a deeper level of involvement and learning.** When everyone participates, the group can do three to four times as much research in approximately the same time as a single person working alone. Discussions also let group members ask and answer questions that clarify confusing ideas and sharpen critical thinking skills. Consequently, many people learn better in small groups.

- **For many people, small group work is enjoyable.** Some people are more motivated and have more positive attitudes when they don't have to deal with a subject or problem alone. Also, social interactions and relationships can make teamwork satisfying.
- **Working in small groups results in the co-creation of meaning.** Because of the nature of information sharing and decision making, small groups are inherently dialogical. Ideally, members form conclusions by bouncing their ideas off one another.

Disadvantages of Group Work

Despite their advantages, group work has disadvantages that you should anticipate.

- **Group work takes more time.** Scheduling meetings and working around the schedules of other busy people takes time, which often frustrates the more task-oriented group members.
- **Some do more work than others.** Some team members work less than they would if they were responsible for the entire project. This can result in tension and resentments within the group.
- **Some group members monopolize the discussion and impose their ideas on others.** Dominators can take over a group if the members aren't careful. One reason is linked to personality: some people are just more extroverted and expressive. Another is linked to gender: women often defer to men in mixed groups.[3]
- **There is a tendency toward groupthink.**[4] Groupthink happens when members try to avoid conflict by subtly pressuring themselves and others to conform to a decision, which may be irrational and unwise. On a national and international level, several world leaders convinced their respective teams that Iraq had weapons of mass destruction and that war was necessary to eradicate them. As we now know, they relied on incorrect intelligence gathering; no weapons were found. Most decisions your group makes won't have such global implications, but you should ensure that you aren't making a bad decision out of politeness or unwillingness to challenge a decision.

In summary, although group work offers many advantages, it also has disadvantages. Groups cannot avoid the time factor, but they can use their available time wisely. Furthermore, most disadvantages can be minimized if group members are accountable to one another, if all members have a chance to voice their opinion, and if they avoid agreement simply for the sake of peace.

Investigative Teams

Instructors commonly ask students to team up to study a subject and present their findings to the entire class. According to one study,[5] biology students learn to do "science thinking" in small groups, and their classroom presentations hone the organizational and speaking skills they will use throughout their careers as scientists.

Investigative reporters, students and professionals alike, also team up to probe complex social issues. Because a seven- to ten-minute informative speech (described in Chapter 15) can present only an overview of a controversy, you may be asked to team up and study a significant issue in greater depth. This typically leads to more learning and more involvement in the subject.[6] When the group shares the research burden, each student can focus on one area. Not only do team members learn more, the class as a whole benefits from the variety of perspectives and the in-depth coverage they hear when the group reports its findings.

Male and Female Tendencies in Group Interactions

DIVERSITY IN PRACTICE

In her book *You Just Don't Understand: Women and Men in Conversation*, Deborah Tannen[7] identifies several differences in the conversational styles associated with males and females. John Cowan[8] traces these differences to boys' and girls' playground experiences, which he suggests are "at least a light-year apart." Male- and female-associated characteristics are tendencies, not absolutes, and men and women, especially college students, are probably more alike than different.[9] Nevertheless, Tannen's conclusions are widely discussed, and the following tendencies have implications for small-group communication.

- Men tend to use *Report Talk*—informative speaking that relies more on facts, figures, and definitions and less on personalized information. In contrast, women tend to use *Rapport Talk*—speaking that stresses relationships and personalizes information with examples and stories.
- Men tend to pursue goals aimed at gaining power, status, and respect, whether or not they offend others. Women, in contrast, tend to help others and build relationships between people. They are less concerned about winning an argument.
- Men tend to speak in a *dominant way*, meaning that they interrupt and display their knowledge and expertise. They also set the agenda. On the other hand, women express more agreement, make connections, and smooth out relationships. Men offer "assertion followed by counterassertion," and women offer "inquiry followed by counterinquiry."[10] Although women suggest more topics than men, men choose which topic to discuss.
- Men explain more than women, and their explanations are lengthy. Women can and do explain, but they have fewer opportunities to do so in mixed gender groups.
- Men speak more in mixed gender groups. Conversational time is one-sided in their favor. Women listen more and speak less in these settings.

To learn more about this topic, search the Internet for *Deborah Tannen*. You'll find interviews, excerpts from her books, and other interesting information about gender differences that affect the way males and females talk in small groups.

To research and report a topic effectively, the team should have several meetings that progress from an initial get-acquainted session through the research stage to the final presentation.

First Meeting: Getting Acquainted

In your first meeting, find out each person's interest, knowledge, and expertise regarding your topic. Exchange contact information. Leadership can develop informally, or you can designate someone to guide the meeting and keep people on task. An important role is *gatekeeper*, the person who makes sure that quiet people participate and that no one dominates the discussion. Another important role is *recorder*, the member who takes notes or minutes on what transpires during the meeting.

During this meeting, divide your subject into subtopics, and let each member select specific aspects to further research in depth. For instance, you might decide to include a definition, the history, numbers and types of people affected, regions or areas affected, proposed solutions, or arguments for and against each solution.

Successful groups find ways to hold members accountable. So before you adjourn, have group members identify what they will do before the next meeting. Then set a date, place, and a time (beginning and ending) to meet again.

Additional Meetings: Discussing the Subject

Start each new meeting by approving the minutes of the previous meeting. Follow an explicit *agenda*, an ordered list of the items you'll discuss. Ask all members to summarize their work and answer any questions that arise. After everyone has contributed, ask: What questions do we still have? Are there gaps in our research? If so, where? What patterns or themes are we finding? Are we beginning to detect a way to organize our final presentation?

Continue to use the gatekeeper and recorder roles. In every meeting, focus on your final goal: to present your material publicly. To achieve this objective, cooperate on organizing ideas and outlining materials into a coherent form. Review the organizational patterns presented in Chapter 9, and think of creative ways to introduce and conclude your presentation (Chapter 10). Identify possible visual aids (assigning a person to create each one), and put someone in charge of equipment needs.

Before parting, have everyone describe what he or she will do before the next session. Then set a date, place, and time for the next meeting.

Final Meeting: Polishing the Presentation

Meet one last time to finalize all the details. Give each group member a written outline or record of what you've done. Rehearse the actual presentation so that everyone knows what to do, and iron out any glitches that arise. Check that visuals are made and equipment is ordered, and then congratulate one another on a job well done.

Problem-Solving Teams

A "problem" can be defined as the difference between *what is* (the present condition) and *what should be* (the goal).[11] It's the gap between what we have and what we want. Problem-solving teams address campus, local, national, and global problems such as parking or housing problems on campus or challenges to free speech locally, nationally, or globally.

In most contexts, a structured approach proves effective, and groups often use a problem-solving method described a century ago by the educator John Dewey and modified several times since. Dewey's analytical, linear process of appraising problems and generating solutions is typical of Euro-American culture, but similar methods are used globally. For example, the Africa Region's Knowledge and Learning Center reported that women's groups in Senegal also use a five-step process to solve community problems.[12] This process is not strictly linear and one directional; your group may circle back to previous steps, and you may revise as you go along. What follows is a modification of John Dewey's original steps.

Step One: Define the Problem

At the outset state the problem clearly, or your task will be more difficult because it is hard to solve a vague problem. Some problems are simple to define: "Whom shall we hire as the new basketball coach?" is an obvious problem to solve when you have a vacancy. However, for most problems, you need to narrow the topic and follow these three general suggestions:

- State the issue as a policy question, using the word *should*. For example, "What should we do to enhance nighttime safety in campus parking lots?"
- Leave the question broad enough to allow for a variety of answers. The yes or no closed question "Should the student council repair acts of vandalism in the student union building?" leads to less effective discussion than the open question "How should the student council ensure that campus buildings remain free from vandalism?"
- State the question as objectively as possible, avoiding emotionally charged language. "How can we get rid of this unfair grading system?" is less useful than "What changes should be made to course evaluations?"

Step Two: Analyze the Problem

Begin collecting pertinent support materials and analyzing the facts, values, and policies that underlie the problem. Divide the relevant issues among group members and have them consult a variety of sources for information. Questions such as these are helpful:

- What are the factual issues involved? What's the history of the problem?
- What causes the problem? Which are primary causes? What secondary factors contribute to it?
- What effects result from the problem?
- What values apply? Are ethical issues involved? In what respects?
- Are any relevant policies involved? Any historical precedents?

After completing these two steps, you're ready as a group to explore possible solutions.

Step Three: Set Criteria for Deciding on a Solution

Because solutions must be realistic in terms of time, money, and ease of enactment, set standards for determining an acceptable solution before you even begin to suggest possible solutions. Ask two vital questions:[13] (1) What must we do? That is, what is *required*? (2) What do we want to do? In other words, what is *desired*? For example, we must solve the problem with less than $10,000; we want to solve it with less than $5,000. We must have the policy in effect by the beginning of the next school year; we want it implemented by the end of the spring term. Budget and time constraints automatically rule out some solutions as too costly or too time-consuming.

Step Four: List Possible Solutions

During this period, generate as many ideas as possible. Groups commonly brainstorm, meaning that individuals offer any ideas that pops into their minds, regardless of practicality. Consider a mind map as described in Chapter 5 to record these ideas.

Here are some tips for a successful brainstorming session:

- Have a recorder write down all the suggestions on a whiteboard or flip chart.
- Record each idea without evaluating it.
- Make sure each person in the group has an opportunity to contribute at least once.
- Piggyback off one another's ideas—that is, encourage group members to use one proposal as a jumping-off point for another.

After everyone has contributed, begin to evaluate each idea against the criteria you decided upon earlier. Your brainstorming session may lead you to rethink your criteria, so don't hesitate to go back and make necessary revisions.

Step Five: Select the Best Solution

The final step is to select the best solution. Evaluate the suggested solutions against your criteria. You'll easily eliminate some ideas because they're too expensive, too time-consuming, or don't fit your criteria for obvious reasons. After you have pared down your options, analyze and weigh the merits of those that remain to find the one that group members can agree on.

Presenting Your Group's Findings

In general, there are three basic ways to present your conclusions: a symposium, a panel, and a final report. To illustrate, we'll look at ways a group that formulated a new night-time campus parking policy might present their recommendations.

A Symposium

In this format, each group member selects one aspect of the issue and presents it in an organized speech. After everyone has spoken, the moderator opens up the floor for a question-and-answer period. For example, group members divide the campus parking topic into subpoints, and assign each person one topic. The first speaker describes the problem; the second overviews possible solutions. The third explains the chosen solution, and the fourth relates a case study of a college that implemented a similar policy. The final speaker provides a summary. After they finish, a moderator invites audience questions.

A Panel Discussion

After group members have formulated their recommendations, they then plan several discussion questions. During the actual presentation, the entire group appears together. A leader or moderator asks a series of questions, and members take turns providing insights, with everyone contributing information and opinions in a free-flowing, dialogical manner. Afterward, the moderator may open the discussion to the audience and encourage listeners to talk with panelists during a question-and-answer period.

A Final Report

In this format, one member presents for the entire group. To communicate with both the college leadership and the public, the task committee collectively writes a final report that details the group's procedures and gives the underlying rationale for the proposed policy. A designated speaker then presents it to the governing boards for approval. A press release generated from this report goes to area news sources. Television stations might pick up the story and send reporters to interview the committee spokesperson, who provides additional information as needed. (Although this format is common in businesses and organizations, most instructors don't assign it because speech classes are settings where everyone is expected to speak.)

In summary, although teamwork is a vital part of modern life, working in teams and groups offers advantages as well as disadvantages. Whether you work on an investigative team or in a problem-solving group, organize each meeting so that everyone participates and all group members understand and carry out their responsibilities. Keep a record of what takes place in each meeting. Problem-solving teams typically go through several steps in which they identify and analyze a problem and formulate a workable solution. Both investigative and problem-solving groups present their findings, whether in a symposium, panel discussion, or group report.

SAMPLE SPEECHES
Professional Speech

MindTap™

Engaging the Mind and the Spirit* (for use with Chapter 3)

By Rodney Smolla, President, Furman University, Inaugural Address
Read this speech or watch it online and note the ways that this university president calls for accommodation on campus in an election year. Notice also how he describes the way we often listen.

. . . In the very last paragraph of Mark Twain's classic, *The Adventures of Huckleberry Finn*, Huck tells us that he is planning to light out for the Western Territory, because his Aunt is out to "sivilize" him, and as Huck laments, "*I can't stand it. I been there before.*" . . . [M]y opening theme this morning is Huck's closing theme, this problem he has with being "civilized."

I invite you to join me in reflection on the state of *our* contemporary civility, and its discontents.

As a nation we are once again poised on the eve of an important political election. Whatever your politics . . . you cannot help but notice that . . . the discourse has often been highly partisan, highly personal, and highly polarized.

What is true of our politics extends more broadly across our culture, in this nation and around the world. At times it seems as if the whole planet is determined to work a cruel twist on the words of Abraham Lincoln, proceeding with malice toward all, and charity for none.

There is a curiosity to this. We might well expect that the health of our public discourse should be at an all time high. Never have so many channels been open to so many voices. From the new media of Facebook, Twitter, and texting, to such old-fangled modes of communication as e-mail, telephone, television, radio, or cable, today we may express and change views with such breathtaking speed and ease that we *ought* to be living in a "golden age" of public discourse, world-wide.

Yet many of us feel a nagging disquiet. Quantity does not equate with quality. Yes, we may talk more than ever before. But when we talk, particularly about issues that really matter—in politics, in religion, in science or the arts—we have, as a culture, become more strident, more shrill, more angry. Our discussions are increasingly laced with personal attacks, increasingly prone to caricature and superficial slogans and sarcastic sound-bites. Perhaps more fundamentally, we may be talking *more*, but we are listening *less*.

And when we do listen, we may not be listening with genuinely open hearts and open minds. We may instead be listening tactically, listening for our cues, listening for our chance to pounce, our opening to launch a counter-attack.

No one political party, no one religious viewpoint, no one space on the cultural spectrum, has a monopoly on these bad habits. We are equal opportunity employers when it comes to the employment of devices that diminish the civility of our debates, and in turn sap the strength of our democracy.

I urge you, however, to not despair!

We have it in our power to effectuate a rescue. It can begin right now, and right *here*.

To all of us in higher education . . . I issue this challenge: [Let us] take on as an assignment the constructive improvement of the civility of our public discourse. . . .

What society sorely needs, and what we are uniquely suited to contribute, are the habits of engaging minds and spirits to the service of civilized and constructive debate and deliberation. Let us be leaders in encouraging such habits as a genuine willingness to listen, an avoidance of gratuitous personal attacks and cheap shots, a commitment to factual accuracy and intellectual honesty in our own advocacy, a de-emphasis on carica-ture, and a re-emphasis on character.

I know, and I *appreciate*, that many of our students and our faculty members, our alumni and our fellow citizens have passionate feelings about the issues of our day. And in our passions we are often deeply and intensely engaged.

Trust me, I am not . . . asking you to curb your enthusiasm. . . . This is not a crusade for blandness, for a discourse that is sanitized and laundered, so that it loses all its color, humor, bite, and zip. Your passions are admirable; they are the stuff of a vibrant democ-racy and a vital marketplace of ideas.

There is a critical difference, however, between being engaged and being enraged. . . . [A]nd we owe it to the nation, and to the world, to stand up and demonstrate the difference.

And so my challenge is for . . . you to rise above the course and the common, and by your leadership advance the common good.

. . . To that end, let me now speak directly to our students.

My hope for you is that every single student . . . will pursue and will receive a dual degree. One in an academic discipline, and a second in the development of character. . . . The purpose of your education here, like the purpose of life itself, is not simply to acquire a credential. . . . [I]ts meaning must extend beyond what appears on your tran-script. . . . [I]t must touch both your mind and your spirit, shape both your intellect and your character.

This effort must be a partnership. . . . We cannot implore you, our students, to refrain from thinking of your education as a compilation of numbers, as the acquisition of credentials, unless we refrain from defining you as numbers or credentials. . . .

We cannot plausibly claim that we . . . graduate [our] students with an academic degree and a degree in character, unless we intentionally seek out students who yearn for engagement in both. . . . And if, as a University, we are serious about attracting a more diverse student body, a student body enriched by peoples of all the cultures of the world, by members of all the great religions of the world, a student body that transcends lines of nationality, race, religion, ethnicity, sex, disability, politics, and poverty, a student body representative of all parts of our country, and all countries of the world, a student body truly engaged in mind and spirit, then we must fulfill the promise of that diversity and that engagement. . . .

Diversity is a shallow and hollow achievement if those who comprise the commu-nity do not genuinely engage, interact, and experience one another once here. . . . [I]f as a University community we do not encourage our students, our faculty, our staff, our alumni, to cross divides of generations and geography and faith and politics, to listen to one another, with authentically open minds and hearts.

Let us be a community that moves beyond mere grudging tolerance or forced politeness into the realm of generous and genuine respect. . . .

Respect is at the heart of the liberal arts tradition. Respect is at the heart of American democracy. For all our differences and all our divisions, what we in America may most proudly and with unalloyed unity proclaim, is our collective passion for democracy, for equality, for freedom of speech, for freedom of religion, for respect for human dignity.

Let all of us in higher education be keepers of that flame. As we participate in the global marketplace, in the global community, let us be a beacon of civility, compassion, and respect.

Let that respect come from our deepest beliefs, in the essential dignity, and the essential worth, of every human being.

Source

Smolla, R. (2010, December). Engaging the mind and the spirit. Speech delivered October 22, 2010, at Furman University. *Vital Speeches of the Day*, 76(12), 570–573 (edited).

Informative Speech with Visual Aids

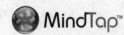

The Chinese Valentine's Day (for use with Chapters 5 and 15)

By Lishan Zeng

Lishan's assignment was to research, outline, and deliver an informative speech using a visual aid. He conducted a survey before he spoke to assess the class's familiarity with his topic. Most did not know about the Chinese counterpart to St. Valentine's Day, and they had only superficial knowledge of the American holiday. He planned his speech accordingly.

Log on to your book's online resources to watch and critique Lishan Zeng's speech. The text of his speech is available both here and in your online resources, which also provide an outline of the speech.

Look at this picture. [*photograph of the Milky Way*] What do you see? The universe? The stars? Or a romantic story? I see love in this picture. It's the story of Niulang and Zhinü, and that's the origin of Chinese Valentine's Day.

According to the survey I did, eighty percent of you did not know that there is a Chinese Valentine's Day, and ninety percent did not know the origin of it. This does not surprise me. What surprises me is that ninety percent of you know the date of the Western Valentine's Day but just ten percent of you know why you have that day.

That motivates me to do the research about the Western Valentine's Day and then tell you the story of the Chinese Valentine's Day. I will compare the Western and Chinese Valentine's Day, and I hope that by the end of my speech you will get to know when the Valentine's Day is and how and why people celebrate the Valentine's Day.

Most of you know that the Western Valentine's Day falls on February 14. But most of you do not know that the Chinese Valentine's Day falls at the seventh day of the seventh lunar month, and it falls on August the 16th this year.

Some of you know why people celebrate Valentine's Day. According to History.com, people in the West celebrate Valentine's Day to remember the death of St. Valentine. St. Valentine was a priest of the third century in Rome. At that time the Emperor of Rome forbade marriage for young men because he thought young men unmarried made better soldiers. Well, St. Valentine went against that law and performed marriages for young lovers in secret. Another version of this story is that St. Valentine's helped Christians escape the harsh Roman prisons where they were often beaten and tortured. In either story, he was bound and sentenced to death.

About the Chinese Valentine's Day. According to chinadaily.com, it's a day when Niulang and Zhinü are allowed to meet with each other. Niulang is a poor, handsome boy, living with his brother and sister-in-law. He owns nothing but an old ox that can talk and is an immortal from the Heaven.

Zhinü is the daughter of the Emperor of Heaven, who is good at handcrafting, especially in weaving clothing. Because the ox is treated nicely by Niulang, the ox wants to fulfill one of Niulang's wishes, so the ox asks Niulang what he wants. "Uh . . . I want

Valentine's Day Western Culture vs. Chinese Culture		
	Western Valentine's Day	**Chinese Valentine's Day**
When	February 14	The seventh day of the seventh lunar month; falls on August 4 this year
Why	The Story of Saint Valentine	The Story of Niulang and Zhinü
How	Flowers, candy, chocolate, cards	Pray for skills and for true love Fruit and incense for Zhinü

[Because Lishan's first language is Chinese and he speaks with an accent, he displayed this table to help his listeners better understand his speech.]

to marry a beautiful girl;" that's Niulang's answer. Then the ox takes Niulang to heaven, and there, Niulang meets Zhinü. And they fall in love. After that, they are married and have two kids.

But their story is not like any of the romantic Disney stories. They do not end up living happily together ever since. The marriage between a human and a god is never permitted, so the Emperor of Heaven takes Zhinü away from Niulang and her kids. But, he's touched by their love and agrees that they could meet each other once a year. And that day becomes the seventh day of the seventh lunar month.

As we can see, no matter if it's the Western or the Chinese cultures, people celebrate Valentine's Day all because of love, but they observe that in different ways. In the West, Valentine's Day is about sharing love with lovers and family members. People send gifts, like flowers, chocolates, candy, and love cards to persons they love.

In China, Valentine's Day is more about the longing for love and in the present. Chinese girls offer fruit and incense to Zhinü, to pray to have good skills and to find a satisfactory boyfriend. Lovers pray that they could get blessed and also pray for their love and happiness.

Now let's do a review about the Valentine's Day. Western Valentine's Day falls on February 14, and Chinese Valentine's Day falls on the seventh day of the seventh lunar month. And the Western Valentine's Day is about a story about St. Valentine, and the Chinese Valentine's Day is the story of Niulang and Zhinü. And people celebrated Western Valentine's day by sharing flowers, chocolate, candy, and love cards with the people they love. Chinese people spend the holiday to pray for good skills and love.

In conclusion, Western Valentine's Day and Chinese Valentine's Day both contribute to love, although they celebrate that in different ways. The longing for love is a strong thing that Chinese and the Western people share. Here are more things we share, even though we come from different cultures. And there will be lots to discover.

Informative Speech Outline

E-Waste* (for use with Chapter 9)

By Jordan Keagle
Jordan's assignment is to create an informative speech that illustrates civic engagement by describing a social issue and an organization founded to help solve it.

---

*© Cengage Learning 2015.

General Purpose: To inform

Specific Purpose: To inform my audience about the growing issue of e-waste in the United States and of an organization created to combat it.

Thesis statement: E-waste is a mounting problem in the United States and around the world, but the Electronics TakeBack Coalition exists to reduce improper technology disposal methods.

Preview: I will discuss how the problem of e-waste came about, the harms it causes, and how the Electronics TakeBack Coalition helps to counteract the problem.

Introduction

I. Raise your hand if you have a cell phone, computer, or video game system.

II. Raise your hand if you, like me, plan to replace one gadget with a new version.

III. I'm a technophile, so I did some research to discover what happens to discarded technology in the United States.

IV. Today, I will discuss how e-waste came about, the harms it causes, and how the Electronics TakeBack Coalition helps to counteract the problem.

Body

I. First, let's look at the problem.

   A. A Swiss government agency, the EMPA (2009), defines e-waste (also called "tech waste") as any out-of-date or otherwise discarded equipment that uses electricity.

     1. This can be computers, cell phones, or household appliances.

     2. If you can plug it in and you throw it out, it's e-waste.

   B. Over the past decades, the amount of US e-waste has grown steadily.

     1. Elizabeth Royte (2005), writing in the *Smithsonian Magazine*, estimated that at least 60 million PCs are buried in US landfills.

       a. That article was from 2005.

       b. The issue has only gotten worse since then.

     2. A 2008 EPA report said that 80–85% of discarded electronics were sent to landfills between 2003 and 2005.

     3. In August of 2010, EPA administrator Lisa P. Jackson announced e-waste as one of the agency's top priorities.

   C. Obviously, piles of electronics are building up in landfills all over the country causing problems.

     1. Sheer space is one concern, as electronics can be bulky.

     2. More importantly, they contain harmful chemicals.

       a. Royte (2005) says one CRT monitor contains between 2 and 8 pounds of lead.

       b. Other devices contain other toxic chemicals like mercury or cadmium.

       c. A 2009 journal article in *Science of the Total Environment* says newer devices like LCD screens may seem better than CRT monitors, but they often just trade one harmful chemical for another (Robinson, 2009).

       d. Waste services must take apart the devices to remove harmful components, which costs time and money.

     3. Companies often discard or destroy electronics, so chemicals enter the environment.

D. Improper disposal of electronic devices can have direct consequences for the environment and the people living near the disposal sites.
   1. Obviously, toxic chemicals can't be all that good for the environment.
   2. A 2010 study in China, where much of the world's e-waste is processed, compared the health of pregnant women living near a facility with those living farther away (Zhang et al., 2010).
      a. Women living closer had up to five times the amount of toxic chemicals in their blood.
      b. They also had lower levels of thyroid hormones, which can cause nervous system issues for their developing children.

Transition: Now that you have a better understanding of some of the problems surrounding e-waste, let's look at an organization that is working for solutions.

II. Electronics TakeBack Coalition (ETBC) exists to help solve the mounting problem.
   A. Its website (n.d.) says it was founded in 2001 as the "Computer TakeBack Campaign"—a project of the Tides Center.
      1. It focused on the Dell Computer Company, which had no recycling program.
      2. In 2007 it became the Electronics TakeBack Coalition, reflecting a concern for the wider field of all electronics.
   B. According to its website (n.d.), the ETBC has a number of programs and initiatives to change the state of e-waste on a national scale.
      1. Its flagship program centers on producer takeback, which urges manufacturers to take back products and properly dispose of them.
         a. In 2007, ETBC ran a campaign called "Take Back My TV," encouraging television companies to offer recycling programs.
         b. Eight companies now offer such programs.
      2. The ETBC also provides information to individuals.
         a. Its website offers advice on finding recyclers in your area.
         b. It has instructions for purchasing environmentally friendly technology.
      3. Finally, the ETBC distributes information and tools to promote and track implementation of anti-e-waste legislation on federal and state levels.

Conclusion

I. After looking at the facts, it is obvious that e-waste is a mounting problem.
II. However, despite the harm e-waste poses to both humans and the environment, organizations like the Electronics TakeBack Coalition show that the problem is not insurmountable.
III. So think back to your own pieces of technology: computers, cell phones, iPods, and the like.
IV. Next time you are thinking of upgrading, consider the cost of throwing out the old device as well as the cost of purchasing the new.

Sources

Electronics TakeBack Coalition. (n.d.). Campaign platform. Retrieved from http://www.electronicstakeback.com/about/platform.htm

EMPA. (2009). E-waste definition. Swiss Federal Laboratories for Materials Science and Technology (EMPA). Retrieved from http://ewasteguide.info/e_waste_definition

Environmental Protection Agency. (2008). Fact sheet: Management of electronic waste in the United States. (EPA 530-F-08-014). Washington, DC: Retrieved from http://www.epa.gov/epawaste/conserve/materials/ecycling/docs/fact7-08.pdf

Environmental Protection Agency. (2010, August 17). Administrator Jackson announces EPA's international priorities /agency to work with other countries to curb pollution at home and abroad. Retrieved from http://yosemite.epa.gov/opa/admpress.nsf/0/C94F5F47E03ECC668525778200642318

Robinson, B. H. (2009). E-waste: An assessment of global production and environmental impacts. *Science of the Total Environment*, 408(2). doi: 10.1016/j.scitotenv.2009.09.044

Royte, E. (2005). E-gad! *Smithsonian*, 36(5), 83–87.

Zhang, J., Jiang, Y., Zhou, J., et al. (2010). Elevated body burdens of PBDEs, dioxins, and PCBs on thyroid hormone homeostasis at an electronic waste recycling site in China. *Environmental Science & Technology*, 44(10). doi: 10.1021/es902883a

Informative Speech Outline with Presentation Aids

Music-Thanatology (for use with Chapters 10, 13, and 15)

By Abby Rine

Abby was assigned to do an informative speech with visual aids.

Specific Purpose:	To inform my audience about comforting music that is played to terminally ill patients as they die.
Thesis Statement:	Music-thanatology, playing comforting music to dying patients, differs from music therapy; it is an ancient practice that is being revived today.

Introduction

[*A recording of harp music plays softly throughout the introduction.*]

I. During Salvatore Villalobos's final battle with throat cancer, he became increasingly anxious until he was offered comfort music through his hospice (Trujillo, 2011).
  A. Judith Shotwell, a harpist and music-thanatologist, soothed his final days with music.
  B. In order to keep dying patients comfortable and give them peace, many hospitals and hospices now provide a similar service.
    1. According to Music-Thanatology Association International (MTAI, 2011), music-thanatology is the prescriptive use of music—harp and voice—to help aid mental, physical, and spiritual symptoms of the dying.
    2. The word comes from the Greek word *thanatos*, which means "death."
    3. The music is live so the musician can tune in to the patient's and family's specific needs.
II. Death is inevitable, but no one wants pain and suffering.
III. I first heard about music-thanatology as a news item; my curiosity was piqued, and I wanted to know more about the technique.
IV. I will explain the difference between music-thanatology and music therapy; then I'll give a brief history of the practice and show how it is currently being revived.

Body

I. Music-thanatology (MTAI, 2011) differs from music therapy according to the American Music Therapy Association website (2011).

[*A PowerPoint list has two columns comparing therapy to thanatology.*]

  A. Music therapy is designed to be life-supporting, but music-thanatology aims to help people "unbind" and move toward the completion of life.
  B. Music therapists engage people actively, often using words; music-thanatologists typically eliminate words.

C. Music therapy is often upbeat and peppy, but music-thanatology is calm and slow, with periods of silence.

D. Music therapy aids the quality of life; music-thanatology aids the quality of death.

   1. Music-thanatology is classified as palliative medicine; the Latin root *pallium* means "cloak" or "shelter."

      a. The World Health Organization defined palliative care as "the active total care of patients whose disease is not responsive to curative treatment. Control of pain, of other symptoms, and of psychological, social, and spiritual support is paramount. The goal of palliative care is the achievement of the best quality of life for patients and their families" (quoted in Fins, p. 17).

      b. When medical procedures fail in an irreversible illness, caregivers shift attention to the welfare of the whole person and provide palliative care until death.

      c. Mary K. Sheehan, MSN, MBA, RN, and CEO of a palliative care center, states, "Music-thanatology brings a new spiritual dimension to the dying process. It is transformative for everyone present. . . . [It is] an amazing gift to the family, an event they will remember in a positive manner" (quoted in Baker, 2010).

   2. Thanatologists adapt music to each patient's needs by using rhythms that correspond with the patients' vital signs.

      a. As the thanatologist learns more about the patient, such as his medication and his handling of his illness, she adapts the music's tone and rhythm.

      b. "You meet the patient where the patient is," says Rebecca Hazlitt, a music-thanatologist from Estes Park, Colorado (Harvey, 2010).

II. Music-thanatology is not a new medical technique.

[*A Gregorian chant plays softly in the background during point II.*]

A. According to Donald Heintz in *The Last Passage: Recovering a Death of Our Own* (2011), the monks of Cluny, France, in the tenth century practiced music to give spiritual, emotional, mental, and physical comfort to the dying.

B. They began to use "infirmary music"—usually Gregorian chants.

   1. Chants have highly developed melodies but lack rhythmic accent and pulse.

   2. Chants are closely related to respiration and can be connected to the brain processes and central nervous system.

   3. [*Pause to listen to a few seconds of the chant.*]

III. Music-thanatology was neglected until Therese Schroeder-Sheker experienced the death of a patient while working as a nurse's aid in a geriatric home.

A. Her 2001 book, *Transitus: A Blessed Death in the Modern World*, tells how she came into a dying patient's room; she instinctively put her head beside his and sang to him until he died.

   1. Later, she studied ways that music could aid the dying, and she added the harp to her vocals.

   2. She founded the Chalice of Repose Project (CORP) to awaken the dormant practice of music-thanatology.

B. Two educational centers now certify music-thanatologists.

   1. The CORP (April 2010, last updated) offers the Contemplative Musicianship Program, the Music-Thanatology Program, and the Masters Degree Program in Music-Thanatology, which is affiliated with the Catholic University of America.

   2. Lane Community College in Eugene, Oregon, also offers a two-year nondegree training program.

C. Currently, music-thanatologists work in the United States and in the Netherlands.

   1. They conduct a 30- to 60-minute vigil in the weeks, days, or hours before death.

a. Vigils are especially helpful during crises periods when hard decisions are made or life-supports are removed (League for Innovation, 2010).

  1) Thanatologists play harps because they are easy to transport and they are polyphonic (meaning they can play more than one note at a time) (Chalice of Repose Project, 2009, last updated).

  2) They play unfamiliar tunes because they don't know what associations a patient has with a particular melody (Trujillo, 2011).

b. Patients, families, and care facilities benefit.

  1. Patients typically experience decreased pain, reduced anxiety, deeper slumber, and lessened fear (League for Innovation, 2010).

  2. Families have opportunities to have closure.

    a) For example, music at Kathleen Corcoran's bedside encouraged her friends and family to sit by her, "pour out their hearts, and verbally express themselves," according to Sister Vivian Ripp, her music-thanatologist (McGowan, 1998).

    b) Each person thanked Kathleen for what she had brought into his or her life, and she died peacefully.

    c) "It was strikingly, overwhelmingly beautiful," her husband said (McGowan, 1998).

c. Facilities report a decrease in pain and delirium medications (Baker, 2010).

2. Music-thanatology has proven effective with cancer, respiratory and infectious diseases, AIDS, dementia, Alzheimer's, and multiple sclerosis patients.

3. Rebecca Hazlett (Harvey, 2010), who has played for hundreds of dying persons, processes her emotions by talking with other thanatologists and by crying in her hot tub.

a. Thanatologists must have a self-care program such as meditating.

b. "The key is you have to have made some sort of peace with the idea of dying," Hazlett says.

Conclusion

[*Replay the harp music from the introduction.*]

I. Today we have looked at the ancient but also contemporary practice of music-thanatology as a way of assisting dying patients.

II. We contrasted it with music therapy, noted its roots in medieval infirmaries, and heard some of its proponents' claims.

III. Death is inevitable, but music-thanatologists do their best to soothe and comfort those who are going through it.

IV. Although Salvatore Villalobos died, his wife said, "Judith and her music were a great inspiration in our lives. She made the last days of my husband's life very comfortable and he found peace" (Trujillo, 2011).

References

American Music Therapy Association. (2011). A career in music therapy. Retrieved from http://www.musictherapy .org/handbook/career.html

Baker, R. C. (2010, July 21, last updated). Music-thanatology. Advance for Nurses. Retrieved from http://nursing .advanceweb.com/Regional-Articles/Features/Music-Thanatology.aspx

Chalice of Repose Project. (2009, July 30). Why the harp for music-thanatology and prescriptive music? Retrieved from http://chaliceofrepose.org/why-the-harp/

Chalice of Repose Project. (2010, April, last updated). Overview of all educational programs offered. Retrieved from http://chaliceofrepose.org/ed-overview/

Fins, J. (2006). *A palliative ethic of care: Clinical wisdom at life's end.* Sudbury, MA: Jones & Bartlett.

Harvey, J. (2010, March 9). The sound of angels moving matter—music and medicine at the end of life. *Estes Park Trail-Gazette.* Retrieved from http://www.eptrail.com/ci_14641088

Heinz, D. (1999). *The last passage: Recovering a death of our own.* Oxford, UK: Oxford University Press.

League for Innovation in the Community College. (2010, June). Musical prescriptions for end of life care. *League Connections,* 11(6). Retrieved from http://www.mtai.org/index.php/press_full/2010/06/

McCowan, K. (1998, December 24). An exceptional death recalled. *The Register-Guard* (Eugene, OR). Retrieved from http://www.mtai.org/index.php/press_full/1998/12/

Music-Thanatology Association International. (2008). What is music-thanatology? Music-Thanatology Association International website. Retrieved from http://www.mtai.org/index.php/what_is

Trujillo, A. M. (2011, February 19). Harpist uses music to soothe hospice patients. *The New Mexican.* Retrieved from http://www.santafenewmexican.com/Soothing-sounds

Persuasive Speeches

Come Watch Lacrosse (for use with Chapters 16 and 17)

By Andrés Lucero

Andrés was assigned to make one claim and support it by giving three criteria and showing how lacrosse meets those criteria.

Have you ever sat and watched a long, boring baseball game? You all know the deal: ball . . . strike . . . ball . . . strike . . . ten minutes later, a popup. Well, if you've endured such "entertainment" and agree that there might be more exciting things to do with your time, you should try watching a sport created by Native Americans—one that is fast and exciting, hard hitting, and very strategic. A sport like lacrosse. As you may know, I play lacrosse for the university. Today, I will explain why you should watch a lacrosse game.

Lacrosse is fast and exciting. In fact, it is called the fastest sport in the world because the clock runs constantly and stops only for a few seconds when the ball goes out of bounds. Unlike baseball or football, players never have time to rest. For that reason, there are many substitutions during the game. Since there is always action on the field, there is never a boring moment. Watching lacrosse is similar to watching a long rally in a tennis match, yet the game itself is as hard hitting as football.

A second reason to watch lacrosse is because it is a very physical game. Since it is a contact sport, not surprisingly, there is lots of rough contact. If I am not careful, I can be seriously injured. I know this from experience. In my first month of college play, I had a painful introduction to Division I lacrosse. On too many occasions, I found myself lying flat on my back, with nothing but sky in view. I discovered that there are many lacrosse players who set up a kill and look to just cream a guy. However, a player does not have to be roughed up. Some players—myself included—try to use strategy to outsmart the opponent.

And this is a third reason you should watch a lacrosse match. Good players and good teams do not just go out and run around the field; they plan what they will do and then they execute their plan. When you watch a game, you can see how the entire team works together to make goals. Most of the finesse teams, those who concentrate on strategy, win more often than those who look for ways to injure their opponents.

In conclusion, you now have three good reasons to watch a lacrosse game: it is a fast, hard-hitting sport that requires much strategy to win. So the next time you find yourself in front of the TV watching a ball . . . then a strike . . . then a ball . . . then ten minutes later, a popup, get up and go watch a lacrosse game—experience it firsthand.

Needed: A Grief Support System on Campus

(for use with Chapters 16 and 17)

By Carrie Weichbrodt

Carrie's assignment was to give a persuasive speech about a campus problem that needed a solution. Her goal is to convince her audience of a need; she is not formulating a policy.

The phone rings. You answer it, and suddenly the world stops. You have just become one of the thousands of college students experiencing the grief of losing a loved one.

On September 13, 2006, my life changed forever when it was my phone that rang. My dad was gone. I was 18.

As a student and Resident Assistant, I know many other people on our campus who are grieving. Somehow we find each other.

To deal with my grief, I went to the Health and Counseling Center and asked for a grief specialist. There were no resources for me. I got a doctoral student in psychology who told me I was fine.

Freud did not believe that normal bereavement is a pathological disturbance requiring professional intervention. In his 1917 essay, "Mourning and Melancholia," he argued that mourning is our reaction to a loss, but we eventually form new attachments and move on without professional help. But I believe he was wrong, and today, I will prove it. I will show that there is a significant and compelling need for grief specialists in the campus Health and Counseling Center. Then I'll outline a plan that will solve this problem.

How extensive is the problem? The number of undergraduates dealing with grief is substantial. In a spring 2008 article in the journal *New Directions for Student Services*, David Balk, the leading researcher in the field of college student bereavement, asserts that at any given time, 20–30 percent of college undergraduates are in the first twelve months of grieving the death of a family member or friend. The National Students of Ailing Mothers and Fathers (AMF) Support Network, initiated at Georgetown University, says that between 35 and 48 percent of college students are dealing with a death that occurred within the previous two years. Counselors at Kansas State University, Oklahoma State University, City University of New York, and the University of Arizona estimate that grief is a defining issue in the lives of no fewer than 50 percent of the students on their respective campuses.

One reason is the mortality rates on college campuses. The numbers are somewhat difficult to assess, but 5,000 to 18,750 students nationwide die annually. That's about 4 to 15 per 10,000. Most deaths are vehicle accidents. Our own small campus has had two traffic fatalities, plus one drowning in recent years. And last year, a popular professor died of cancer. In addition, many students have parents or other close relatives and friends who are struggling against terminal illnesses.

In an often-cited article, "College Student Loss and Response, Coping with Death on Campus," Louis E. LaGrand, professor of health science at the State University of Arts and Science, Potsdam, New York, argues that colleges and student communities too often dismiss the serious and continuing impact of unresolved grief among young adults.

My goal today is not to depress you with staggering statistics, but to assure you that there *is* a need that we should address. Irreparable loss can devastate any young adult.

Now that we know some of the numbers, let's look at five areas affected by grief: physical, behavioral, interpersonal, cognitive, and spiritual.

Physical effects include insomnia and exhaustion. Insomnia is especially significant during the first twenty-four months of bereavement. That's the first two years! Grieving students also suffer from exhaustion as a result of the emotional struggle they are going through.

There are *behavioral* effects as well. Students struggle to stay organized, manage their time, and meet deadlines. They lose their typical patterns of conduct as they try to absorb the loss of the loved one.

Interpersonal effects result when friends dismiss the intensity and duration of the grief cycle and begin to shun the griever. Let's face it, ongoing grief is uncomfortable to be around.

There are also *cognitive* effects. Grieving students have problems concentrating, studying, and remembering what they've studied, which has obvious effects on grades and test taking. They typically experience a drop in test scores in the first six months of bereavement, and a timely response by institutions is warranted.

Finally, there are *spiritual* effects. Bereaved students ask "why?" and begin to question their assumptions about reality, fairness, and goodness.

Now that we understand the extent of the problem and its effect on students, let's discuss what can be done.

First, I propose that the university hire a bereavement specialist who would work with campus personnel to design a program for educating professors, Residence Life personnel, and Resident Assistants in ways they can assist grieving students. This would include annual professional workshops on grief and grieving.

Second, many students feel more comfortable expressing their grief in an informal environment with someone who has had a similar experience. The bereavement specialist would recruit students who have skillfully walked through grief to be peer counselors; these students can further process their own experience when they mentor fellow students.

There is a model for this. Georgetown University is the home of the National Students of Ailing Mothers and Fathers (AMF) Support Network. It was started by David Fajgenbaum, whose phone call came July 17, 2003. His mother had stage four brain cancer, and she died while he was still a student. The group's name Ailing Mothers and Fathers (AMF) includes his mother's (Anne Marie Fajgenbaum) initials: A.M.F. The group's website says its mission is to support all grieving college students, to empower them to fight back against terminal illnesses, and to raise awareness about the needs of grieving college students.

Our university's Health and Counseling Center's web page states its goal as "Helping students stay healthy so they may achieve the highest personal growth and intellectual success." Providing effective resources for grieving students, allows these students to achieve their highest personal growth and intellectual success. David Balk says:

> Rather than deciding that bereaved college students are on their own and merely wish them good luck, we should make the effort to determine whether appropriate institutional responses can be put in place to help students get beyond a life event that can obstruct their best academic performance and may ultimately affect a school's retention and graduation rates.

So we have the opportunity to make a difference in the lives of hundreds of students on our campus. This number may be as high as 720 undergraduates each year. Creating a grief support program would further the university's commitment to holistic health for all students.

Today we've seen there is a significant need and that grief affects a student's ability to be a competent scholar. However, specialists can make a difference, and it's been done before.

I hope that none of you get that devastating, life-changing phone call during your college career. But I hope that if you do, a program will be in place to help you work through the grief that inevitably follows.

References

Balk, D. (2001). College student bereavement, scholarship and the university: A call for university engagement. *Death Studies, 25,* 67–84.

Balk, D. (2008, Spring). Grieving: 22 to 30 percent of all college students. *New Directions for Student Services,* 121, 5–14.

Berson, R. (1988). A bereavement group for college students. *Journal of American College Health,* 37.

Cusick, A. (2007). Death response plans in universities: A structural approach. Unpublished manuscript.

Floerschinger, D. (1991). Bereavement in late adolescence: Interventions on college campuses. *Journal of Adolescent Research,* 6.

Freud, S. (1957). Mourning and melancholia. *The complete psychological works of Sigmund Freud, Vol. 14.* London: Hogarth Press.

LaGrand, L. (1986). College student loss and response: coping with death on campus. *New Directions for Student Services, No. 31.* San Francisco, CA: Jossey-Bass.

McGowan, K. (2008, March 7). OPTIMISM: Make the road by walking. Retrieved March 12, 2008, from http://www.studentsofamf.org/National_Students_of_AMF_featured_in_Psychology_Today_Magazine!-nid-39.html

National Students of Ailing Mothers and Fathers. (n.d.). AMF mission statement. Retrieved March 12, 2008, from http://www.studentsofamf.org/

Commemorative Speech

A Tribute: Jorge Oteiza (for use with Chapter 18)

By Ryan McGonigle
Ryan was assigned to pay tribute to a cultural hero. As a student of Basque descent, he praises the life of a famous Basque artist who is revered in his culture.

The name Jorge Oteiza may not exactly raise any eyebrows or provoke any curiosity among the American public, but to the Basque people and to me—an American of Basque descent—he is a legend. Oteiza was arguably the greatest Basque artist and poet of the twentieth century.

Jorge Oteiza was born in Guipuzcoa Province in Spain, near the famous coastal Basque city of San Sebastian at the beginning of the twentieth century. As a child he was raised according to Basque tradition: Honor your father and mother; persevere under hardships; give generously to your neighbors; speak respectfully to others; and most of all, keep your word—which is better than gold. These ideals, centuries old, were later reflected in Oteiza's poetry and art.

As the son of a sheepherder, Oteiza was accustomed to adversity. At home he worked what seemed to be eternities every day. At school he struggled to learn Castilian Spanish—which, by the way, no one in his family spoke. He had no choice in learning it, however; it was either learn it or get whipped by the teachers. Later, he would write poetry in this, his second language. Ironically, it was through that very same school system that he became interested in art—his first love.

Following the death of his father, he was obliged to continue in his father's footsteps as a sheepherder. Traditionally, in Basque country, sons follow the family occupation. If your father was a fisherman, most likely you will be one too. Breaking with tradition is not only very hard to do, but it is also dishonorable. Fortunately for Jorge, his sister soon married, and the sheep became part of the dowry given to his brother-in-law. This released Oteiza to realize his true potential as an artist. His style of sculpture became well known in the area, and soon his work was in demand. Oteiza made sculptures for the city in which he lived, San Sebastian, as well as for other cities throughout the Basque area.

In the mid-1930s during the Spanish Civil War, three major events occurred for Oteiza. First, he married Itziar Carrieco Etxendia. Throughout his life, she was the inspiration for much of his work. Not only did she support him, she encouraged him to create both poetry and art. The second event happened when the Basque region declared its independence from Spain. This resulted in a war, and his home came under fire. In the conflict, he lost his best friend, the photographer Nicolas de Lekuona. Finally, Oteiza was incarcerated in a mass roundup of Basque intellectuals, priests, and artists. He spent almost two years in jail.

It was in one of Spain's infamous prisons that Ortiza became a man worthy of his surname. "Oteiza" in the Guipuzcoan dialect of Basque sounds very much like the word that means "prickly bush," and like a thorn—or a prickly bush in the side of the

Spaniards—he caused a bit of irritation. In prison, he became nationalistic, and his later sculpture and poetry shows the positive and negative effects of his identification with the revolutionary Basque movement. He frequently put his neck on the line by sculpting pro-Basque and/or anti-Spain works. For example, some of his work portrays the hardships of the Basque people that resulted from the policies of the Spanish dictator Franco. Eventually, the regime of Franco got to him, and he took a hiatus from sculpture to work on his poetry.

In his poetry, the pro-Basque theme or the Basque experience is prominent. One phrase recurs throughout his work—"*Gora Euzkadi Ederra*" or "Long live the beautiful Basque country." This is a strongly nationalistic phrase that arouses Basque emotions. It is somewhat similar to the African American slogan from the 1960s: "Black Is Beautiful."

During this time, he took on an apprentice—a man by the name of Eduardo Txillida.* Oteiza put all of his efforts into teaching Txillida his art form, but all Txillida could do was to copy or imitate his master. Eventually, the two split and to this day Oteiza accuses his pupil of not being able to do anything original. All of Txillida's works resemble Oteiza's, just on a grander scale. He copied his master without permission instead of developing his own style, and in Oteiza's eyes, he failed to keep his word.

Basque critics consider Oteiza to be a true master because he maintained traditional art forms. He received honors from the Basque school *Euskertz Aindia*, the official academy of the Basque people. He did not care so much about money or fame—although he had both. Instead, he cared about his people and their welfare. Throughout the long ordeal of the war and in the ensuing years, Jorge Oteiza persevered under hardships. For these reasons, he is the true master.

Historical Speeches

Inaugural (for use with Chapters 12 and 18)

By John F. Kennedy

President Kennedy's 1960 inaugural speech, composed with the aid of speechwriter Ted Sorensen, is number two on many lists of 100 best speeches of the 20th century (behind King's "I Have a Dream" speech). It has become the standard to which other presidents aspire. It's a good example of a special occasion speech that uses memorable language to highlight US ideals. Note the elements of oral style throughout the speech: familiar words, short phrases, pauses, repetitions, and colorful imagery—especially metaphors.

Vice President Johnson, Mr. Speaker, Mr. Chief Justice, President Eisenhower, Vice President Nixon, President Truman, Reverend Clergy, fellow citizens:

We observe today not a victory of party, but a celebration of freedom—symbolizing an end, as well as a beginning—signifying renewal, as well as change. For I have sworn before you and Almighty God the same solemn oath our forebears prescribed nearly a century and three-quarters ago.

The world is very different now. For man holds in his mortal hands the power to abolish all forms of human poverty and all forms of human life. And yet the same revolutionary beliefs for which our forebears fought are still at issue around the globe—the belief that the rights of man come not from the generosity of the state, but from the hand of God.

We dare not forget today that we are the heirs of that first revolution. Let the word go forth from this time and place, to friend and foe alike, that the torch has been passed

---

*Txillida is sometimes spelled Chillida.

to a new generation of Americans—born in this century, tempered by war, disciplined by a hard and bitter peace, proud of our ancient heritage, and unwilling to witness or permit the slow undoing of those human rights to which this nation has always been committed, and to which we are committed today at home and around the world.

Let every nation know, whether it wishes us well or ill, that we shall pay any price, bear any burden, meet any hardship, support any friend, oppose any foe, to assure the survival and the success of liberty.

This much we pledge—and more.

To those old allies whose cultural and spiritual origins we share, we pledge the loyalty of faithful friends. United there is little we cannot do in a host of cooperative ventures. Divided there is little we can do—for we dare not meet a powerful challenge at odds and split asunder.

To those new states whom we welcome to the ranks of the free, we pledge our word that one form of colonial control shall not have passed away merely to be replaced by a far more iron tyranny. We shall not always expect to find them supporting our view. But we shall always hope to find them strongly supporting their own freedom—and to remember that, in the past, those who foolishly sought power by riding the back of the tiger ended up inside.

To those people in the huts and villages of half the globe struggling to break the bonds of mass misery, we pledge our best efforts to help them help themselves, for whatever period is required—not because the Communists may be doing it, not because we seek their votes, but because it is right. If a free society cannot help the many who are poor, it cannot save the few who are rich.

To our sister republics south of our border, we offer a special pledge: to convert our good words into good deeds, in a new alliance for progress, to assist free men and free governments in casting off the chains of poverty. But this peaceful revolution of hope cannot become the prey of hostile powers. Let all our neighbors know that we shall join with them to oppose aggression or subversion anywhere in the Americas. And let every other power know that this hemisphere intends to remain the master of its own house.

To that world assembly of sovereign states, the United Nations, our last best hope in an age where the instruments of war have far outpaced the instruments of peace, we renew our pledge of support—to prevent it from becoming merely a forum for invective, to strengthen its shield of the new and the weak, and to enlarge the area in which its writ may run.

Finally, to those nations who would make themselves our adversary, we offer not a pledge but a request: that both sides begin anew the quest for peace, before the dark powers of destruction unleashed by science engulf all humanity in planned or accidental self-destruction.

We dare not tempt them with weakness. For only when our arms are sufficient beyond doubt can we be certain beyond doubt that they will never be employed.

But neither can two great and powerful groups of nations take comfort from our present course—both sides overburdened by the cost of modern weapons, both rightly alarmed by the steady spread of the deadly atom, yet both racing to alter that uncertain balance of terror that stays the hand of mankind's final war.

So let us begin anew—remembering on both sides that civility is not a sign of weakness, and sincerity is always subject to proof. Let us never negotiate out of fear, but let us never fear to negotiate.

Let both sides explore what problems unite us instead of belaboring those problems which divide us.

Let both sides, for the first time, formulate serious and precise proposals for the inspection and control of arms, and bring the absolute power to destroy other nations under the absolute control of all nations.

Let both sides seek to invoke the wonders of science instead of its terrors. Together let us explore the stars, conquer the deserts, eradicate disease, tap the ocean depths, and encourage the arts and commerce.

Let both sides unite to heed, in all corners of the earth, the command of Isaiah—to "undo the heavy burdens, and [to] let the oppressed go free."

And, if a beachhead of cooperation may push back the jungle of suspicion, let both sides join in creating a new endeavor—not a new balance of power, but a new world of law—where the strong are just, and the weak secure, and the peace preserved.

All this will not be finished in the first one hundred days. Nor will it be finished in the first one thousand days; nor in the life of this Administration; nor even perhaps in our lifetime on this planet. But let us begin.

In your hands, my fellow citizens, more than mine, will rest the final success or failure of our course. Since this country was founded, each generation of Americans has been summoned to give testimony to its national loyalty. The graves of young Americans who answered the call to service surround the globe.

Now the trumpet summons us again—not as a call to bear arms, though arms we need—not as a call to battle, though embattled we are—but a call to bear the burden of a long twilight struggle, year in and year out, "rejoicing in hope; patient in tribulation," a struggle against the common enemies of man: tyranny, poverty, disease, and war itself.

Can we forge against these enemies a grand and global alliance, North and South, East and West, that can assure a more fruitful life for all mankind? Will you join in that historic effort?

In the long history of the world, only a few generations have been granted the role of defending freedom in its hour of maximum danger. I do not shrink from this responsibility—I welcome it. I do not believe that any of us would exchange places with any other people or any other generation. The energy, the faith, the devotion which we bring to this endeavor will light our country and all who serve it. And the glow from that fire can truly light the world.

And so, my fellow Americans, ask not what your country can do for you; ask what you can do for your country.

My fellow citizens of the world, ask not what America will do for you, but what together we can do for the freedom of man.

Finally, whether you are citizens of America or citizens of the world, ask of us here the same high standards of strength and sacrifice which we ask of you. With a good conscience our only sure reward, with history the final judge of our deeds, let us go forth to lead the land we love, asking His blessing and His help, but knowing that here on earth God's work must truly be our own.

Ain't I a Woman?[1] (for use with Chapter 9—the wave pattern)

By Sojourner Truth [Isabella Van Wagenen] (1797–1883)
Men in the audience at the Women's Convention (Akron, Ohio, 1851) argued against woman suffrage for three reasons: (1) man's superior intellect; (2) Christ was a man; and (3) the sin of the first woman, Eve. No manuscript exists of Sojourner's speech refuting each point. However, History of Woman Suffrage (1902) gave an eyewitness summary of the points, including Truth's dramatic delivery. This is the most commonly published version:

Well, children, where there is so much racket there must be something out of kilter. I think that between the Negroes of the South and the women at the North, all talking about rights, the white men will be in a fix pretty soon. But what's all this here talking about?

That man over there says that women need to be helped into carriages, and lifted over ditches, and to have the best place everywhere. Nobody ever helps me into carriages, or over mud-puddles, or gives me any best place!

And ain't I a woman? [*Said raising herself to her full height and her voice to a pitch like rolling thunder.*]

Look at me! Look at my arm! [*She bared her right arm to the shoulder, showing her muscles.*]

I have ploughed and planted, and gathered into barns, and no man could head me! And ain't I a woman?

I could work as much and eat as much as a man—when I could get it—and bear the lash as well! And ain't I a woman?

I have borne thirteen children, and seen them most all sold off to slavery, and when I cried out with my mother's grief, none but Jesus heard me! And ain't I a woman?

Then they talk about this thing in the head; what did they call it? [*Someone whispered* "Intellect"]

That's it, honey. What's that got to do with women's rights or Negro's rights? If my cup won't hold but a pint, and yours holds a quart, wouldn't you be mean not to let me have my little half-measure full? [*To loud cheers, she pointed and gave a "keen glance" at the minister who made the argument.*]

Then that little man in black there, he says women can't have as much rights as men, 'cause Christ wasn't a woman! Where did your Christ come from? [*In deep, wonderful tones, outstretched arms and eyes ablaze*]

[*Still louder.*] Where did your Christ come from? From God and a woman! Man had nothing to do with Him.

[*Turning to another man*] . . . If the first woman God ever made was strong enough to turn the world upside down all alone, these women together [*glancing across the platform*] ought to be able to turn it back, and get it right side up again! And now they are asking to do it, the men better let them. [*Sustained cheering*]

Obliged to you for hearing on me, and now old Sojourner has got nothing more to say. [*Roars of applause*]

[*Note: Originally reported in dialect and translated into Standard English.*]

GLOSSARY

A

absent audiences listeners who are separated from the speaker and receive the message through some form of media

absolute listening listening without interrupting or inserting oneself into the talk

academic journals journals that pertain to a specific area of academic research

Accidental plagiarists plagiarists who lack knowledge about the rules

accommodation response to diversity in which you listen and evaluate the views of others; both sides adapt, modify, and bargain to reach mutual agreements

actuate motivate the audience to do something

ad hominem an attack on the messenger rather than the message

ad populum an appeal to popular opinion

affective effects influences on listeners' feelings

ageist language language that negatively influences the way listeners think about older people

alliteration word with a recurring initial sound

alternation varying numbers and letters in a consistent pattern for different levels of points

ambiguous word identifies more than one object or idea; its meaning depends on the context

analogies state similarities between two things

analogy comparison of one item that's less familiar or unknown to something concrete and familiar

annotate to summarize a book or article's contents on a source card

anticipatory speech anxiety tension experienced at the mere thought of giving a speech

antimetabole saying words in one phrase, and reversing them in the next phrase

archetypal symbol recurring metaphor and simile that arises from shared human and natural experiences

argument an intentional, purposeful set of reasons created to explain disputed beliefs and conclusions

articulation the way you enunciate or say specific sounds, an element of pronunciation

artistic proofs reasons the speaker creates to accept an argument

assimilation response to diversity in which you embrace new perspectives and lifestyles and reject or surrender some or most of your previous beliefs and actions

attitudes our tendency to like or dislike something or to have positive or negative feelings about it

audience analysis identifying audience characteristics to communicate more effectively

B

backing additional reasons to support or defend a warrant

bar graph compares data from several groups by using bands of various lengths

behavioral effects influences on audience actions

belief mental acceptance of something as true or false, correct or incorrect, valid or invalid

bicultural knowing and applying different rules for competent behaviors in two cultures

blame the cause of the problem

burden of proof responsibility of the speaker who argues against the status quo to make the case for change

C

canon a set of principles, standards, norms, or guidelines

canon of delivery rules or standards for presenting a speech

canon of disposition or arrangement guidelines for organizing a speech

canon of invention principles for designing a speech that meets a need of a specific audience

canon of memory guidelines to help you remember your ideas

canon of style principles for choosing effective language

canons of rhetoric principles, standards, norms, or guidelines for creating and delivering a speech

causal claim claim about the relationship links between occurrences

causal reasoning linking two factors in such as way that the first occurs before the second and regularly leads to the second as a matter of rule

cause–effect or causal pattern presents reasons (causes) and implications (effects) of a topic

central idea a synonym for thesis statement

chronological pattern presents points in a sequential or time order

civic engagement working with others to help solve issues of public concern

civility a social virtue grounded in courtesy that chooses to understand and work with others

claim a debatable point or proposal, conclusion, or generalization that some people won't accept without some sort of evidence or backing

claims of prediction claim that something will or will not happen in the future

clarification questions requests to clear up confusing ideas

classification a method of presenting information by explaining things that are put into categories according to a principle

closed question request for a brief, specific answer

co-cultures subgroups of culture, characterized by mild or profound cultural differences that coexist within the larger culture

code switching changing from one dialect to another

cognitive dissonance theory humans seek stability or equilibrium; when faced with inconsistency they seek psychological balance; this may motivate them to change in order to be consistent

cognitive effects influences on beliefs, understandings, and other mental processes

cognitive modification identifying negative thoughts and replacing them with positive ones

cognitive preferences the way you prefer to perceive, reason, remember, and solve problems; it's culturally influenced but unique to you

collectivist cultures members of these cultures are integrated into an in-group that protects them throughout their lives

comments information from personal experience or research

common ground specific areas or concerns that both speaker and audience consider important

communication apprehension (CA) the fear or dread of negative responses you might experience because you speak out

communication style a culture's preferred ways of communicating, given its core assumptions and norms

communicative competence the ability to communicate in a personally effective and socially appropriate manner

comprehensive listening listening to understand information

concrete word specific, rather than general or abstract, term

confident style a way of speaking characterized by effective vocal variety, fluency, gestures, and eye contact

connectives words, phrases, and sentences used to lead from idea to idea and tie the parts of the speech together smoothly

connotative meanings emotional overtones, related feelings, and associations that cluster around a word

content outline formal record of your major ideas and their relationship to one another in your speech

conversational style speaking that's comparatively calmer, slower, and less intense, but maintains good eye contact and gestures

convince a persuasive purpose that targets audience beliefs

coordination arranging points into levels, giving the points on a specific level the same basic value or weight

core cultural resources beliefs, attitudes, and values (BAV) along with behaviors that provide a logical basis for a culture to define what is necessary, right, doubtful, or forbidden

correlation two things occur together, but one does not necessarily lead to the other

cost advantages weighed against the disadvantages

creative work poem, dance, painting, writing, or other aesthetic creation

credibility listeners' impressions of your character, intentions, and abilities that make you more or less believable

criteria the standards used for making evaluations or judgments

criteria-satisfaction pattern good for value or definition speeches; sets forth standards for judgment or for inclusion in a category and then shows how the proposal meets or exceeds these standards or fits into the category

critical listening listening that requires you to reflect and weigh the merits of messages before you accept them

critical thinking the ability to think analytically about ideas

cultural allusion reference to historical, literary, and religious sources that are culturally specific

culture an integrated system of learned beliefs, values, behaviors, and norms that include visible (clothing, food) and underlying (core beliefs, worldview) characteristics of a society

cure the solution

cut-and-paste plagiarism copying material word for word and then patching it together without quotation marks or citations

cynical speakers presenting verbal or nonverbal messages they don't believe in an attempt to create a false image

D

debatable points disputable statement about facts of existence or history

deductive reasoning starting with a principle (the premise) and applying it to a specific case

deliberate fraud knowing, intentional plagiarism

delivery the verbal and nonverbal behaviors you use to perform your speech

demagogue a polarizing speaker who appeals to audiences more on the basis of emotion and personal charisma than on reasoned arguments

demographic analysis identifying audiences by populations they represent, such as age or ethnicity

demonstrated or intrinsic credibility obvious knowledge the speaker shows during the speech

denotative meaning what a word names or identifies

diagram drawing or design that explains, rather than realistically depicts, an object or process

dialect a variant form of a language

digital object identifier (DOI) series of numbers and letters that locate intellectual property online

digital oratory an emerging form of public address housed online in new media platforms such as YouTube, Vimeo, or iReport

direct methods asking audience members directly for their opinion by questionnaires, interviews, and so on

disclaimer word or phrase that leads the audience to doubt your competence or expertise

discourse consistency using a repetitive style such as alliteration of main points throughout the speech

dismissive language put-downs; language that discounts the importance of someone's viewpoint

dissonance inconsistency or clash

division a method for presenting information by breaking the whole into parts and explaining each one

document cameras high-resolution cameras that display documents and three-dimensional objects

domain the type of site such as .com, .edu, or .org that tells the site's purpose and tax status

D-R-E method Describe-Respond-Evaluate; a feedback method that describes content, shares personal responses, and gives evaluation

dual coding theory (DCT) theory that our brains process material two ways: through language and through images

dual processing combining words and images to create meanings

E

empirical facts information verifiable by observation

enthymeme omitting part of the syllogism in an argument and letting listeners supply what's missing; inherently dialogical

enumeration a count

epithet word or phrase with a powerful negative connotation, used to describe some quality of a person or group

established fact information verified consistently by many observers

ethical communication the conscious decision to speak and listen in ways that you, in light of your cultural ideals, consider right, fair, honest, and helpful to all parties involved

ethnicity heritage and cultural traditions, usually stemming from national and religious backgrounds

ethos personal credibility or character traits that make a speaker believable and worthy of the audience's confidence

euphemism word or phrase that substitutes an inoffensive term for a potentially offensive, embarrassing, or unpleasant thing

exemplum speech pattern built around a quotation and developed by at least one narrative

experts people whose knowledge is based on research, experience, or occupation

expository speech the "speech to teach" that explains an idea in detail

expressive cultures cultures that encourage members to give their opinions, speak their minds, and let their feelings show

extemporaneous delivery preparing a speech carefully in advance but choosing the exact wording during the speech itself

eye contact looking audiences in the eye; communicates friendliness in the United States

F

fabrication making up information or repeating information without sufficiently checking its accuracy

factual claims argument about debatable points, causation, or predictions

fair use provision the provision in the federal Copyright Act that allows free use of materials for educational and research purposes

fallacy failure in logical reasoning that leads to unsound or misleading arguments

false analogy comparing two things too dissimilar to warrant the conclusion drawn

false dichotomy an either–or fallacy that ignores other reasonable options

faulty generalization a fallacy of induction; generalizing too broadly, given the evidence

fight-or-flight mechanism physiological mechanism your body automatically activates when threatened; helps you fight or flee

figurative analogies state similarities between two otherwise dissimilar things; requires an imaginative connection

filled or vocalized pause saying *um* or *uh* or other sounds during a pause

flip chart tablet you prepare in advance or create on the spot; turn to a new page or tear off and display pages as you finish them

flowchart shows the order or directional flow in which processes occur; may simply be a series of labeled shapes and arrows

G

gender clusters of traits culturally labeled as masculine, feminine, or androgynous

general purposes four general purposes are to inform, to persuade, to entertain, or to commemorate

geographic map shows mountains, deserts, and other natural features; not easily outdated

grounds, data, or evidence supporting material for claims

H

habituation lessening anxiety by successfully repeating an experience over time

harm the problem in a stock issues case; also called ill

hearing physical process involving sound waves, eardrums, and brain receptors

heckling disrupting a speech by interrupting or shouting down a speaker

hedges words such as *kinda* or *I think* that can lead listeners to distrust your competence or your knowledge of your topic

homogeneous audiences listeners who are similar in attitude

hostile audiences listeners who are negative toward the topic or the speaker

hypothetical example not a real incident or person, but true-to-life

I

identification, or co-orientation concerns shared among speakers and listeners that help overcome divisions and bring diverse people together

image-based visuals carry meaning in visual images; written words are secondary

impromptu delivery speaking with little advanced preparation

Improper paraphrase changing some words of a source but keeping the basic structure and ideas intact without citing the source

Inclusive language ethical terminology that affirms and includes, rather than excludes, persons or groups of people

indentation formatting by spacing various levels of points toward the right

indirect methods assessing audiences by observation or secondhand sources

individualistic cultures members of these cultures depend mainly on themselves and are judged on personal merits

inductive reasoning starting with specific instances or examples, then formulating a reasonable conclusion

information card card for recording and categorizing important data

information imbalance some people or groups having very little access to information while others have it in abundance

interactive whiteboards connects to other technology; you can overwrite material and then save your markups

internal monologue (I-M) self-talk

internal preview brief in-speech summary that foretells the subpoints you'll develop under a major point

internal summary restates the ideas within a point or points

invitational rhetoric inviting audiences to enter and understand the rhetor's world and then share their own perspectives; focuses on mutual understanding and mutual influence, not winning or change per se

J

Jargon a specialized, technical vocabulary that serves the interests and activities of a particular group

K

key words important words and phrases that will jog the speaker's memory

L

language verbal code consisting of symbols that a speech community uses for communication

laypeople or peers ordinary people whose knowledge comes from everyday experiences

lecture capture use of technology to upload class materials in digital formats

legacy journalism traditional news sources such as local and national newspapers

line graph displays in a linear form one or more variables that fluctuate over a time period

listening active process that receives, distinguishes, attends to, assigns meaning, and remembers what you hear

listening speaker dialogical speaker who hears audience interests and concerns before, during, and after a speech

literal analogies compare two actual things that are alike in important ways

literal images show the actual subject

loaded questions questions containing implications intended to put the speaker on the defensive

logical elements a speech's major ideas with supporting materials and their relationship

logos arguments from the words of the speech itself; often called rational proofs

M

manuscript delivery reading a speech

MAPit strategy developed by librarians that evaluates material according to message, author, and purpose

mean average of a group of numbers

median middle number in a set of numbers arranged in a ranked order

memorized delivery learning the speech by heart, then reciting it

metaphor comparison of two dissimilar things

metaphorical image implies the subject

mixed metaphor combining metaphors from two or more sources, starting with one comparison and ending with another

mode most frequently occurring number

model a facsimile of an object you can't easily bring to the speech

Monroe's Motivated Sequence a call to action in five steps: attention, need, satisfaction, visualization, and action

motivated audiences listeners who listen for a reason

motivation internal, individualized factor that results when we understand how topics affect our lives in a personal way

multivocal society society that actively seeks expression of a variety of voices or viewpoints

N

native digital news news outlets on the Internet that hire trained journalists and editors

nonexpressive cultures cultures that value privacy and encourage members to keep their emotions and ideas to themselves rather than to express them publicly

nonparallel language language that does not treat the two sexes equally

O

online public access catalog (OPAC) digital catalog to help you locate books and materials in your library's holdings

open question giving opportunity for a range of answers or a more lengthy response

oral culture culture with no writing and no technology for recording messages apart from face-to-face interactions

oral style characteristics of spoken language compared to written language

organic pattern alternative pattern that provides a clear speech structure in a less linear form

organizational chart shows hierarchies and relationships

original document evidence recorded by a primary source such as a letter or autobiography

P

pandering providing messages audiences want to hear, not necessarily what they need to hear

parallel case or literal analogy comparing likenesses between two similar things; arguing that what happened in a known case will likely happen in a similar case

parallel points points that are similar in kind and length

participatory question question that listeners answer overtly

passive audience unmotivated listeners who listen to accomplish other goals

pathos appeals or reasons directed toward audience emotions

perceived behavioral control our opinion about our ability to do a behavior

percentage figure that shows the relationship of the part to the whole, which is represented by the number 100

performance anxiety fear of forgetting or of poorly presenting a speech

personification giving human characteristics to nonhuman entities

perspective taking trying to imagine something from another person's point of view

persuasion the symbolic process in which a communicator intentionally creates an argument in an attempt to convince others to change their attitudes or behaviors in an atmosphere of free choice

physical factors bodily conditions that can limit your desire or ability to listen

physiological anxiety bodily responses to a perceived threat (increased heart rate, adrenaline rush)

picture graph or pictograph presents data in pictures, each representing a certain number of individual cases

pie graph represents parts of the whole or divisions of a population by circles divided into portions

plagiarism presenting the words, images, or ideas of others as if they were your own

policy claim disputed claim about the need to act or the plan for taking action

political map shows current borders for states and nations; can be outdated in a fast-changing world

post hoc a fallacy of causation; a false cause

power posing assuming the open and expansive postures associated with powerful people

prejudice preformed biases or judgments, whether negative or positive

presentation aids visual, audio, and multimedia support that helps audiences understand and remember information

presentation software program computer software to create a package of lists, tables, graphs, and clip art

presumption assumption that change is not necessary until proven otherwise

preview short summary of the major points you'll develop in the speech

primary source information from a person actually involved in the event

prior or extrinsic credibility credibility that speakers bring to the speech because of their experience and reputation

problem–solution pattern describes a problem and a possible solution or solutions to it

process anxiety fear due to lack of confidence in knowing how to prepare a speech

process speech describes a sequence of steps or stages that follow one another in a fairly predictable pattern

pro–con pattern presents arguments in favor of and arguments against an issue

psychological anxiety mental stress about a perceived threat

psychological factor mental stressors or distractions that take away from your desire or ability to focus

psychological profile assessment of an audience's beliefs, values, and attitudes regarding a topic

public speaking a person delivers a presentation to a group that listens, generally without interrupting the speaker's flow of ideas

public speaking anxiety (PSA) fear or dread specifically related to speaking in public

Q

qualifier word or phrase that limits the scope of the claim

R

race category, often associated with stereotypes, based on physical characteristics

racist language language that privileges one racial or ethnic group over another

random audiences listeners who are initially doing something else but are attracted by a message that catches their attention

ranked questions asking for responses to be placed in an order

rates of increase or decrease percentage that uses an earlier baseline figure to compare growth or decline

ratio relationship shown by numbers, such as 1 in 10

reasoning by metaphor comparing two things that are generally different but share a recognizable similarity

rebuttal counterargument the audience might have

receiver apprehension (RA) anxiety that people experience while listening to messages that make them uncomfortable

redundancy repeating the same idea more than once, but developing it differently each time

reference librarian librarian at the reference desk who is specifically trained to help people find information

relic or artifact culturally significant creation such as a building, jewelry, or a tool

repetition saying the same thing more than once

request for elaboration question asking for more information

resistance response to diversity in which you refuse to change, and you defend your own positions or attack others

re-sourcement creatively framing a divisive issue or viewpoint in a different way that may be less threatening

reversibility of perspectives an attempt to think from the other's perspective as well as one's own

rhetoric the study of persuasion in its various forms; this helps develop critical thinking skills

rhetorical question question that listeners answer in their minds

rhetorically sensitive the ability to adapt fairly successfully to a variety of social situations

rhymes words that end in the same sound

rightsabilities phrase coined by Professor Vernon Jensen to highlight the tension between our right to free speech and our responsibility for our speech

S

salient relevant or significant

sans serif fonts a simple font with no cross lines on each letter

scaled questions asking for responses along a continuum, used to assess attitudes

schemas mental model that guides your perception, interpretation, storage, and recollection of a speech

scholarly book book based on research that advances knowledge in an academic field

script the written text containing every word of the speech

secondary source summary or interpretation of an event or a person provided by a nonparticipant

self-selected listeners who choose to listen to a selected subject or speaker

serif font a font with cross lines at the top and bottom of letters

sex biological categories of male and female

sexist language language that privileges males and their activities and interests

signpost connective such as *first, most importantly*, and *consequently* that links ideas, lends emphasis, and helps listeners keep their place in the speech

simile short comparison that uses the word *like* or *as* to compare two items that are alike in one essential detail

sincere speakers presenting verbal and nonverbal messages they themselves believe

six-by-six rule limit information to six lines, six words per line

slippery slope a fallacy of causation; saying one small thing will lead to larger things without offering proof

social category culturally constructed category such as race or gender

solvency the proposed plan will actually solve the problem

source card card used to record bibliographic information

spatial pattern presents points by place or location

speaking notes the notes you use to deliver your speech

specialized encyclopedia text that summarizes information in a specific subject area

specific purpose the cognitive, affective, or behavioral response a speaker desires

speech–thought differential the difference between the rate you think (about 500 words per minute) and the average speaking rate (about 150 words per minute)

spinning selecting material that favors the speaker's interests and point of view

spiral pattern repetitive pattern with a series of points that increase in drama or intensity

Standard English the English dialect most commonly used in public speaking and in US institutions

star pattern presents relatively equally weighted speech points within a thematic circle that binds them together; order of points may vary

statement of reasons pattern pattern that lists reasons and then explains each one

status quo Latin phrase that means "the existing state of affairs"

stereotyping place someone in a category and then assume the person fits the characteristics of that category

stock issues the questions a reasonable person would need to have answered before forming a reasoned decision about a topic

stress accenting syllables or words

structural elements a speech's introduction, body, and conclusion

style in rhetoric, style refers to language

subject librarian librarian who also has an advanced degree in a particular subject such as law or medicine

subjective norms our perceptions of what significant people think we should do

subordination placement of supporting points under major points

systematic desensitization process designed to lessen physical reactions to stress; teaches how to relax while thinking about frightening speech events

T

taboo topics a culture considers inappropriate

tag question short question tagged onto the end of a sentence; some can be helpful but others are annoying

terminal credibility final impression listeners have of a speaker

tertiary source condenses primary and secondary materials into collections such as encyclopedias

text-based visual carries meaning in the written words rather than in visual images

theory of reasoned action (TRA) links behavioral intentions with attitudes, subjective norms, and perceived behavioral control; assumes we rationally weigh costs and benefits of our actions

thesis statement a single sentence that names the subject and establishes its significance

topical pattern divides a subject into subtopics, each of which is part of the whole

Toulmin's Model of Reasoning a linear model designed to show six elements of reasoning common in the United States

trade book book aimed at a general audience

trade journal journal that pertains to a specific occupation

transactional model of communication represents communication as a process in which speakers and listeners work together to create mutual meanings

transition summarizes where you've been and where you're going in your speech

U

unfilled pause silent pause

unmotivated audience listeners who lack a listening purpose or goal

unsupported assertion unsupported claim

V

vague word imprecise term that has indefinite boundaries

value claim argument about right or wrong, moral or immoral, beautiful or ugly

values standards used to make evaluative judgments such as good or bad

verbiage nonessential language

visualization rehearsing by using your imagination to envision your speech from start to finish

vocal variations changes in volume, rate, and pitch that combine to create impressions of the speaker

vocalics or paralinguistics all aspects of spoken language except the words

W

warmth using behaviors that signal positive interest and engagement, especially through pleasant facial expressions

warrant assumption that justifies or logically links the evidence to the claim

wave pattern repetitive pattern that presents variations of themes and ideas, with major points presented at the crests

word verbal symbol that stands for or represents an idea

REFERENCES

CHAPTER 1

1. Jensen, K. K., & Harris, V. (1999). The public speaking portfolio. *Communication Education, 48*, 221–227.

2. Smith, D. (1996, February). Globalization of the general education curriculum. Discussion leader. George Fox University, Newberg, OR.

3. Galvin, K. M., & Cooper, P. J. (2000). Perceptual filters: Culture, family, and gender. In K. M. Galvin & P. J. Cooper (Eds.), *Making connections: Readings in relational communication* (2nd ed., pp. 32–33). Los Angeles: Roxbury.

4. Collier, M. J. (2006). WSCA presidential address: Cultural positioning, reflexivity, and transformative third spaces. *Western Journal of Communication, 70*, 263–269.

5. Conrad, C. (1994). *Strategic organizational communication: Toward the twenty-first century* (3rd ed., p. 31). Fort Worth, TX: Harcourt Brace.

6. Gray, G. W. (1946). The precepts of Kagmenmi [sic] and Ptah-hotep. *Quarterly Journal of Speech, 31*, 446–454.

7. Halledén, P. (2005). What is Arab-Islamic rhetoric? Rethinking the history of Muslim oratory art and homiletics. *International Journal of Middle East Studies, 37*, 19–38. doi: 10.1017. S0020743805050038.

8. *Dao De Jing* 81.185 is quoted in Xing, L. (1998). *Rhetoric in ancient China, fifth to third century, B.C.E.: A comparison with classical Greek rhetoric.* Columbia, SC: University of South Carolina Press, p. 87.

9. Hart, R. P., & Burks, D. O. (1972). Rhetorical sensitivity and social interaction. *Speech Monographs, 39*, 90.

10. Pearce, W. B. (1989). *Communication and the human condition.* Carbondale: Southern Illinois University Press.

11. Ong, W. J. (1982). *Orality and literacy: The technologizing of the word.* New York, NY: Methuen.

12. Clark, R. A., & Jones, D. (2001). A comparison of traditional and online formats in a public speaking course. *Communication Education, 50*(2), 109–124.

13. Hofstede, G. (n.d.). Dimensions of national cultures. Geert Hofstede website. Retrieved from www.geerthofstede.nl/dimensions-of-national-cultures.

14. Oddou, G. (2006, Spring). Hofstede's dimensions of culture. California State University, San Marcos. MGMT 461. Retrieved from courses.csusm.edu/-mgmt461go/Hofstede-correlations.doc.

15. FIU Oral Presentation Lab. (n.d.). Cultural issues and public address. Miami: Florida International University. Retrieved from http://opl.fiu.edu/cultural.htm.

16. Lai, A. (2006, June). Eye on religion: Cultural signs and caring for Chinese patients. *Southern Medical Journal, 99*, 688–689.

17. Sallinen-Kuparinen, A., McCroskey, J. C., & Richmond, V. P. (1991). Willingness to communicate, communication apprehension, introversion, and self-reported communication competence: Finnish and American Comparisons. *Communication Research Reports, 8*, 54–65.

18. Marsella, A. J. (1993). Counseling and psychotherapy with Japanese Americans: Cross-cultural considerations. *American Journal of Orthopsychiatry, 63*, 200–208. ISSN: 00029432.

19. Klopf, D. W. (1997). Cross-cultural apprehension research: Procedures and comparisons. In J. A. Daly, J. C. McCroskey, J. Ayers, T. Hopf, & D. M. Ayres (Eds.), *Avoiding communication: Shyness, reticence, and communication apprehension* (2nd ed., pp. 269–284). Creskill, NJ: Hampton Press.

20. Messenger, J. (1960). Anang proverb riddles. *Journal of American Folklore, 73*, 235.

21. Weider, D. L., & Pratt, S. (1990). On being a recognizable Indian. In D. Carbaugh (Ed.), *Intercultural communication and intercultural contacts* (pp. 45–64). Hillsdale, NJ: Erlbaum.

22. Jenefsky, C. (1996). Public speaking as empowerment at Visionary University. *Communication Education, 45*, 343–355.

See also Jaasma, M. A. (1997, Summer). Classroom apprehension: Does being male or female make a difference? *Communication Reports, 10*, 218–228.

23. Clasen, P., & Lee, R. (2006). Teaching in a sanitized world: An exploration of the suburban scene in public communication pedagogy. *Communication Education, 55*, 438–463.

24. Lind, S. J. (2012). Teaching digital oratory: Public Speaking 2.0. *Communication Teacher, 26*(3), 163–169. doi: 10.1080/17404622.2012.659193.

25. Stewart, E. C., & Bennett, M. J. (1991). *American cultural patterns: A cross-cultural perspective* (rev. ed.). Yarmouth, ME: Intercultural Press.

26. Evans, R. W., & Avery, P. G. (1999, September/October). Taboo topics: Cultural restraint on teaching social issues. *Social Studies, 90*(5), 218–225. ISSN: 00377996.

27. DeJong, J., Jawad, R., Mortagy, I., & Shepard, B. (2005). The sexual and reproductive health of young people in the Arab countries and Iran. *Reproductive Health Matters, 13*(25), 49–59. doi: 10.1016/S0968-8080(05)25181-9.

28. Sayer, D. (2010). Who's afraid of the dead? Archaeology, modernity, and the death taboo. *World Archaeology, 42*(3), 481–491.

29. Ugwu-Oju, D. (1993, November 14). Pursuit of happiness. *The New York Times Magazine.*

30. Pearce, *Communication.*

31. California State Senate. (2002, January 20, last updated). Definition of critical thinking. Quoted on B. Dowden, Philosophy 4, California State University Sacramento. Retrieved from www.csus.edu/indiv/d/dowdenb/4/ct-def/def-of-ct.htm.

32. King, A., & Kuypers, J. (2013). Scholarly definitions of rhetoric. Retrieved from www.americanrhetoric.com/rhetoricdefinitions.htm.

33. The first three definitions can be found at the previous site.

34. Quoted in Xing, *Rhetoric in ancient China*, p. 88.

35. Allen, M., Berkowitz, S., Hunt, S., & Louden, A. (1999). A meta-analysis of the impact of forensics and communication education on critical thinking. *Communication Education, 48,* 18–30.

36. American Association of Colleges and Universities. (2013). It takes more than a major: Employer priorities for college learning and student success. Retrieved from www.aacu.org/leap/presidentstrust/compact/2013SurveySummary.cfm.

37. Rhodes, T. (2010, November). Learning across the curriculum: Communication departments hold vital role. *Spectra, 46*(1), 12–15.

38. Darling, A. L., & Dannels, D. P. (2003). Practicing engineers talk about the importance of talk: A report on the role of oral communication in the workplace. *Communication Education, 52,* 1–16.

39. Waugh, T. (2004, June). The tide is turning. Are you ready? *The Practical Accountant, 37,* 16–17.

40. Goldfinger, J. (2009). Democracy Plaza: A campus space for civic engagement. *Innovative Higher Education, 34,* 69–77. doi 10.1007/s10755-009-9096-1.

41. Wahl-Jorgensen, K. (2001). Letters to the editor as a forum for public deliberation: Modes of publicity and democratic debate. *Critical Studies in Media Communication, 18,* 303–320.

42. Roper Starch. (1999). How Americans communicate. Poll commissioned by the National Communication Association. Retrieved from www.natcom.org/research/Roper/howamericanscommunicate.htm.

43. Witt, P. L., & Behnke, R. R. (2006, April). Anticipatory speech anxiety as a function of public speaking assignment type. *Communication Education, 55,* 167–177.

44. The transactional model appears in almost every communication text.

45. Crooks, R. (1998, May 11, last modified). Noise. English Department, Bentley College. Retrieved from http://web.bentley.edu/empl/c/rcrooks/toolbox/common_knowledge/general_communication/noise.html.

CHAPTER 2

1. Bodie, G. D. (2010). A racing heart, rattling knees, and ruminative thoughts: Defining, explaining, and treating public speaking anxiety. *Communication Education, 59*(1), 40–105.

2. McCroskey, J. C. (1977). Oral communication apprehension: A summary of recent theory and research. *Human Communication Research, 4,* 78–96.

3. Richmond, V. P., & McCroskey, J. C. (1995). *Communication: Apprehension, avoidance, and effectiveness* (4th ed.). Scottsdale, AZ: Gorsuch Scarisbrick.

4. Beatty, M., McCroskey, J. C., & Heisel, A. D. (1998). Communication apprehension as temperamental expression: A communibiological paradigm. *Communication Monographs, 65,* 197–219.

5. Bodie, A racing heart.

6. Tschan, M. (2009). Personal interview. See also USTA. (2014). Sports psychology: Mental skills for achieving optimum performance. Retrieved January 6, 2014, from www.usta.com/Improve-Your-Game/Sport-Science/117746_Sports_Psychology_Mental_Skills_for_Achieving_Optimum_Performance/.

7. Robinson, T. E. (1997). Communication apprehension and the basic public speaking course: A national survey of in-class treatment techniques. *Communication Education, 46,* 188–197.

8. Witt, P. L., & Behnke, R. R. (2006). Anticipatory speech anxiety as a function of public speaking assignment type. *Communication Education, 55*(2), 167–177.

9. Bippus, A. M., & Daly, J. A. (1999). What do people think causes stage fright? Naïve attributions about the reasons for public speaking anxiety. *Communication Education, 48,* 63–72.

10. Duff, D. C., Levine, T. R., Beatty, M. J., Woolbright, J., & Park, H. S. (2007). Testing public anxiety treatments against a credible placebo control. *Communication Education, 56*(1), 72–88.

11. Cicero, M. T. (1981). *Ad herennium: De ratione dicendi (Rhetorica ad herennium)* (H. Kaplan, Trans.). The Loeb Classical Library. Cambridge, MA: Harvard University Press.

12. Quintilian. (1920–1922). *The instituto oratoria of Quintilian* (4 vols., H. E. Butler, Trans.). The Loeb Classical Library. Cambridge, MA: Harvard University Press.

13. Style. (2008). *Compact Oxford English Dictionary.* Accessed June 3, 2008, from www.askoxford.com/concise_oed/style?view5uk.

14. Pearson, J. C., Child, J. T., & Kahl, D. H., Jr. (2006). Preparation meeting opportunity: How do college students prepare for public speeches? *Communication Quarterly, 54*(3), 351–366.

15. Sawyer, C. R., & Behnke, R. R. (1999). State anxiety patterns for public speaking anxiety and the behavior inhibition system. *Communication Reports, 12,* 33–41.

16. Behnke, R. R., & Sawyer, C. R. (2001). Patterns of psychological state anxiety as a function of anxiety sensitivity. *Communication Quarterly, 49,* 84–95. See also Young, M. J., Behnke, R. R., & Mann, Y. M. (2004). Anxiety patterns in employment interviews. *Communication Reports, 17,* 49–57.

17. McGlynn, F. D., Smitherman, T. A., & Gothard, K. D. (2004). Comment on the status of systematic desensitization. *Behavior Modification, 28*(2), 194–205. doi: 10.1177/0145445503259414.

18. This process came from Richmond, R. L. (2011). Systematic desensitization: A guide to psychology and its practice. Retrieved from www.guidetopsychology.com/sysden.htm.

19. Behnke, R. R., & Sawyer, C. R. (2000). Anticipatory anxiety patterns for male and female public speakers. *Communication Education, 49*(2), 187–195. doi: 10.1080/03634520009379205.

20. Yaikhong, K., & Usaha, S. (2013). A measure of EFL public speaking class anxiety: Scale development and preliminary validation and reliability. *English Language Teaching, 5*(12), 23–35. doi: 10.5539/elt.v5n12p23.

21. Matsuoka, R. (2008). Communication apprehension among Japanese college students. *Journal of Pan-Pacific Association of Applied Linguistics, 12*(2), 37–48.

22. Howell. W. (1990). Coping with internal-monologue. In J. Stewart (Ed.), *Bridges not walls: A book about interpersonal communication* (5th ed., pp. 128–138). New York, NY: McGraw-Hill.

23. Mount Sinai Medical Center. (2007). Stress: Diseases and conditions. Retrieved from www.mssm.edu/cvi/stress.shtml#q2. See also Vîslă, A., Cristea, I. A., Tătar, A. S., & David, D. (2013). Core beliefs, automatic thought and response expectancies in predicting public speaking anxiety. *Personality and Individual Differences, 55,* 856–859.

24. Bippus & Daly, What do people think.

25. Kane, L., & Helmer, L. (2006, October 6). Conquering podium paralysis: Public speaking skills for doctors. *Medical Economics, 83*(19), 31–32.

26. MacIntyre, P. J., & MacDonald, J. R. (1998). Public speaking anxiety: Perceived competence and audience congeniality. *Communication Education, 47*, 359–365.

27. Finn, A. N., Sawyer, C. R., & Behnke, R. R.(2003). Audience-perceived anxiety patterns of public speakers. *Communication Quarterly, 51*, 470–482. See also Elfering, A., & Grebner, S. (2012). Getting used to academic public speaking: Global self-esteem predicts habituation in blood pressure response to repeated thesis presentations. *Applied Psychophysiological Feedback, 37*, 109–120.

28. Ayers, J., & Sonandre, D. M. A. (2003). Performance visualization: Does the nature of the speech model matter? *Communication Research Reports, 20*(3), 260–268.

29. Mount Sinai Medical Center, Stress.

30. Ayres and Hopf have been studying visualization for many years. See Ayres, J. & Hopf, T. S. (1989). Visualization: Is it more than extra-attention? *Communication Education, 38*, 1–5; see also Ayres, J., Hopf, T. S., & Ayres, D. M. (1994). An examination of whether imaging ability enhances the effectiveness of an intervention designed to reduce speech anxiety. *Communication Education, 43*, 256.

31. Ayres, J., Hopf, T., & Edwards, P. A. (1999). Vividness and control: Factors in the effectiveness of performance visualization? *Communication Education, 48*, 287–293.

32. Carney, D. R., Cuddy, A. J. C., & Yap, A. J. (2010). Power posing: Brief nonverbal displays affect neuroendocrine levels and risk tolerance. *Psychological Science, 21*(10), 1363–1368. doi: 10.1177/0956797610383437.

33. Stel, M., van Dijk, E., Smith, P. K., van Dijk, W. W., & Djalal, F. M. (2012). Lowering the pitch of your voice makes you feel more powerful and think more abstractly. *Social Psychological and Personality Science, 3*(4), 497–502. doi: 10.1177/1948550611427610.

34. Ayers, J. (2005, April). Performance visualization and behavioral disruption: A clarification. *Communication Reports, 18*(1), 55–63.

35. Finn, A., Sawyer, C. R., & Schrodt, P. (2009). Examining the effect of exposure therapy on public speaking anxiety. *Communication Education, 58*(1), 92–109.

36. Clark, R. A., & Jones, D. (2001). A comparison of traditional and online formats in a public speaking course. *Communication Education, 50*(2), 109–124.

37. Stockstill, C. J., & Roach, K. D. (2007). Communication apprehension in high school athletes. *Texas Speech Communication Journal, 32*(1), 53–64.

CHAPTER 3

1. U.S. Constitution Online. (2010, January 24, updated). Amendment 1: Freedom of religion, press, expression. Retrieved from www.usconstitution.net/xconst_Am1.html.

2. Dobner, J. (2012, April 27, updated). Jeremiah Hill in trouble over "joke" to "hijack plane, kill Obama." *Huffington Post.* Retrieved from www.huffingtonpost.com/2012/04/27/jeremiah-hill-obama-letter_n_1457440.html.

3. Turley, J. (2012, October 12). Shut up and play nice: How the Western world is limiting free speech. *The Washington Post.* Retrieved from www.washingtonpost.com/opinions/the-four-arguments-the-western-world-uses-to-limit-free-speech/2012/10/12/e05.

4. Jensen, J. V. (1997). *Ethical issues in the communication process.* Mahwah, NJ: Erlbaum.

5. Jensen, *Ethical issues.*

6. Pearce, W. B. (1989). *Communication and the human condition.* Carbondale: Southern Illinois Press.

7. Berger, P. (1969). *A rumor of angels: Modern society and the rediscovery of the supernatural.* Garden City, NY: Doubleday.

8. Berger, *A rumor.*

9. Tannen, D. (1998). *The argument culture: Moving from debate to dialogue.* New York, NY: Random House.

10. Berger, *A rumor.*

11. Ibid.

12. Gates, H. L. (1992). *Loose cannons: Notes on the culture wars.* New York, NY: Oxford University Press.

13. Pearce, W. B., & Pearce, K. A. (2000). Combining passions and abilities: Toward dialogic virtuosity. *Southern Communication Journal, 65*, 161–175.

14. Tannen, *The argument culture,* 289.

15. Papacharissi, Z. (2004). Democracy online: Civility, politeness, and the democratic potential of online political discussion groups. *New Media and Society, 6*(2), 259–283. doi: 10.1177/1461444804041444.

16. Barrett, H. (1991). *Rhetoric and civility: Human development, narcissism, and the good audience.* Albany, NY: SUNY Press.

17. Obama, B. H. (2011, January 12). Remarks by the president at a memorial service for the victims of the shooting in Tucson, Arizona. McKale Memorial Center, University of Arizona, Tuscon, AZ. Retrieved from www.whitehouse.gov/the-press-office/2011/01/12/remarks-president-barack-obama-memorial-service-victims-shooting-tucson.

18. Jensen, *Ethical issues.*

19. Khadaroo, S. T. (2011, February 24). Does Facebook boost civic engagement among American youths, too? *The Christian Science Monitor.* Retrieved from www.csmonitor.com/USA/Education/2011/0224/Does-Facebook-boost-civic-engagement-among-American-youths-too.

20. Jensen, *Ethical issues.*

21. Yankelovich, D. (1999). *The magic of dialogue: Transforming conflict into cooperation.* New York, NY: Simon & Schuster.

22. Etzioni, A. (1996). *The new golden rule: Community and morality in a democratic society* (pp. 104–106). New York, NY: Basic Books.

23. Mallory, B. L., & Thomas, N. L. (2003, September/October). When the medium is the message: Promoting ethical action through democratic dialogue. *Change,* 2–9. Retrieved from www.collegevalues.org/pdfs/galleyproofsCHANGEfinal.pdf.

24. The Regents of the University of Michigan. (2013). Teaching strategies: Incivility in the college classroom. Center for Research on Learning and Teaching. Retrieved from www.crlt.umich.edu/tstrategies/incivility.

25. A Google search for "classroom civility" turned up more than 500,000 hits. Here are just two: Center for Teaching and Learning. (2009). Classroom civility. UC Santa Cruz. Retrieved from http://ctl.ucsc.edu/resources/tips/tips-civility.html; and Faculty Development Center. (n.d.). Civility in the classroom. University of Maryland, Baltimore County. Retrieved from www.umbc.edu/fdc/topics/civility.php.

26. Goedde, B. (2013, May 24). A course in online civility. *Chronicle of Higher Education, 59*(37).

27. Hexham, I. (1999). Academic plagiarism defined. University of Calgary Department of Religious Studies. Retrieved from www.ucalgary.ca/hexham/study/plag.html.

28. UCDavis Student Judiciary Affairs. (2001, October 25, updated). Avoiding plagiarism. Retrieved from http://sja.ucdavis.edu/avoid.htm#guidelines.

29. UCDavis Student Judiciary Affairs. (2008, February 25, updated). Why academic integrity matters. Retrieved from http://sja.ucdavis.edu/academic-integrity-page2.html.

30. Plagiarism.com. (2011). Plagiarism and the Internet. Retrieved from http://plagiarism.org/plag_article_plagiarism_and_the_internet.html.

31. Plagiarism.com, Plagiarism and the Internet.

32. Many Internet sites explain plagiarism. See Purdue Online Writing Lab. (2011, January 14, last edited). Avoiding plagiarism. Purdue University. Retrieved from http://owl.english.purdue.edu/owl/-resource/589/03/. See also The Writing Center. (2013). Plagiarism. University of North Carolina at Chapel Hill. Retrieved from http://writingcenter.unc.edu/handouts/plagiarism/.

33. Purdue Online Writing Lab.

34. Writing Center, Plagiarism.

35. UCDavis Student Judiciary Affairs. (2001). Avoiding plagiarism.

36. Gilday, B. (2010, Fall). The dark side of product placement [Student speech]. George Fox University, Newberg, OR.

37. Stern, J. (2009, August). Making smarter movies. Speech delivered June 20, 2009, at the Los Angeles Film Festival, Los Angeles, CA. *Vital Speeches of the Day, 75*(8), 347–352.

38. A video on YouTube demonstrates the WorldCat.org Citation Tool and advises this. Retrieved from www.youtube.com/watch?v=X8W7kWMrVNk.

39. The material in this box draws from N. Carbone. (2001, December 3). Thinking and talking about plagiarism. Bedford St. Martins Technotes. Retrieved from http://bedfordstmartins.com/technotes/techtiparchive/ttip102401.htm.

40. Hunter, J. (1997). Confessions of an academic honesty lady. Grinnell College Writing Lab. Retrieved from www.grinnell.edu/academic/writinglab/forum/con_hj.pdf.

41. Reuters. (2011, January 6). Journal says doctor faked data linking autism to vaccines. *The Washington Post*. Retrieved from www.washingtonpost.com/wp-dyn/content/article/2011/01/05/AR2011010507052.html.

42. Department of Journalism. (n.d.). Academic integrity handbook. University of Arizona. Retrieved from http://journalism.arizona.edu/publications/academic_integrity/integrity_handbook.pdf.

··

CHAPTER 4

1. This quotation has been attributed to many philosophers including Confucius, Epictetus, Zeno of Citium, and Laertius Diogenes.

2. Burleson, B. R. (2011). A constructivist approach to listening. *International Journal of Listening, 25*, 27–46. doi: 10.1080/10904018.2011.536470.

3. Maes, J. D., Weldy, T. B., & Icenogle, M. L. (1997, January). A managerial perspective: Oral communication competency is more important for business students in the workplace. *Journal of Business Communication, 34*, 6–14.

4. Treuer, P. (2006, July 17, last updated). Listening skills. *Student Handbook*. University of Minnesota Duluth. Retrieved from www.d.umn.edu/kmc/student/loon/acad/strat/ss_listening.html.

5. Salopek, J. J. (1999). Is anyone listening? *Training and Development, 53*(9), 58–60. See also Ramsey, R. D. (2007, November). The most important skills for today's supervisors. *Supervision, 68*(11), 3–5.

6. Lenckus, D. (2005, November 28). Physician apologies, listening skills found to reduce medical malpractice claims. *Business Insurance, 39*(48).

7. Burley-Allen, M. (2001). Listen up: Listening is a learned skill and supervisors need it to improve their employee relationships. *HR Magazine, 46*(11), 115–117.

8. Jaecks, K. M. S. (2009, Spring). Current perceptions of the role of dental hygienists in interdisciplinary collaboration. *Journal of Dental Hygiene, 83*(2), 84–91.

9. Owen, J. (2007, June 2). Interior decorator cites listening skills as key to satisfying clients. *Walton Sun* (Santa Rosa Beach, FL). Retrieved from InfoTrac College Edition database.

10. Olsztynski, J. (2008, December). Master the art of listening. *Roofing Contractor, 28*(12), 18–19.

11. Golen, S., & Lynch, D. H. (2008, September). The importance of listening skills in tax preparation. *The CPA Journal, 78*(9), 56–59.

12. This quotation is in the public domain. It is available at many quotation collections websites.

13. Janusik, L. (2011). Listening facts. Paragon Resources. Retrieved from www.paragonre sources.com/library/listen.pdf.

14. TAMU Student Counseling Service. (2008). Listening skills. Texas A&M University. Retrieved from http://scs.tamu.edu/selfhelp/elibrary/listening_skills.asp.

15. This axiom traces back to Richards, I. A. (1936). *The philosophy of rhetoric*. London: Oxford University Press. D. Berlo is often credited with it.

16. Chen, H. (2011). Brief analysis of strategies to improve English listening competence among non-English undergrad students. *Asian Social Science, 7*(12), 68–71. doi: 10.5539/ass.v7n12p68.

17. Winiecki, K. L., & Ayers, J. (1999). Communication apprehension and receiver apprehension in the workplace. *Communication Quarterly, 47*(4), 431–440.

18. Lundsteen, S. W. (1993). Metacognitive listening. In A. D. Wolvin & C. G. Coakley (Eds.), *Perspectives on listening* (pp. 106–123). Norwood, NJ: Ablex.

19. Lundsteen, Metacognitive listening.

20. Imhof, M. (1998). What makes a good listener? Listening behaviors in instructional settings. *International Journal of Listening, 12*, 81–105.

21. Burleson, B. R. (2011). A constructivist approach to listening. *International Journal of Listening, 25*, 27–46. doi: 10/1080/10904918.2011.536470.

22. Imhof, M. (2001). How to listen more efficiently: Self-monitoring strategies in listening. *International Journal of Listening, 15*, 2–19.

23. Lundsteen, Metacognitive listening.

24. Imhof, M. (2003). The social construction of the listener: Listening behaviour across situations, perceived listener status, and culture. *Communication Research Reports, 20*(4), 357–366.

25. EDUCAUSE. (2008). 7 things you should know about lecture capture. EDUCAUSE Learning Initiative. ELI 7044.pdf.

26. Edwards, R., & McDonald, J. L. (1993). Schema theory and listening. In Wolvin & Coakley, *Perspectives*, 60–77.

27. Bierhorst, J. (1985). *The mythology of North America*. New York, NY: William Morrow.

28. Daniel, J., & Smitherman, G. (1990). How I got over: Communication dynamics in the black community. In D. Carbaugh (Ed.), *Intercultural-communication and intercultural contacts* (pp. 45–64). Hillsdale, NJ: Erlbaum. See also Smith, A. L. (Molefi Asanti). (1970). Socio-historical perspectives of black oratory. *Quarterly Journal of Speech, 61*, 264–269.

29. Sitkaram, K. S., & Cogdell, R. T. (1976). *Foundations of intercultural communication*. Columbus, OH: Charles E. Merrill.

30. Kiewitz, C., Weaver, J. B. III, Brosius, H.-B., & Weimann, G. (1997). Cultural differences in listening style preferences: A comparison of young adults in Germany, Israel, and the United States. *International Journal of Public Opinion Research, 9*, 233–248.

31. Ridge, A. (1993). A perspective of listening skills. In Wolvin & Coakley, *Perspectives*, 1–14.

32. Snyder, M. D. (2002, March/April). Free speech and the 'heckler's veto.' *Academe 88*(2), 01902946.

33. Epstein, J. (2013, May 23). Code Pink heckler interrupts Obama counter-terror speech. Politico 44. Politico. Retrieved from www.politico.com/politico44/2013/05/code-pink-heckler-interrupts-obama-drone-speech-164687.html.

34. Bruce, M. (2013, June 4). Michelle Obama, heckled by gay rights advocate, threatens to leave event. *ABC Early Morning News*. Retrieved from http://abcnews.go.com/blogs/politics/2013/06/first-lady-heckled-by-gay-rights-advocate-threatens-to-leave-event/.

35. Boyd, S. D. (2001, October). The human side of teaching: Effective listening. *Techniques, 76*(7), 60.

36. Goodman, G., & Esterly, G. (1990). Questions—the most popular piece of language. In J. Stewart (Ed.), *Bridges not walls: A book about interpersonal communication* (9th ed., pp. 69–79). New York, NY: McGraw-Hill.

37. Becker, C. B. (1986). Reasons for the lack of argumentation and debate in the Far East. *International Journal of International Relations, 10*(1), 75–92. doi: 10.1016/0147-1767(86)90035-0; see also Sueda, K. (1995). Differences in the perception of face: Chinese *mien-tzu* and Japanese *mentsu*. *World Communication, 24*(1), 23–31.

38. Anonymous reviewer. (2004).

....

CHAPTER 5

1. Christensen, M. D. (1998, March). An idea is only the bait. *The Writer, 111*, 20–21.

2. Bitzer, L. F. (1999). The rhetorical situation. In J. L. Lucaites, C. M. Condit, & S. Caudill (Eds.), *Contemporary rhetorical theory: A reader* (pp. 217–225). New York, NY: Guilford; see also Vatz, R. E. (1999). The myth of the rhetorical situation. In Lucaites, Condit, & Caudill, *Contemporary rhetorical theory*, 226–231.

3. McKeon, R. (1998). Creativity and the commonplace. In T. B. Ferrell (Ed.), *Landmark essays on contemporary rhetoric* (pp. 33–41). Mahwah, NJ: Hermagoras Press.

4. Michaud, J. (2013, December 22). Sweet morsels: A history of the chocolate-chip cookie. *The New Yorker*. Retrieved from www.newyorker.com/online/blogs/culture/2013/12/sweet-morsels-a-history-of-the-chocolate-chip-cookie.html.

5. Weinstein, B. (2008, January 15). The ethics of talking politics at work. *BusinessWeek*. Retrieved from www.businessweek.com/managing/content/jan2008/ca20080115_994641.htm.

6. Murray, D. M. (1998, May). Write what you don't know. *The Writer, 111*, 7–9.

7. Christensen, An idea.

8. Daisak, W. (2008, January). What not to talk about. Toastmasters International. Retrieved from www.toastmasters.org/ToastmastersMagazine/ToastmasterArchive/2008/January/Articles/WhatNot-toTalkAbout.aspx.

9. Grant, H. (2007, January). Sabina Xhosa and the new shoes. Address delivered November 1, 2006, at the IBM Lecture, Westminster College, Fulton, Missouri. *Vital Speeches of the Day, 73*(1), 36–40.

10. Scofield, S. (1999, August). An end to writer's block. *The Writer, 111*, 7–9.

11. Augustine. (397–426, 1958). *On Christian doctrine: Book IV* (D. W. Robertson Jr., Trans.). New York, NY: Liberal Arts Press.

12. Campbell, G. (1963). *The philosophy of rhetoric* (L. Bitzer, Ed.). Carbondale: Southern Illinois University Press. (Original work published 1776)

13. Monroe, A. H. (1962). *Principles and types of speech* (5th ed.). Chicago: Scott Foresman.

14. Gwynne, R. (2005, March 12, last updated). Topic organization. University of Tennessee Knoxville. Accessed from http://web.utk.edu/gwynne/topic_organization.html.

15. Borough of Manhattan Community College. (n.d.). What's the difference between a specific purpose and a central idea? e-tutoring FAQS. City University of New York. Retrieved from www.bmcc.cuny.edu/faq/faq_detail.jsp?faq_id=715&course_id=156.

16. Gwynne, Topic organization.

17. Anonymous reviewer. (2005). College of Marin.

18. Griffin, C. W. (1998). Improving students' writing strategies: Knowing versus doing. *College Teaching, 46*, 48–52.

....

CHAPTER 6

1. Holman, P. (1970). *The psychology of speakers and audiences*. Glenview, IL: Scott Foresman.

2. Bitzer, L. F. (1999). The rhetorical situation. In J. L. Lucaites, C. M. Condit, & S. Caudill (Eds.), *Contemporary rhetorical theory: A reader* (pp. 217–225). New York, NY: Guilford. See also Garrett, M., & Xiao, X. (1993, Spring). The rhetorical situation revisited. *RSQ: Rhetorical Society Quarterly, 23*(2), 30–40.

3. Garrett & Xiao, The rhetorical situation.

4. Psychologists have written about audience motivations for decades. An early book was Hollingsworth, H. L. (1935). *The psychology of audiences*. New York, NY: American Book.

5. Manson, N. C. (2012). Making sense of spin. *Journal of Applied Philosophy, 29*(3), 200–213. doi: 10.1111/j.1468-5930.2012.00566.x.

6. Editorial. (2006, July 3). Pander-monium: Our view: Congress is angling for votes, not solving problems. *Spokesman-Review* (Spokane, WA). Retrieved from InfoTrac College Edition.

7. Simon, P., quoted in Editorial, Pander-monium.

8. Reider, J. (2008). *The Word of the Lord is upon me: The righteous performance*

of Martin Luther King, Jr. Cambridge, MA: Belknap Press of Harvard University Press.

9. Reider, J. (2008, May 22). Interview. Tavis Smiley. PBS. Retrieved from www.pbs.org/kcet/tavissmiley/archive/200805/20080522_rieder.html.

10. Reider, Interview.

11. Rothenberg, P. S. (Ed.). (1998). *Race, class, and gender in the United States.* New York, NY: St. Martin's Press.

12. New London Group. (1996). A pedagogy of multiliteracies: Designing social futures. *Harvard Educational Review* 66(1), 60–92.

13. Collier, M. J. (1994). Cultural identity and intercultural communication. In L. A. Samovar & R. E. Porter (Eds.), *Intercultural communication: A reader* (7th ed., pp. 36–45). Belmont, CA: Wadsworth.

14. O'Neil, D. (2006, July 5, last updated). Overview. Ethnicity and Race Tutorial. Palomar College, San Marcos, CA. Retrieved from http://anthro.palomar.edu/ethnicity/ethnic_1.htm.

15. Crowley, S. (2011, January 29). Black? White? Asian? More young Americans choose all of the above. *The New York Times.* Retrieved from www.nytimes.com/2011/01/30/us/30mixed.html?pagewanted=all.

16. Marmor, J. (1996, December). Blurring the lines. *Columns, 16*(8), 22–27.

17. Jameson, D. A. (2007, July). Reconceptualizing cultural identity and its role in intercultural business communication. *Journal of Business Communication, 44*(3), 199–235.

18. Jayson, S. (2010, February 10). Tech-savvy "iGeneration" kids multitask, connect. *USA Today.* Retrieved from http://usatoday30.usatoday.com/tech/news/2010-02-10-igeneration10_CV_N.htm.

19. Halstead, T. (1999, August). A politics for Generation X. *Atlantic Monthly, 284*(2), 33ff.

20. Oblinger, D. (2003, July/August). Boomers & Gen Xers & millenials: Understanding the new students. *EDUCAUSEreview.* Retrieved from https://net.educause.edu/ir/library/pdf/erm0342.pdf.

21. Jameson, Reconceptualizing cultural.

22. Jeanes, W. (2010, December 3). Does where you live determine what you drive? The Garreau Group. Retrieved

from http://autos.aol.com/article/what-people-drive-where/.

23. Rokeach, M. (1972). *Beliefs, attitudes, and values.* San Francisco: Jossey-Bass.

24. Jaffe, C. I. (1995). Chronemics: Communicating mainstream cycles to Russian Old Believer children. *World Communication, 15,* 1–20.

25. Levine, R. (1997). *A geography of time.* New York, NY: Basic Books.

26. McCroskey, J. C. (1993). *An introduction to rhetorical communication* (6th ed.). Englewood Cliffs, NJ: Prentice-Hall.

27. Weider, D. L., & Pratt, S. (1990). On being a recognizable Indian. In D. Carbaugh (Ed.), *Intercultural communication and intercultural contacts* (pp. 45–64). Hillsdale, NJ: Erlbaum.

28. Miller, A. N. (2002). An exploration of Kenyan public speaking patterns with implications for the American introductory public speaking course. *Communication Education, 5*(2), 168–182.

29. Charlesworth, D. (2009). Assign this: Considering lyrics as public speeches: Extending the application of audience analysis. *SPECTRA, 45*(7), 10.

CHAPTER 7

1. Purcell, K., Rainie, L., Heaps, A., Buchanan, J., Friedrich, L., Jacklin, A., Chen, C., & Zickuhr, K. (2012, November 1). How teens do research in the digital world. Pew Research Internet Project. Retrieved from www.pewinternet.org/2012/11/01/how-teens-do-research-in-the-digital-world/.

2. *Internet Wire.* (2006, November 14). College students fall short in demonstrating the ICT skills necessary for success in college and the workplace. Market Wire via Comtex.

3. Lieggi, L. (1999, July 20). Personal interview. George Fox University, Newberg, OR.

4. Janes, J. (2009, October). At the last minute. *American Libraries, 40*(10), 44.

5. Rolfe, A. (2008, May 21). Personal interview. George Fox University, Newberg, OR.

6. Leiggi, Personal interview.

7. Orwell, M. (n.d.). Job description of a reference librarian. eHow Money. Retrieved from www.ehow.com/facts_5548214_job-description-reference-librarian.html.

8. Head, A. J., & Eisenberg, M. B. (2009, December 1). Lessons learned: How

college students seek information in the digital age. Project Information Literacy Progress Report. The Information School. University of Washington. Downloaded from projectinfolit.org/pdfs/PIL_Fall2009_Year1Report_12_2009.pdf.

9. Yu, H., & Young, M. (2004). An impact of web search engines on subject searching in OPAC. *Information Technology and Libraries, 23,* 168–181. See also Abram, S., & Luther, J. (2004, May 1). Born with the chip: The next generation will profoundly impact both library service and the culture within the profession. *Library Journal, 129,* 34–38.

10. Johnson, F. C., & Craven, J. (2010). Beyond usability: The study of functionality of the 2.0 online catalogue (OPAC). *New Review of Academic Librarianship, 16,* 228–250. doi: 10.1080/13614533.2010.511845. p. 230.

11. Rand, A. D. (2010). Mediating at the student-Wikipedia intersection. *Journal of Library Administration, 50,* 923–932. doi: 10.1080/01930826.2010.488994.

12. Head & Eisenberg, Lessons learned; see also Schweitzer, N. J. (2008). Wikipedia and psychology: Coverage of concepts and its use by undergraduate students. *Teaching of Psychology, 35,* 81–85.

13. Janes, Last minute.

14. Lever, T. (2009, Autumn). Wikipedia: What's in it for teachers? *Screen Education, 53,* 38–42.

15. Economist Intelligence Unit N.A. Incorporated. (2011, January 15). Wikipleadia: User-generated content. *The Economist US, 398*(8716), 69. Retrieved from www.economist.com/node/17911276.

16. Snyder, J. (2013). Wikipedia: Librarians' perspectives on its use as a reference source. *Reference & User Services Quarterly, 53*(2), 155–163.

17. Rand, Mediating at.

18. Lever, Wikipedia.

19. Shaw, D. (2008, February/March). Wikipedia in the newsroom. *American Journalism Review,* 40–45.

20. Peck, R. (2012, May 28). New media versus legacy journalism. NoLaVie: Life and Culture in New Orleans. Retrieved from http://nolavie.com/2012/05/new-media-versus-legacy-journalism-33958.html.

21. Jurkowitz, M. (2014, March 26). The growth in digital reporting. Pew Research Journalism Project. Retrieved

from www.journalism.org/2014/03/26/the-growth-in-digital-reporting/.

22. Olmstead, K., Mitchell, A., & Holcomb, J. (2014, March 26). Developments in online news video content. Pew Research Journalism Project. Retrieved from www.journalism.org/2014/03/26/developments-in-online-news-video-content/.

23. Sullivan, A. (2008, November 1). Why I blog. *The Atlantic*. Retrieved from www.theatlantic.com/magazine/archive/2008/11/why-i-blog/307060/2/.

24. Yale University. (n.d.). Informational steps & tips. Yale Undergraduate and Career Services. Retrieved from http://ucs.yalecollege.yale.edu/sites/default/files/InformationalInterviews.pdf.

25. This is the slogan of TED: Ideas worth spreading at www.ted.org.

26. Miller, A. N. (2002). An exploration of Kenyan public speaking patterns with implications for the American introductory public speaking course. *Communication Education*, 5(2), 174.

27. *Internet Wire*, College students fall short.

28. O'Hanlon, N., & Diaz, K. R. (2010, March). Techniques for enhancing reflection and learning in an online course. *MERLOT Journal of Online Learning and Teaching*, 6(1), 43–54.

29. Calkins, S., & Kelley, M. R. (2007, Fall) Evaluating Internet and scholarly sources across the disciplines: Two case studies. *College Teaching*, 55(4), 151–156.

30. O'Hanlon & Diaz, Techniques for enhancing.

31. University of Maryland Libraries. (2014). Primary, secondary, and tertiary sources. University of Maryland. Retrieved from www.lib.umd.edu/tl/guides/primary-sources.

32. Calkins & Kelley, Evaluating Internet.

33. Newsy. (2014). About Newsy. Retrieved from www.newsy.com/about/.

34. www.msnbc.com.

35. www.nationalreview.com.

36. Bruft, D. (2014, February 27). Student notetaking for recall and understanding: A lit review review. Center for Teaching. Vanderbilt University. Retrieved from http://cft.vanderbilt.edu/2014/02/student-notetaking-for-recall-and-understanding-a-lit-review-review/.

37. Anonymous reviewer. (2008).

38. Paragraph 107: Fair use. (2004, April 30). Copyright Law of the United States of America. Title 17. Circular 92. Chapter 1. Retrieved from www.copyright.gov/title17/92chap1.html.

39. The International DOI Foundation. (n.d.). Frequently asked questions about the DOI system: What is a DOI name? Retrieved from www.doi.org/faq.html#1.

40. APA Style. (n.d.). Basics of APA Style tutorial. Retrieved from http://flash1r.apa.org/apastyle/basics/index.htm.

CHAPTER 8

1. Ridley, M. (2014, March 27). Climate forecast: Muting the alarm. *The Wall Street Journal*. Retrieved from http://online.wsj.com/news/articles/SB10001424052702303725404579460973643962840?mg=reno64-wsj&url=http%3A%2F%2Fonline.wsj.com%2Farticle%2FSB10001424052702303725404579460973643962840.html.

2. The Internet has many articles about dissenters such as Bjorn Lomborg. Some issues are outlined in Elmhirst, S. (2010, September 27). I didn't want to be the gay guy who talks about the environment. *New Statesman*, 132(5020), 30–31. See also Bailey, R. (2008, October). The rational environmentalist: Bjorn Lomborg on the priorities that should come before global warming. *Reason*, 40(5), 46–54.

3. BIO Classroom. (2013). Black history little known facts. Biography.com. Retrieved from www.biography.com/tv/classroom/black-history-little-known-facts.

4. Stoner, R., Chow, M. L., Boyle, M. P., Sunkin, S. M., Mouton, P. R., Roy, S., Wynshaw-Boris, A., Colamarino, S. A., Lein E. S., & Courchesne, E. (2014). Patches of disorganization in the neocortex of children with autism. *New England Journal of Medicine*, 370, 1209–1219. doi: 10.1056/NEJMoa1307491.

5. *Merriam-Webster Dictionary*. (n.d.). Scholar. Retrieved from www.merriam-webster.com/dictionary/scholar.

6. Isaacs, E. (2012, July). What does it mean to be a scholar in the 21st century? Address delivered April 19, 2012, at the Lewis University Celebration of Scholarship, Romeoville, IL. *Vital Speeches*, 78(7), 238–243.

7. Skoloff, B., & Baumann, L. (2014, March 27). Mudslide crews face daunting task in body search. Associated Press. Retrieved from http://hosted.ap.org/dynamic/stories/U/US_WASHINGTON_MUDSLIDE?SITE=AP&SECTION=HOME&TEMPLATE=DEFAULT&CTIME=2014-03-27-12-54-19.

8. Hagen, S. (2011, August). The commencement address I won't give. Address delivered May 14, 2011, at Birmingham-Southern College, Birmingham, AL. *Vital Speeches*, 77(8), 291–294.

9. BreakTheChain.org. (2001, July 26, last updated). That's one dumb shrub. Retrieved from www.breakthechain.org/exclusives/bushiq.html.

10. Snopes.com. (2013, April 10, last updated). Water works. Urban Legends Reference Pages. Retrieved from www.snopes.com/medical/myths/8glasses.asp.

11. Freeman, A. (2014, Spring). Criminalizing mental illness. Informative speech. George Fox University, Newberg, OR.

12. Sepich, R. (2010–2011). America's infrastructure problem [Competitive speech]. Northwest Forensics Conference: Mount Hood Community College.

13. Statistic Brain. (2013, January 1). Twitter statistics. Retrieved from www.statisticbrain.com/twitter-statistics/.

14. Stephenson, S. (2011, May 19). Pile of debt would stretch beyond stratosphere. Reuters News. Retrieved from www.reuters.com/article/2011/05/19/us-usa-debt-size-idUSTRE-74I5TL20110519. See also Demonocracy.Info. (n.d.). U.S. Debt ceiling visualized in $100 bills. Retrieved from http://demonocracy.info/infographics/usa/us_debt/us_debt.html.

15. IHTD. (2013). How much is a trillion dollars? If I Had a Trillion Dollars Youth Film Festival. Retrieved from http://ihtd.org/festivalguide/resources/how-much-is-a-trillion-dollars/.

16. Lehner, U. C. (2011, July 19). If health is wealth, cities are richer. Letter From the Editor. *DTN: The Progressive Farmer*, Retrieved from www.dtnprogressive-farmer.com/dtnag/common/link.do;jsessionid=0F0776EB2971F0BAEC164E14B0ED37BE.agfreejvm2?symbolicName=/free/news/template1&product=/ag/news/bestofdtnpf&vendorReference=03c04f6a-bd64-4713-ac52-9066f87bb730_-1311938424149&paneContentId=88&paneParentId=0.

17. *CNN Money*. (2014, April 17). Cost of living: How far will my salary

go in another city? Retrieved from http://money.cnn.com/calculator/pf/cost-of-living/.

18. Szalavitz, M. (2010, October 12). The marijuana number that was too good to check. *Time*. Retrieved from http://healthland.time.com/2010/10/12/the-marijuana-number-that-was-too-good-to-check/.

19. The Free Library. (2004). CDC admits obesity stats flawed, other serious errors documented in CCF report; pharmaceutical and weight loss industry heavily involved in misleading research. Retrieved from www.thefreelibrary.com/CDC+Admits+Obesity+Stats+Flawed,+Other+Serious+Errors+Documented+in. . . -a0125154558.

20. The Free Library, CDC admits.

21. National Center for Victims of Crime. (2000). Crime and victimization in America: Statistical overview. Retrieved from www.ncvc.org.

22. MacIntyre, A. (1981). *After virtue: A study in moral reasoning* (2nd ed.). South Bend, IN: University of Notre Dame Press.

23. Camacho, N. (2012, Fall). Obsessive-compulsive disorder [Student speech]. George Fox University, Newberg, OR.

24. Weichbrocht, C. (2008, Spring). Needed: A grief support system on campus [Student speech]. George Fox University, Newberg, OR.

25. Miller, A. N. (2002). An exploration of Kenyan public speaking patterns with implications for the American introductory public speaking course. *Communication Education, 5*(2), 168–182.

26. Jones, N. (2014, March). Latchkey children [Student speech]. George Fox University, Newberg, OR.

27. Associated Press. (2008, March 4). Gang memoir is a total fabrication. CBS News. Retrieved from www.cbsnews.com/stories/2008/03/04/entertainment/main3903246.shtml.

28. Perkins, J. (2011, April 22). Letter to the Editor. *Virginia Law Weekly, 63*(26). University of Virginia. Retrieved from www.lawweekly.org/?module=displaystory&story_id=3368&edition_id=180&format=html; see also Press release. (2011, May 6). Law student who alleged police misconduct recants story, clears university police. *UVA Today*. Retrieved from www.virginia.edu/uvatoday/newsRelease.php?id=14982.

29. Glover, M. (2012, September 6). Boy describes rear-end school bus crash in Byron, Minn. KMSP-TV. Retrieved from www.myfoxtwincities.com/story/19468727/victim-witness-of-rear-end-school-bus-crash-describe-scene. See also Capacio, S. & Beno, L. (2012, October 23). Police: Byron teen killed in crash on first day of school was texting. KMSP-TV. Retrieved from www.myfoxtwincities.com/story/19897049/police-teen-killed-in-crash-on-first-day-of-school-was-texting.

30. Healing Horse Therapy Center. (2013). Retrieved from http://healinghorsecenter.wix.com/healing-begins#!services1/c1gth.

31. Wilson, P. (1983). *Second-hand knowledge: An inquiry into cognitive authority.* Westport, CT: Greenwood.

32. Both examples come from Edde, A. (2014, January 20). Special needs children find help in horses through equine therapy programs. *Miami Herald.* Retrieved from www.miamiherald.com/2014/01/20/3882411/finding-help-in-horses.html.

33. Edde, Special needs children.

34. Aboseh, M. B. M. (2012). Proverbs as theoretical frameworks for lifelong learning in indigenous African education. *Adult Education Quarterly, 63*(3), 236–250. doi: 10.1177/0741713612462601. See also Tembo, M. S. (1999, April). Your mother is still your mother. *World and I, 14,* 4.

35. Owomoyela, O. (2005). *Yoruba proverbs,* 1179 (p. 138). Omaha: University of Nebraska Press.

36. Odom is quoted in McMenamin, D. (2011, February 11). Lamar Odom gets stitches to close gash. ESPN. Retrieved from http://sports.espn.go.com/los-angeles/nba/news/story?id=6111516.

37. Khan, L. A. (2002, January 15). A century of great awakenings: "We have learned much about ourselves." Speech delivered May 4, 1950, at the US Senate, Washington, DC. *Vital Speeches of the Day, 68*(7), 222–225.

38. Sepich, America's infrastructure problem.

39. Hagen, Most commencement addresses.

40. Slade, C. (2003). "Seeing reasons": Visual argumentation in advertisements. *Argumentation, 17,* 14–160. ISSN: 0920-427X.

41. Jeong, S.-H. (2008, March). Visual metaphor in advertising: Is the persuasive effect attributable to visual argumentation or metaphorical rhetoric? *Journal of Marketing Communication, 14*(1), 59–73.

42. Jeong, S.-H. (2006). Persuasive effect of visual metaphor in advertising: Is it attributable to metaphorical rhetoric or visual argumentation? Conference Paper. International Communication Association. Communication and Mass Media Complete database.

43. LaWare, M. R. (1998). Encountering visions of Aztlan: Arguments for ethnic pride, community activism and cultural revitalization in Chicano murals. *Argumentation and Advocacy, 34,* 140–153.

44. LaWare, Encountering visions, p. 153.

CHAPTER 9

1. Choi, E. (2010). Personal interview (edited remarks).

2. Miller, G. A. (1956). The magical number seven, plus or minus two: Some limits on our capacity for processing information. *The Psychological Review, 63,* 81–97.

3. Anonymous reviewer. (2010).

4. Spradling, J. (n.d.) The cycle of violence. Office of the Kansas Attorney General. Retrieved from www.hruth.org/files/library/CycleofViolence.pdf.

5. Fuentes, E. (2014, March). Rap influence around the world [Student speech]. George Fox University, Newberg, OR.

6. Fekkes, T. (2010). Negative political advertisements [Student speech]. George Fox University, Newberg, OR.

7. Gentry, R. (2010). Perceptions of beauty: The media's influence over Asian women [Student speech]. George Fox University, Newberg, OR.

8. Hewitt, E. J. (2014). The importance of maintaining the attendance policy [Student outline]. George Fox University, Newberg, OR.

9. Grozav, E. (2014). Class attendance in college [Student outline]. George Fox University, Newberg, OR.

10. These stereotypes came from Merskin, D. (2007). Three faces of Eva: Perpetuation of the hot-Latina stereotype in *Desperate Housewives. Howard J. of Communications, 18,* 133–151. doi: 10.1080/106-4170701309890.

11. McMinn, M. (2011, March 1). Faculty lecture. George Fox University, Newberg, OR.

12. Bloch, M. (1975). *Political language and oratory in traditional society*. London: Academic Press.

13. Miller, A. N. (2002). An exploration of Kenyan public speaking patterns with implications for the American introductory public speaking course. *Communication Education, 5*(2), 168–182.

14. Keagle, J. (2011). Tech waste: A growing American problem [Student speech]. George Fox University, Newberg, OR.

15. Engen, D. E. (2005). The civic awareness and imagination assignment. *Communication Teacher, 10*(3), 80–83.

16. Zhang, Z. (2014). Chinese traditional wedding customs [Student speech]. George Fox University, Newberg, OR.

17. Burchett, C. (2014). *Rosca de Reyes* [Student speech]. George Fox University, Newberg, OR.

18. Jorgensen-Earp, C. (n.d.). "Making other arrangements": Alternative patterns of disposition [Unpublished course handout]. Lynchburg, VA: Lynchburg College.

19. Zediker, K. (1993, February). Rediscovering the tradition: Women's history with a relational approach to the basic public speaking course. Panel presentation at the Western States Communication Association, Albuquerque, NM.

20. King, M. L. Jr. (1963, August 28). I have a dream [Speech delivered at the March on Washington]. Retrieved from www.youtube.com/watch?v=smEqnnklfYs.

21. Anonymous reviewer. (2010).

CHAPTER 10

1. Quintilian. (1920–1922). *The instituto oratoria of Quintilian* (4 vols., H. E. Butler, trans.) The Loeb Classical Library. Cambridge, MA: Harvard University Press.

2. Veninga, R. L. (2010, June 22). Floods, oil spills, tornados: The psychology of resilience. Speech delivered June 9, 2010, at the Detroit Economic Club, Detroit, MI. *Vital Speeches of the Day, 76*(9), 390–392.

3. Cutter, L. (2014, Spring). Walt Disney [Student speech]. George Fox University, Newberg, OR.

4. Holiday, A. (2010, Fall). ACL injuries in the female athlete [Student speech]. George Fox University, Newberg, OR.

5. Li, Z. (2014, Spring). Anerobic and aerobic exercise [Student speech]. George Fox University, Newberg, OR.

6. Manninen, A. (2014, Spring). Sleep deprivation [Student speech]. George Fox University, Newberg, OR.

7. Hingston, T. (2014, Spring). Show jumping [Student speech]. George Fox University, Newberg, OR.

8. Cooper, J. (2014, Spring). Division I athletes should be paid [Student speech]. George Fox University, Newberg, OR.

9. Garvison, K. (2014, Spring). Power napping [Student outline]. George Fox University, Newberg, OR.

10. Lapahie, H., Jr., (2001). Diné clans. LAPAHIE 5.1. Retrieved from www.lapahie.com/Dine_Clans.cfm; see also Office of Diné Culture, Language, and Community Services. (n.d.) Unit 11: NAHAT'/ / Division of Diné Culture. Retrieved from www.nmcn.org/heritage/dine_-culture/nahatagvt.pdf.

11. Braithwaite, C. A. (1997). *Sa'ah Naagháí Bak'eh Hòzhóón:* An ethnography of Navajo educational communication practices. *Communication Education, 46,* 219–233.

12. Grozav, E. (2014, Spring). Safe drinking water [Student speech]. George Fox University, Newberg, OR.

13. Centers for Disease Control and Prevention. (2014, February 11, last updated). Zombie Preparedness. Office of Public Health Preparedness and Response. Retrieved from www.cdc.gov/phpr/zombies.htm.

14. Rimes, H. (2014, Spring). The pros and cons of yoga [Student speech]. George Fox University, Newberg, OR.

15. Weinert, J. (2012, Fall). Dueling in America [Student speech]. George Fox University, Newberg, OR.

16. Grozav, Safe drinking.

17. Roppe, Z. (2012, Fall). Musical frisson [Student speech]. George Fox University, Newberg, OR.

18. Nevils, B. (2010, Fall). Retirement planning [Student speech]. George Fox University, Newberg, OR.

19. Grozav, Safe drinking.

20. Elmer, R. (2010, Fall). Photoshopped perfection [Student speech]. George Fox University, Newberg, OR.

21. Lamebull, S. (1997). Industrial hemp [Competitive student speech]. Mt. Hood Community College, Gresham, OR.

22. Grozav, Safe drinking.

23. Nordstrom, L. (2010). No-wheeled car or dry boat? [Student speech]. George Fox University, Newberg, OR.

24. Persons, B. (2004, Fall). Driving while drowsy [Student speech]. George Fox University, Newberg, OR.

25. Anonymous Reviewer. (2010).

26. Choi, E. (2010). Personal interview.

27. Dodge, L. (2012). Homelessness in Portland [Student speech]. George Fox University, Newberg, OR.

28. Elmer, Photoshopped.

29. Duncan, C. (2011, December). Virtue and vocation: Habits for the journey. [Address delivered at the opening convocation, Wittenberg University, Springfield, OH, August 28, 2011]. *Vital Speeches of the Day, 77*(12), 414–419.

CHAPTER 11

1. McCombs, C. (2014, Spring). Campaigns [Student speech]. George Fox University, Newberg, OR.

2. Gentry, R. (2010). Perceptions of beauty: The media's influence over Asian women [Student speech]. George Fox University, Newberg, OR.

3. Freeman, A. (2014). Criminalizing mental illness [Student speech]. George Fox University, Newberg, OR.

4. Nordstrom, L. (2010). No-wheeled car or dry boat? [Student speech]. George Fox University, Newberg, OR.

5. Riverdale School. (1999, December 14). Preparing the delivery outline. Riverdale School speech class, upper grades. Retrieved from www.teleport.com/beanman/english/delivout.html.

6. *SNOW*. (1999). Thinking and learning skills. University of Toronto. Retrieved from http://snow.utoronto.ca/learn2/introll.html.

7. Irvine, J. J., & York, D. E. (1995). *Learning styles and culturally diverse students: A literature review.* (ERIC Document Reproduction Service No. ED382 722 UDO3046)

8. Riding, R., & Cheerman, I. (1991). Cognitive styles—an overview and integration. *Educational Psychology, 11,* 193–215.

9. Tomlinson, C. A. (2009, February). Learning profiles and achievement: Do learning preferences have a place in promoting student success in the classroom? *School Administrator, 66*(2), 28–34.

10. Hermann-Nehdi, A. (2010, May). Whole brain thinking: Ignore it at your peril. *T+D, 64*(5), 36–42.

11. Jorgensen-Earp, C. (n.d.). "Making other arrangements": Alternative patterns of disposition [Unpublished course handout]. Lynchburg, VA: Lynchburg College.

CHAPTER 12

1. Berman, J. (2012, February 28). How to talk like a local. *ABC Nightly News*. Retrieved from www.abcnews.go.com/WTN/video/dictionary-celebrates0diversity-language015812788.

2. Kimble, J. (2006). Lifting the fog of legalese. Durham, NC: Durham Academic Press, p. xii. Retrieved from www.cap-press.com/pdf/1549.pdf.

3. Trudgill, P. (2000). *Sociolinguistics: An introduction to language and society* (4th ed.). New York: NY: Penguin Books.

4. Gozzi, R. (1990). *New words and a changing American culture*. Columbia, SC: University of South Carolina Press.

5. Cited in R. Engnell. (2010). Senior capstone: Ethical and spiritual dimensions of communication. George Fox University, Newberg, OR.

6. Whorf, B. L. (1956). *Language, thought, and reality*. Quotations from Benjamin Lee Whorf. Retrieved from http://mtsu32.mtsu.edu:11072/Whorf/blwquotes.html.

7. *Oxford English Dictionary*. (2014, March). What's new: March 2014 update. Oxford University Press. Retrieved from http://public.oed.com/whats-new/.

8. ESPN Classic. (2002, August 16). Lakers broadcaster Chick Hearn dies at 85. Associated Press. Retrieved from https://espn.go.com/classic/obit/s/2002/0805/1414492.html.

9. Gozzi, *New words*.

10. Range. (2002). Oxford dictionaries. Retrieved from www.oxforddictionaries.com/definition/english/range.

11. Kluger, J. (2013, January 15). The end of an epithet: How hate speech dies. *Time*. Retrieved from http://healthland.time.com/2013/01/25/the-end-of-an-epithet-how-hate-speech-dies/.

12. Delwiche, A. (2002, September 29). Propaganda: Euphemisms. Propaganda Critic. Retrieved from www.propagandacritic.com/articles/ct.wg.euphemism.html.

13. Dialects doing well. (1998). InSCIght on Apnet. Retrieved from www.apnet.com/inscight/02181009/graphb.htm.

14. Reider, J. (2008). *The Word of the Lord is upon me: The righteous performance of Martin Luther King, Jr*. Cambridge, MA: Belknap Press of Harvard University Press.

15. Quoted in Oral Communication Center. (2011). Spoken vs. written language. Hamilton College, Hamilton, Clinton, NY. Retrieved from www.hamilton.edu/oralcommunication/spoken-language-vs-written-language.

16. DeVito, J. A. (1965). Comprehension factors in oral and written discourse of skilled communicators. *Speech Monographs, 32*, 124–128.

17. Ferraro, V., & Palmer, K. C. (n.d.). Differences between oral and written communication. Retrieved from www.mtholyoke.edu/acad/intrel/speech/-differences.htm.

18. Stern, J. D. (2009, August). Making smarter movies. Speech delivered June 20, 2009, to the Los Angeles Film Festival, Los Angeles, CA. *Vital Speeches of the Day, 75*(8), 347–352.

19. Greidanus, S. (2007). *Preaching Christ from Genesis: Foundations for expository sermons*. Grand Rapids, MI: Eerdmans.

20. Anderson, J. W. (1991). A comparison of Arab and American conceptions of "effective persuasion." In L. A. Samovar & R. E. Porter (Eds.). *Intercultural communication: A reader* (5th ed., pp. 96–106). Belmont, CA: Wadsworth.

21. Thyne, C. (2012). Stem-cell research [Student speech]. George Fox University, Newberg, OR.

22. Lessing, D. (2008, February). Not winning the Nobel Prize: Lecture given December 7, 2007, to the Nobel Peace Prize Committee, Oslo, Norway. *Vital Speeches of the Day, 74*(2), 72–73.

23. Reagan, R. (1986, January 31). Address on the *Challenger* disaster. Nationally televised speech. Available on www.youtube.com/watch?v=gEjXjfxoNXM.

24. Scherer, J. J. (2010, August). Go for tov: Learning to "come home to yourself." Speech delivered May 1, 2010, at the commencement ceremony for Roanoke College, Salem, VA. *Vital Speeches of the Day, 76*(8), 351–354.

25. The first two examples came from www.americanrhetoric.com.

26. Lamm, R. D. (2005). How to make an environmentalist. Speech delivered January 27, 2005, at the Thorne Ecological Institute 50th Anniversary, *Vital Speeches of the Day, 71*(10), 304–306.

27. Brody, W. J. (2007, November). What's promised, what's possible. Speech delivered September 7, 2007, to the National Press Club, Washington, DC. *Vital Speeches of the Day, 73*(11).

28. Peters, D. (2000, May). Sweet seduction. *Chatelaine, 73*(5), 53.

29. Osborn, M. (1997). The play of metaphors. *Education, 118*(1), 84–87.

30. Panelist. (2008, June 12). *Life on the Rock* (Encore). EWTN Television.

31. Seattle. (1971). The Indian's night promises to be dark. In W. C. Vanderwerth (Ed.), *Indian oratory: Famous speeches by noted Indian chieftains* (pp. 118–122). Norman: University of Oklahoma Press. (Original work published 1853)

32. Osborn, M. (1967). Archetypal metaphor in rhetoric: The lightdark family. *Quarterly Journal of Speech, 53*, 115–126. See also Osborn, M. (1977). The evolution of the archetypal sea in rhetoric and poetic. *Quarterly Journal of Speech, 63*, 347–363.

33. Seattle. The Indian's night.

34. Blankenship, K. L., & Holtgraves. (2005, March). The role of different markers of linguistic powerlessness in persuasion. *Journal of Language and Social Psychology, 24*(1), 3–24. doi: 10.1177/0261927X04273034.

35. Blankenship, K. L., & Craig, T. Y. (2007, March). Powerless language markers and the correspondence bias. *Journal of Language and Social Psychology, 26*(1), 28–47. doi: 10.1177/0261927X06296470.

36. Johannesen, R. L., Valde, K. S., & Wheedbee, K. E. (2008). *Ethics in human communication* (6th ed.). Long Grove, IL: Waveland Press.

37. Emory University Department of Religion. (2001, December 6). *Statement on inclusive language*. Retrieved from www.emory.edu/COLLEGE/RELIGION/about/statement.html.

38. Seiter, J. S., Larsen, J., & Skinner, J. (1998). "Handicapped" or "handicapable"? The effects of language about persons with disabilities on perceptions of source credibility and persuasiveness. *Communication Reports, 11*(1), 21–31.

39. Currey, J., & Mumford, K. (2002, September 18). Just talk: Guide to inclusive language. University of Tasmania. Retrieved from http://student.admin.utas.

edu.au/services/just_talk/Disability/
disability.htm.

40. Lean In. (2014, March 14). Ban bossy—I'm not bossy. I'm the boss. Retrieved from http://youtube.com/watch?v=6dynbzMiCcw#aid=P9LGX_U3Oug.

41. Thiederman, S. (1991). *Bridging cultural barriers for corporate success: How to manage the multicultural workforce*. New York, NY: Lexington; see also Thiederman, S. (1991). *Profiting in American multicultural market places: How to do business across cultural lines*. New York, NY: Lexington.

42. Lustig, M. W., & Koester, J. (1993). *Intercultural competence: Interpersonal communication across cultures*. New York, NY: HarperCollins; see also Simons, G. F., Vazquez, C., & Harris, P. R. (1993). *Transcultural leadership: Empowering the diverse workforce*. Houston, TX: Gulf.

CHAPTER 13

1. Widder, E. (2010, April). Glowing life in an underwater world. Retrieved from www.ted.com/talks/lang/eng/edith_widder_glowing_life_in_an_underwater_world.html.

2. Clark, J. (2008, Winter). PowerPoint and pedagogy: Maintaining student interest in university lectures. *College Teaching, 56*(1), 39–45.

3. Wall, T. (2004, October). PowerPoint pitfalls that can kill an audience's will to stay awake. *Presentations, 18*(10), 46.

4. Hartland, W., Biddle, C., & Fallacaro, M. (2008, June). Audiovisual facilitation of clinical knowledge: A paradigm for dispersed student education based on Paivio's dual coding theory. *AANA Journal, 76*(3), 194–198.

5. Marketwire Canada. (2009, October 7). m62 highlights difference between visual aids and useless photos. Canadian Corporate News/Comtex.

6. Mackiewicz, J. (2008). Comparing PowerPoint experts' and university students' opinions about PowerPoint presentations. *Journal of Technical Writing and Communication, 38*(2), 149–165.

7. Wall, PowerPoint pitfalls.

8. Quoted in Martinez, M. (2010, November). New literacies for a new era: Learning to read words is no longer enough; students must learn to be visually literate too. *Phi Delta Kappan, 92*(13), 72–74.

9. Marketwire Canada, m62 highlights.

10. Wall, PowerPoint pitfalls

11. Comtext, m62 highlights.

12. Mackiewicz, Comparing PowerPoint.

13. Katt, J., Murdock, J., Butler, J., & Pryor, B. (2008). Establishing best practices for the use of PowerPoint as a presentation aid. *Human Communication, 11*(1), 193–200.

14. Ezekiel 4:1–3.

15. Cicero, De Orator 2:266–267. Summarized in Beacham, R. C. (1999). *Spectacle entertainments of early Imperial Rome* (p. 38). New Haven, CT: Yale University Press.

16. Muhovic, E. (2000). Visual aids for presentations. Center for Managerial Communications, Denver University. Retrieved from www.du.edu/emuhovic/visualpresentations.html.

17. Tufte, E. (2004). PowerPoint is evil. Wired. Retrieved from http://archive.wired.com/wired/archive/11.09/ppt2_pr.html.

18. Doumont, J.-L. (2005, February). The cognitive style of PowerPoint: Slides are not all evil. *Technical Communication, 52*(1), 64–71.

19. Radel, J. (1999, July). *Effective presentations*. University of Kansas Medical Center online tutorial series. Retrieved from http://KUMC.edu/SAH/OTEd/jradel/effective.html.

20. AV Technology. (2009, March 6). Document cameras. NewsBay Media. Retrieved from http://avtechnologyonline.com/article/27094.aspx.

21. Presentation tips: "Document camera." (2004, February 18). University of Wisconsin–Madison. Retrieved from www2.fpm.wisc.edu/support/PresentationTips.htm.

22. Anonymous reviewer (1994).

23. Hernandez, T. (2004, December). Digital whiteboards allow design teams to capture plan markups. *Building Design & Construction, 45*, 19–21.

24. Anonymous reviewer. (1994).

25. Five keys to effective handouts. (1997, October 13). *Buffalo Business First*. Retrieved from http://buffalo.bizjournals.com/buffalo/stories/1997/10/13/smallb3.html.

26. Anonymous reviewer.

27. Katt et al., Establishing best practices.

28. Reynolds, G. (2006, August 30). From design to meaning: A whole new way of presenting? Retrieved from www.presentationzen.com/presentationzen/2006/08/from_design_to_.html.

29. Glazer, E. (2009, Summer). A process for Web design. TC801. Retrieved from https://www.msu.edu/~glazered/tc801/index.html.

30. Reynolds, G. (2005, September 5). What is good PowerPoint design? Retrieved from http://presentationzen.blogs.com/presentationzen/2005/09/whats_good_powe.html.

31. Poole, A. (2010). Which are more legible: Serif or sans serif typefaces? Retrieved from http://alexpoole.info/which-are-more-legible-serif-or-sans-serif-typefaces.

32. Shaikh, A. D., Chaparro, B. S., & Fox, D. (2006, February). Perception of fonts: Perceived personality traits and uses. *Usability News, 8*(1). Retrieved from http://psychology.wichita.edu/surl/usabilitynews/81/PersonalityofFonts.asp.

33. The facts about fonts. (2003, December). *PR Newswire*. Retrieved from InfoTrac College Edition database.

34. Bennett, J. (2008, April 7). Just go to Helvetica. (Design). *Newsweek, 151*(14), 54.

35. Great FX Business Cards. (2005, March 21). Using color to your marketing advantage. Retrieved from www.greatfxbusinesscards.com/colorandemotions.htm.

36. Great FX Business Cards, Using color.

37. Anonymous reviewer.

CHAPTER 14

1. Decker, B., & Decker, K. (2012, December 18). The top ten best (and worst) communicators of 2012. Decker Communications. Retrieved from http://decker.com/blog/tag/top-ten-best-and-worst-speakers/.

2. Hypes, M. G., Turner, E. T., Norris, C. M., & Wollferts, L. C. (1999, January). How to be a successful presenter. *Journal of Physical Education, Recreation & Dance, 70*(1), 50–53.

3. Unless noted otherwise, most suggestions in this section come from Schwartz, A. E. (1988, August). Rehearsing: Key to avoiding training chaos. *Training and Development Journal, 42*(8), 15–17.

4. Kaye, S. (1999, March). Make an impact with style: Presentation tips for leaders.

IIE Solutions, 31(3), 26(2). Retrieved from InfoTrac College Edition database.

5. Kampmann, M., & Rosen, J. (1991, January). Speaking with confidence. *Supervisory Management, 36*(1), 3.

6. Schwartz, Rehearsing.

7. McDonald, C. A. (2008, June). Email interview.

8. Schwartz, Rehearsing.

9. Kaye, Make an impact.

10. These tips draw from Schwartz, Rehearsing.

11. Reider, J. (2008). *The Word of the Lord is upon me: The righteous performance of Martin Luther King, Jr.* Cambridge, MA: Belknap Press of Harvard University Press.

12. Anonymous reviewer. (2010).

13. Hoogestraat, W. E. (1960). Memory: The lost canon? *Quarterly Journal of Speech, 46*(2), 141–148.

14. Anonymous reviewer. (2008).

15. Keefe, J. (1988, August) Drama lessons for speakers. *Meetings & Conventions 33*(9), 30.

16. Schwartz, Rehearsing.

17. Keefe, Drama lessons.

18. Montalbo, T. (1980). Churchill: A study in oratory. Seven lessons in speechmaking from one of the greatest orators of all time. The Churchill Centre. Retrieved from www.winstonchurchill.org/i4apages/index.cfm?pageid+814.

19. Bippus, A. M., & Daly, J. A. (1999). What do people think causes stage fright? Naïve attributions about the reasons for public speaking anxiety. *Communication Education, 48*, 63–72.

20. Arthur, A. (1997, July). Keeping up public appearances: Master the fine art of public-speaking and give a great presentation every time. *Black Enterprise, 27*(12), 5.

21. Goffman, E. (1959). *The presentation of self in everyday life*. Garden City, NY: Doubleday Anchor.

22. Gullberg, M., & Holmqvist, K. (2006). What speakers do and what addressees look at: Visual attention to gestures in human interaction live and on video. *Pragmatics & Cognition, 14*(1), 53–82.

23. Ekman, P., & Friesen, W. V. (1969). The repertoire of nonverbal behavior: Categories, origins, usage, and coding. *Semiotica, I*, 49–98.

24. Morgan, N. (2004, Winter). Preparing to be real. *Harvard Management Communication Letter, 1*(1), 3–5.

25. Hansen, J. (2010, September). Teaching without talking: Teachers need to be aware of more than just the words they speak to children. They also need to monitor the nonverbal messages that they're sending to students through proximity, eye contact, gestures, and touching. *Phi Delta Kappan, 91*(10), 35–41.

26. Kempmann & Rosen, Speaking with confidence.

27. Brody, M. (1998, August). Delivering your speech right between their eyes. *American Salesman, 43*(8), 29–31.

28. Brody, M. (1994, June). Delivering your speech right between their eyes. *Supervision, 55*(8), 18.

29. Richmond, V. P., & McCroskey, J. C. (2000). *Nonverbal behavior in interpersonal relations* (4th ed.). Scottsdale, AZ: Gorsuch Scarisbrick.

30. Lev-Ari, S., & Keysar, B. (2010). Why don't we believe non-native speakers? The influence of accent on credibility. *Journal of Experimental Social Psychology, 46*, 1093–1096. doi: 10.1016/jesp2010.05.025.

31. Montalbon, Churchill.

32. Richmond, V. P., McCroskey, J. C., & Payne, S. K. (1991). *Nonverbal behavior in interpersonal relations* (2nd ed.). Englewood Cliffs, NJ: Prentice Hall. See also FIU Oral Presentation Lab. (n.d.). Cultural issues and public address. Florida International University, Miami, FL. Retrieved from http://opl.fiu.edu/cultural.htm.

33. FIU Oral Presentation Lab, Cultural issues.

34. Krompacky, Y. H. (1993, March 21). Immigrants, don't be in such a hurry to shed your accents. *The New York Times*, Sec. 4, p. 16.

35. Aristotle. (1984). *The Rhetoric*. (H. R. Roberts, Trans.). New York, NY: The Modern Library. (Original translation published 1954)

36. Summarized in Burgoon, J. K., Buller, D. B., & Woodall, W. G. (1989). *Nonverbal communication: The unspoken dialogue*. New York, NY: Harper & Row; see also Ray, G. B. (1986). Vocally cued personality prototypes: An implicit personality theory approach. *Communication Monographs, 53*, 266–276.

37. Burgoon et al., Nonverbal communication.

38. Morgan, Preparing to be real.

39. Morgan, Preparing to be real.

40. The next three suggestions come from Toastmasters International. (n.d.). Vocal variety. Retrieved from www.angelfire.com/tn/bektoastmasters/Toastmasters5.html.

41. Davidson, W., & Kline, S. (1999, March). Ace your presentations. *Journal of Accountancy, 187*(3), 61. See also Hypes et al., Successful presenter.

42. Humphrey, J. (1998, May 15). Executive eloquence: A seven-fold path to inspirational leadership. Speech delivered November 25, 1997, to the Board of Trade, Metropolitan Toronto, Canada. *Vital Speeches, 64*(15), 468–471.

43. Hart, R. P., & Burks, D. O. (1972). Rhetorical sensitivity and social interaction. *Speech Monographs, 39*, 90.

44. Branham, R. J., & Pearce, W. B. (1996). The conversational frame in public address. *Communication Quarterly, 44*(4), 423–439.

45. Brookhiser, R. (1999, November 22). Weird Al: A troubled and alarming vice president. *National Review, 60*(22), 32–34. See also Shipman, C. (2000, December/January). Searching for Al. *George, 102*, 9.

46. Democracy in America [blog]. (2008, June 23). Sexism at the *Times*? *The Economist*. Retrieved from www.economist.com/blogs/democracyinamerica/2008/06/sexism_at_the_times.cfm.

47. Speech Studio. (2010). Guidelines for videotaping your speech. Cengage Learning.

48. Advanced Public Speaking Institute. (2014). Public speaking: Tips for television, videotape, and videoconferencing. Retrieved from www.public-speaking.org/public-speaking-tvvideo-article.htm.

49. Goffman, *The presentation of self*.

50. Anonymous reviewer, 2004.

CHAPTER 15

1. Neuman, W. R. (2010, February 4). Appraising information abundance: The Chronicle review. *Chronicle of Higher Education*. Retrieved from http://chronicle.com/article/Appraising-Information/63744/.

2. Davidson, J. (2005, January 15). Bombarded on all sides: Handling everyday information. Speech delivered September 29, 2004, to Land America,

Las Vegas, NV. *Vital Speeches of the Day,* 71(7), 212–217.

3. Edwards, R., & McDonald, J. L. (1993). Schema theory and listening. In A. D. Wolvin & C. G. Coakley (Eds.), *Perspectives on Listening* (pp. 60–77). Norwood, NJ: Ablex.

4. Information in this section comes from Fillible, R. (1988). Public speaking course handout. Oregon State University, Corvallis, OR.

5. Quotation retrieved from www.quotedb.com/quotes/1382.

6. General Assembly of the United Nations. (1948, December 10). Universal Declaration of Human Rights. Retrieved from www.un.org/Overview/rights.html.

7. UN News Centre. (2014, April 26). Senior UN official welcomes release of full preliminary results in Afghan vote. Retrieved from www.un.org/apps/news/story.asp?NewsID=47661#.U1w6vcfB30s.

8. UN News Centre. (2014, April 10). Providing West African communities with sound information crucial to preventing spread of Ebola. Retrieved from www.un.org/apps/news/story.asp?NewsID=47546&Cr=disease&Cr.

9. ACTFL. (n.d.). ACTFL certified proficiency testing programs (oral and written). American Council on the Teaching of Foreign Languages. Retrieved from www.actfl.org/i4a/pages/index.cfm?pageid=3642.

10. Patterson, M. (n.d.). Demonstrative speech (how to). Brazosport College. Retrieved from www.brazosport.cc.tx.us/,comm/demon.html.

11. Flynn, K. R. (n.d.). Demonstration or "how to" speech topics. Copia-Lincoln Community College. Retrieved from www.colin.edu/flynn/Speech/Demo_Speech.htm.

12. Kuzmovich, E. (2005). How to draw a hand [Student speech]. George Fox University, Newberg, OR.

13. Nguyen, N. (2005, March). *Ha Noi, Thanh pho yeu dau* (my beloved city) [Student speech]. George Fox University, Newberg, OR.

14. Sakhashchik, A. (2014, Spring). Dong Nguyen [Student speech]. George Fox University, Newberg, OR.

15. Taylor, P. M. (1839). *Confessions of a Thug.* Released by Gutenberg.org, February 12, 2014.

16. Associated Press. (2005, July 7). Reporter jailed for refusal to name leak source. Retrieved from www.msnbc.msn.com/id/8417075/.

17. U.S. Department of State (2008). Freedom of Information Act (FOIA). Retrieved from http://www.state.gov/m/a/ips/.

18. Risen, J., & Poitras, L. (2013, September 28). NSA collects data on US citizens' social connections. NBC News. Retrieved from www.nbcnews.com/news/other/nsa-collects-data-us-citizens-social-connections-f8C11285369.

19. Martin, A. (2012). Obama campaign uses Facebook to collect data on citizens. Retrieved from www.examiner.com/article/obama-campaign-uses-facebook-to-collect-data-on-citizens.

20. Rowan, K. (1995). A new pedagogy for explanatory public speaking: Why arrangement should not substitute for invention. *Communication Education, 44*(3), 235–250.

21. von Till, B. (1998, November). Definition speech. San Jose State University. Poster session. National Communication Association meeting, New York City, NY.

22. Boerger, M. A., & Henley, T. B. (1999). The use of analogy in giving instructions. *Psychological Record, 49*(2), 193.

23. wiseGEEK. (n.d.). What does the term "Main Street" mean? Retrieved from http://www.wisegeek.com/what-does-the-term-main-street-mean.htm.

24. Gardner, H. (1993). *Multiple intelligences: The theory in practice.* New York, NY: Basic Books.

25. Goodall, H. L., & Waaigen, C. L. (1986). *The persuasive presentation: A practical guide to professional communication in organizations.* New York, NY: Harper & Row.

26. Rubin, D. L. (1993). Listenability 5 oral-based discourse + considerateness. In Wolvin & Coakley, Perspectives, 261–268.

27. Rowan, A new pedagogy.

28. Rubin, Listenability 5 oral-based.

29. Thompson, F. T., & Grandgenett, D. J. (1999). Helping disadvantaged learners build effective learning skills. *Education 120*(1), 130–135.

CHAPTER 16

1. Oliner, S. P., & Oliner, P. M. (1988). *The altruistic personality: Rescuers of Jews in Nazi Germany.* New York, NY: Free Press.

2. Perloff, R. M. (2003). *The dynamics of persuasion: Communication and attitudes in the 21st century* (2nd ed.). Mahwah, NJ: Erlbaum, p. 8.

3. Aristotle. (1984). *The Rhetoric* (H. R. Roberts, Trans.). New York, NY: The Modern Library 1356, 356, 20. (Original translation published 1954)

4. Aristotle, *The Rhetoric.*

5. Quintilian. (1920–1922). *The instituto oratoria of Quintilian* (4 vols., H. E. Butler, Trans.). The Loeb Classical Library. Cambridge, MA: Harvard University Press.

6. Quintilian, *The instituto oratoria.*

7. Cuddy, A. J. C., Glick, P., & Benninger, A. (2011). The dynamics of warmth and competence judgments and their outcomes in organizations. *Research in Organizational Behavior, 31,* 73–98.

8. Burke, K. (1983, August 12). Dramatism and logology. *The Times Literary Supplement,* p. 859.

9. Allen, S. A. (1993, February 15). To be successful you have to deal with reality: An opportunity for minority business. Speech delivered October 20, 1992, to the National Minority Supplier Development Council, Cleveland, OH. *Vital Speeches, 59,* 271–273.

10. Kochman, T. (1990). Cultural pluralism: Black and white styles. In D. Carbaugh (Ed.), *Cultural communication and intercultural contacts* (pp. 219–224). Hillsdale, NJ: Erlbaum.

11. Anderson, J. W. (1991). A comparison of Arab and American conceptions of "effective persuasion." In L. A. Samovar & R. E. Porter (Eds.), *Intercultural communication: A reader* (5th ed., pp. 96–106). Belmont, CA: Wadsworth.

12. Gentry, R. (2010). The prevalence and implications of food waste [Student speech]. George Fox University, Newberg, OR.

13. Clinton, H. R. (2010, March). A new nervous system for our planet. Speech delivered January 21, 2010, at the Newseum, Washington, DC. *Vital Speeches of the Day, 76*(3), 108–114.

14. Roczak, T. (1992, June 9). Green guilt and ecological overload. *The New York Times,* p. A23.

15. Maslow, A. H. (1987). *Motivation and personality* (3rd ed.). San Francisco: Harper & Row.

16. Maslow, A. H. (1943). A theory of human motivation. Originally published in *Psychological Review, 50,* 370–396. Posted

by Green, C. D. (2000, August). Classics in the history of psychology website. Retrieved from http://psychclassics.yorku.ca/Maslow/motivation.htm.

17. Brigance, W. N. (1961). *Speech: Its techniques and disciplines in a free society* (2nd ed.). New York, NY: Appleton-Century-Crofts.

18. Anonymous reviewer. (1994).

19. Huey Long Official website. (2010). Long legacy project. Retrieved from www.hueylong.com.

20. Gunn, J. (2007). Hystericizing Huey: Emotional appeals, desire, and the psychodynamics of demagoguery. (Huey Pierce Long). *Western Journal of Communication, 71*, 1–27.

21. Roberts-Miller, P. (2005). Democracy, demagoguery, and critical rhetoric. *Rhetoric & Public Affairs, 8*(3), 462.

22. Roberts-Miller, Democracy, demagoguery.

23. Gunn, Hystericizing Huey.

24. Gunn, Hystericizing Huey.

25. Wicker, B. (1975). *The story-shaped world: Fiction and metaphysics, some variations on a theme.* South Bend, IN: University of Notre Dame Press.

26. Hilliard, A. (1986). Pedagogy in ancient Kemet. In M. Karenga & J. Carruthers (Eds.), *Kemet and the African world view* (p. 257). London: University of Sankore Press.

27. Aristotle. (1984). *Poetics* (1459, 5) (I. Bywater, Trans.). New York, NY: The Modern Library. (Original translation published 1954)

28. McClain, F. J. (2001, November 1). The music in your soul: A celebration of life. Speech delivered September 18, 2001, at the Fall Convocation, Queens College, Charlotte, NC. *Vital Speeches of the Day, 68*(2), 59–61.

29. Cohn, J. (2012, August). To heal a nation: You're also being drafted into public service. Speech delivered May 28, 2012, as Nova Southeastern University Health Professions Division, Fort Lauderdale, FL. *Vital Speeches of the Day, 78*(8), 250–253.

30. Pence, M. (2010). My subject today is the presidency. Speech delivered September 20, 2019, at Hillsdale College, Hillsdale, MI. *Vital Speeches of the Day, 76*(11), 504–508.

31. Shapiro, J. (2014, April 30). Campus rape reports are up, and assaults aren't the only reason. *All Things Considered*, 5:24 p.m., KOPB 91.5, Portland, OR.

32. Sullivan, P. A. (1993). Signification and African-American rhetoric: A case study of Jesse Jackson's "Common Ground and Common Sense" speech. *Communication Quarterly, 41*(1), 1–15.

33. Griffiths, M. (1988). Feminism, feelings, and philosophy. In M. Griffiths & M. Whitford (Eds.), *Feminist perspectives in philosophy* (pp. 131–151). Bloomington: Indiana University Press; see also Jaggar, A. (1989). Love and knowledge: Emotion in feminist epistemology. In A. Garry & M. Pearsall (Eds.), *Women, knowledge, and reality: Explorations in feminist philosophy* (pp. 129–155). London: Unwin; McMillan, 1982.

34. Jaggar, Love and knowledge.

35. Griffiths, Feminism, feelings.

36. Frank, D. A. (1997). Diversity in the public space: A response to Stepp. *Argumentation and Advocacy, 33*, 195–197.

37. Dunbar, K. (2000). Gender, science & cognition. Retrieved from www.psych.mcgill.ca/perpg/fac/dunbar/women.html.

38. Asen, R. (1999, Winter). Toward a normative conception of difference in public deliberation. *Argumentation and Advocacy, 35*(3), 115–116.

39. Craig, K. (2010–2011). Ocean acidification [Competitive speech]. Northwest Forensics Conference: Mount Hood Community College, Gresham, OR.

40. Morris, H. J. (2002, June 17). League of their own. *U.S. News & World Report, 131*(21), 50–51.

41. Smith, A. (2009, April). Effects of chewing gum on mood, learning, memory, and performance of an intelligence test. *Nutrition Neuroscience, 12*(2), 81–88. doi: 10.1179/147683009X423247.

42. Owen, N., Sparling, P. B., Healy, G. N., Dunstan, D. W., & Matthews, C. E. (2010, December). Sedentary behavior: Emerging evidence for a new health risk. *Mayo Clinic Proceedings, 85*(12), 1138–1141.

43. Gass, R. (1999). Fallacy list: SpCom 335: Advanced argumentation. California State University, Fullerton. Retrieved from http://commfaculty.fullerton.edu/rgass/fallacy31.htm.

44. Hilliard, Pedagogy in ancient, 287.

45. Hilliard, Pedagogy in ancient, 287.

46. Combs, S. C. (2004). The useless-/usefulness of argumentation: The DAO of disputation. *Argumentation and Advocacy, 41*(2), 58–71.

47. Combs, The useless-/usefulness.

48. Foss, S. K., & Griffin, C. (1995). Beyond persuasion: A proposal for an invitational rhetoric. *Communication Monographs, 62*, 2–18.

....

CHAPTER 17

1. Aristotle. (1984). *The Rhetoric* (H. R. Roberts, Trans.). New York, NY: The Modern Library. (Original translation published 1954)

2. Liu, L. (2008). *Yang* and *yin* in communication: Towards a typology and logic of persuasion in China. *Diogenes, 217*: 120–132. ISSN 0392-1921.

3. Uskul, A. K., & Oyserman, D. (2010). When message-frame fits salient cultural-frame, messages feel more persuasive. *Psychology and Health, 25*(3), 321–337. ISSN 1476-8321.

4. Mullins, D. (1993). Guest lecture. St. John's University, Jamaica, NY.

5. STATS. (n.d.). What's the difference between correlation and causation? Statistical Assessment Services. Affiliated with George Mason University, Washington, DC. Retrieved from http://stats.org/in_depth/faq/causation_correlation.htm.

6. Kaufman, W. (2011, July 14). Google announces Global Science Fair winners. NPR News. Retrieved from www.npr.org/2011/07/12/137783968/google-announces-global-science-fair-winner.

7. Tucker, P. (2014, May 6). Every country will have drones within ten years. Defense One. Retrieved from www.defenseone.com/technology/2014/05/every-country-will-have-armed-drones-within-ten-years/83878/?oref=d-skybox.

8. Stewart, R. A., & Roach, K. D. (1998). Argumentativeness and the theory of reasoned action. *Communication Quarterly, 46*(2) 177–193.

9. Anonymous reviewer. (1994).

10. Toulmin, S. (1958). *The uses of argument.* Cambridge, UK: Cambridge University Press; Toulmin, S., Rieke, R., & Janik, A. (1984). *An introduction to reasoning* (2nd ed.). New York, NY: Macmillan.

11. Rex, L. A., Thomas, E. E., & Engel, S. (2010). Applying Toulmin: Teaching logical reasoning and argumentative writing. *English Journal, 99*(6), 56–62.

12. Horne, M. P. (2008). Teaching religious doubt with Toulmin's Model of Reasoning. *Teaching Theology and Religion, 11*(4), 203–212. ISSN 1368-4868.

13. Anonymous reviewer. (2011).

14. "Attitude." (n.d.). Definition retrieved from www.cogsci.princeton.edu/cgi-bin/webwn2.1.

15. Anonymous reviewer. (1994).

16. Boster, F. J., Kenzie, A. C., Campo, S., Liu, W.-Y., Lillie, J. K., Baker, E. M., & Yun, K. A. (2000). The persuasive effects of statistical evidence in the presence of exemplars. *Communication Studies, 51*(3), 296–306.

17. Hoecker, K. (2010, Fall). A doll's effect on young girls' concepts of beauty [Student speech]. George Fox University, Newberg, OR.

18. Norton, K. I., Olds, T. S., Olive, S., & Dank, S. (1006). Ken and Barbie at life size. *Sex Roles, 34*(3–4), 287–294. doi: 10.1007/BF01544300.

19. Kuther, T. L., & McDonald, E. (2004, Spring). Early adolescents' experiences with, and view of, Barbie. *Adolescence, 39*(153), 39–51.

20. Dittmar, H., Halliwell, E., & Ive, S. (2006). Does Barbie make girls want to be thin? The effect of experimental exposure to images of dolls on the body image of 5- to 8-year-old girls. *Developmental Psychology, 42*(2), 283–292. doi: 10.1037/0012-1649.42.2.283.

21. Kuther & McDonald, Early adolescents' experiences.

22. Bartanen, M. D. (n. d.). Application of the issues-agenda paradigm to speaker duties and stock issues in value debates. Cross Examination Debate Association. Retrieved from cedadebate.org/CAD/index.php/CAD/article/view/115/101.

23. Sims, H. (2011, Spring). Snakes make good pets [Refutation speech, modified]. George Fox University.

24. Hill, B., & Leeman, R. W. (1997). *The art and practice of argumentation and debate*. Mountain View, CA: Mayfield, 163–164.

25. Tobin, S. J., & Weary, G. (2008). The effects of causal uncertainty, causal importance, and initial attitude on attention to causal persuasive arguments. *Social Cognition, 26*(1), 44–56.

26. Editorial. (2007, November 25). The high cost of health care. *The New York Times*. Retrieved from www.nytimes.com/2007/11/25/opinion/25sun1.html?pagewanted=1.

27. Festinger, L. (1957). *A theory of cognitive dissonance*. New York, NY: Row, Peterson.

28. This theory, developed by Fishbein and Ajzen, is summarized in Trafimow, D., & Finlay, K. A. (2001). Evidence for improved sensitivity of within-participants' analyses in test of the theory of reasoned action. *The Social Science Journal, 38*(4), 629–638. See also Muse, L. A., & Stamper, C. L. (2007). Perceived organizational support: Evidence for a mediated association with work performance. *Journal of Managerial Issues, 19*(4), 517–538.

29. Poss, J. E. (2001, June.) Developing a new model for cross-cultural research: Synthesizing the health beliefs model and the theory of reasoned action. *Advances in Nursing Science, 23*(4), 1–16.

30. Park, H. S. (2000). Relationships among attitudes and subjective norms: Testing the theory of reasoned action across cultures. *Communication Studies, 51*(2), 162–175.

31. Monroe, A. H. (1962). *Principles and types of speeches* (5th ed.). Chicago: Scott Foresman.

32. Pugh, T. (2007, Fall). Organ donation [Student speech]. George Fox University, Newberg, OR.

CHAPTER 18

1. Goodall, H. L., & Phillips, G. M. (1984). *Making it in any organization*. Upper Saddle River, NJ: Prentice Hall.

2. Pacanowsky, M. E., & O'Donnell-Trujillo, N. (1983). Organization communication as cultural performance. *Communication Monographs, 50*, 126–147.

3. Bormann, E. G. (1985). Symbolic convergence theory: A communication formulation. *Journal of Communication, 35*, 128–138.

4. Ouchi, W. B. (1998, Fall). The concept of organizational culture in a diverse society. SIETAR International. Retrieved from http://208.215.167.139/sij-98-12/keynote03.htm.

5. Obama, B. H. (2009, May 26). Remarks by the president in nominating Judge Sonia Sotomayor to the United States Supreme Court. Retrieved from www.whitehouse.gov/the-press-office/remarks-president-nominating-judge-sonia-sotomayor-united-states-supreme-court.

6. Vest, G. G. (1870). Tribute to the dog. Retrieved from www.historyplace.com/speeches/vest.htm.

7. Howlett, S. (2003, Fall). Beyond batting [Student speech]. Radford University, Radford, VA. Retrieved from www.radford.edu/~llanc/manuscriptsample.htm.

8. Goldberg, J. (2005, June 17). The hop bird: My dad, 1931–2005. *National Review Online*. Retrieved from www.nationalreview.com/goldberg/goldberg200506170746.asp.

9. O'Malley, M. (2011, May). If I were to sing tonight. Speech delivered March 16, 2001, at the American Ireland Fund's National Gala, Washington, DC. *Vital Speeches of the Day, 77*(5), 166–167.

10. Coleman, M. S. (2011, May). I was a teenage scientist. Speech delivered March 11, 2011, at the Intel Talent Search Alumni Dinner, Washington, DC. *Vital Speeches of the Day, 77*(5), 181–184.

11. McCardell, J. M. (2011, November). From tentative twig to mighty branch. Speech delivered August 22, 2010, at the welcoming ceremony, University of the South, Sewanee, TN. *Vital Speeches of the Day, 76*(11), 492–495.

12. Gillard, J. (2011). I always remember thinking: Americans can do anything. Speech delivered March 9, 2011, to a Joint Session of Congress, US House of Representatives, Washington, DC. *Vital Speeches of the Day, 76*(11), 492–495.

13. Hawken, P. (2009, May 3). The earth is hiring. Commencement address delivered at the University of Portland, Portland, OR. Retrieved from www.humanity.org/voices/commencements/speeches/index.php?page=hawken_at_uportland.

14. Servis, M. (2007, July). Myth, mystery, and meaning in medicine. Speech delivered June 9, 2007, Commencement, UC Davis School of Medicine, Davis, CA. *Vital Speeches of the Day, 73*(7), 309–311.

15. McNally, J. R. (1969). Opening assignments: A symposium. *The Speech Teacher, 18*, 18–30.

16. Steph. B. (2010, January 29). Growing up deaf [Student speech]. George Fox University, Newberg, OR.

APPENDIX A

1. Burbach, M. E., Matkin, G. S., Gambrell, K. M., & Harding, H. E. (2010, September). The impact of preparing faculty in the effective use of student teams. *College Student Journal, 44*(3), 752–761.

2. Beebe, S. A., & Masterson, J. T. (1990). *Communicating in small groups: Principles and practices* (3rd ed.). New York, NY: HarperCollins. See also Cooper, P. J. (1995). *Communication for the classroom teacher* (5th ed.). Scottsdale, AZ: Gorsuch Scarisbrick.

3. Tannen, D. F. (1990). *You just don't understand: Men and women in conversation.* New York, NY: William Morris.

4. Janik, I. (1971, November). Groupthink. *Psychology Today*, 43–46.

5. Eisen, A. (1998). Small group presentations in teaching "science thinking" and context in a large biology class. *Bioscience, 48*(1), 54–57.

6. Burbach et al., Impact of preparing.

7. Tannen, *You just don't.*

8. Cowan, J. (2000). Lessons from the playground. In K. Galvin & P. Cooper (Eds.), *Making connections: Readings in relational communication* (2nd ed., p. 307). Los Angeles: Roxbury.

9. Grob, L. M., Meyers, R. A., & Schuh, R. (1997). Powerful/powerless language use in group interactions: Sex differences or similarities? *Communication Quarterly, 45*(3), 282–303.

10. Cowan, Lessons from.

11. Henson, J. (n.d.). Problem solving using group challenges. Retrieved from www.bvte.ecu.edu/ACBMEC/p1998/henson.htm.

12. Sengalese women remake their culture. (1998, December). *IK Notes World Bank, No. 3.* Retrieved from www.africapolicy.org.

13. Kepner, C. H., & Tregoe, B. B. (1965). *The rational manager: A systematic approach to problem solving and decision making.* New York, NY: McGraw-Hill.

APPENDIX B

1. Truth, S. (1997). Ain't I a Woman? *Modern History Sourcebook.* Retrieved from http://www.fordham.edu/halsall/mod/sojtruth-woman.html. (Original speech delivered 1851, Women's Convention, Akron, OH.)

INDEX